THE STAR AND THE STRIPES

THE

STAR

AND THE

STRIPES

A HISTORY OF THE FOREIGN POLICIES OF AMERICAN JEWS

MICHAEL N. BARNETT

PRINCETON UNIVERSITY PRESS

Princeton and Oxford

Published by Princeton University Press, 41 William
Street, Princeton, New Jersey 08540

In the United Kingdom: Princeton University Press, 6
Oxford Street, Woodstock, Oxfordshire OX20 1TR

press.princeton.edu

First paperback printing, 2018
Paper ISBN: 978-0-691-18072-4

The Library of Congress has cataloged the cloth edition as follows:

Names: Barnett, Michael N., 1960–

Title: The star and the stripes : a history of the foreign
policies of American Jews / Michael Barnett.

Description: Princeton : Princeton University Press, [2016]
| Includes bibliographical references and index.

Identifiers: LCCN 2015031272 | ISBN 9780691165974
(hardcover : acid-free paper)

Subjects: LCSH: Jews—United States—Politics and government. | Jews—
United States—Attitudes. | United States—Foreign relations—21st century.
| United States—Ethnic relations. | BISAC: POLITICAL SCIENCE / Civics
& Citizenship. | POLITICAL SCIENCE / Political Process / Political
Advocacy. | SOCIAL SCIENCE / Jewish Studies. | POLITICAL SCIENCE
/ Government / International. | POLITICAL SCIENCE / General.

Classification: LCC E184.36.P64 B37 2016 | DDC 973/.04924—
dc23 LC record available at http://lccn.loc.gov/2015031272

British Library Cataloging-in-Publication Data is available

This book has been composed in Linux Libertine

Printed on acid-free paper. ∞

Printed in the United States of America

CONTENTS

ACKNOWLEDGMENTS

As I sit down to write these acknowledgments, I am reminded of the conclusion to most Bar and Bat Mitzvah ceremonies. This joyful religious event celebrates the moment when the child becomes an "adult" in the Jewish community, with all the rights and responsibilities that entails. The Bar and Bat Mitzvah is a rite of passage, and, as with all such rites, there are tests; the two most important are the reading from the Torah and crafting a speech that pulls meaning from the ancient text. Upon completion, the celebrant proceeds to thank everyone who helped him reach this milestone. Invariably, there is a rehearsed sequence, which goes roughly in the following order. It begins with those who were directly responsible for his religious training: his teachers, rabbi, cantor, and perhaps the tutor his parents hired out of a desperate fear that he would never be ready and would embarrass himself and his family at this public event that was several years and thousands of dollars in the making. Israel is often next in line, credited with being a source of inspiration and living expression of the Jewish people. Best friends are then thanked for cushioning the pain of the experience. Relatives, both living and dead, come next. There are grandparents, aunts, and uncles who need to be acknowledged. There are the dearly departed, present in spirit only. Often, at this point, there is a pause to mention a relative who perished in the Holocaust. Then comes the immediate family. There are siblings to be named, and, last but hardly least, the parents, who, of course, made everything possible and were wonderfully supportive. It is easy to poke fun at this part of the ceremony, but it also contains an important element of truth: there is a long history building up to this moment, and it did not begin the first day of Bar Mitzvah training.

I find myself in a similar situation. As I prepare to thank all the many who helped me along the way, I am not certain where to begin because I am not exactly sure when to mark the book's point of conception. There was the moment, sometime around 2011, when I decided to write a book on American Jews. If I stick to this calendar, then my list should be limited to those who directly commented on the contours and contents of the book. Yet as with many books, and especially those written by "mature" scholars, there is a long prehistory. Looking backward, I can identify several epiphanic moments. There was a summer 2010 trip to Israel. I had decided years before to stop working on Israel and the Middle East (more on this in a moment), but that summer I traveled with Academic Exchange, an educational group that takes scholars of international relations to Israel. I felt jolted by the experience. Like any good academic, I began to think about exploring my questions through research and writing. So I must thank the organizers, my dear friends Charlie Kupchan and Rabbi Nachum Braverman. Soon thereafter I received and accepted an invitation from Emanuel Adler to contribute to an edited volume on Israel and the world, and I decided to explore the question of global cosmopolitanism and Israeli victimhood.

Yet there are earlier, equally influential moments. As I write in the introduction, there was the time I drove to the synagogue and was struck by the replacement of the banner supporting Israel with a banner mobilizing action to stop the killing in Darfur. But the only reason this exchange struck me as curious was because I was writing on humanitarian action. Accordingly, many of the folks I thanked in these articles and books should be mentioned again. Humanitarianism, though, was far from my point of origin as an academic; I was trained in international relations and the Middle East. In retrospect, I think one reason I wandered into humanitarianism was because I needed something to rescue me from a field of study that offers no hope whatsoever. So I should thank the sectarianism of the region and the American Jewish community for driving me into an area of life that resists tribalism and nurtures cosmopolitanism. And before then, there were my childhood experiences of being raised in a very small Jewish community in downstate Illinois, so there are Jewish educators and leaders to acknowledge. The most memorable and formative experience of my childhood occurred in the sixth grade when my mother took my brother and me to Israel for a year; I would never be the same. So I find myself wanting to mention the enduring influence of Israel. This book would never have been written if my grandparents had not decided to flee Lithuania and Ukraine around World War I for the United States. And, of course, they never would have left had it not been for the pogroms and centuries of anti-Semitism, so I suppose I also should thank the anti-Semites. And now that I have mentioned the omnipresent theme of Jewish suffering, I know that I have fulfilled every requisite of a Bar-Mitzvah speech.

Other individuals and institutions deserve special mention because of their support. I have learned much from those who attended the talks I delivered at the following places: School of Oriental and African Studies, University of London; the Reut Institute, Tel-Aviv; the Hebrew University of Jerusalem; Tufts University; the B'nai B'rith Elderhostel Retreat at Wildacres; University of Illinois; the University of Minnesota; the University of Wisconsin; the University of Virginia; and conferences on human rights at the University of Chicago and New York University.

I was fortunate to have research assistants who often took deep, personal interest in the book and provided support and feedback beyond the usual: thank you Amir Stepak, Shannon Powers, Katherine Hurrelbrink, Danielle Gilbert, Charmaine Chau, and Jessica Anderson.

I benefited greatly from several institutions that provided financial support: the Stassen Chair at the University of Minnesota, Humphrey School of Public Affairs; the George Washington University; and the Transatlantic Academy, associated with the German Marshall Fund.

Thanks to those who attended a book manuscript workshop: Michael Abramowitz, Marc Lynch, Ian Hurd, Melani McAlister, Ilana Feldman, James Loeffler, Lisa Leff, and Daniel Schwartz. Although I didn't do everything they suggested (I wanted to write one book, not a series), I hope they don't think their efforts have gone to waste.

I interviewed lots of people. The good news about interviewing American Jews (and non-Jews) about American Jews is that everyone has something to say, and no one ever said, "I am sure I am saying something you have heard before." I have had countless conversations, some scheduled and some impromptu, that effected my thinking. I greatly benefited from conversations and exchanges with many people over the years, including Ron Krebs, Theodore Sasson, Walter Reich, Leonard Fein, Dyonna Ginsburg, Natan Sznaider, Aaron Dorfman, Shmuel Rosner, Jonathan Rynhold, Emanuel Adler, Gal Beckerman, Samuel Moyn, Eric Weitz, Elizabeth Borgwardt, Robert Bernstein, Roberta Cohen, Elliot Abrams, Abigail Green, Michelle Lackie, Ori Soltes, Jacob Sztokman, Sally Gottesman, Marty Friedman, Jerry Fowler, Micha Odenheimer, Raymond Duvall, Dafna Kaufman, Rabbi Marci Zimmerman, Jim Gerstein, Kathryn Sikkink, Martha Finnemore, Aryeh Neier, Joel Migdal, Nadav Shelef, Oded Halevi, Rabbi Yosef Kanefsky, Rabbi David Rosenn, and Rabbi Jill Jacobs.

I am indebted to four premier American Jewish organizations. Early on I approached the American Jewish World Service, and, by the end, I not only became a contributor but also even urged my daughter to go on one of its youth service trips to Ghana. I owe a tremendous thanks to Aaron Dorfman. At my invitation, I traveled with the United States Holocaust Memorial and Museum as part of the delegation that visited Rwanda on the occasion of the twentieth anniversary of the genocide. I am still trying to process that trip. Thanks to Michael Abramowitz for making it happen. The archivists at the American Jewish Committee were welcoming beyond belief. And thanks also to the American Jewish Joint Distribution Committee, and especially Misha Mitsel for his help with the archival materials.

Several others deserve special recognition. Nachum Braverman, for his friendship and Torah sessions; I know I wasn't your best student, but I learned a tremendous amount. Victoria Shampaine for her support, careful reading, and cogent editing. Stephen Hopgood and Janice Stein read and reread the manuscript at various stages, and, being good friends, kept telling me that I had more work to do. I thank them for their close reading and their closer friendship.

I greatly appreciate the feedback I received from two anonymous reviewers at Princeton who provided sharp critiques and excellent recommendations for how to proceed. As so many of us know from personal experience, the review process is not here to make us feel better; the best it can do is make the book's argument stronger, and hopefully it served that purpose. I also received very helpful comments from my good friends Roger Haydon and David McBride. Michael Levine read early versions and provided sage advice for making the argument more accessible. Although he was not given enough time to work miracles, Ken DeCell did what he could to improve the book's readability. I am grateful for his efforts.

Much thanks to Eric Crahan, who not only guided the book through the editorial process but also spent a considerable amount of time talking through the argument and its presentation. Others at Princeton also deserve thanks: Ben Pokross and the remarkably patient Leslie Grundfest steered the book through the production process, and Dawn Hall had the unenviable chore of copyediting the manuscript.

When I started this book my daughters, Maya and Hannah, were children; now they are two amazing young adults. For the moment, they also represent two different segments of the younger generation of American Jews. Maya has constantly attempted to find a way to link her Jewish identity and her cosmopolitan identity—volunteering at religious school, going to Ghana for a summer with the American Jewish World Service, interning for grassroots organizations, traveling to Israel on two occasions (three if we count the trip when she was six months old), and working toward a career in public health. Hannah, on the other hand, shows considerable interest in everything about the world—except her Jewish heritage. She was Bat Mitzvahed, but wrote a speech about her reservations regarding her Jewish identity. In response, the rabbi deftly told Hannah that dissent and skepticism are classic Jewish traits. And if humor is another, then despite her protests, she is very Jewish.

My wife, best friend, and in-house psychiatrist, Victoria, does not deserve me. And I do not deserve her. However, we probably deserve each other. Forever.

I am dedicating this book to my mother. None of "this"—not my life and not this book—would have happened without her. I don't know if she will be proud of the book, but I trust that she won't hold it against me.

THE STAR AND THE STRIPES

INTRODUCTION

THIS MIGHT BE THE FIRST BOOK EVER CONCEIVED AS A RESULT OF driving kids to religious school. In 2008 my life seemed consumed by two activities: writing a book on the history of humanitarianism, and carpool duty. On one occasion as I was driving up to the temple I noticed that the large banner above the entrance exclaiming the temple's support for Israel had been replaced by another: "Save Darfur." I then walked into the foyer and took a long look at the announcement board. For as long as I could remember items on Israel-related activities had dominated the space. They were now few and far between and arrayed on the edges, seemingly shunted aside by the far more abundant notices of opportunities to volunteer outside the Jewish community: serve in a homeless shelter, work in a soup kitchen, help distribute foodstuffs at a food bank, deliver used furniture to the needy, assemble care packages for victims of humanitarian emergencies. Darfur and other social action programs were part of the broader phenomenon of *tikkun olam*, a Hebrew expression that means "to repair the world." Tikkun olam had become quite popular at my temple, just as it had in much of the American Jewish world.

What accounted for all this activity around humanitarian action? Some self-congratulatory explanations credited Judaism and Jewish ethics. But these essentialist arguments require several miracles and leaps of faith to draw a straight path from ancient text to contemporary tikkun olam. If religious commitment correlated with tikkun olam, then the Orthodox Jewish community would put the Reform and Conservative movements to shame. Yet the former focused almost exclusively on the needs of the Jewish community while the latter wanted to repair the entire world. And tikkun olam was not sweeping all Jewish communities alike; it was popular among American Jews but far less prominent among Israeli Jews.

My work on humanitarianism gave me a broader perspective. I knew that since the 1990s voluntarism and humanitarianism had grown in scale across the secular and religious worlds. Individuals and communities increasingly wanted to "give back." While most gave at home, more and more were donating to global causes and even traveling abroad to build schools, staff public health clinics, and work in orphanages. Many intersecting factors contributed to the expanding scale of humanitarianism: the end of the Cold War provided opportunity for Americans to think about how most of the world lives; new communication technologies made it possible for people to know instantly about the suffering of others; new logistical technologies made it possible to make a difference; a renewed cosmopolitanism and intensifying discourse on human rights was encouraging the fortunate to think about their responsibilities to distant strangers; and rising incomes meant they had more to spare and more guilt to relieve. Religious communities were doing more than their secular brethren in a period of religious resurgence, as there was a growing emphasis on compassion to express one's religious identity, and the integration of secular notions of humanness into religious doctrine and practice.

These secular and religious forces could easily account for the rise of tikkun olam in the Jewish community. American Jews have a long history of favoring doctrines, traditions, and movements that emphasize a duty to help the poor and vulnerable, that there is no basis for favoring one group over another, and that the same ethical principles should be applied to all people. Notwithstanding the cosmopolitan sentiments, in practice the American Jewish community focused on the overwhelming needs of a large, impoverished immigrant population. Beginning in the mid-twentieth century, the American Jews were becoming a success story, and the circumstances of the Jews around the world were improving, allowing American Jews to begin practicing what they had preached for over a century. Most Jews now lived in liberal democracies where they were accepted rather than reviled. Israel once needed help protecting its borders and resettling hundreds of thousands of impoverished Jews who had outlasted the Holocaust and fled Arab lands, but no more. It has been decades since Israel's survival was in mortal danger, and the river of immigrants has slowed from a flood to a trickle. Israel no longer depends for its survival on American Jewry's financial support. As the comedian Sarah Silverman put it in her plug for the American Jewish World Service (AJWS): "This is Jews helping *goyim*. Let's face it. The Jews are doing quite well."

Yet the images lingered in my mind of a Darfur banner replacing the one supporting Israel and the relative absence of Israel from the announcement board. Although I worried about taking the symbolism too far, I began to think about the possible relationship between tikkun olam and Israel. My temple had not withdrawn its support for Israel. But I also knew that many members, much like the broader American Jewish community, were increasingly ambivalent about Israel and its policies. But was tikkun olam part of this "distancing" from Israel? I kept running through four possibilities: One, there might be no relationship whatsoever. Two, tikkun olam might be crowding out Israel. There could be only one banner at the temple, and Israel had made way for Darfur. Three, American Jews might be turning to tikkun olam as a consequence of their distancing from Israel. In other words, they were first souring on Israel, then finding their way to tikkun olam. And, four, American Jews could choose to enact their identity either through Israel or through tikkun olam, and they were increasingly choosing the latter. If so, why? Was it because Israel raised ethical quandaries while Darfur had a presumed purity? Might tikkun olam demonstrate that Jews could be on the right side of social justice, especially at a time when the Jewish state seemed to be living on the borderline? Perhaps they share the view of the American Jewish World Service's Ruth Messinger, that tikkun olam will "deter anti-Semitism by demonstrating that Jews work to provide social justice and dignity for all people regardless of race, religion, or ethnicity."[1]

My research on humanitarianism led me to try and address these possibilities by asking a broader question: how do political communities understand their obligations to others? The ethical core of humanitarianism is a consideration of our duties to distant strangers in need. Modern humanitarianism rests on the presumption of a shared humanity that leads us to care about all those in need and not just those we like or who look and act like us. These sorts of arguments draw heavily on normative theory and theology because they tell us how we should feel and what we should do. Yet, as a practical matter, we do play favorites, often because of blood and feelings of belonging. To capture this moral unevenness, scholars sometimes refer to concentric circles of compassion, suggesting how our felt duties start at the most intimate and intensive and then dissipate as they move outward. Our family before our friends. Our friends before our village. Our village before our nation. Our nation before the world. Our religious brethren before other religious communities. This is a reasonable starting point, but it cannot explain why the moral imaginations of political communities shift over time. For centuries slavery was an accepted practice, but a movement developed in the late eighteenth century that eventually led to its global prohibition. Public and private giving to distant strangers has dramatically expanded over the decades. What accounts for these changes in the moral imagination? This is a central issue in the study of practical ethics: how a political community, religious or otherwise, defines its obligations to others.

My research on humanitarianism linked these issues in ethics to both material circumstances and identity. There are political communities whose socioeconomic conditions improved but whose compassion remained constricted. Conversely, there are political communities whose socioeconomic circumstances have not changed but who nevertheless increased their concern for strangers. What does the identity of American Jews suggest?

The American Jewish identity is both American and Jewish. American Jews are Jews, and Jews are a transnational and diasporic people. And as a transnational people that exist in a world of states, the states system has weighed heavily on them. The modern history of world Jewry can be told as a story of a transnational and diasporic people attempting to adjust to a world carved into different territories that are intended to circumscribe identities and loyalties. Jews have responded in all kinds of ways to this challenge: assimilate into the national and Christian woodwork; join cosmopolitan movements such as socialism that imagine the disappearance of sectarian identities and territorial boundaries; champion a diaspora nationalism that imagines retaining the Jewish identity while residing in separate states; fight for liberalism, pluralism, and equal rights; advocate international law and institutions to protect minorities and other vulnerable populations; align with forms of liberal internationalism and the spread of democracy, human rights, and rule of law; and, finally and most famously, support a Jewish nationalist movement and a Jewish state.

American Jews have addressed this challenge largely by advocating the development and defense of liberalism and pluralism, creating international law and institutions, and supporting the establishment and defense of a Jewish state. While these beliefs and strategies could be pursued simultaneously, they had an order of appearance and could be in tension with each other. Early on, American Jews held that the best defense against anti-Semitism was the enshrinement of principles of equality in domestic law and institutions. A Jewish state was another option, but its particularity clashed with the commitment of many American Jews to principles of equality and inclusivity. Eventually American Jews did join the Zionist movement and became diehard supporters of the State of Israel, but they first had to be convinced that their American identity could be compatible with their Zionism. The desire to see an Israel that was consistent with their American identity reflects how American Jews have wanted Jewish nationalism and Israel to address the physical *and* spiritual survival of the Jews. American Jews did not imagine that they would need to flee to Israel as a place of refuge; they were safe and snug in their "golden Medina." Instead, they invested Zionism and Israel with considerable meaning: they were a sign of the eternal struggle and indefatigable spirit of the Jewish people; a memorial to suffering and a testimony to their tenacity; a bridge between the ancient and modern; a Jewish point of light among the world's nations; a spiritual and tangible reminder to hold onto their Jewish identity as they live in an America where the pressure to assimilate is constant.

For many American Jews, Israel has become part of their soul. A trip to Israel is a pilgrimage and, for many, an unexpected homecoming. Most American Jews trace their family trees to somewhere in Europe or Russia, but rarely does the old country spark any wistful longing. Little remains of the centuries-long Jewish presence in Europe except for artifacts collected in museums; plaques marking where a synagogue once stood; ancient synagogues that stand empty and whose upkeep is paid by Diaspora Jews; memorials for labor, concentration, and death camps; and run-down cemeteries and mass graves.

In stark contrast, many American Jews who visit Israel, including those who go without any prior attachment, report a surprising sense of being "at home." The Israeli novelist Amos Oz describes it as a "tribal feeling," intimate and comforting.[2] Although American Jews pledge allegiance to the United States, and relatively few have emigrated, a trip to Israel nevertheless unleashes a feeling of warmth, comfort, and belonging that many never realized they had missed.

America is deeply ingrained in the American Jewish identity. American Jews closely identify with their nation's ideals of human dignity, equality, and freedom of conscience. Jewish religious leaders have insisted on the centrality of these values to Judaism, which, not coincidentally, also foster Jewish survival. As a minority people, the Jewish people's survival and well-being depends on being tolerated and accepted by their hosts; when their hosts have embraced these humanistic ideals, Jews have enjoyed security and its fruits. America has defined itself as a country that is constituted by these ideals. Although America does not always live up to them, life for the Jews was certainly better because Americans judged themselves against these ideals. It would be a mistake, however, to reduce Jews' attachment to the United States to self-interest alone. American Jews are proud of the contributions they have made to American life. The chosen people in this chosen land helped to create a Judeo-Christian country.

American Jews have largely integrated their Jewish and American sides in much the same way other immigrant populations have created their own hyphenated identities, yet their attachments to Israel and America, at times, pull in different directions. I am not speaking of dual loyalty, the anti-Semitic canard that accuses the Jews of favoring their "own" over their country and that often becomes implicitly and explicitly resurrected in contemporary discussions of American Jewry's support for Israel. Instead, I am referring to the fact that American Jews' identification with the Jewish people and Israel pulls toward particularism and an inward-looking nationalism, while the values they associate with the American identity pull toward universalism and an outward-looking cosmopolitanism. American Jews are frequently living examples of F. Scott Fitzgerald's saying that the "test of a first-rate intelligence is the ability to hold two opposed ideas in mind at the same time and still retain the ability to function."

Particularism and universalism are enduring features in Jewish theology and history, providing different answers to the identity-defining issues of how Jews see themselves in relation to Gentiles, their obligations to those inside and outside the Jewish community, and their sense of the purpose of the world. Particularism inscribes Jews as a chosen people that dwells alone, with a calling to maintain their covenant with God and an obligation to help their own first to the relative neglect of others. Universalism calls on the Jews to be a prophetic people with obligations to Jews and non-Jews alike and with a mission to help create a world of peace, justice, and harmony.

A persistent theme in Jewish theology is the tension between particularism and universalism, present throughout the Torah, in sayings, and religious debates. What kind of people are they? Are they *Am Segulah*, a chosen people? Are they *Am Yoshev Lavad*, a people that dwells alone? Or are they *Or LaGoyim*, a "light unto nations"? What is their purpose in the world—to maintain their covenant with God or to be a prophetic people and serve humanity? How does their identity relate to their duty to their fellow Jews and others? Should they follow the Talmudic expression *Anijei Ircha Kodmim*, your city's poor comes first, which advises Jews to tend primarily to their own? Hillel's inspiring words, though, urge Jews to look beyond their own needs: "If I am not for myself, who will be for me? But if I am only for myself, who am I? If not now, when?" Jews have been asking themselves these questions for as long as they have been a people, and because there is unlikely to be a settled view, they will keep asking them.

The relationship between particularism and universalism also has been a feature of modern Jewish history. I am less concerned with the insolvable question of what the ideal balance would be, and more concerned with how different Jewish communities have imagined what balance might be more or less acceptable. Although best known for her inspiring words inscribed on the Statue of Liberty, Emma Lazarus also captured this challenge with these memorable words: "The truth is that every Jew has to crack for himself this nut of his peculiar position in a non-Jewish country."[3]

A good starting point for understanding how different Jewish communities have cracked this nut is the following adage: If you want to understand the Jews, start by looking at the Gentiles. This piece of advice is attributed to Heinrich Heine, the nineteenth-century poet and writer who was born a Jew and then converted to Christianity. Not everyone is ready to accept the insights of a former member of the tribe. A Yiddish proverb offers a similar, though more fatalistic, conclusion: *Vy es kristit zikh, azoy yidlt zikh* (As the Christians go, so go the Jews).[4] And then there is the unsettling statement by a nineteenth-century Jewish novelist: "Every country has the Jews it deserves."[5] These sayings underscore the insight that the Jews are a product of their environment. The Jews of course, predated Christianity; their foundational texts, religious beliefs, and prayers, many of their rituals, and their sense of themselves as a distinct community were forged centuries before the Jewish sect of Christianity became hegemonic. But once Jews lived in a Christian world, the opinion of the Gentiles could have as great an impact as God's.

American Jews have cracked this nut in a way that favors the universal, but nevertheless sees the particular as flowing into the universal and the universal as providing a space for the particular. This makes American Jews slightly different from many other Jewish communities, past or present, that have tended to be more comfortable closer to the particular end of the spectrum. The American experience explains why American Jews are different. As scholars of American Jewish history are fond of saying: American Jews are different because America is different. And America is different because it did not treat its Jews as different. Although anti-Semitism certainly existed, and continues to exist, from the beginning Jews in America enjoyed greater rights than they ever had in Europe, lived in a land where politicians found it more politically advantageous to court the Jewish vote than to whip up anti-Semitism, and were allowed to live as both Jews and Americans. In the United States, Jews started with a clean slate in a country that was in the process of forming its national character around principles of individual liberty, equality, freedom of conscience, and the rule of law. And they did not just take advantage of the opportunities America afforded; they helped create their own opportunities by contributing to the development of an America that was safe for them.

The American experience had two enduring effects on the American Jewish identity. The first is a strong preference for political ideologies of liberalism and pluralism, which allow them to navigate the shoals of chauvinism and assimilation. The second is a strong attraction to non-Orthodox Judaism and its goal of fitting Judaism into the modern world. Simply put, the American experience produced American Jews who are overwhelmingly liberal and whose "liberalism is central to their conception of Judaism."[6] The fusing of the political and the theological produced what I will call a political theology of Prophetic Judaism—a belief that the Jews are a people connected to the world who should demonstrate their religiosity through acts of compassion to all, and whose diaspora will help catalyze global justice and a common humanity. This political theology addresses central demands of both identity and interests. By stressing what they share with others, by emphasizing universalism, and by championing political ideologies that are premised on equality, Jews, a minority population with a long history of persecution, are best able to safeguard their security and survival.

Scholars of American Jewish history have extensively cataloged how the American experience shaped the identity and political culture of American Jews, but they have neglected the ways it also has shaped their foreign policies. I will argue that this political theology has produced a foreign policy that is more cosmopolitan than tribal. Tribalism is an extreme form of communalism, where one's identity and loyalty is tied to the group. A tribal foreign policy has the characteristics of a severe realpolitik: consumed by self-interest and survival; drawing stark boundaries between us and them; viewing the world as threatening and filled with dangers immediate or lurking around the corner; believing that values, ideals, and ethics are dangerous distractions from the primary goal of survival; and holding that security is best accomplished through might rather than mutual accommodation or acceptance. In this view, Jews can evaluate world events by asking that simple question: "Is it good or bad for the Jews?"

Cosmopolitanism, on the other hand, holds that one's identity and duties extend to all of humanity. It includes a belief that self-interest is intertwined with the community's interests; all humans are equal and deserving of equal dignity, respect, and treatment; our obligations are not restricted to "our kind" but rather are universal; international law and institutions can help states and peoples settle their disputes through peaceful means; and peace is possible. For these Jews, the cosmopolitan spirit flows from Prophetic Judaism and its call for Jews to be a "light unto the nations" and to help the world "beat its swords into ploughshares." As they think about the world, they imagine how their own safety and well-being are bound up with global justice and peaceful coexistence of all peoples.

As I define it, "Jewish foreign policy" is the attempt by Jewish individuals and institutions to mobilize and represent the Jewish community for the purpose of protecting Jewish interests and advancing a vision of global justice inspired by Jewish political and religious thought. Jewish foreign policy has two overriding concerns: the Jewish Problem and the Jewish Question. The Jewish Problem is the potential of harm by non-Jews. To put the matter bluntly: when non-Jews see Jews as a problem to be solved, Jews are endangered. When Jews are under threat, this is a concern for Jews everywhere— not only for those in the line of fire but also for those watching from a relatively safe distance. Jews fortunate enough to be watching securely from afar instinctively sympathize with the plight of their coreligionists and want to help. They also worry that anti-Semitism is contagious and, like a virus, can jump across borders and quickly infect non-Jews at home. The Jewish Question concerns the relationship between Jews and the world. Are the Jews a people *apart from* the world or *a part of* the world? Are they a "people who dwells alone" or a "light unto the nations"? The mixture of universalism and particularism shapes Jews' instinctual response to these questions.

So far I have emphasized how the American experience has shaped the foreign policies of American Jews, but three global factors also figure prominently. American Jews have been influenced by Israel, but, as we will see, Israel's influence is difficult to predict and much depends on the form that Jewish nationalism takes. Global anti-Semitism has made a deep impression on American Jews. Conventional wisdom predicts that when anti-Semitism goes up, American Jews will go tribal, and when anti-Semitism goes down, they will go soft. Yet American Jewish tribalism is surprisingly uncorrelated with the ebb and flow of anti-Semitism; American Jews did not become more tribal during the interwar period when life was becoming more precarious at home and deadly in Europe, but they did when things were better than ever beginning in the late 1960s. Another global force is cosmopolitanism—not the cosmopolitanism of the Jews but rather the world's feelings about cosmopolitanism and how those feelings shape its views of the Jews. There have been times when being labeled a cosmopolitan people is the kiss of death, while at other times that label has been bestowed as a compliment. Israel, anti-Semitism, and global cosmopolitanism have combined in different ways to alter the balance between universalism and particularism.

This book is an interpretive history of the foreign policies of American Jews. It immerses itself in the history of American Jews and traces how the American experience shaped the identity of American Jews; how this identity is intertwined with the political theology of Prophetic Judaism; how the political theology accounts for an outward orientation that is more cosmopolitan than tribal; and how this foreign policy orientation shaped American Jews' responses to the Jewish Problem and the Jewish Question. As a work of history, this book is deeply informed by the historical record and draws from memoirs, archives, secondary research, and interviews. As a work of interpretation it is informed by what the social sciences and humanities tell us about the relationships between various kinds of political communities and their relations with others.

American Jewry's approaches to the Jewish Problem and the Jewish Question exhibit several defining continuities and some striking differences. While struggling to identify solutions to the Jewish Problem, American Jews have instinctively gravitated toward policies of integration rather than segregation. Much as they have embraced liberalism and pluralism to maintain their communal security and identity at home, American Jews have stressed how similar institutions and values can help Jewish communities abroad. Simply put, what is good for American Jews is good for Jews elsewhere—and for the world. American Jews, in the main, are not pacifists—they recognize that often there is no alternative but to use force to protect Jews in danger. Yet because of principle and pragmatism, they have advocated forms of liberal internationalism that encourage the export of democracy and the rule of law; lobbied for the creation of international institutions, norms, and laws to protect Jews and other minorities and vulnerable populations; and generally pushed hard for universal human rights principles and institutions. In short, as American Jews have sought solutions to the Jewish Problem, they have tended to link their own fate to that of all humanity.

The other side of this cosmopolitan orientation to the Jewish Problem is a wariness by American Jews of tribalism and nationalism, both their own and others'. American Jews are committed to the survival of the Jewish people, but they have been of several minds regarding whether nationalism helps or hurts their cause. Jews know from personal experience how nationalism, especially when it turns exclusionary and vainglorious, can breed violence. American Jews, morover have been highly skeptical of the claim that Jewish nationalism would increase their security. Instead of fighting nationalism with nationalism, American Jews have preferred to present themselves as a community that fits seamlessly into the American nation. The American Jewish establishment initially saw the first stirrings of Jewish nationalism and Zionism as potentially playing into the hands of anti-Semites who claimed the Jews were a separate people that could never live harmoniously with others. American Jews were relative latecomers to political Zionism and the belief that Jews needed a separate state. After World War II and the Holocaust they threw their support behind Zionism, but also continued to preach at international forums that nationalism represented a threat to world peace and security, and that international human rights, institutions, and law constituted the path to peaceful coexistence. Their nationalist sentiments were a labor of love and fear. Conventional wisdom proclaims that American Jews are deeply attached to Israel, always have been and always will be, but in fact the relationship is much more complicated, and the love affair began much more recently (and is possibly much more fragile) than is generally presumed.

Their cosmopolitan orientation also has influenced their answer to the Jewish Question. First and foremost, because of the American experience, American Jews have devoted more time to the Jewish Question than has perhaps any other Jewish community in modern history. Unfortunately, most Jewish communities have never felt secure enough to look beyond their own needs (the Jewish Problem) to consider what contributions they might make to human progress. American Jews, though, have enjoyed more security and acceptance than nearly any other Diaspora Jewish community in recent memory;

consequently, they have been able to worry about the Jewish Question. When Jews no longer have to worry about their survival, they can worry about their values and purpose in the world. The American Jews, so to speak, have "fancy" problems. This is yet another example of how the American Jews are different because America did not treat its Jews as different.

The American Jewish response to the Jewish Question is complex. Cosmopolitanism comes in many shapes and sizes. The variegated nature of cosmopolitanism, how it is actually practiced, is sometimes neglected because of the literature's bias for normative over political analysis. As a student of humanitarianism I have been interested in why a political community comes to see its ethics in a particular way, not whether it lives up to some abstract principles as defined by self-anointed keepers of the flame. Consequently, my instinct is not only to ask "why humanitarianism now?" but also "why humanitarianism rather than some other sort of cosmopolitan politics?"

Adjusting the question ever so slightly illuminates a curiosity in the foreign policies of American Jews. American Jewish organizations were at the forefront of international human rights, and played a leading role at home and abroad for much of the twentieth century. The cause of international human rights rose to prominence in the last part of the century, and has been on the international agenda ever since. Had American Jews said to those who joined after them, "What took you so long?" it would have been understandable. In fact, though, the more popular human rights became, the more American Jews appeared to distance themselves from that mission. What happened? The simplistic answer is that human rights no longer served American Jewish interests; in other words, the passion for human rights owed probably much less to their prophetic heritage and much more to their circumstances. But it was not simply a matter of Jews' abandoning human rights; the shift in their commitment stemmed also from the fact that they saw the United Nations and the human rights movement as having become shamelessly politicized, stalking Israel, and harboring anti-Semites. If American Jews are turning toward tikkun olam but want to keep their distance from human rights, where do they go? Humanitarianism and social justice, which are viewed as more apolitical and thus more acceptable. In general, the

American Jewish experience and the broader Jewish experience remind us to treat cosmopolitanism as part of politics.

Thus far I have discussed cosmopolitanism and tribalism as if they are separate and independent categories, but the history of the foreign policies of American Jews reveals how intertwined and mutually constituted they are. A prevailing view is that the two exist in a zero-sum relationship—more of one means less of the other. Cosmopolitanism's rise will be twinned with tribalism's demise. There is only so much room on the announcement board at my temple. Yet American Jews have not necessarily seen the two as antonyms but rather as potentially existing in a positive-sum relationship. American Jews, even at their most cosmopolitan, have wanted to retain their communal identity. American Jews, even at their most tribal, have seen the Jews as part of humanity. There are times when American Jewish organizations see humanitarianism as a way to strengthen the Jewish community. We also will see how American Jews attempt to integrate Zionism into their universalism and cosmopolitanism. Israel, for many, was not supposed to be just an expression of tribalism but also another arm of Jewish cosmopolitanism.

I explore these themes of how particularism and universalism, and tribalism and cosmopolitanism, integrate, separate, and intersect in ways that alter the foreign policies of American Jews in two areas: human rights and humanitarianism, and Israel. For the prophetically minded, human rights and humanitarianism are the quintessential expressions of cosmopolitanism. To that extent, they are a direct reflection of identity. Yet, as I have suggested, political commitments are formed not just by spiritual connections but also by interests.

Israel looms over this book. However, this is not a book about the relationship between American Jewry and Israel. It is a book about the foreign policies of American Jews and their responses to the Jewish Problem and the Jewish Question. Israel is part of that history, but it is not all of it. My hope is that situating Israel in this broader perspective will illuminate how American Jewry's feelings about Israel are shaped and reshaped by these broader questions. What are American Jews talking about when they talk about Israel? Israel, but much more. Conversations about Israel are never just about Israel. They are also about Jews' concern for Jewish survival in body and spirit, their sense of place and purpose in the world, their obligations to those inside and outside the community, and how they want to see themselves and how they want others to see them.

OVERVIEW

Chapter 1 offers a manual for understanding the foreign policies of the American Jews, exploring how their beliefs were an outgrowth of, primarily, the American experience, and, secondarily, the world. It begins by situating American Jews in historical context, contrasting their history with that of the Jews of Western and Eastern Europe, and highlighting how the American experience explains American Jewry's affinity for liberalism and non-Orthodox Jewry. These commitments explain the rise and endurance of the political theology of Prophetic Judaism, which, in turn, explains American Jews' cosmopolitan sensibility when addressing the Jewish Problem and the Jewish Question. The chapter ends with a discussion of the foreign policy of a transnational people and considers how the foreign policy process is informed by the linking of identity, interests, and institutions. Although there is no such thing as a Jewish foreign policy, a central point of debate within and between Jewish communities is: how should Jews best protect their interests and promote their values in the world?

The changing American and global contexts have led to five distinct periods in the foreign policies of American Jews, periods distinguished by a changing balance between cosmopolitanism and tribalism and different ways that American Jews thought about the Jewish Problem and the Jewish Question. Chapter 2 examines the period from the mid-nineteenth century to the turn of the century, when American Jews were absorbed by the task of acculturation. As American Jews grew more settled, accepted, and confident, they began asking the US government to use its growing power to stop the persecution of Jews abroad. In the long run, American Jews placed their faith in the same sort of liberalism and rule of law that had been so good to them. Because illiberal states that were tormenting Jews were unlikely to become converts to liberalism, the Jews of France, Britain, and the United States hoped that their governments would impose these reforms. Additionally, they were antinationalists and anti-Zionists. In their view, the answer to the Jewish Problem was not a Jewish homeland in some godforsaken backwater in the Middle East where they were not wanted. Zionism was unrealistic, and it could potentially lead to questions American Jews would prefer were never asked.

Chapter 3 explores the period from 1914 and the beginning of World War I through the end of World War II. The world changed, and so too did the foreign policy beliefs of American Jews—but not as much as might have been expected given this long stretch of murderous anti-Semitism. The American Jewish Committee went to Paris after World War I with the agenda of convincing the victors to force the new national states of Europe to recognize the fundamental rights of minorities and to lobby for a League of Nations with responsibility for monitoring and enforcing those rights. At the same time, there was a slow, cautious acceptance of Zionism. However, not all Zionisms are alike, and as American Jews increased their support for Zionism, they also gravitated toward a version that did not hinge exclusively on the Jewish state. The first American Jewish Zionists imagined a homeland for the Jews in Palestine—a place where Jews would enjoy security and share power with the indigenous, non-Jewish inhabitants. It took the Holocaust to convince the American Jews that a homeland for the Jews was not good enough and, instead, a state controlled by and for the Jewish people was needed.

Chapter 4 covers the period between World War II and 1967. In many ways 1948 was a decisive moment in the foreign policies of American Jews. This is the year that two different solutions to the Jewish Problem and the Jewish Question took firm institutional shape— the State of Israel and the creation of the Universal Declaration of Human Rights. American Jews were involved in both developments. In retrospect, two elements stand out in this period. After decades of worrying about the tensions between nationalism and cosmopolitanism, they began to relax. It also is surprising how little the creation of Israel affected American Jewry, and that tepidness stems partly from the fact that American Jews had never been die-hard nationalists.

Chapter 5 examines the two decades following 1967—the year when American Jews turned into the zealots they are said by some to have always been. Israel's victory in 1967's Six-Day War gave American Jews a renewed sense of power and pride, and their Jewishness became increasingly defined by the twin experiences of suffering (the Holocaust) and redemption (Israel). This new Jewish identity created something of a tension for American Jews: their domestic political theology continued to run toward liberalism, but their foreign policy beliefs began exhibiting greater traces of tribalism. Moreover, global cosmopolitanism was developing in ways that were not necessarily sympathetic to Jewish concerns. The human rights movement, once seen as their friend, was increasingly viewed as a possible threat to Jews and especially to Israel. Fortunately, this was also a moment when American Jews could rely on something better than human rights—American power. An American Jewry that once saw security as bound up with a culture of acceptance now found greater reassurance in the threat and use of force. The campaign to free Soviet Jews was a product of these various elements—a concern for Jewish survival, a growing disenchantment with human rights, and a rising tribalism.

Chapter 6 explores the most recent period, from 1990 to the present. There are growing signs that American Jewry's tribalism is tapering off and cosmopolitanism is experiencing a revival. Part of the reason for this shift is generational. We are now seventy years removed from the Holocaust and almost a half-century from the 1967 war; the Holocaust is an increasingly distant memory, and this generation of American Jews has few direct memories of beleaguered Israel but lots of images of Israel as a powerhouse. American Jews remain pro-Israel, but they also exhibit a growing ambivalence because of Israel's ethnonational character and concern that the failure to solve the Palestinian conflict will erode Israel's ability to be both Jewish and democratic. This generation also has few personal experiences with anti-Semitism, and it is increasingly affected by globalization and a cosmopolitanism of suffering that emphasizes obligations to those most in need—and Jews, increasingly secure, wealthy, and citizens of liberal states, no longer automatically claim the attention of those seeking to help the world's victims. American Jews have embraced tikkun olam, social justice, and humanitarianism. But not necessarily human rights, which has its eyes on Israel and, at times, carries the stench of anti-Semitism. If American Jews are becoming distant from Israel and reacquainted with cosmopolitanism, they might simply be returning to where they have always been most comfortable. The aberration, historically speaking, is quite possibly their post-1967 tribalism.

A book about the history of the foreign policies of American Jews must conclude by addressing the years ahead. Yet the future tense is likely to sound much like the past tense. American Jews will continue to have a political identity that is equal parts Jewish and American—a belief that they have special responsibilities to their fellow Jews as well as an obligation to show compassion to all peoples and to help the world find a common humanity. In other words, the tension between tribalism and cosmopolitanism will continue, although because of a more multicultural America and globalized world, cosmopolitanism is likely to be more attractive than before. Cosmopolitanism might become even more alluring if American Jews perceive Israel to be an ethnonational state whose values clash with their own. There is no reason to imagine a rupture—such histrionics belie the evidence that American Jews continue to support Israel. Yet to ignore the signs of a fraying relationship is to engage in willful disbelief. If it does come to pass, history can tell us why.

CHAPTER ONE

HEINE'S LAW AND JEWISH FOREIGN POLICIES

A PEOPLE'S POSITION AND CONDITION HAVE A POWERFUL INFLU-
ence on its foreign policy. The position of a people concerns its physical security, its vulnerability to external forces, and the extent to
which it controls its own fate. Its condition is how settled it feels
and its sense of itself in the world. All peoples live with some degree of uncertainty on both counts. There is no absolute security, either physical or ontological. However, the Jewish people reside in
the margins—and their uncertainty about who they are is intertwined
with their uncertainty about their safety.

Why are Jews such an uncertain people? According to Martin
Buber, one of the most beloved Jewish philosophers of the twentieth
century, Jews' uncertainty starts with the simple fact that they are a
diasporic people:

> When Jerusalem ceased to be a Jewish city, when the Jew was
> no longer permitted to be at home in his own country—it was
> then that he was hurled into the abyss of the world. Ever since,
> he has represented to the world the insecure man. Within that
> general insecurity which marks human existence as a whole,
> there has since that time lived a species of man to whom destiny
> has denied even the small share of dubious security other beings
> possess.[1]

Yet the reason for the insecurity goes deeper. Gentiles have never quite known what to make of the Jews. From the Gentile perspective, Jews defy all existing "historical categories and general concepts."[2] The Jews have a "spectral" quality. Gentiles have often defined the Jews, because of their mysterious nature, as a threat to whatever they believed was the ideal.[3] Because of their conceptual elusiveness, Buber continues, the Jew is "always living on ground that may at any moment give way beneath its feet."[4] Not only were Gentiles unsure of what to make of the Jews, the Jews themselves could not decide. Over the centuries they have been a tribe, a nation unto itself, and a nation that strives to "develop humanity."[5] Which is it? "To understand our position in the world," Buber concluded, "we must realize that a twofold desire comes to the fore in the history of Diaspora Jewry: the insecure Jew strives for security, the Jewish community which cannot be classified strives to be classified."[6] The only thing certain for this uncertain people is the twinned existence of the Jewish Problem and the Jewish Question.

Heine's law—if we want to understand the Jews we should begin by looking at the Gentiles—is a good starting point for understanding how the external world has influenced the internal world of the Jews, which, in turn, has shaped the Jewish orientation toward the external world. Identity is the link between the two—the external world of the Gentiles affects the identity of the Jews, and the identity of the Jews shapes their own beliefs toward the world outside their community. What makes Jewish identity particularly complicated is that the particular and the universal share joint custody. Since the Enlightenment, the tension between the particular and the universal has been central to Jewish political thought and life.[7] Whether the particular or the universal is the North Star depends on formative historical circumstances—specifically, whether the Jewish community resides in a culture of inclusion or exclusion. A tribal people will have a tribal or realist sensibility, and a prophetic people a cosmopolitan sensibility. Living under the influence of an American society more open than almost any other, American Jews resisted seeing themselves as separate and envisioned their identity and interests as best served by a cosmopolitan ethos. America's impact was immense, but the story, in fact, begins in Europe.

A WORLD OF CHANGE

For most of their history in the diaspora among the Christians, Jews had little say about the Jewish Problem, and the Jewish Question was a Talmudic exercise. When the Gentiles had a problem with the Jews, they decided how it would be handled—usually through some form of sequestration and ghettoization, but sometimes through exile, forced conversion, and extermination. Regardless of whether they were barely tolerated or openly persecuted, Jews had little choice but to be a people that dwells alone. They could spend time in their yeshivas debating the alternatives, but the answers they came up with had no significance for practical politics. Given such a harsh and unforgiving environment, and given how isolated Jewish communities were from each other, the foreign policy of Jews, such as it was, was not much more than attempting to appease those who had the power of life, death, and taxes.

Beginning in the nineteenth century and as a consequence of the Enlightenment, liberalism, and nationalism, Christians in some parts of Europe began to rethink the Jewish Problem, which invested the Jewish Question with political significance. By favoring reason over superstition, change over tradition, science over religion, and, most important, humanity over discrimination, Enlightenment thought held that people should be judged as individuals and on their achievements, not on their religion. Because the Enlightenment made it less defensible to treat some people as inherently inferior and undeserving of equal treatment and respect, it represented the beginning of the emancipation of the Jews and other minorities. "The Jews," writes Isaiah Berlin, "were emancipated under the great banner of humanism, equality, toleration, internationalism, enlightened ideals in the name of which men rose against kings and priests, ignorance and privilege."[8] Whereas once Jews were locked into a second-class status at best, the promise of their emancipation meant they could expect something better for themselves—and for their children.

The Christian offer of emancipation was not unconditional but instead came with a catch: Jews had to abandon those traditions, mannerisms, and traits that Gentiles believed kept Jews from fitting in.[9] The Jewish Question now spilled out of the yeshivas and into the streets and became part of daily politics. In synagogues, cafés, clubs, and gymnasiums, Jews in Vienna, London, Berlin, and Paris began asking themselves: How much of our Jewishness are we willing to sacrifice? Which customs, traditions, and laws are expendable? What are the core features of being Jewish? What distinguishes Jews from others? Are we a chosen people? If not, and we are just like everyone else, why stay Jewish? Being Jewish now became a *choice*—Jews could decide for themselves if they wanted to remain Jews, what being Jewish meant to them, and what bound them as a people.[10] The day that Gentiles decided they might not have a Jewish Problem was the day the Jewish Question became a matter of critical political importance for Jews.

Jews responded in three ways, ranging from rejection to assimilation. Some Jews refused temptation and, instead, retreated into fortified religious communities, interacting as little as possible with the outside world. Assimilation was a second response. Jews were ready to be rid of the "disaster" of being Jewish, as the American sociologist Horace Kallen indelicately put it.[11] After centuries of being banished from public life and restricted in residency, dress, occupation, movement, and education, many Jews were ecstatic to be able to be just like everyone else. Some accomplished this through conversion—good-bye Judaism, hello Christianity. Others joined ecumenical and interfaith movements with Christians also drawn to Enlightenment-influenced spiritual movements. Other cosmopolitan-oriented movements had many Jewish adherents.[12] Rationalists like Karl Popper believed that an "open society" would create a world in which universal values would dissolve parochial identities.[13] Others preached the end of difference through the end of private property. To socialists, religion was a narcotic that kept all people sedated, and socialism would sober them up. Socialism—the great assimilator. The classic and notorious example of such thinking is Karl Marx's *On the Jewish Question.*[14] He argued that emancipation was a confidence trick, that Jews were delusional if they thought Christians would ever truly accept them, that Jews had acquired many unsavory characteristics because of the combination of anti-Semitism and capitalism, and that their true rehabilitation and liberation was dependent on a socialist revolution.

For those desiring to avoid the extremes of self-imposed isolation and deracination, there was a very large, undefined middle ground that mixed the particular and the universal. Many Jews wanted to expand their horizons while retaining their Jewish identity; others wanted to preserve the past without becoming living fossils. The Jews were not the only people to confront the challenge of maintaining a sense of self in an age of secularization, modernization, and other homogenizing pressures. Every group was experiencing its version of the Jewish Question. Yet arguably these dilemmas were acutely felt by the Jews because the stakes seemed to be so high.

Perhaps because of the severity of the stakes, many of the most influential social theorists of this period were Jews who used their personal encounters with the Jewish predicament to reflect on broader historical currents and the Jewish condition. Karl Marx, Émile Durkheim, Georg Simmel, Karl Popper, Claude Lévi-Strauss, Franz Boas, Norbert Elias, Sigmund Freud, Herbert Marcuse, Hannah Arendt, and Isaiah Berlin are some of the Jewish intellectuals of the age who made important contributions to modern social and political thought and to the debate within the Jewish community regarding its confrontation with modernity.[15]

This internal debate among the Jews was not for the thin-skinned. Jews who defended a Jewish communal identity accused Jews seen as leaning too far toward cosmopolitanism of being self-hating Jews. For instance, Isaiah Berlin endorsed the existence of a Jewish identity on the grounds that all humans have an urge to be members of a group, and he intimated that cosmopolitans suffered from various emotional maladies and psychoanalytic neuroses.[16] Conversely, Jews who leaned toward cosmopolitanism condemned the more communally oriented for being insular, irrational, backward, clannish, and chauvinistic. While the Jewish intellectual class was exchanging ideas and insults, many European Jews were voting with their feet, happily leaving the smallness of the Jewish community and forging new connections with a world that had previously been declared off limits to them.[17] But, the moment they left the ghetto, they faced the predicament of how far to go and how much to leave behind.

Jews seeking a comfortable middle ground found a home in pluralism and liberalism. Pluralism's fundamental belief is that humans participate in society not only as individuals but also as members of community, which provides a source of identity, meaning, and emotional and physical security. Our desire to be part of a group is quite human—and having a group identity keeps us human. Modernization, however, can detach us from others and ourselves. Modernization shreds tradition, culture, and the comforts of identity and offers mainly autonomy and material freedom in its place. Alienated from themselves and others, individuals are left struggling to find a home in an unfamiliar and soulless world. Pluralism can be an antidote, protecting us from these dispiriting effects by keeping us comfortably connected to the communal. Indeed, one argument, which early American Zionists advocated, is that without a secure group identity, individuals are unable or unwilling to be full and productive members of society.

Pluralism made it safe to be a member of a group, and liberalism ensured that all individuals, regardless of the groups they belonged to, would be treated equally and fairly. As Irving Horowitz observes: "If Jewishness is to be 'defeated,' it will be done precisely by the same forces of fanaticism assaulting liberalism. For Judaism has become, perhaps against its own theological predilection, a cardinal expression of liberalism. And for the liberal society, the attitude toward Jews has become a test case of whether liberalism is possible."[18]

There are two kinds of liberalism, and Jews have been drawn to both. There is a liberalism of equality, which holds that humans have rights because of their humanity; individuals should have liberty in body, thought, and soul; the best state is a limited state that protects rather than crushes individual liberties; and the principle of self-interest should shape the institutions of economy, society, and polity. Jews savored the promise of equality and the opportunity to be seen as "men on the street." There also is a liberalism of egalitarianism, which aspires to level political, economic, and cultural inequalities.

Jews are associated with both movements, but it is the liberalism of equality that offered the initial promise of deliverance.[19] Although liberalism is now identified as a conservative force in society, it was quite radical for its time. Prior to liberalism a person's privileges, rights, and station in life were determined by religion, national identity, family name, gender, and tradition. Liberalism, a rebellion against "inherited

ways of life," changed all that.[20] Christians now began thinking the
unthinkable: Jews and other outcasts were free and equal members of
society. Liberalism was the modern-day Moses, and everywhere liberalism went, the Jews were sure to follow. Word that Napoleon and
the French revolution had liberated the Jews had a convulsive effect
among the Jews of Europe. In Martin Buber's novel, *For the Sake of
Heaven*, Orthodox Jews in a central European ghetto believe that Napoleon must be the messiah, symbolizing liberalism's nearly divine
status among the Jews.[21] In France, Jews flocked to republicanism and
its promise of equality under the law and citizenship for all, and, in
doing so, opposed the clerical and conservative wings of French society.[22] Similar events occurred in Britain, Germany, and other parts
of Europe. On the occasion of Rabbi Dov Meisels's election to the
provisional Austrian Reichsrath in 1848, he explained, playfully, why
he sat on the left side of the aisle: "Juden haben keine Rechte—Jews
have no right(s)."[23] Jews, moreover, did not just passively wait for
liberalism's arrival; they were among its most vocal advocates and
at times claimed co-creator status, insisting that the values of Judaism and liberalism not only coincided but that Judaism also inspired
liberalism.[24]

In addition to the Enlightenment and liberalism, nationalism also
was disrupting European politics and the world of the Jews. A nation is a political community that is bound by a common history,
language, religion, spirit, and sense of fate. Nationalism and the goal
of statehood give the nation a special status in modern politics. And
as self-defined nations went about their business of nation and state
building, some had open membership while others were restricted.

The classic distinction, introduced by the Zionist and Jewish scholar
of nationalism Hans Kohn, is that between civic and ethnic nationalism.[25] In ethnic nationalism, blood, lineage, kinship, and tribe determine membership; that is, "an individual's deepest attachments are
inherited, not chosen."[26] States that are constituted by ethnic nationalism typically privilege one group over another, and such favoritism
and discrimination is often manifest in law, politics, economics, and
culture. Israel, for instance, has strong elements of ethnic nationalism because the Jewish identity dominates Israel's culture, institutions, politics, and law. In civic nationalism, on the other hand, the

nation is "a community of equal, rights-bearing citizens, united in patriotic attachment to a shared set of political practices and values."[27] The United States has a civic nationalism, accepting the possibility that all individuals, regardless of their origins, backgrounds, or heritage, belong to a single union. Simply put, ethnic nationalism is exclusive, whereas civic nationalism is inclusive.

The rise of nationalism profoundly affected Jewish life. This transnational political community, the Jews, was being forced to find a place in a world increasingly carved into different territories that demanded exclusive loyalty or defined the nation in ways that excluded Jews.[28] After centuries of having little choice but to be a people apart, Jews now were being expected to shift their loyalties to the state, to demonstrate greater obligation to their fellow citizens than to their brethren in another country, and to think about what was in the best interest of the state rather than the Jewish community. To some Jews this represented a new kind of prison because their ties to the Jewish people were being severed. For others it was liberation. Whether nationalism was more positive than negative depended on which form prevailed.

Civic nationalism and its accompanying liberal tenets meant that Jews had the opportunity to be accepted as equal citizens of the nation-state, but only if they abandoned those features of Jewish life that Gentiles found offensive and pledged their loyalty to the state and not to Jews. In the debate over the Jewish emancipation in France in 1789, Count Stanislas de Clermont-Tonnerre declared: "To the Jews as a nation—nothing; to the Jews as human beings, everything."[29] If the Jews wanted to be a nation, then they could not be French, and if they wanted to be French, then they had to rid themselves of any thoughts of being a nation. Jews had to make a choice. Accepting their place in the French nation, Jews recategorized themselves as a religious community and became card-carrying, flag-waving Republicans.[30]

In France and other countries where Jews received citizenship, they inherited new rights and responsibilities, including military service. Although hardly thrilled about the idea of getting shot and worried that they might be forced to shoot at a fellow Jew, Jews nevertheless saw military service as (1) a necessary evil, (2) the price of admission, or (3) a welcoming rite of passage.[31] Regardless of their feelings about military service, Jews were often overrepresented in the ranks. According to the early Zionist thinker Max Nordau, nearly 900,000 Jews served during World War I—out of a total population of thirteen million Jews and comprising about 7 percent of the total number of soldiers.[32] Jewish communities proudly memorialized Jewish soldiers who had sacrificed their lives for their country.

In those countries where ethnic nationalism took root, Jews did not have to consider which features of their Jewishness they were prepared to surrender to become part of the nation because they were, for all intents and purposes, automatically disqualified from membership. In the emerging folk nationalisms of Eastern Europe in the late nineteenth century, Jews were defined as outsiders because of their heritage, dress, religion, and Yiddish tongue. Life got progressively harder and more dangerous as boundaries between "us" and "them" became more rigid and legalized. Under such circumstances Jews had very limited choices: prepare for a life of ostracism; join movements such as socialism that aspired to remove all differences between peoples; become Jewish nationalists; or immigrate to Jewish-friendly lands.[33]

The Golden Land

America made Western Europe look like Eastern Europe. From the very beginning Jews in America enjoyed more rights than they ever had in Europe, faced anti-Semitism but never on the scale that existed in Europe, and were allowed to be both Jews and Americans. Consequently, American Jews worried less about the Jewish Problem than they did the Jewish Question. America, quite simply, posed a nearly unprecedented dilemma—and one that continues today.[34] If Jews assimilated into the American society, they might disappear completely. Yet if they insisted on their distinction, they might lose out on the American promise. The challenge was to balance their Jewishness and their Americanness. As Irving Howe poignantly wrote, "The Jewish immigrant world branded upon its sons and daughters the mark of separateness even while encouraging them to dream of universalism. This subculture might have been formed to preserve ethnic continuity, but it was the kind of continuity that would reach its triumph in self-disintegration. It taught its children both to conquer the Gentile world and to be conquered by it, both to leave an intellectual impression and to accept the dominant social norms."[35] America's hospitality threatened to do to the Jews what centuries of hatred, exclusion, and ostracism could not.

The desire to be equally American and Jewish drove American Jews into the arms of liberalism, pluralism, and other ideologies of inclusion and tolerance.[36] Committed to the fundamental principles of reason, rationality, and humanity, American Jews viewed the liberalism of equality as the key to political, economic, and cultural security. Until the 1930s Jews were not strongly identified with one party or the other. In fact, many of the most prominent American Jewish leaders were stalwart members of the Republican Party, the party of Lincoln, and were opponents of hardened traditions that restricted the right and opportunity to be a "real" American.[37] Pluralism was equally attractive, because it made belonging to the group both organic and beneficial to society. Horace Kallen offered one of the earliest and most influential statements on the relationship between the communal identity and American pluralism. Writing against the claim that a "melting pot" does and should exist, Kallen developed the concept of "cultural pluralism" and the idea that different cultural groups can have one foot in the particular and the other in the universal, and that diversity is a strength, not a weakness. Such thinking reassured both an American society that was attempting to integrate millions of immigrants and American Jews who wanted to be both Jewish and American. Jews in America could enjoy a virtuous circle of identity, but only if they saw themselves as an enlightened and inclusive people.

REFORMING JEWS

The Enlightenment, liberalism, and nationalism shaped not only Jewish political life but also Judaism. Although there have always been important historical and regional variations in the practice of Judaism, until the eighteenth century these were relatively minor. But then massive societal change led to considerable experimentation and fragmentation. Eventually three major branches emerged—Orthodox, Conservative, and Reform, distinguished in part by the compromises they were willing to make with the modern world. Orthodox Judaism became the branch that refused to surrender, and in the Orthodox world Judaism continued to influence nearly everything, including how to pray, marry, raise children, eat, dress, work, shop, move around the city, and socialize. Conservative Judaism attempted to find a midpoint between a Judaism that makes no compromises and a Judaism that makes (too) many.

Directly influenced by Enlightenment thought, the promise of emancipation, and the desire to remain Jews, Reform Judaism was not just a proper noun but also a verb—it became the name of a branch of Judaism and a movement to alter Judaism to accommodate the world. It emerged first in Germany, spread throughout Europe and then America—that is, wherever the outside world extended an open hand.[38] Reform Judaism affected all aspects of Jewish life.[39] It influenced how Jews saw Judaism and interpreted texts. Whereas once Jews treated the Torah as God-given, new "scientific" methodologies encouraged them to see it as a human artifact, written over centuries by many different hands that interjected the politics, culture, and intrigues of the times. From this perspective, the Enlightenment and rationalism would help rejuvenate a Judaism that was suffocating from years of insularity. Whereas once Jews accepted religious laws as eternally relevant, they now began to see them as anachronistic, embarrassing artifacts ill-suited for the modern age and desperately needing revision. Influenced by emerging rationalist perspectives that emphasized the progressive spirit, Jews began treating religious texts not as backward-looking but instead as supporting an interpretation of Judaism that was enlightened and forward-thinking. Judaism, insisted the nineteenth-century German Orthodox Rabbi Samson Raphael Hirsch, is a "religion tied to progress."[40]

Reform Judaism also made it easier for Jews to practice Judaism and to do so in a way that resembled their churchgoing neighbors. Jews were no longer expected to keep kosher inside and outside the home, to observe all Jewish holidays, to make the Sabbath a strict day of rest, or to separate men and women in the synagogue. If Jews were not devoting themselves to Judaism, then they needed help being Jews, including rabbis to lead them in services and prayer books translated from Hebrew into the local language. In order to appear less alien to their Christian neighbors, choirs and organs were brought into many temples.

In addition to reforming the internal world of Judaism, Reform Judaism reconceived how Jews should relate to the external world. For much of their history, the Jews believed they had a covenant with God, were sworn to uphold all 613 commandments, and were models of stoic religious devotion. They were a chosen people, their exile from their homeland was punishment for their sins, and they must be steadfastly pious until the day of redemption.[41] Reform Judaism saw things quite differently. Instead of dedicating themselves to arcane religious laws that did little more than advertise their strangeness, Jews should emphasize "the ethical, hence universal, teachings of Judaism, teachings presumably shared with Christians."[42] Instead of being chosen and in exile, Jews now saw themselves as no better than others but having a special responsibility to heal the world, which they could do only if they scattered to all corners of the earth. Reform Judaism flourished on fertile American soil because it allowed Jews to remain Jews and become just like all Americans.

Prophetic Theology

Reform Judaism found its religious feet in Prophetic Judaism.[43] The prophetic tradition refers to the sayings of the prophets who lived in the seventh and eighth centuries BCE, a period in which the Jewish tribes were having difficulty sustaining themselves, religiously or politically. They were a divided kingdom, and Hebrews frequently, and quite literally, were at war with each other. They also were battling other peoples on a regular basis. In order to escape this unending conflict, the Hebrews proposed to create a unified monarchy.

Although this might have been the go-to solution for other peoples in this age, it was a controversial proposal for the Hebrews. The Jews had long considered monarchy to be an illegitimate form of rule. The only king was God. A human king not only would see himself as godlike but might also impose laws that violated God's command-ments. Despite warnings from those like the prophet Samuel, the He-brews created a monarchy, perhaps responding to the real dangers of the here and now instead of the hypothesized dangers of the future. However, Samuel's fears were becoming less speculative and more tangible. These mortal kings began presenting themselves as deities. They were incorporating into Judaism other gods and the pagan reli-gions of their neighbors. Under the cover of pietism and righteousness, they were sinning, violating God's commandments, and committing all kinds of injustices, including accumulating wealth and power while neglecting the needs of the people, engaging in corruption, and permitting slavery. In response to these transgressions, dozens of prophets, including Amos, several Isaiahs, Hosea, and Micah, pro-fessed that God had spoken directly to them, commanding them to exhort the Jews to return to a path of righteousness, to reaffirm that there was only one, invisible God, to choose good over evil, and to work for justice. As the twentieth-century Orthodox Rabbi Abraham Joshua Heschel wrote, "Prophecy is the voice that God has lent to si-lent agony, a voice to the plundered poor, to the profane riches of the world. It is a form of living, a crossing point of God and man. God is raging in the prophet's words."[44]

The prophetic theology not only drew from a different part of text but also shifted the emphasis of Judaism from ritual to ethics. God's message was clear: to be righteous requires more than unthinkingly following commandments, reflexively holding ceremonies, and per-forming rituals—it also demands an ethical life of treating others kindly and working for justice. A house of worship that becomes a "den of thieves" is not pious.

> Do I need your endless sacrifices? I am stuffed with burnt offerings. . . . I cannot stand your pomp and solemnity. I am disgusted by your ceremonies of time and season. . . . Wash yourselves clean, put away your evil acts, cease from doing evil, learn to do good. Seek justice, aid the wronged, defend the powerless, the orphan and the widow. (Isaiah 1:11–19)
>
> I hate your holy days and despise your festivals; I am not moved by your solemn gatherings. Your offerings are rejected; I ignore

your slaughtered gifts. Spare me the sound of your hymns, and let the music of your lutes fall silent; I am not listening. Rather let justice well up like the water, let righteousness flow like a mighty stream. (Amos 5:21–24)

The prophets wanted to restore ethics in Judaism.[45]

Prophetic Judaism called on Jews to expand their ethical horizon from the particular to the universal. All people must be treated equally. Jews, many reform-minded Jewish leaders boasted, practically conceived the principles of nondiscrimination and humanity; this was the revolutionary revelation of the Noahide Code. Some also claimed to have invented the Golden Rule, citing the saying of the first-century Rabbi Hillel the Great: "That which is despicable to you, do not do to your fellow, this is the whole Torah, and the rest is commentary, go and learn it." Jews also needed to widen their circle of compassion. The proverb "whoever saves a single life saves the world" applies equally to Jews and non-Jews. Universalism also demands that Jews extend their spatial horizons, expanding their commitments from the local to the global. The result of this sacred work, the prophets vowed, would be moral progress, justice, and peaceful coexistence. Some of the most famous passages in Prophetic Judaism contain visions of this coveted setting:

> The wolf will live with the lamb; the leopard will lie down with the kid; the calf, the lion cub, and the fatling will walk together, and a little child will lead them. (Isaiah 11:6–9)
>
> You shall beat your swords into ploughshares and your spears into pruning knives. Nations will not lift up sword against nation; nor will you study war any more. (Micah 4:3)

The prophetic image of the Jews as possessing a universalizing mission became a staple of modern Jewish political thought.

To fulfill their responsibilities, Jews would have to disperse across the world. They would be a light unto nations.

> Yea, He saith, "It is too light a thing for you to be My servant, to establish the tribes of Jacob, and to restore the offspring of Israel. I shall submit you as a light unto the nations, to be My salvation until the end of the earth." (Isaiah 49:6)

I the LORD have called unto you in righteousness, and have taken hold of your hand, and submitted you as the people's covenant, as a light unto the nations. (Isaiah 42:6)

According to Rabbi Leo Baeck, who led a Berlin congregation during the Nazi years, was later deported to a concentration camp, then settled in America after the war: "This mission goes beyond Israel itself; it is an election for the sake of others. All Israel is the messenger of the Lord, the 'servant of God' who is to guard religion for all lands and from whom the light shall radiate to the nations."[46] Exile, consequently, lost its traditionally negative meaning and became an unfair characterization of the Jewish diaspora. The Jews were scattered to the far corners of the earth not because they were being punished but rather to help the cause of social justice.

The prophetic vision of Jews helping to create new bonds of humanity and bringing about moral progress, peace, and justice worked in favor of integration in several ways. It instructed Jews to find their place among the nations and discover what they had in common with other peoples. Jews should acculturate—but not to the point that they completely assimilated. In other words, the prophetic vision allowed Jews to have the particular and the universal. In addition to helping Jews harmonize the possible tensions between the two, it gave them a new purpose and reason to stay Jews—they needed to maintain their group if only because it would benefit the greater good. Historically speaking, Jews have offered a litany of reasons for why they must continue as a people. Torah. They are the chosen people. It is their birthright. Their ancestors did not defend Judaism to the death so that a future generation could abandon it once the going got easy. Parents want to give their children a core identity in a fluid world. Anti-Semitism is still a global menace and Jews need to identify with and protect their own. And, after the Holocaust, the need to refuse Hitler a posthumous victory. The prophetic tradition added to the list of reasons as it suggested that Jews must survive in order to serve humanity.

Serving humanity would also serve the immediate and long-term interests of the Jews. Bringing out the more humanistic aspects of Judaism would help ward off their enemies.[47] For many reform-minded

Jews who were seeking a way to escape tradition and demonstrate to their Gentile neighbors that they were model citizens, the prophetic emphasis on ethics was a godsend. It was always a good thing for a vilified minority with a reputation for clannishness and particularism to demonstrate its connection to and concern for others. In addition to enhancing their security through greater acceptance, they would be rewarded for their good behavior. God pledged to give the Jews peace and plenty if they did what was expected of them. They would receive "granaries . . . piled high with grain . . . and barrels over-flow[ing] with wine and oil" (Joel 2:22). A world organized around universal values, moreover, will not only create a world of peace but will also be a world that embraces the Jews. In general, Prophetic Judaism addressed both the Jewish Problem and the Jewish Question —by recognizing their particularism through universalism, Jews would create a space for themselves in the world, help to create a better world, and secure their own survival.

Relatedly, in the hands of Reform Judaism, Prophetic Judaism crossed the line from theology into political theology.[48] An ongoing challenge for any religious community is the translation of theological concepts rooted in text into political choices shaped by context. In short, polit-ical theology is the result of connecting the transcendental to the im-manent. The search for a "usable past" is central to this exercise.[49] All three Abrahamic religions contain a wealth of admonitions, sayings, and commandments created by many different hands over centuries and often containing contradictory values. Every statement of "thou shalt not kill" has a parallel statement that offers some shockingly liberal exemptions. There is no one, true meaning. Religious texts do not speak for themselves; there is an active, human, process of inter-pretation. Consequently, all religious communities debate both the meaning of texts and which elements are most urgent and salient. And they often favor some interpretations over others depending on how well they answer the challenges of the times. For instance, the American Jewish World Service's Ruth Messinger described the pro-cess by which the agency developed its training manuals: "The edu-cation department at AJWS mines Jewish texts and tradition to create learning materials that demonstrate the intersection of Judaism and social justice."[50] It would have been just as easy to find support for the

Hebrew maxim *aniye ircha kodmim*—"the poor of your town come first." If American Jews are more attracted to AJWS's message than to the tribal-sounding parts of the Talmud, it is because it better reflects their Americanized state of mind.

Like members of all religious communities, Jews have struggled to convert religious tenets into political practice.[51] For Jews attempting to retain some degree of communal identity while also participating in a welcoming society, reform Judaism signaled their "political accommodation with the emerging state," presenting a "Judaism that would not only be amendable to modern politics, but would also provide the foundation for participation in the political order."[52] But the very process of attempting to search for a usable past to accommodate themselves to the emerging political order invariably provoked a debate about identity.

As they imagined their relationship to the new political order, Jews were forced to ask, "What kind of people are we?" In the abstract there are innumerable ways to categorize a people—tribe, nation, ethnicity, civilization, race, religious community, clan, creed, sect, caste, and on and on. Yet how a people chooses to define itself and others is limited by conceptual imagination and the political language of the historical moment. Until the nineteenth century the "nation" was not on the ballot because the concept was not part of lived politics. Moreover, the meaning of these concepts is open to interpretation. A people might consider itself to be a nation, but which kind, ethnic or civic? Were these peoples an enlightened or backward nation? This process of classification is better understood as a political exercise in branding than as a scientific exercise in taxonomy.[53]

For much of their history, Jews had considered themselves to be something of a tribe.[54] A tribe is a social group—often existing long before the emergence of the state—defined by kinship, blood, and lineage. In fact, one of the earliest uses of the term, from twelfth-century Middle English, referred to the twelve tribes of Israel. It is nearly impossible to become a member of the tribe if not born into it, and once a member, exit is difficult. Membership, in short, is involuntary. Tribes can be associated with a piece of territory, but often they are nomadic or stateless. Tribes tend to keep to themselves, are wary of outsiders, and typically do not engage the world except to protect their survival. Although they can be hospitable to strangers, their principal obligation is to fellow members, and outsiders are often treated differently and severely.

Beginning in the nineteenth century most political communities looking for respectability and dignity referred to themselves as nations. Except for an emerging handful of Jews in Eastern Europe toward the end of the century, the reform-minded, stirred by the possibilities offered by the Enlightenment, did not see the Jewish people as a nation.[55] To be a nation, according to the political vernacular of the time, implied that a people sees itself as distinct from all others, deserves self-determination, and can be secure and fulfill its national destiny only if it has its own national state. If Jews were a nation, then they were poor candidates for citizenship in the newly emerging national states of Europe. In the debate in the French Assembly in 1789 about Jewish emancipation, the question centered on whether the Jews could be anything other than a tribe. On one side were those who accepted the possibility but who also noted that it meant that Jews had to lose their clannish mentality and ways. On the other were those who believed that the Jews were a tribe that forever saw itself as a people apart and that constantly looked to another homeland.[56] Many Jewish intellectuals of the period either condemned the idea that the Jews were a nation or labored to distinguish those nations that are unto themselves from those nations that are striving for the collective good—and insisting that Jews were the latter. Martin Buber, for instance, could accept that the Jews were a nation, but only if it was a nation that acted on behalf of humanity.

The Jews in America were more certain about what kind of people they were *not* than the kind they were. They were not a chosen people, if "chosen" meant some sort of divine mission that only they could undertake.[57] They were not a tribe or anything that bore a family resemblance to a people that appeared unto itself. Yet neither did they want to become cartoonish cosmopolitans. Instead, American Jews wanted to retain their communal identity, to continue to see themselves as descending from a "cohesive ancestral group with particular customs, traditions, and values—religious, linguistic, and otherwise."[58] In short, they wanted to retain their sense of distinction but to avoid self-love.

Accordingly, some American Jews accepted that the Jews were a nation, but insisted it was the kind with a universalizing spirit. Other important voices who maintained a prophetic outlook objected to the category of the nation on the grounds that it was too closely identified with insularity. For instance, Mordecai Kaplan feared that if the Jews were called a nation they would be presumed to be the regressive kind. Instead he proposed the concept of "civilization." Although many other modernizing and non-Orthodox Jewish theologians rejected Kaplan's notion of a civilization (in part because it seemed to trivialize Judaism), they generally agreed with the prophetic idea that Jews were a people connected to the world. Later in his life Kaplan did write of the Jews as a nation, but insisted that it was an "ethical nationhood." In general, American Jews have considered many labels over the decades—from religious community to nation to civilization—but most of these labels describe a Jewish people as sketched by the prophets. Such beliefs have influenced how American Jews have seen themselves and the world.

THE FOREIGN POLICIES OF A
TRANSNATIONAL PEOPLE

Political communities that have a collective identity, a need to manage their relations with the external world and to reflect on their place in the world and their obligations to others, are likely to be concerned with foreign policy. Foreign policy is the process by which a political community organizes its relations with "outsiders" for the purpose of protecting its fundamental interests and values. In modern international relations we tend to assume that these political communities are states, but any political community, including a nation without a state, will have the basic elements of a foreign policy: a collective identity, a set of interests, and institutions that attempt to protect it from dangers posed by the outside world.

There is not a Jewish foreign policy, and Jewish political communities struggle over what it should be. Yet the existence of this struggle indicates a fundamental feature of Jewish political life: there is a Jewish political community. As in all communities, there are debates about who is a member and has the privileges, responsibilities, and burdens of membership. But Jews do talk about themselves as if they are a political community, and they articulate a set of interests, including the survival of the community. The foreign policies of a Jewish community are designed to serve two immediate functions—to alleviate Jewish suffering (the Jewish Problem) and to assure its identity in the world (the Jewish Question).

No political community, not a state or transnational people, will easily agree on how to protect its identity, interests, and values. But the community will nevertheless feel the need to organize to do so. The moment the Jewish community became a transnational political community beginning in the nineteenth century, it began the difficult process of trying to organize transnationally to protect Jewish interests. There is nothing insidious about a political community organizing to protect itself to advance its interests in the world.[59] It is quite normal. Indeed, to do otherwise in a world that has demonstrated considerable hostility to that political community would be self-destructive. If the Jews have a longer tradition of organizing transnationally, it is because of a healthy survival response to the intensity and relentlessness of global anti-Semitism.[60]

Beginning in the nineteenth century and mirroring the developing internationalism of the times, Jews began to organize transnationally to address their common concerns. Who represented the Jews, or at least attempted to defend their interests? Sometimes it was well-connected bankers such as Baron de Rothschild. In 1860 the French Jewish elite established the Alliance Israélite Universelle, which soon sprouted chapters around the world. British and German versions emerged thereafter. When Jewish leaders met with government officials, they were said to be engaged in diplomacy.[61] Herzl presented himself, and was often received by foreign governments, as something of an ambassador of the Jews. Jewish organizations were present at many multilateral meetings in Europe during the late nineteenth century, in part because the Jewish Problem was almost always on the agenda. In the late nineteenth century Zionist organizations began popping up around Europe and the United States, organizations that represented every shade of Zionism.[62] In the attempt to improve their influence by speaking with a single voice, Zionists occasionally created umbrella organizations. Leo Motzkin, a Russian Jew who held a series of leadership posts in Jewish and Zionist institutions, helped establish the Committee of Jewish Delegations in 1918 to try to align the many Jewish organizations that descended on Paris to represent Jewish interests at Versailles. This committee was the forerunner to the World Jewish Congress, which was established in 1936. However, the attempt to instill unity in the ranks often triggered the creation of rival transnational organizations. The search for consensus could sow division.

"Jewish diplomacy" ended with the creation of the State of Israel. Now there existed a self-proclaimed Jewish state that defended the "national" interest defined by the interests of the Jewish people rather than by the state's interests.[63] Israeli leaders often sounded as if they spoke on behalf of all Jews, and not just Israelis. When they did, diaspora leaders often objected vehemently, not only did different Jewish communities have very different interpretations of what Jews wanted, but such pronouncements from Israel also made it seem as though the Jews had not only dual loyalties but also privileged Jewish interests over the interests of, say, the United States. To try and reduce the conflict, American Jewish and Israeli leaders have sometimes established a modus operandi that defines their mutual roles and responsibilities and have occasionally called for a consensus-making body, but they have come no closer than holding periodic meetings for a "healthy exchange of views."[64]

Before and after the establishment of the State of Israel, American Jews tried to address their common foreign policy concerns. The American Jewish community has employed all sorts of foreign policy instruments. They have raised money through high-profile fund-raising campaigns and placed *tzedakah* boxes in homes and stores to collect change. They have helped develop international law, norms, and institutions they hope will simultaneously address the Jewish Problem and the Jewish Question. They have sent representatives to multilateral meetings and international conferences and to meet with foreign governments. In 1919 an American Jewish delegation attended the postwar talks in Paris, and in 1945 several American Jewish nongovernmental organizations held consultative status at the preparatory talks in San Francisco for the creation of the United

Nations. American Jews and Jewish organizations have used quiet diplomacy. They also have created a sophisticated lobbying arsenal in Washington. The American Israel Public Affairs Committee (AIPAC) is the best known, but unsung organizations have been responsible for lesser-known but equally impressive legislative victories. Twice in the twentieth century American Jews successfully defied the White House to pass congressional legislation to pressure Russia (in 1911) and the Soviet Union (in 1974) to improve the treatment of its Jewish minority.

American Jews are a divided people, and it can appear as if there is an association for every possible combination of religious and political outlook. The American Jewish Year Book lists the astounding figure of 17,500 organizations.[65] Assuming a population estimate of 6,800,000 American Jews, there is one organization for every 388 Jews. No single organization represents or speaks for American Jews, though many pretend otherwise. The Conference of the Presidents of Major Jewish Organizations claims to represent the voice of American Jewry, but this restrictive club has only fifty members. A century ago the American Jewish Committee, the establishment organization, opposed an increasingly popular Zionism, especially among Jewish immigrants from Eastern Europe. Today the American Jewish "establishment" is arguably more tribal than are most American Jews. AIPAC does very little to correct the perception that it is the American Jewish community's representative on all things Israel, though recently its title is being challenged by the "pro-Israel and pro-peace" J Street.[66] To write a book that intends to provide a comprehensive review of associational life in the American Jewish community would be quite a task. Fortunately, that is not my ambition. Instead, I will selectively discuss a handful of organizations that are the best known and the longest-standing—such as AJC, AIPAC, AJJDC, and AJWS— that provide a window into the relationship between tribal and cosmopolitan sentiments in the foreign policies of American Jews. In general, the diversity of opinion is why I emphasize the foreign poli*cies* of American Jews.

Jewish political communities might agree that there is a need to address the Jewish Problem and the Jewish Question, but they exhibit considerable differences of opinion on how best to do so. One of the distinguishing features of this debate among Jews, in America and around the world, is that they are self-consciously wrestling with which categories of identity best reflect Jewish political thought and action; how these categories relate to practical politics; and which category would best advance Jewish interests and be least disquieting to non-Jews.

For more than 150 years the terms of the debate about identity have implicated the concepts of nationalism and internationalism. Nationalism, both in the Jewish community and in the broader world, largely meant that a people or nation would attempt to develop itself and defend its interests in the territorial confines of a state and worry about its relative power because competing nationalisms do not just exist but also exhibit aggressive tendencies. Depending on the times, the prevailing meaning of nationalism, and its vernacularization by nationalists, Jewish communities treated nationalism as either acceptable or mephitic. As we will see, a century ago it was only after Zionism had been Americanized—that is, drained of its more exclusionary and tribal elements—that it became more acceptable to an American Jewish community that was attempting to prove it could become truly American. For those who objected to the image of the distinct communities of the world building garrisons, and instead favored the vision of the peoples of the world establishing harmonious relations based on their shared interests and common values, the discourse of internationalism became the preferred alternative. Internationalists imagined just that—national communities interacting for their mutual betterment and understanding.

How do these concepts relate to tribalism and cosmopolitanism? We can think of each as containing a set of dispositions and sensibilities, almost a philosophical orientation to the world, which reflects the differences between particularism/tribalism and universalism/cosmopolitanism. Consequently, these concepts map onto each other in the following way:

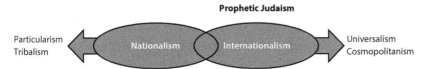

Figure 1.1. Jewish Identity and Foreign Policy Beliefs

Particularism/tribalism and universalism/cosmopolitanism are religious and political orientations that exist in the margins. Nationalism and internationalism are broad kinds of foreign policy projects, often rivals but sometimes borrowing so much from each other that they almost become distinctions without a difference. Prophetic Judaism overlaps with internationalism and can include elements of a nationalism that encourages cooperation among peoples. For simplicity's sake, I will refer mainly to cosmopolitanism and tribalism, and proceed as if internationalism is inclusive of cosmopolitanism and nationalism of tribalism.

Tribes beget tribalism and nationalism. The doctrine of realpolitik, for all intents and purposes, encompasses tribal foreign policy beliefs and practices. A realist foreign policy has several characteristics. It assumes the world to be a hostile place. This bleak environment requires that states and other political communities attend first and foremost to their security, which is best achieved through the threat of and use of force. Peace through superior firepower. Realists also advise against trusting others. In this world there are no friends, only relationships of convenience. Actors will keep their agreements when it suits their needs—not the needs of those they are pledged to help. Relatedly, international law and global institutions such as the League of Nations and the United Nations offer limited or no protection. The weak might put their hope in these false promises, but they do so because they lack power and have no other alternatives. Ethics, morality, and principles will not save the weak. The world is a lonely and nasty place, always has been and always will be, with no hope for progress.

Sometimes the Jewish people are portrayed as quintessential realists.[67] They are products of an environment that, historically, has been harsh beyond belief. For good reasons Jews have been concerned with their survival.[68] Even those Jewish philosophers who want the Jews to embrace their prophetic selves acknowledge that they live in a world that leaves them little margin for error. The Jews are a living example of the Greek historian Thucydides' classic statement that the strong do what they can and the weak suffer what they must. The history of the Jewish people exhibits considerable uncertainty regarding their condition and their position, but exhibits near certainty that they can depend on no one but themselves. Buber, once again, effectively summarizes this view:

> Every symbiosis it enters upon is treacherous. Every alliance in its history contains an inevitable termination clause, every union with other civilizations is informed with a secret divisive force. It is this inescapable state of insecurity which we have in mind when we designate the Jewish Diaspora as *galut*, i.e., exile.[69]

For realist-minded Jews, the best way to ensure Jewish security is to act like all other peoples: get a state, acquire a military, and show the world that Jewish life is not expendable. And the realist admonition to not be distracted by the plight of others and to avoid the false promises of law and institutions are lessons well learned.[70]

The foreign policy beliefs of a prophetic people trend toward cosmopolitanism and internationalism.[71] Cosmopolitanism can be broadly understood as the belief that all individuals are part of a shared humanity and common morality. Like realism, cosmopolitanism has many varieties. There are "thick" versions that portray humans as easily malleable and the global community as something of a kaleidoscope. There are "thin" versions that value connectedness but not to the point of surrendering inherited identities. The goal is not to eradicate all differences, just those that are parochial and limit one's worldview. In fact, "particular cultures and subcultures are . . . repositories for insights and experiences that can be drawn upon in the interests of a more comprehensive outlook on the world."[72] The universal and the particular can coexist—and nourish each other.

Whether thick or thin, cosmopolitanism begins with humanity. Each person is of equal worth and a subject of moral concern. A common humanity, moreover, compels us to transcend our particularistic identities and see ourselves as connected to all others, near and far. By expanding our moral vision from the self to the other, we will create a healthy distance from our own culture, achieving a more complex and complete human experience. Cosmopolitanism also imposes negative and positive duties. We must avoid taking action that produces unnecessary and foreseeable harm. We also must act to "prevent and alleviate human suffering wherever it may be found," "protect life and health and . . . ensure respect for the human being," and "promote mutual understanding, friendship, cooperation and lasting peace amongst all peoples."[73] Cosmopolitans envisage a world in which a common humanity radiates peace and justice from the earth to the heavens.

There is a chasm between the world that exists and the world that cosmopolitans hope will exist. However, unlike realists who assume that the world will never change, cosmopolitans have not given up on humans; instead, many cosmopolitans believe that the paramount political challenge is to get humans to act like humans. Individuals are rational and capable of reason, can learn from their mistakes, and can develop habits of cooperation, trust, and mutual understanding. Importantly, security can be established not through military force and a policy of deterrence but rather through mutual reassurance. Toward that end, the globally minded recommend the creation of international law, norms, and institutions that can help peoples learn to trust one another and adopt nonviolent ways of solving their disputes. These international arrangements not only help to foster mutual security but also can create a genuine spirit of solidarity.

Prophetic Judaism is the Jewish people's version of cosmopolitanism. The Jews are not chosen or a people apart but rather are part of humanity. They must constantly attempt to see what they share with others—not what separates them. By expanding their horizons, they will have a better understanding of humanity and realize the idea of justice.[74] By taking into account the circumstances of others, Prophetic Judaism also demands that Jews act to avoid preventable harm and remove suffering.[75] By living these cosmopolitan principles, the Jews will help the world achieve a new level of peace, security, and justice. "The prophets," writes Martin Buber, "call upon a people which represents the *first real attempt at 'community'* to enter world history as a prototype of that attempt. Israel's function is to encourage the nations to change their inner structure and their relations to one another."[76] This priestly mission cannot be achieved through force. Instead, it requires reason, rationality, and a genuine dialogue that leads to the recognition of a shared humanity and universal ethics. Swords *can* be pounded into ploughshares.

This universalism, however, did not envision the end of the Jewish people but instead a more enlightened way to situate the particular in the universal. This is thin, not thick, cosmopolitanism. During World War I, Julian Mack, one of the most respected leaders of the American Jewish community of the early twentieth century, articulated the difference between the two:

> There are two ideals in this world along the lines of statehood. Cosmopolitanism and internationalism. There are dreamers who say, "Wipe out all these lines of division. Let us no longer have Englishmen, Americans, Frenchmen, when the war is over; let us have one great country, the world. Let us all be citizens in it." This is cosmopolitanism. Internationalism, while based upon nationalism, does not involve a clashing of nations, or the domination of one nation. True internationalism aims at the highest self-development by each nation, not in conflict but in friendly rivalry with other nations, each endeavoring to work out the best that is within it for the good of its own people, and through them, as its contribution to the world. And in that spirit of internationalism, the Jewish people want again to become of the nations of the world, a nation that will develop that best that is in it.[77]

Similarly, Horace Kallen reflected, "Prophetic 'universalism' did not abolish the nations, it harmonized the nations; and it was nationalistic to the point of giving to Israel a dominant tone in the international harmony and to Zion the foremost place. Indeed, when it was most 'universal' it was most nationalistic."[78] Jews, in other words, are able to articulate and maintain a sense of who they are through their "mission."

Not only can the prophetic theology safeguard the Jewish identity, it also can enhance Jewish people's survival and security. "By maintaining such relations with the nations and being involved in the development of humanity," Buber writes, "Israel may achieve its unimperiled existence, its true security."[79] Conversely, warned other Jewish intellectuals such as Ahad Ha'am, to reject cosmopolitanism and follow the path of tribalism would bring out the worst in the Jewish people, making them self-absorbed, shortsighted, reactive, xenophobic, and self-destructive.[80]

A Jewish political community that sees itself as a prophetic people will seek solutions to the Jewish Problem and the Jewish Question that incorporate strong elements of cosmopolitanism and internationalism.[81] In many respects, a prophetic foreign policy has many of the elements that define what international relations scholars call liberal internationalism. In brief, liberal internationalism is a foreign policy doctrine that recommends that states organized around liberal values actively promote the expansion of markets, democracy, and the rule of law around the world; doing so is not only in the interests of liberal states, it also is in the long-term interests of the world because liberalism is the foundation for prosperity, peace, and justice.

A prophetic foreign policy (at least its post-Enlightenment variants) resembles liberal internationalism and has several defining qualities. To begin, it accepts a role for power and even force. Internationalists might have ideals, but they are hardly idealists to the extent that they put their faith in good intentions of others; they recognize that there is a continuing role for power. Moreover, power might not only be important for protecting communities at risk but also for creating a more humane world. In the nineteenth century French Jews favored the imperial expansion of the French republic and its civilizing mission, viewing it as a way to extend a French security umbrella to lands, such as North Africa, where there were significant Jewish populations. Yet power alone will not create the conditions for mutual security; that also requires the adoption of the right values and institutions at home and abroad. Toward that end, those who have developed the proper (liberal) mentality and institutions have a responsibility to help others do the same through democratization and the spread of human rights and the rule of law; the spread of liberal values, in short, will help produce a world of peace and justice. Finally, a prophetic foreign policy also recommends the establishment of international law and institutions.

Heine's law helps us understand the sources of the foreign policy beliefs of American Jews—but as a transnational people with a strong sense of collective identity, shared memories, and common fate, they also are very much affected by the world outside of America. Three global factors are ever-present. The first and most obvious is world-wide anti-Semitism, the threat to other Jewish communities, and the enduring shadow of the Holocaust. American Jews feel a special re-sponsibility for the welfare of other Jews and the survival of the Jew-ish people and often worry that anti-Semitism can spread and even infect an America that has been largely immune to its most virulent forms. The conventional wisdom is that when the world turns more dangerous, Jews will become more particularistic and tribal. Not necessarily so. Much depends on the existing political theology. In the 1930s and 1940s, when anti-Semitism was destroying the Euro-pean Jews and American Jews were seeing worrisome signs of some-thing similar at home, they responded by clinging to the American ideals of equality and liberty, by opposing segregation and champi-oning integration.

The second is the global culture of cosmopolitanism. Global cos-mopolitanism has experienced its ups and downs, often depending on how it compares to its sometime rival, nationalism. In the era of nationalism in the nineteenth and early twentieth centuries, nation-alism was *in* and cosmopolitanism was *out*. Societies were attempting to build up the state and were jealously demanding that all members abandon other particularistic identities and reject cosmopolitanism. As one observer pointedly put it, the cosmopolitan "is a kind of parasite who depends on the quotidian lives of others to create various local flavors and identities in which he dabbles." Or, as Jean-Jacques Rous-seau observed, cosmopolitanism is an "excuse to love the Tartars so that one did not have to love one's neighbors."[82] Those movements that imagined an alternative political project, such as socialism, and those peoples who were seen as incapable of shifting their loyalties, such as the Jews, became stigmatized and perceived as an immediate and pernicious threat to the nation—they were "rooted cosmopolitans," directed by the Elders of Zion.[83]

The twentieth century's thirty years' war from 1914 to 1945 caused even the most hardened nationalist to despair and give cosmopolitan-ism a second look. Cosmopolitanism now became seen as an anti-dote to nationalism's violent excesses, and the language of humanity became heavenly. But this was not just an ordinary, run-of-the-mill

cosmopolitanism. This was a cosmopolitanism of suffering: we identify with distant strangers because of their suffering. In this new
global environment the Jewish association with cosmopolitanism became a blessing. Because of the Holocaust, the world's treatment of
the Jews became something of a measure of its moral progress. The
world's sympathy for the Jews, however, would last as long as they
were deemed deserving victims. Once other peoples knocked off the
Jews from the list of top-ten suffering populations in the world, and
once Israel was seen as not just a haven for homeless Jews but as the
creator of another homeless people, then cosmopolitanism no longer
was a source of support. In general, there is no settled relationship
between cosmopolitanism and nationalism, and Jews have experi-
mented with, and experienced, nearly every possible combination.[84]

The global climate of cosmopolitanism also affects how American Jews orient themselves toward the world. As a prophetic people,
American Jews can be expected to respond favorably toward inter-
nationalizing forces. Globalization, to the extent that it breaks down
barriers and borders, is likely to open up opportunities for American
Jews to contribute to a world of growing connections. For American
Jews already feeling the assimilationist pull at home, the cosmopolitan spirit potentially further reduces their primary identification with
the Jewish people. American Jews are also affected by the cosmopolitanism of suffering. They not only want to be involved in humanitarian action, they also feel a desire to help based on need—and not
identity. Simply put, why privilege Jewish suffering? In general, we
can expect that a universalizing world is likely to lead American Jews
to rally for ideologies that emphasize what makes them like all others, not what makes them different.

Last, the existence of Israel and the Israeli political culture contributes to the foreign policies of American Jews.[85] The birth of Israel
required Diaspora Jews to make some adjustments, especially to the
extent that Israel claimed to represent the Jewish people and Jews
in the diaspora were expected to form their Jewish identity through
Israel. But the way American Jews feel about Israel is greatly affected
by whether they believe they share the same values. For instance,
American Jews are fond of liberalism and like their nationalism to
honor basic rights and be respectful of minorities. To the extent that

Israel is perceived to ascribe to these values, American Jews have had relatively little difficulty squaring their own commitments with their support for Israel. But the ideology of liberalism has always been second to forms of collectivism in Israel—socialism, Judaism, and nationalism. Israel, quite simply, is an ethnonational state whose democracy heavily depends on Jews having a supramajority. And many students of Israeli politics suggest that liberalism's breath is becoming increasingly labored as Israel becomes more nationalist, tribal, and inclined to allow religious texts and not citizens and principles of equality to decide Israel's laws. Israel's values are likely to make an impression, and not always a favorable one.

American Jews, because they are American and because they are Jews, have a prophetic political theology that generates a cosmopolitan sensibility. This became evident once American Jews became a full-fledged, organized, and active community in the nineteenth century. For the biologically inclined, this is genetic imprinting. For the more culturally inclined, this is path dependence—the way history and culture lock in beliefs, habits, and interests.[86] Yet however powerful, American Jews are not a pure type or kind. There is diversity in thought, experience, and belief. No political community, Jewish, American Jewish, or any other, will practice a pure form of anything—this is politics, not piety. When Jews have been most universalistic, they have also guarded against assimilation and have wanted to retain elements of their communal identity. Because of history and circumstances, American Jews have blended and balanced universalism and particularism in varying ways, and the growing dominance of one has, from time to time, led to a countermovement by partisans of the other. Part of the story of the foreign policies of the American Jews is not the struggle of a people who are never fully certain about their position and condition, but a struggle that always takes place against a backdrop that is more universal than particular.

CHAPTER TWO

THE MAKING OF A
PROPHETIC PEOPLE

In September 1654, twenty-three Jews arrived from Brazil in the new settlement of New Amsterdam, soon to be called New York. Originally from the Sephardic community in the Netherlands, they had gone to Recife, Brazil, a region controlled by religiously tolerant Dutch. Soon after they arrived, however, Portuguese forces, Catholic and unfriendly to Jews, overran the area. Some Jews returned to the Netherlands, others sailed for Dutch colonies in the Caribbean, and a group traveled thousands of miles north on the *Sainte Catherine*. These were not the first Jews to land on American soil—a handful had arrived over the previous decades—but it was the first organized party interested in establishing a Jewish community. Although they thought the Dutch-controlled settlement of New Amsterdam would be a safe haven, the governor, Peter Stuyvesant, wanted nothing to do with them and wrote to his superiors at the Dutch West India Company for permission to send them on their way. Given their "customary usury and deceitful habits," he thought it advisable to "require them in a friendly way to depart."[1] The company responded by sympathizing with his desire to ensure that the new territory not be "infected by the people of the Jewish nation," but suggested that the governor take pity on the Jews from Brazil and remember that Dutch Jews had invested a large amount of capital in the company.[2] A decade later the British took over the colony, renamed it New York, and granted the Jews greater civil rights.

Over the next century the Jewish community slowly expanded from a few dozen in the mid-seventeenth century to a few thousand by the time of the American revolutionary war in 1776. Jews predominantly settled in colonies that granted religious freedom, most prominently in Charleston, South Carolina, where the English philosopher John Locke had helped to write a charter granting liberty of conscience to all, including "Jews, heathens, and dissenters." Indeed, many Jews enjoyed rights and a measure of acceptance far exceeding anything previously experienced. And while anti-Semitism arose in the new world, it was nothing compared to the old world. In fact, Christian sects probably faced more persecution than Jews.

Several factors explain these relative comforts. Jews were so few in number that they did not draw much attention or seem to pose any threat. The Puritans exhibited some amount of philo-Semitism. The principle of religious freedom was written into law and constitutions, offering legal protections.[3] Jews usually occupied the lowest rung in society, but now Africans had that distinction. Jews did not have a huge stake in the outcome of the War for Independence, but they tended to favor the revolutionaries because they had no natural allegiance or affinity for England and its political order based on inheritance and tradition. With few Jews in America at the time, not many Jews distinguished themselves in the war; but two are routinely cited with pride. Francis Salvador was the first Jew to die fighting for independence, and the well-known banker Haym Solomon helped finance the war. The very small Jewish community had begun to establish its patriotic credentials.

Although Jews worried that America's changed political status might make life difficult for them, America's founding fathers delivered reassuring messages to the Jewish community. Most famously, in 1790 President George Washington sent a letter to the Sephardic synagogue in Newport, Rhode Island, pledging that Jews had nothing to fear. In words the American Jewish community still cherishes, Washington wrote: "The Government of the United States, which gives to bigotry no sanction, to persecution no assistance, requires only that they who live under its protection should demean themselves as good citizens in giving it on all occasions their effectual support. . . . May the children of the stock of Abraham who dwell in this land continue to merit and enjoy the good will of the other inhabitants—while every one shall sit in safety under his own vine and fig tree and there shall be none to make him afraid." It was a remarkable statement for its time and a defining moment in the history of the Jews in America. However, the historian Hasia Diner recommends a close look at the fine print. America's acceptance of the Jews was not unconditional but rather dependent, as Washington wrote, on Jews comporting themselves as "good citizens."[4] Jews walked a thin line between acceptance and ostracism.[5]

Over the next century Jewish immigration to the United States largely corresponded with the ebbs and flows of political instability and anti-Semitism in Europe and Russia. America had only 4,000 Jews in 1820, but afterward that number increased steadily: 15,000 in 1840, 50,000 in 1850, and 150,000 in 1860. Although the Jewish population as a percentage of America's population did not change perceptibly, the growth in absolute numbers produced some notable changes in the American Jewish community. For one thing, it became more Ashkenazi and less Sephardic. Sephardic Jews, who originated from Spain, Portugal, and other parts of the Mediterranean, had been the first to settle in the new world. The post-1815 Jewish immigrants, however, were largely Ashkenazi, coming from Germany and the Austro-Hungarian Empire. Between 1820 and 1880, nearly 250,000 Jews came to America, most of them from Germany or those countries heavily influenced by German culture. As the Jewish population grew in number, so too did associational life. In 1825 there were roughly six active congregations, but by 1848 there were nearly fifty, most of them founded by German Jewish immigrants. And because these synagogues needed rabbis, and America had no seminary, nearly all of the rabbis came from Europe. As the number of Jewish immigrants grew, so did the number of Jewish communities scattered throughout an expanding United States. German Jewish peddlers appeared in nearly every reasonably sized community with the westward expansion, trading with Native Americans, supplying miners, and establishing general stores in frontier towns and growing cities like San Francisco.

This was the first generation of American Jews to wrestle collectively with the Jewish Question, but it did so in rather exceptional circumstances. Jews were not made to feel like permanent outsiders. They did not have to dismantle laws regulating and banning their presence because no such laws were on the books. They did not have to tear down ghetto walls because no such walls existed. Unlike European states, the United States had no national church that formally blurred private and public life. Unlike the romantic nationalisms of Europe that excluded Jews because they were alien to folk traditions, the United States was forming a national identity that was nominally inclusive. When Christians emigrated from Europe to the United States, they had not left behind their prejudices, but the ocean air seemed to have reduced their hatred. America was a land of opportunity and relative security.

Relative security. Jewish security was based on acceptance. Gentiles had to be willing to accept Jews as equals—not just in law but in everyday society. The Jewish experience, however, was not acceptance but rather rejection, persecution, and oppression. And while the age of enlightenment was making life easier, there were everyday reminders that modest improvements could be instantaneously erased by deadly setbacks. Just as they had in Europe, the Jews of America began trying to purge themselves of everything that might cause Christians to doubt whether Jews could fit in. Jews began changing their dress, mannerisms, accents, and expressions—and also their Judaism—to rid themselves of the old country.

Reform Jewry might have been made in Europe, but it was tailor-made for the Jews in America who wanted to be both Jews and Americans. The Jews of America flocked to Reform Judaism, and it quickly grew from a minor movement to a dominant wing in American Judaism by the early 1900s.[6] In America there was greater demand for a reform movement because American society was more willing to integrate its Jews, encouraging Jews to be more willing to do what they could to avoid giving Christians a reason to reject them. And America provided fertile soil for the reform movement because, compared to Europe, it was more conducive to religious experimentation, more of an open marketplace where ideas could compete. Christian denominations expanded in America because there was no national church, people had freedom of conscience, and there were lots of new territories and towns to minister to. Reform Judaism thrived in America in part because, unlike in Europe, it did not have to compete with well-established institutions, venerated religious authorities, and rooted traditions. In fact, many reform-minded rabbis emigrated from Europe to America for the opportunity to establish their own brand of Judaism. America was a virtual blank slate.

Beginning in the 1840s "reform societies" emerged with the goal of modernizing and Americanizing Judaism, frequently drawing inspiration from the reform movement in Europe. Reform Judaism aggressively pursued an agenda of integration—which did not mean making America safe for Jews, but making Jews safe for America. The leaders of the reform movement had various motives. Some were sincerely desirous of modernizing Jewry, believing that as a progressive religion it had to keep pace with the times. They also worried that if Judaism were not reformed, making it more consistent with American society and more user-friendly, Jews would assimilate into Christian society. They and others were determined to "change Judaism in order to save it."[7]

There was almost no aspect of Judaism or Jewish life that was not up for negotiation, especially if it eased Jewish acculturation. Because Jews increasingly worked on Saturdays, they needed religious services to shift to Sundays, like their Christian neighbors. Because childhood could no longer be devoted to religious instruction, they needed English to replace Hebrew as the language of prayer and text, and they needed rabbis to give sermons to remind them of the week's Torah portion and its meaning. Because the traditional separation of men and women in the synagogue appeared inconsistent with Christianity and the American culture of equality, congregations began removing the *mechitza*, the dividing wall. Kashruth (traditional dietary laws) was increasingly abandoned because of its inconvenience and perceived backwardness. Synagogues increasingly resembled churches on the inside, with services now accompanied by organs and choirs.

Reform Judaism also drew inspiration and justification from Prophetic Judaism and its stress on universalism instead of particularism, the emphasis of ethics rather than archaic laws, and its call on Jews to widen their moral universe from their own to all of humanity. Not only was this form of Judaism more modern and progressive, but it also would help the Jews integrate by increasing their prospects of acceptance by Gentile America. The prophetic theology would show non-Jews that Jews were not the clannish tribe they were rumored to be. Reform Judaism also would help fight off the dangers of assimilation because energized Jews would see themselves as having a sacred duty to create heaven on earth; in other words, they could see themselves as being part of the American creed even as they maintained their communal identity. Prophetic Judaism in the American context also demanded that American Jews either disown or find a new interpretation for two theological concepts that were steeped in Jewish thought and liturgy but were barriers to their acceptance—the chosen people and exile.

"The essence of Judaism," writes the historian Rabbi Arthur Hertzberg, "is the affirmation that the Jews are the chosen people: all else is commentary."[8] Jewish texts make constant reference to the Jews as chosen and special. It is written in Deuteronomy 7:6–8:

> For you are a people holy to the Lord your God: the Lord your God has chosen you to be for Him a treasured people above all the peoples who are on the face of the earth. It was not because you were more in number than any other people that the Lord set his love upon you and chose you for you were the fewest of all peoples but it is because the Lord loves you, and is keeping the oath which He swore to your fathers.

In a later passage (Deuteronomy 27:17–18): "You have distinguished the Lord today to be a God for you . . . and the Lord has distinguished you today to be ready for Him a treasured people." Before reading from the Torah, a Jew recites the following blessing: "Blessed art thou, our God king of the universe, who has chosen us from all peoples and hast given us thy Torah." Jews have debated the meaning of chosen, whether they were chosen or did the choosing, what the consequences and obligations of being chosen are; and even whether God chose the Jews because of some unflattering traits—they are a "stiff-necked people" and thus have the ability to persevere in the face of harsh opposition. Regardless of how they became that way, the moral of the story is the same: Jews are the chosen people.[9]

With the help of Reform Judaism, American Jews began to distance themselves from the idea that they are a chosen people. To put themselves on a pedestal, to intimate that they are better than other Americans, was hardly consistent with the principle of equality and could potentially play into the hands of anti-Semites who argued that Jews were the cause of the Jewish Problem because of their belief in their superiority. Operating under the influence of the Enlightenment and aiming to integrate into America, American Jews began emphasizing principles of humanity. On the occasion of a major gathering in Philadelphia in 1869, the leaders of the reform movement disavowed the concept of the "chosen people" and stressed the "unity of all rational creatures." And at that same meeting, Rabbis David Einhorn and Samuel Hirsch declared that the "messianic aim of Israel is not the restoration of the old Jewish state . . . but the union of all the children of God."[10] In 1899 American Reform Rabbi Henry Berkowitz credited the prophets, who predated Jesus by several centuries, with establishing the unity of all: "It was the great discovery of the prophets of the eighth century that the God of Israel is the God of mankind, the God of Judea is the God of the universe. This great thought then for the first time broke through the bonds of nationality and announced the Universal religion."[11] There was little denying that American Jews were attracted to notions of humanity because it appealed to the self-interest and morality of the secularizing Jew. However, to demonstrate to others and themselves that this was not an affectation of convenience but rather deeply rooted in Judaism, Jewish scholars and theologians began returning to texts to find trace elements of such thinking.[12] In general, Jews began to develop a "special American feeling for humanity."[13]

Yet it was no trivial matter to banish the concept of "chosen people." Because the concept had "sustained Jewish identity and Jewish faith through the ages," the fear was that its expulsion might accelerate assimilation.[14] After all, if Jews truly were just like everyone else, why go through the inconvenience of being Jewish? Consequently, non-Orthodox rabbis proposed alternative meanings that were intended to make the concept less obnoxious and offensive, more consistent with America's egalitarian ethos, and yet nevertheless gave reason to retain their communal identity. The Jews were just like everyone else, but they still had special responsibilities. Their teachings had broader significance and timeless lessons, and their history gave them experiences and insights that other peoples did not have and that they could use to improve the world.[15] Jews were now "perpetual teachers to Gentiles."[16] They were commanded to conduct themselves in an ethically righteous manner and to serve as role models for Americans. Jews, for instance, understood democracy. Democracy, according to those in the reform movement, was part and parcel of Judaism. This "bond between Judaism and democracy" helped define "the role of the Jews in America—a chosen people in God's new chosen land."[17] Jews might not be chosen, but they were different, and perhaps even special, within reason.

Exile was the other troublesome concept. Jews once had a home called Palestine, and now they were homeless, scattered around the world. Why God would subject his chosen people to such a fate is a source of considerable speculation in Jewish theology, but the standard answer is that they sinned by failing to follow their commandments and thus suffered the ultimate punishment of exile.[18] Wherever they have wandered over the centuries, Jewish communities have uttered the prayer: "For our sins we have been banished from our country and removed far from our land." When they return to a life of righteousness, or perhaps when they have fulfilled God's plan, then Jews will be allowed to go home. And there is no exit option because God closed the door on assimilation: "And you shall not walk in the customs of the nation which I am casting out before you. . . . I am the Lord your God who has separated you from people. . . . [Y]ou shall be holy to Me, for I the Lord am holy and have separated you from the peoples, that you should be Mine." Jews have the mark of Cain, a people protected by God but nevertheless forced to wander the world. Exile, moreover, is more than a physical state. It also cripples the spirit and the psyche. The Jew in exile is not only living outside the homeland but also is trying to survive as a persecuted minority under alien rule, which takes a toll on the soul. There is a largely derogatory term for this kind of physical and spiritual crippling—the *galuth*. Zionist political thought portrays the *galuth* Jew as weak, sniveling, cowardly, and self-hating. If anti-Semites ever require new ways to stereotype Jews, they can always turn to the Zionist playbook.

Yet could Jews in America continue to consider themselves to be in exile? America was prepared to accept them, and Jews were prepared to accept that they were home.[19] America was a promised land, not perdition. In fact, returning to an impoverished, backward Jerusalem for anything more than a short visit at Passover seemed like punishment. Within a few decades American Jews were actively denying that the *galuth* had any relevance to them and espousing the existence of a shared "Judeo-Christian" culture and heritage.[20] If they were no longer in exile because of their wickedness or waiting for the right moment to return to Palestine, then why had they wandered for centuries? Drawing from the prophetic tradition, America's Jews began suggesting that they had a mission to improve the condition of the world. Whereas once their departure from their ancient homeland was seen as divine punishment for their sins, now they saw themselves on a mission from God to spread universal values of equality, justice, and peace.[21] At that same 1869 conference in Philadelphia, the delegates asserted that the destruction of the Jewish state was not a punishment for their sinfulness but rather a "result of the divine purpose . . . [of] dispersing the Jews to all parts of the world for the realization of their high priestly mission, to lead the nations to the true knowledge and worship of God."[22] God dispersed his chosen people around the world not because they were bad but rather because they were supposed to do good.

Of all the Jewish leaders of the period, Rabbi Isaac Mayer Wise had arguably the most profound impact articulating and institutionalizing these themes. Born in 1819 in Steingrub, Bohemia (currently part of the Czech Republic), he earned a reputation as a brilliant student at the yeshiva and later at the University of Prague and the University of Vienna. He became a rabbi at twenty-three, with the ambition of reforming traditional Judaism. He found himself, though, frustrated by the objections of ensconced religious authorities who opposed any sort of reform (though he was not a member of the reform movement at this time). In search of more religious freedom and opportunities for experimentation, he departed for America in 1846. He soon became the rabbi of Temple Beth El in Albany, New York, but his congregation gave his efforts to introduce reforms a weak reception. Looking for greener pastures, in 1850 he founded a reform synagogue, which he humbly called Anshe Emet—"men of truth." Then in 1854 he moved to Cincinnati, Ohio, where he became the rabbi of a new Reform synagogue, Beth Eichim, where he found not just a home but his long-sought-after platform.

Demonstrating considerable organizational skills, Wise began working with other reform-minded rabbis and developing a network of reform institutions. In 1873 he helped establish the Union of American Hebrew Congregations. In 1875 the union founded the Hebrew Union College, the first Jewish seminary in the United States, and Wise became its inaugural president. In 1889 he helped found the Central Conference of American Rabbis (CCAR) and became its first leader. He also helped write the Union Prayer Book, which became the central text for reform synagogues. When he died in 1900, he had altered American Jewish life and helped to create many of the religious institutions that to this very day remain central.

Wise's voluminous body of sermons and writings both reflected and influenced American Jewish political thought, and an 1877 lecture titled "The Wandering Jew" captures the political theology of the period. Inverting nearly every unflattering image of the wandering Jew, Wise transformed a mark of Cain into a light unto nations.[23]

He opens his lecture by observing how Ahasverus, the original Wandering Jew, is an invention of medieval Christianity. The Jew is cursed because he did not accept Christ as the messiah and is condemned to wander the world. His physical appearance matches his emotional crippling. He is an "old, feeble, sickly, bent, and broken man, with a hook nose and an evil eye, disheveled hair and beard, peeping looks, a squealing voice and trembling steps, weary of life, exhausted by misery, always at the brink of despair, yet unable to die and condemned to suffer forever." Although death might be a blessing for this wretched creature, he is "cursed with eternal life to be miserable forever."

Wise, though, gently observed that Christians have, once again, completely misunderstood the "character of the Jew," in much the same way Shakespeare did with his Shylock. Specifically, Christians have overlooked the progressive role Jews played throughout human history. Some of Wise's observations were already familiar to many

Figure 2.1. *The Legend of the Wandering Jew* by Gustave Doré, 1856. Courtesy of the Poetry Collection of the University Libraries, University at Buffalo, The State University of New York.

in Jewish circles, religious and otherwise. Jews were responsible for bringing monotheism to the world. They had been scattered around the world after the destruction of the Second Temple not because they had sinned but rather "for the realization of [their] high priestly mission, to lead the nations to the true knowledge and worship of God."[24]

What is it about the Jews that accounts for their contributions to human progress? According to Wise, it is because they wander the world toppling dogmas and sowing doubt, uncertainty, and skepticism. They are, in essence, the "source and exponent of perpetual doubt."

> Could the human family exist and reach this state of civilization without skepticism? I say, no, no, no. Without skepticism, hence without the Jew, the human family could not advance, as little, indeed, as a planetary body could move in its orbit without the cooperation of the centrifugal and centripetal powers.

In Wise's re-reading of history, the Jew wanders into an existing civilization characterized by hubris and confidence and plants seeds of doubt. This task is not likely to endear the Jew to existing communities, and he is hated for it.

Fortunately, Jews are not alone in their skeptical sensibility toward the world. Wise then cites the example of Luther. According to Wise, skepticism's movement from the margins to the center of thought occurred with the Reformation, when Luther broke the grip of the Catholic Church. Thus began a period of religious experimentation, the questioning of truths—religious, cultural, and scientific—and the mentality required for the scientific method. But standing behind Luther was the Wandering Jew.

> It was again the Wandering Jew who stepped between the hostile factions and brought progression and reformation. The Jew rendered in Latin what had been written in the Semitic. He brought in Latin and in Hebrew the new ideas from the other camp into Christendom. He brought to Christians the new philosophy, the new criticism, the science, learning, letters, arts and industries of other countries. Christians began to study Hebrew, read, and inhaled new ideas in a new atmosphere. The Wandering Jew had sown the seeds of skepticism, the tender plants of progression and reformation began to show in the Humanitarian School. The soil was prepared, the seed was sown, and upon the soil there rose Martin Luther and the Christian Reformation.

The critical figure, according to Wise, is the heretical Jew, Baruch Spinoza. His philosophy smashed everything around him, humbling true believers of all kinds. For his efforts, the Jewish community cursed and excommunicated him. Wise insists that Jews correct this miscarriage of justice and restore Spinoza's place in the pantheon of great Jewish thinkers.

Why have Jews been fated to play this historical role and perform this thankless task? Tiptoeing around any suggestion that the Jews are a chosen people, Wise suggests that this penchant for challenging conventional wisdom began with Jews' introduction of monotheism into a world crowded with idols. In addition, as Jews began wandering the world they absorbed the best ideas from their hosts, carried those ideas to new regions, and, in the process, challenged existing dogmas. The Jew as rebel and liberator.

> If it had not been for those Jewish thinkers and the Wandering Jew to carry their ideas and thoughts into Christendom, theology would have remained the divine comedy for the men in power, and a fabric of oppression for two-thirds of the human family, an ingenious contrivance of words to terrify the masses and to satisfy despotic rulers. . . . He [the Wandering Jew] destroyed the small and the big gods of his persecutors. He dispersed the illusions, exposed superstition, battled against pious ignorance, protested against slavery, claimed freedom of belief, thought and speech, and raised his voice powerfully against all kinds of folly, prejudice, and oppression. He carried skepticism and learning from land to land, was persecuted and cursed for it, gave the impulses to the world's main progressions and reformations, and stood watchfully at the cradle of every new born idea of light and freedom. That was the Jew's revenge.

The Jew has a thankless, perhaps even cursed, role to play, and yet he must continue to play it.

> Little is left for the Wandering Jew to do. Still he has no rest. He must reappear and do his work; until there shall be no more superstition, no ignorance and no intolerance, no hatred, no self-delusion and no darkness among sects. He must reappear and wander on to the end of all woe and misery in society, till the habitable earth shall be one holy land, every city a Jerusalem, every house

a temple, every table an altar, every parent a high priest, and Jehovah the only God. . . . Then the curtain will drop on the grand drama of the Wandering Jew.

The Jew is fated to wander. His hardship and suffering are necessary for human progress. Jews will suffer in order to repair the world, and as the world repairs, Jews will rest more easily.

By revising the meaning of chosenness so that it was consistent with pluralism, by giving exile a universalistic interpretation, by suggesting that Jewish values were consistent with American values and that Jewish and American values were universalistic, and by repudiating any claim to being a nation, Reform Jewry crafted a political theology for America that had several distinct advantages. It was consistent with Reform Jews' campaign for acceptance. They could emphasize the universal without surrendering Jewish identity; indeed, by retaining the particular they would help to nourish the universal. "Like the other innovations of the Reformers, it was offered not as a rejection of the Jewish past, but as a higher form of continuity with Judaism's religious ideals."[25] Jews also had a new purpose. Other religions might be out trying to win converts to their cause, but Jews were working for the betterment of humanity. "This was the stuff of Judaism. The struggle for progress on these matters was truly divine service."[26]

Divine service was the transcendental, and public service and social justice was the immanent. Beginning in the early nineteenth century, American Jews, "from the wealthiest to those of relatively modest means, launched a mammoth enterprise of social service, which included caring for the sick, the elderly, orphans, the unemployed, prison inmates, the hungry, and the destitute." Over the century Jews increasingly opened up welfare institutions and benevolent societies for the Jewish poor and immigrants, but they also made sure to demonstrate that their hearts and centers were open to all, regardless of religion.[27]

The emphasis on philanthropy, social justice, and welfare served multiple functions. Volunteering in the world as Jews helped bind the Jewish community. It gave Jews a sense of being a part of the world, not apart from it. Scrupulously following daily commandments and laws could become mundane and introverted, but a Judaism with a "prophetic concern for justice and brotherhood . . . gave the rhetorical illusion of activity to congregants whose role both inside and outside the synagogue was largely passive."[28] It allowed those in the Jewish community to feel as if they were just like their Christian neighbors; the Christians had their social gospel and the Jews had Prophetic Judaism. It helped improve the reputation of the Jews among Christians, making Jews appear to be model citizens and full-fledged members of the nation.[29] Manuel Noah, one of America's first Jewish leaders, believed that by performing good deeds he could confront anti-Semitism and prove that Jews could be patriotic Americans.[30] Over time the Jewish concern for public welfare became one of the "hallmarks of American Jewry and one of the characteristics of the Jews most admired by non-Jews."[31] By pursuing social justice America's Jews could live their identity and pursue their strategy of security through acceptance.

Not all Jews in America were pleased with this accommodation to modernity, secularism, and American nationalism. In their view, accommodation was a euphemism for assimilation. Social justice was all well and good, but, according to some critics, it came at the expense of traditional religious practice and commandments. Judaism was losing its religion, and the boundaries between Judaism and the rest of the world were eroding so quickly that Judaism seemed at risk of losing its distinctiveness. Synagogues were being built to look like federal buildings on the outside and churches on the inside. The seminaries seemed less and less Jewish. In 1875, at a banquet honoring the first rabbinical graduates of the reform-minded Hebrew Union College in Cincinnati, the hosts served shellfish, which dietary laws forbid. It became known as the "*treyfah* (nonkosher) banquet." Outraged, the more traditional rabbis responded by launching Conservative Judaism and establishing the Jewish Theological Seminary in New York to train Conservative rabbis. Critics railed that Judaism was in danger of becoming a "Christianless Christianity" and Jews were beginning to have "more in common with Unitarians than with Orthodox Jews."[32]

A related criticism was that ethics was increasingly displacing the religious aspect of Judaism. The golden rule was increasingly replacing the 613 commandments and Judaism was in danger of becoming nothing more than a person being good and a good American.[33] American Jews seemed to be keener on volunteering in soup kitchens and raising money for the poor than they were on attending services, lighting Shabbat candles, or keeping kosher. When the members of the men's club of Temple Beth El were asked what makes a good Jew, they answered with a combination of nationalism and universalism, articulating the belief that Jews had a duty to be charitable, merciful, and to expound social justice for all.[34] In 1907 Rabbi Stephen Samuel Wise opened the Free Synagogue in New York City, where he preached social responsibility; nominally Reform, the synagogue emphasized the ethical and moral teachings of Judaism and their application to contemporary social conditions. The religious dimension became marginalized. To follow the ideas of Reform Judaism and the Enlightenment to their logical conclusion of universalism meant that there was no rational reason for maintaining a religious identity.

JEWISH INTERNATIONALISM

Historically, Jews have had two ways of defending themselves: through arms or through accommodation. Because they were minorities in exile, violent resistance was often a last resort or symbolic response, producing little more than a Pyrrhic victory or martyrdom. Accommodation took numerous forms, but usually it involved Jewish leaders trying to persuade rulers to tolerate the ancient religious community. Since medieval Europe, those representing the Jewish community and serving this mediating function were often called the *shtadlan*. Jews in this position are sometimes derogatorily called "court Jews" and accused of placating Christians by making fools of the Jews. Perhaps. But their diplomatic skills often made the difference between survival and destruction. In any event, such negotiations between the Jewish elite and local rulers were usually highly personalistic and limited to the defense of the local Jewish community.

Beginning in the nineteenth century, two important developments changed this arrangement. The rise of liberalism increasingly meant that Jews fortunate enough to live in liberal societies could use legal means to defend and extend their rights; institutions, constitutions, and legal norms became as important as personal ties. The rise of liberalism, the acceptance of Jews as a minority with rights, and the growth of associational life also gave rise to Jewish protection and defense organizations, and one of the strategies of these organizations was to link the rights of Jews to the defense of all minorities and the enshrinement of liberal principles.

The second development was the first wave of globalization. Over the nineteenth century the accelerating movement of people, goods, and ideas caused once insular communities, cities, and countries to be affected by one another and aware that they might have common interests and responsibilities. Militaries covered longer distances, leading to the emergence of global empires. Trade and production occurred on an ever-widening scale, causing producers and consumers, owners and workers to consider the gains and losses from commercial exchange. Communication and transportation revolutions made it easier for people, products, and ideas to move across distances at greater speed. These cross-border and cross-cultural exchanges compelled governments to negotiate new kinds of international organizations and arrangements, some designed to make sure that all this contact did not lead to conflict, and others to capture the rewards of cooperation. These expanding and intensifying networks also widened the moral imagination, causing people in one part of the world to consider their obligations and responsibilities to strangers in another part of the world. States and peoples began coordinating their actions for the purpose of maintaining their identity, advancing their interests, and fostering peace and justice in the world. The world was becoming simultaneously bigger and smaller. Internationalism had arrived.

These global changes also nurtured a Jewish internationalism, most evident in the attempt by the transnational mobilization of Jews to protect Jewish communities under threat. Several events stood out as both examples and causes of this growing internationalism.[35] In Damascus in 1840, local rulers accused the Jewish community of blood libel; in protest, Jews in several postemancipation countries appealed to their governments to halt the anti-Semitic campaign.[36] In 1858 the infamous Mortara affair had an electrifying effect on Jewish communities from Italy to the United States. The Vatican, with Pope Pius IX's authorization, had kidnapped a Jewish boy in Italy on the grounds that he was a Catholic because a house servant had baptized the child without his parents' knowledge. The fact that the baptism had been performed without their permission was irrelevant; the child was now Catholic, and Jews could not raise a Catholic. Officials in Romania were constantly at the throats of Jews, restricting their movements, introducing laws that diminished their lives, condoning if not sanctioning violence, and threatening to expel them. Jews in France, Germany, England, the United States, and elsewhere not only responded individually, they also began to coordinate their campaigns through correspondence and conferences.

The rise of Jewish internationalism shares many features associated with the growth of internationalism more generally, but several stand out.[37] The first is the emergence of a transnational Jewish political identity. For centuries Jews had a transnational religious identity, but in fact they knew very little about the fates of Jews in other countries. Until the nineteenth century they generally lived, prayed, and dreamed in isolation from one another, unaffected by what other Jewish communities were experiencing because they had little knowledge of them and, because of their lowly status, were unable to do much on their behalf even if they did. Beginning in the nineteenth century things began to change as Jews became more aware of Jewish communities in other parts of the world; at this moment their shared religious identity began to have political significance.[38] In addition to feeling obligations to other Jews, they now had knowledge of their needs and the capacity to act. Like most others during this period, Jews were expanding their horizons. When word reached them that Jews were under threat in Romania, Damascus, or the Pale of Settlement, Jews elsewhere began to rally to their defense and raise money to help them through hard times. Drawing from the Talmud, French Jews began saying *"Kol Yisrael arevim zeh bazej"* ("All Jews are responsible for one another").[39]

It was not until Jews became more than a barely tolerated minority, acquired citizenship, and achieved some level of security that they could begin to mobilize politically on behalf of foreign Jews. Jews certainly did not need acceptance, security, and citizenship to send aid to Jewish communities under threat, which they often did. But effective, immediate action—action that went toward stopping the violence and addressing the causes of suffering—required the power of the state. And why would a state that barely tolerated the Jews, was a source of their insecurity, and denied them their basic rights ever go out of its way to help Jews in foreign lands? Political mobilization, in short, could only occur where liberalism had taken root.

Once they began to organize domestically in liberalizing countries such as Germany, England, and France, it was only a matter of time before this diasporic people began to organize transnationally. The rise of the Alliance Israélite Universelle (AIU) illustrates this development. In 1860 the French Jewish elite established the world's first Jewish international defense organization with the goal of "promoting Jewish rights around the globe by emphasizing the liberal values of tolerance, equality, and religious freedom."[40] As they did so, they blended Jewish and French interests. For instance, in their campaigns to protect Jews in foreign lands they often used the language of tikkun olam and the "rights of man," blurring social justice and self-interest.[41] This was not only about promoting the interests of foreign Jews in places like Algeria but also was believed to improve their own capacity to be better Frenchmen.[42] By campaigning for the defense of Jews on civilizational grounds, French Jews would hasten their integration by demonstrating their secularism and French loyalty, strengthening their political alliance with other liberals in France, and reducing the chance that the anti-Semitic attitudes of French colonial officials did not work their way back home.[43]

The rise of the AIU also signaled the movement of transnational mobilization from ad hoc responses to periodic crises to the development of permanent transnational organizations dedicated to Jewish interests.[44] Until its formation, Jewish diplomacy largely reflected the globalization of the traditional statecraft used at home—namely, the *shtadlanut*, often financial magnates and leaders of some of the most important banking houses, such as the Rothschilds, practiced statecraft of the stateless by using their personal connections to intercede with political authorities on behalf of the local Jewish community.[45] In contrast, the AIU was a transnational entity, with more than 345 branches established between 1862 and 1880, stretching from western and central Europe to Serbia, North Africa, Egypt, and the broader Middle East, the United States, and even Brazil and Colombia.[46] Comparable Jewish organizations emerged in Britain, Germany, Holland, and in other parts of Europe. Some of these organizations dedicated themselves to the protection of Jewish communities, while others were designed to develop a collective identity. These different organizations also exhibited something quite different from associational life until this point: they were outside of the standard religious spaces. Although it would be inaccurate to call them secular, for religious leaders often played an important role, these organizations articulated a view of Jews as ethnonational rather than as a religious community and undertook secular forms of philanthropy.[47]

One indirect consequence of Jewish internationalism deserves mention: it led to a fear of "Jewish power." Jews were organizing to protect their interests and the survival of Jewish communities under siege. Such activities, whether visible or imaginary, were the stuff of anti-Semitism. Beginning in the 1880s in France, anti-Semites argued that this coordinated effort by different Jewish communities was the product of a separatist campaign, quest for world domination, and the appropriation of liberalism and republicanism for their malevolent goals.[48] Soon thereafter, attacks on Jews were accompanied by charges that a Jewish cabal was exaggerating and exploiting anti-Semitic outbursts for its own devious purposes. Such sentiments would soon become part of anti-Semitic screeds such as *The Protocols of the Elders of Zion.*

What did the AIU and other Jewish defense organizations recommend to protect Jewish lives? In the short term they petitioned their governments to use their diplomatic, political, and economic tools to force the offending or indifferent governments to protect their Jewish populations. In the long term, though, they believed that these Jewish communities would benefit from the same political and legal breakthroughs—that is, liberalism—that accounted for their own rising fortunes. As they attempted to defend Jews abroad and imagine their long-term acceptance, these Jewish organizations began using the language of rights. There was no appeal to *human* rights—that is, the rights that individuals have because of their status as human beings.

Rather, this was an appeal to group rights, the rights of minorities and religious communities. Peoplehood, not personhood. This rights-based strategy became a central feature of many protection societies in the West. Most of these organizations, especially those in the West, were not recommending the solution that would become ascendant in a few decades: a return to Palestine. For reasons to be discussed, Zionism not only was barely part of the vocabulary, but was considered to be part of the profane. In general, as Jews began to entertain possible solutions to the Jewish Problem and to imagine whether they were consistent or inconsistent in their preferred response to the Jewish Question, they focused on rights at home and not on Palestine or some other contrived all-Jewish sanctuary.

Jewish internationalism was also aided by European imperialism.[49] To deter existing threats, Jews appealed to the combination of imperial power and international norms of liberalism. To blunt future threats, Jews hitched their wagon to civilizing missions and the spread of liberalism, believing that such a development would help societies accept and integrate their Jews—the ultimate form of protection. The liberal empires of England and France became the headquarters for these strategies of Jewish protection. Jews had achieved a level of security and acceptance in these imperial countries, which had the requisite diplomatic, economic, and military power to intervene abroad. But having power is different from being willing to deploy it for the protection of others, which was not something that governments did with any regularity. Sometimes they did so to assist nationals or Christian communities, but there was no reason to expect any imperial powers, or any European state for that matter, to inconvenience itself for the Jews. After all, these governments had only just emancipated this religious minority, and emancipation did not necessarily mean that they suddenly were fond of Jews, especially those who were probably as backward as their countries of origin.

To persuade their governments to come to the aid of Jewish communities under threat in places like Romania, Russia, and the Ottoman Empire, the French and British Jews linked the fate of the Jews to the interests and identity of the imperial state.[50] Accordingly, as they appealed to their governments to defend Jewish lives abroad, they argued that protecting Jews was in the national interest, important for the national reputation, was the proper, Christian thing to do, and part of their sacred mission of defending humanity and spreading civilization.[51] In short, these nascent forms of Jewish internationalism frequently tapped into the same discourses that drove Western imperialism. In mid-nineteenth-century England, "the question of Jewish rights in Muslim lands became a test for British efforts to spread the values of Victorian civilization through an imperialism of human rights."[52] The AIU explicitly tied the protection of Jews to the broader French *mission civilisatrice*. That the protection of Jews abroad was dependent on imperial power does not necessarily mean that Jews were imperialists, but rather that it would have been difficult for European Jews to protect Jews abroad without associating with imperialism.

Perhaps the most stunning, and underappreciated, aspect of Jewish internationalism during this period was that the Jewish Problem was becoming a constant presence on the international agenda.[53] The christening moment occurred after the Napoleonic wars, when the European governments at the Congress of Vienna received an appeal from German Jews to maintain the rights they had gained under French occupation.[54] From this moment on, the Jewish Problem was discussed at every major European multilateral gathering, and, during each and every conversation, Jews, often represented by new transnational bodies such as the AIU and the Hilfsverein der Deutschen Juden, pushed the European powers to restore, extend, and enforce the rights of citizenship to Jews in illiberal lands.[55] In 1872 Jewish delegations convened a special congress in Brussels to address Romanian anti-Semitism. The Treaty of Berlin of 1878 also exhorted international intervention into the Jewish Question, and an important precedent of religious freedom was set as a term for recognition of statehood. Although some consequential language for protecting Jews was removed from the final treaty, Jewish leaders celebrated this victory of "humanitarianism and justice."[56]

Further away from the action, less well-organized, overwhelmed by the need to settle hundreds of thousands of impoverished Jewish immigrants, and citizens of a country still decades away from having a global reach, American Jews had a distant relationship to this emerging Jewish internationalism.[57] The first instance of internationalism by American Jews occurred in 1840, when a few well-placed Jews, led by the Westphalian-born Isaac Leeser, urged Washington to join with European governments in condemning the accusations of blood libel against Jews in Damascus. In 1859, nearly three hundred years after first arriving in America, American Jews established their first self-defense organization to combat anti-Semitism, but its activities were largely domestic. Over the next several decades American Jews formed ad hoc groups in response to other deadly outbreaks. After the American Civil War American Jews lobbied President Grant to protest anti-Semitic legislation in Russia and Romania. Against strong opposition by secretary of state Hamilton Fish and other members of the political establishment, Grant decided in favor of B'nai B'rith's claim that in some instances human rights should trump diplomatic protocols.[58] Why Grant would make these unprecedented interventions on behalf of a Jewish minority owes to his own personal history during the Civil War and his subsequent effort to make amends; specifically, he issued Order No. 11, which dictated the expulsion of all Jews from parts of Kentucky (an order that Lincoln overturned).[59] In any event, American Jewish groups could now boast that their effort to promote "one universal law of humanity" had the backing of the highest office in the land.[60]

By the turn of the century, a better organized, more prosperous, and more secure American Jewry with better ties to a more geopolitically powerful Washington became more actively involved in the effort to protect Jews abroad. In 1891 three major Jewish figures, Oscar Straus, a New York businessman and former ambassador to Turkey, and the bankers Jacob Schiff and Jesse Sigelman—all active in the Republican Party—appealed to Republican President Benjamin Harrison to intervene to protect Russian Jews. He responded by creating a commission of inquiry, included his concern in a speech to Congress, and released a report that defended the involvement of foreign powers where minority issues were concerned. Buoyed by this success, American Jews kept pressing Washington to do more. In 1902 Schiff and Straus successfully lobbied another Republican president, Theodore Roosevelt, to respond forcefully to the Romanian ban on Jewish workers from any trade.[61]

Events in Russia caused American Jewry's leadership to consider the need for a more permanent organization. On April 19, 1903, the city of Kishinev in southwestern Russia experienced a particularly bloody pogrom. Three days of unrelenting and sadistic violence left forty-five Jews dead; hundreds were maimed and injured, and the Jewish community of 50,000 was virtually destroyed. Russian authorities did little to stop the violence or punish the perpetrators—their familiar position of complicity. The same scenario repeated itself over the next several years, with an increase in the number of pogroms from several dozen in 1903 and 1904 to several hundred from 1905 to 1906. These events represented a turning point in the development of American Jewish protection efforts.[62] Existing American Jewish institutions, such as B'nai B'rith, turned their focus from domestic welfare to the welfare of all Jews.

This was also the moment of creation of what would become American Jewry's premier rights-based organization, the American Jewish Committee. In early 1906 Jacob Schiff sent a letter to fifty-seven prominent Jews around the country, inviting them to New York to discuss the need for a formal committee to protect the rights and lives of Jews in America and the world. (See figure 2.2.) They met, and a few months later they formed the American Jewish Committee (AJC).[63] Although the Russian pogroms had triggered its formation, one of the original members reflected that the AJC was "merely a phase in the evolution of Jewish consciousness and Jewish solidarity."[64] The AJC became one of the most important Jewish organizations in the country and arguably the most important foreign policy voice for American Jews for the next several decades.[65]

The AJC had several defining characteristics. It was a self-selected, small, exclusive, and like-minded group headed by a fifteen-member executive committee. They were all men, and almost all wealthy, newcomers to New York City, with German Jewish heritage. They were strong-minded, strong-willed, well-established, and well-connected. In addition to Schiff, the original members included others who had succeeded in the business and financial world. The second in command was the renowned lawyer Louis Marshall, who was said to have argued more cases before the US Supreme Court than any private lawyer of his time. Another founding member was Adolph Ochs, owner

HEBREW CHARITIES BUILDING,

356 Second Avenue,

New York, January 8, 1906.

<u>PERSONAL.</u>

Dear Sir:

The horrors attending the recent Russian massacres, and the necessity of extending to our brethren, a helping hand in a manner most conducive to the accomplishment of a permanent improvement of their unfortunate condition, have, with remarkable spontaneity, induced thoughtful Jews in all parts of the United States, to suggest the advisability of the formation of a General Committee to deal with the serious problems thus presented, which are likely to recur, even in their acute phases, so long as the objects of our solicitude are subjected to disabilities and persecution, owing to their religious belief.

Appreciating the importance of such a project, and the absolute necessity that, if such a Committee be organized, it shall be on such lines as shall not only meet with the approval of the general public, but shall be free from all objectionable tendencies, the undersigned have concluded to invite a number of representative Jews from the several States in which there is a considerable Jewish population, for the purpose of consulting as to this important subject, and, if it is concluded that such a Committee be formed, to devise a plan and basis for an organization, and to consider the ways and means of effecting

its purposes and objects.

You are therefore earnestly requested to meet for such a consultation on Saturday, February 3, 1906, at 8 P. M., and if necessary on the following day, at the Hebrew Charities Building in the City of New York.

If it is your intention to come, will you kindly so state, on enclosed postal card.

Cordially yours,

LOUIS MARSHALL,

SAMUEL GREENBAUM,

NATHAN BIJUR,

CYRUS L. SULZBERGER,

JOSEPH JACOBS, Secretary.

Figure 2.2. Letter of Invitation from Jacob Schiff to attend the meeting that led to the establishment of the American Jewish Committee. Reprinted with permission. New York: American Jewish Committee, ©1906. www.AJC.org. All rights reserved.

of the *New York Times*, who was married to the daughter of Rabbi Isaac Wise. The members of the AJC also had close ties to other great Jewish families of the time, including the Warburgs, the Strauses, the Guggenheims, and the Sulzbergers. They saw themselves as representatives of the American dream. In many cases they or their families had come to America with nothing in their pockets and had worked their way to the top. And unlike some Jewish immigrants who were prepared to assimilate once they landed in the United States, they were proud of their Jewish heritage, sensitive to perceived slights and hints of anti-Semitism, and deeply troubled by rising anti-Semitism at home and around the world.[66]

In addition to their common personal characteristics, the members of the AJC also shared a political outlook. They were deeply committed to liberal values, believing they were consistent with their Judaism and a natural protector of Jewish interests. "Their Judaism and Americanism were more than compatible, they were complementary, for neither was restrictive or narrow in its demands upon the individual. Americanism involved no total conformity or uniformity; rather, it was fluid and receptive."[67] Many of the members, moreover, were committed to protecting and deepening the values they believed were critical to the relative success and security of the Jews. Louis Marshall believed wholeheartedly in the moral power of the US Constitution and that its principles were good for all Americans, including the Jews. One biographer wrote that, beginning in his early professional life, Marshall "operated on assumption that the Jews' greatest protection in America was the Constitution and that Jewish advocacy should therefore focus upon strengthening of constitutional norms of religious toleration and free speech."[68] He lived his principles. He made exceptional contributions to the fight for civil and political rights for minorities, including helping to write the 1913 Civil Rights Act that prohibited discrimination in any place of public accommodation or amusement.[69] On his passing, the National Association for the Advancement of Colored People (NAACP) paid tribute to him by crediting him for having participated in almost all important cases on racial equality.

The members of the AJC did not believe it was enough, though, that America be accepting of Jews; Jews also had to accept their place in America and demonstrate that they understood what it means to be Americans. Accordingly, the AJC and its members used their considerable resources to establish philanthropic, welfare, and social service organizations for the millions of indigent Jewish immigrants. In addition to providing material assistance, these welfare institutions also had an "educational" function designed to teach these newcomers how to fit into American society. This dimension of their welfare network reflected not only an attempt to ease the immigrants' transition from the old world to the new, but also the anxiety of the German Jewish aristocracy that these eastern Jews might be an embarrassment and potential danger to the Jewish community in America. Simply put, they worried that too many Jews were coming to America too quickly and from the wrong places. In 1880 there were 250,000 Jews in America, and then nearly two million Jews arrived from Eastern Europe between 1881 and 1924, most after the turn of the century. These Eastern European Jews were backward, uneducated, loud, filthy, and, generally, an embarrassment to the German Jews who thought of themselves as a breed apart, refined, cosmopolitan, and educated.

In addition to being unsightly and unseemly, these eastern Jews also had other challenging attributes. Unlike the German Jews who had arrived with some exposure to the demands of an open society, these Jews were coming from relatively insulated and isolated Jewish communities. Some were meeting non-Jews for the very first time. The German Jews worried that these Jews might prefer to live in ghettos and wanted to teach them to become part of a world of diversity with principles of tolerance and respect for difference.[70] They also had different political and religious orientations. The German Jews, who thought of the Jews as a religious community and not as a nation, were relatively conservative politically and were attracted to the reform movement. In fact, the most influential members of the German-Jewish leaders in the early twentieth century supported the Republican Party. In contrast, the Eastern European Jews thought of themselves as a nation; some associated themselves with radical, antireligious movements, including socialism, others Orthodox Judaism. And unlike the previous waves of Jewish immigration that spread across America, most of these Jews settled on the eastern seaboard and in tenement housing in urban areas like New York. In general, the American

Jewish leadership felt a genuine obligation to help their brethren yet also worried that these *ostjuden* would reflect poorly on them.[71]

The German Jewish fear that these backcountry relatives were giving Jews a bad name was not unfounded: many of these new immigrants were making a poor first impression on the American public. In 1882 the *New York Tribune* wrote of the teeming numbers of Jews living in filthy conditions, which, it added, was not a surprise given who they were. Another publication editorialized that while Jews accounted for almost 25 percent of New York's population, they accounted for 50 percent of its growing crime rate, which, it added, was to be expected given the character of the Jews. Feeling obligated to Americanize these new immigrants, and fearing the consequences for all Jews if they did not, the German Jews became their spokesmen, mentors, and benefactors, defining for them their physical and spiritual needs, ensuring that they did not become a public burden by helping with their resettlement, getting them jobs—most notably in the needle trades—and teaching them how to be proper Americans. At first these new immigrants were thankful to their Jewish protectors but after a while grew resentful of their paternalism.

The AJC organized to protect Jews abroad, and its underlying traits shaped the way it thought about protection and how it went about it. The AJC operated in the *shtadlanic* tradition as it attempted to further American Jewry's interests by lobbying, often quietly and behind the scenes. And while the members demonstrated a willingness to use American power when it was available, they believed that the ultimate source of protection resided in rights. Simply put, an article of faith among them was that the same rights that provided for their welfare and security in America was the ultimate solution to the Jewish Problem elsewhere. Accordingly, they formulated their vision around the importance of liberties and rights: "to prevent infringement of the civil and religious rights of Jews, and to alleviate the consequences of persecution." Yet because they were aiming to protect the rights of Jews in places where those rights were not yet recognized, they also saw the expansion of rights as a necessary part of their mission. And while they were focused on the rights of Jews, they also believed that the rights of all minorities and peoples were inextricably intertwined. Consequently, they emphasized the importance of rights for all people. Because it would take more than a good argument to convince these illiberal governments to begin the process of liberalization and protecting their Jews, the AJC also counted on the power of the United States. And similar to the AIU, to convince the politicians that they should help vulnerable Jews, they often tied the ideals and status of the United States to the fates of Jews. The AJC also noted another advantage of this protection mission: if these eastern Jews began to feel secure and accepted at home, then they would not feel the need to immigrate to the United States, and reducing the number of the wrong kinds of Jews flooding American shores would help the continued integration of American Jewry.

An early and defining moment in this rights-based strategy occurred in the context of Russian-American relations.[72] In 1832 the United States and Russia signed a treaty to promote commerce and navigation, and it survived the ups and downs of US-Russian relations until the 1890s, when Russia announced that it would no longer abide by Article 1, which pledged to treat all American citizens equally. Specifically, Russia decided that it would no longer honor the passports of American Jews, partly on the grounds it would be hypocritical to extend to American Jews rights that it denied to its own Jewish population. Although it is not clear how many American Jews were actually affected by this change in policy, for American Jews the issue was not numbers affected but principles violated. "Abrogation was a fight for Jewish self-respect and for American self-respect."[73] Capturing the significance of the moment for an American Jewish community that wanted to prove it was American but nevertheless felt an obligation to fellow Jews, in a public address Marshall thundered that American Jewish responsibilities were to their identity as Jews and as Americans: "He is now more than a Jew—he is also an American citizen, and the hand that smites him inflicts a stain on his citizenship. It is not the Jew who is insulted; it is the American people. And the finding of a proper remedy against this degradation is not a Jewish, but an American question."[74] For the United States to acquiesce in this discriminatory behavior was tantamount to agreeing that American Jews were not equal to other American citizens.

The combination of the Kishinev pogroms and the State Department's decision in 1907 that it would, in essence, help enforce this restriction on American Jews, raised considerable ire among American Jews. Led by the AJC, American Jewish leaders began pushing Washington to pressure Russia to change its passport policy. They used all variety of reasons to argue the case. For America to accept Russian discrimination was to violate the cherished American principle of equality for all citizens. Using the treaty to change Russian policy would be consistent with American principles and might nudge the Russian government to relax its restrictions on Jews. If Russia made life better for its Jews, they would be inclined to stay at home rather than immigrate to the United States. And the AJC appealed to the Republican administration's political interests: if the Taft administration was seen fighting on behalf of Jewish interests, Democratic-leaning Jewish voters might switch their party affiliation.

At first the American Jewish leadership pinned its hopes on a diplomatic resolution, but when that failed it turned to the more radical and dramatic proposal of ending the treaty. This move infuriated the State Department and other defenders of the agreement on the grounds that abrogation would harm American interests and indicate that a small minority could hijack them. When Taft sided with the State Department and others who opposed abrogation, the AJC and other Jewish organizations decided to appeal to Congress. Knowing that a campaign to assist a handful of Jewish Americans to get access to Russian markets was unlikely to be a winning message, organized Jewry argued that a despotic Russia was violating its agreements with the United States and assailing the American principles of liberty and equality. This was not a Jewish issue; it was an American issue. To the shock of nearly everyone involved, Congress voted to nullify the treaty, and on December 17, 1911, the United States informed Russia that it would end the seventy-five-year-old agreement.

THE ZIONIST THREAT

Until the late nineteenth century, it seemed that Gentiles were keener on seeing Jews return to Palestine than were the Jews in exile. It was not just anti-Semites who held such dreams. For many Christians, the Jewish return to their ancient homeland was a romantic undertaking and even necessary for Christ's return. Over the eighteenth and nineteenth centuries the idea of a Jewish return captured the imagination of many European (and some American) elites, including some unlikely figures. Thirty-five years before Herzl traveled to Basel, Switzerland, for the first Zionist conference, the Geneva-born Henry Dunant, who at the time was busy establishing the International Committee for the Red Cross (ICRC), helped to found the International Society for the Revival of the Orient in 1864. Although he had managed to persuade self-interested governments and battle-hardened generals to make war a little less barbaric, he could not convince the Alliance Israélite Universelle, the leading Jews of Berlin, or the Anglo-Jewish Association that they should be less concerned with cementing their rights at home and more concerned with a Jewish return to Palestine.[75] The idea of a Jewish homeland in Palestine held little appeal to the Jews of Europe, Russia, and America because they wanted to stay at home, to enjoy the same political, religious, economic, and civil rights that other citizens possessed, and to live peacefully and harmoniously with their Gentile neighbors. In other words, their answer to the Jewish Problem and the Jewish Question was that Jews should not segregate themselves in some ancient homeland but rather integrate into their existing homeland.

Yet the Jewish drive for normalization encountered two brutal obstacles. Many societies were evolving in ways that reinforced the idea of Jewish abnormality. The Eastern European countries, for instance, were developing a form of nationalism that relied on narrow ethnic loyalties, religious allegiances, and folk traditions that excluded Jews, even casting them as threats to the nation. Romania's vicious and vocal anti-Semitism could give the appearance that the only thing that held together a Romanian identity was hatred of the Jews. In response, Jews began developing countermovements, but arguably the "first line of defense . . . against the new, crude nationalisms" was cosmopolitanism, most famously in the form of socialism.[76]

The news was better in the liberalizing societies in Western Europe, where Jews were beginning to savor civil and political rights, shedding the poverty of the ghettos and enjoying some of the fruits of economic development. Yet the promised equality was partial and incomplete. And here resided the second obstacle. Jews might enjoy formal legal equality, but they confronted many barriers, some cultural and some official. Consequently, many Jews found themselves increasingly alienated from both their heritage and their societies. Even when they rejected their old world customs, habits, and traditional ways of practicing Judaism, the Gentiles continued to treat them as outcasts. They could vote, but they could not live where they wanted, join the right clubs, or gain admission to the best schools. Denied acceptance to the new and despising the old, Jews found themselves in a space of spiritual misery and alienation.

That Jews would never be accepted by liberal society was the famous conclusion of Theodor Herzl, the patriarch of modern Zionism. The basics of his story have been told often enough that they can be repeated briefly. In 1896 the Austrian journalist was sent by his newspaper to France to report on the trial of Colonel Alfred Dreyfus. The French government had accused Dreyfus, a distinguished officer in the French military, of treason. Many, though, believed he was innocent and that anti-Semitism was behind the trumped-up charges. His trial had an electrifying effect in France—and on Herzl. France believed itself to be the cradle of emancipation and often saw its treatment of Jews as evidence of its civilizing characteristics. According to those who rallied to the side of the accused, it was not Dreyfus who was on trial but rather France itself. The trial caused Herzl, largely assimilated and hardly religious, to reconsider his confidence in the prospects for the integration of the Jews in European society. His bitter conclusion was that if France, the first European country to liberate its Jews, could have such anti-Semitic outbursts then there was little hope for the Jews elsewhere. Jews needed a national homeland.

Herzl was not the first to reach this conclusion, for there were others, mainly in Eastern Europe and Russia, who were attempting to nurture Jewish nationalism in one form or another. They were in general agreement that Zionism meant the recognition and creation of some form of national identity, but they were at odds regarding whether this Jewish renaissance also required a nation-state of their own.[77] Some argued for a Zionism that meant little more than a recognition by Jews that they were a nation that shared a past and a common fate. Others argued that the Jews needed a homeland. Why did they need a homeland? There were differences of opinion. Some believed that it would hasten the collective identity of the Jewish people, while others believed that the more pressing challenge was not the Jewish soul but rather Jewish lives. What form of homeland? Some argued that it was enough that Jews have political autonomy, and argued that national self-determination could exist without a state of their own. Others argued that the Jewish nation needed to be just like all other nations and establish its own sovereign state. Where should the Jewish homeland or state be? Most Zionists insisted that it could only be the ancient Jewish home of Palestine. However, there were others who felt that almost any place where the Jews could have safety and sovereignty was sufficient.

Herzl can be credited with helping create a unified front, transforming a disjointed set of parlor conversations into a credible movement, and in doing so, putting it on the agenda of European and world politics. One reason for his success with Jews and Gentiles was because he articulated a vision of a Jewish homeland that was consistent with the times. As famously sketched in his futuristic novel, *Altneuland*, he imagined a Jewish state that was a testimony to liberal, progressive politics. This would be a Jewish homeland where Jews could be normal and could have normal relations with Gentile states. As Hannah Arendt wrote, "In Herzl's view reality could hardly express itself in any other form than that of the nation-state. In his period, indeed, the claim for national self-determination of peoples was almost self-evident justice as far as the oppressed peoples of Europe were concerned, and so there was nothing wrong or absurd in a demand made by Jews for the same kind of emancipation and freedom."[78] He also understood that any success was dependent on support from the imperial powers and the Ottoman Empire and, accordingly, labored to connect the cause of Zionism to a progressively inclined imperialism. He envisioned European Jews bringing development, civilization, and progress to a Palestine that he saw as either relatively uninhabited or underdeveloped by its Arab inhabitants, but in either case Jewish immigration would be a boon to the native population.

The Zionist movement offered a new answer to the Jewish Problem and began to organize transnationally, but it was still a very minor movement. Jews had several other options when considering how to increase their security, including immigrating to the West and fighting for liberalism and socialism at home. Migrating to Palestine was not high on their list. As a general rule, Zionism's popularity was directly related to the Jews' wretchedness. "The misery and unhappiness of Jews in Eastern Europe," observed Horace Kallen, "can be measured by their support for Zionism."[79] In countries that had undergone emancipation and political liberalization, Zionism remained a minor movement, the last possible solution to the Jewish Question.

Because Jews in America had every reason to be hopeful, they had every reason to be indifferent or even opposed to Zionism.[80] Of the two-hundred delegates attending the First Zionist Congress in 1897, there was a single American.[81] On the eve of World War I, American Jewish donations supporting Zionist pioneers totaled somewhere between $10,000 and $12,000.[82] By coming to America, Jews had already voted with their feet on what they thought was the best answer to the Jewish Problem. Not many Jews saw the long and arduous journey to Ellis Island as a transit point to Palestine. And even those who supported Zionism never imagined making aliyah, the Jewish expression for returning to Palestine. Instead, as the old but still resonant joke goes, Zionism in America meant that one Jew gave money to a second Jew to help a third Jew go to Palestine. Yet at the time, even giving money was too much for most American Jews.

But American Jews were more than unimpressed by Zionism—many were openly hostile. Jewish leaders issued one stinging rebuke after another. At the 1885 Pittsburgh conference a leading Reform theologian bitterly complained: "If anti-Semitism sets the brain of Herzl on fire, must we act as madmen too?"[83] Rabbi Isaac Mayer Wise railed against "Ziomania."[84] In 1898, in response to the first Zionist conference in Basel, Switzerland, the Union of American Hebrew Congregations was unequivocal in its anti-Zionism. Many of the founding members of the American Jewish Committee also opposed Zionism, and the organization became one of the gathering spots for the opposition.

Why did so many American Jews see Zionism as such a threat? One reason was its perceived impracticality. Zionists were scrambling for a state—not just any state, but a state in a Palestine that was controlled by the Ottoman Empire and populated by Arabs who had little interest in receiving hundreds of thousands of Jews from *shtetllach* with messianic dreams of creating a utopian society. This was madness. Jewish philanthropists were exploring alternative destinations. In 1891 Baron Maurice de Hirsch, for instance, helped to found and fund the Jewish Colonization Society, which was dedicated to assisting European and Russian Jews moving to North and South America. American Jews also thought that Zionism was a distraction of time and resources. Rather than fighting for Jews to migrate to Palestine, Jewish leaders should be fighting for equality at home. "Zionism was . . . a flight from this sacred responsibility . . . a gloomy abdication of the struggle against anti-Semitism."[85]

The principle reason why this speck of a movement managed to attract outsized attention from the Jewish political and religious elite was because of the fear that Zionism would threaten their acceptance and integration.[86] It was not just American Jews who had this worry. So too did Jewish communities in other countries that were on the cusp of acceptance. Lucien Wolf, a leading member of the British Jewish community, argued that Zionism would do much harm to and little good for the Jews. French Jews, working through the AIU, seemed to be dedicating as much time to combating Zionism as they did to stopping good, old-fashioned anti-Semitism. Zionism sent all the wrong signals. After decades of constantly reminding Gentiles that Jews were just like everyone else and that Judaism was a religion that was a purely private matter, here came Zionists claiming just the opposite. In the United States the reform movement became associated closely with anti-Zionism, as classical Reform became the antithesis of Zionism.[87] The rule of thumb was that "the wealthier and the more secularized the congregation, the louder was its rabbi in his insistence on its religious spirituality, its universalism, and its mission, and the bitterer he was in his denunciation of Zionism."[88]

The core concern was that Zionism was a form of nationalism; nationalism was premised on the notion that a distinct people required political sovereignty, and if the Jews were a nation then they probably could not or would not be full-blooded patriots. "Before the charge of nationalism," Irving Howe remarked, "courageous men quailed, as their grandfathers might have quailed before the charges of heresy."[89] The 1898 denunciation of Zionism by the Union of American Hebrew Congregations rejected Zionism's basic premise: "We are unalterably opposed to political Zionism. The Jews are not a nation, but a religious community. Zion was a precious possession of the past, the early home of our faith where our prophets uttered their world-subduing thoughts and our psalmists sang their world-enchanting hymns. As such, it is a holy memory, but it is not our hope of the future. America is our Zion."[90]

American Jewish leaders worried that Zionism played into the hands of anti-Semites who claimed that Jews would never fit in and always wanted to remain apart. Zionism was based on the claim that Jews were a separate nation—which is precisely what many Christians had been saying all along. The Jewish Problem was exactly this—a Jewish problem.[91] Writing in a periodical in 1921, a Christian critic of Zionism said that Jews needed to decide whether they were a people apart or a light unto nations and that Jews always get themselves into trouble when they choose to keep themselves apart from others. When they have chosen to be "an unassimilated mass," Jews have been "equally obnoxious to Roman paganism, to Christianity and to Islam."[92] In a similar spirit, Harvard University professor Albert Bushnell exclaimed that Jews needed to "fish or cut bait."[93] Many American Jews, working hard to ingratiate themselves in America, worried that Zionism was undoing all their hard work.

CHAPTER THREE

PROPHETS MUGGED
BY REALITY

Beginning in 1914 and continuing over the next thirty-one years, the Jewish Problem entered its bloodiest chapter. Tens of thousands of Jews died during and after World War I, not just as casualties of war but also because they were Jews. After the war a venomous nationalism swept across Europe and engulfed Jewish villages in its path. Against this murderous backdrop, the Jewish Problem was on the international agenda at the Paris Peace Conference, just as it had been at almost every major postwar multilateral conference since 1815. However, this conference differed from all others because it accepted not one but two possible solutions—minority rights in Jews' home countries and a Jewish homeland in Palestine. This was the good news. The bad news was that the Great Powers were no more willing to make credible commitments than before. Hitler then instigated his own final solution to the Jewish Problem. The international community's response split: some said and did nothing, some protested and did little, and some used Hitler as a role model.

American Jews watched in horror and grief as European Jews slipped away. It took American Jewry a while to fully comprehend the gravity of the situation, which made them equal to almost everyone else. Knowing more, though, did not mean they were any more prepared to deliver meaningful action. They were relatively safe but not without their own worries. Also, there was relatively little they could do. The immigration doors had been closed in the early 1920s, and they were not going to swing open during these hard economic times, no matter how desperate the situation of European Jewry became. Although minority rights were formally on the books, the League of Nations had been reduced to a joke, and American Jews were in no position to give it a backbone. Britain was paralyzed by its inability to satisfy the nationalist aspirations of both the Jews and the Arabs in Palestine. It is a testament to the deep-seated fear by American Jews that they might give off the whiff of tribalism, be accused of dual loyalty, and endanger their own safety in their American home, that it took as long as it did for them to accept not only Zionism but also the idea of a state for the Jews. The period between the wars is not a story of the power of ideology over reality. However, it does underscore the influence of the prophetic theology and suggest how fearful American Jews were of seeing their struggle for acceptance become challenged by the appearance of a nationalism that might be mistaken for advocating separatism.

WORLD WAR I

Jewish existence had been moving in opposite directions in different parts of Europe and Russia for nearly a century. As a consequence of their increasingly liberal and inclusionary character, Western European states were gradually granting Jews citizenship and accepting them as equals. As a consequence of their growing illiberal and exclusionary character, the Eastern European states and Russia were making life more and more difficult for Jews, with insecurity a daily fact of life and violent pogroms a regular occurrence. The war caused misery for everyone, but especially for the Jews in Eastern Europe. When the war broke out in August 1914, the world's Jewish population totaled thirteen million, the vast majority of whom lived in Eastern Europe and Russia. Already isolated from their societies, the Jews were easy targets and scapegoats.

War and the rise of chauvinistic nationalisms provided pretext and cause for violent campaigns against the Jews, or, in contemporary language, ethnic cleansing. The Russian plan to expel two million

Jews from a war zone in Lithuania and Poland was halted when German troops took control of the area.[1] Eastern Jews, increasingly anxious and insecure, became ever more alienated from their societies and sympathetic to Zionism, which had the unintended effect of intensifying anti-Semitism. American Jews, fortunate to be separated by an ocean from the fighting but worried about their loved ones on the continent, did what they could by mobilizing a fervent relief effort.[2]

The Jews of Europe, though, were not the target of the first relief campaign. Instead, it was the Jews of Palestine—the first time this Jewish community became a matter of intense concern for American Jewry. On August 31, 1914, Henry Morgenthau, the US ambassador to Turkey, cabled the AJC's Jacob Schiff an urgent message regarding the deteriorating condition of the Jews as a consequence of disruptions caused by the war; 78,000 Jews, he wrote, were rumored to be near starvation. The American Jewish community, largely through the American Jewish Committee, responded quickly.

As the war intensified and as Europe's Jews found themselves in similar straits, American Jews increased their relief efforts, though not without some hesitation.[3] America was formally neutral, though sympathetic to the allies. American Jewish leaders were largely of German descent and wanted to raise funds to distribute on both sides of the war, and they were especially sensitive to the possibility of being seen as unpatriotic if they were perceived to be siding with Germany. Notwithstanding this fear, American Jews began contributing generously to the relief effort. Indeed, because "no segment of the Jewish community denied a responsibility to provide assistance,"[4] a thousand fund-raising drives appeared to bloom. Overcoming their stark ideological and religious divisions, in 1914 three of the largest collectors of funds—the American Jewish Committee's American Jewish Relief Committee, the Orthodox community, and the socialist and labor organizations—created a unified mechanism to disperse funds: the American Jewish Joint Distribution Committee, chaired by the influential New York banker Felix Warburg.

The "Joint," as it came to be known, was the most successful and organized effort by American Jews to help their kin in foreign lands.[5]

Figure 3.1. Refugees Being Fed by the Joint Distribution Committee-sponsored Kindergarten and Community School in Byalostok, Ukraine. American Jewish Joint Distribution Committee Archives.

In addition to proving that Jewish groups could put aside their differences to work for a common cause, it also "represented practical confirmation of the concept that philanthropy could bring together essentially all American Jews in a way that no religious (or secular) ideology or other institution could."[6] German and Eastern European Jews might have their differences, but they could rally around the idea of helping fellow Jews.[7] The Joint raised contributions from individuals, families, and magnates such as Julius Rosenwald, the founder of Sears Roebuck, and by the end of the war had collected more than $16 million—nearly equaling the total raised by the American Red Cross. In addition to its successful fund-raising, the Joint also created an extensive network of distribution centers throughout Europe.

The end of the war did not mark the end of the suffering. In 1917 the Russian Revolution erupted, tumbling into a civil war, widespread famine, and anti-Jewish violence. Roughly 200,000 Jews died, and even more would have without the action of the Joint and other Jewish aid agencies.[8] Life was equally horrific for Jews in other parts of the East. There were regular outbursts of anti-Semitic violence; the vast majority of Jews in major urban areas were near starvation, dependent on whatever charity was available, and there were reports of whole families lying down to die in the middle of town squares.[9]

Whenever and wherever they could, American Jewish relief agencies provided aid. After survival was reasonably assured, then came the challenge of rebuilding lives. Using the increasingly recited expression of "helping people to help themselves," American Jewish agencies began helping Jewish families and communities get back on their feet. And because the Zionist organizations had the best connections in Eastern Europe, they played a leading role in distributing the aid, strengthening Zionism in the process.[10] Although the Zionists might have been expected to aid only those who wanted to leave for Palestine, they made little distinction between those who wanted to immigrate and those who wanted to rebuild their lives at home. A principle was emerging—Jews, like all people, should not be forced to immigrate but rather should have the option to stay in their countries of origin or adoption. This principle coincided with the political calculations of many American Jewish organizations, including the AJC, that the United States was not prepared to accept any more Jews. Like all principles, it was informed by a healthy dose of pragmatism.

The American Jewish response resembled those of other ethnic and religious communities in the United States in several ways. First, it operated on the principle of partiality rather than impartiality. Not until after World War II did aid organizations begin to embrace the principle of aid based on need rather than identity. In a tribal division of labor, American Jews mobilized to help Jews in need, Catholics for Catholics, Polish for Poles (though not Polish Jews), and so on. No one expected Jews to direct their operations toward non-Jews, nor was there any realistic expectation that non-Jews would go out of their way to help Jews. Second, the relief effort relied on grassroots action, and the state played relatively little role. On rare occasions it provided modest financial support, and if it had excess logistical capacity it might help transport and distribute aid, but most of the state's support was in spirit only. The biggest contribution to the American Jewish relief efforts by the United States came when President Wilson declared January 7, 1916, Jewish Relief Day. Third, the combination of the deep desire to help and the severity of suffering meant that American society became mobilized to provide relief like never before, creating new aid organizations that became permanent players in the humanitarian world after World War I. Many of these organizations, accordingly, went from providing emergency relief to postwar reconstruction. Fourth, because the very countries that once headed relief efforts now required assistance, and because it was on the verge of becoming a world power, the United States became a central player in the humanitarian world. American Jews experienced a similar trajectory. German, British, and French Jews could no longer perform their traditional leadership roles, and American Jews assumed positions of responsibility for the first time.

ZIONISM, AMERICAN STYLE

By the eve of World War I, American Jews began lowering their guard against Zionism. This turnaround owed to several factors. The alternatives for protecting Jews were disappearing quickly. Eastern European societies and states were as nasty as ever. Decades before, Jews might have escaped persecution by fleeing to the West, but now the West would accept only a fraction of the requests. Zionism, might be a lifesaver for the Jews of Europe after all. And while American Jews had once seen Zionism as a threat to their own existence, it might not be so ominous now. Indeed, assimilation was increasingly viewed as a threat to the community. Perhaps Zionism could save American Jews from deracination, giving them a mechanism to maintain their collective bonds.[11] And while Jews of Western European origin continued to harbor suspicion about Zionism, among Jews from the East it became particularly popular; for them, providing them food for the soul as they Americanized and purged themselves of traits from the old country. Moreover, they did not have the same faith in universalism as the German Jews had.[12] In short, where the Jews of Europe saw Zionism as a way to save themselves from physical destruction, the Jews of America appreciated Zionism's ability to possibly save them from spiritual emptiness.

American Jews were softening their resistance to Zionism, but to a particular kind of Zionism. There were many different kinds of Zionism at the time. Some advocated a homeland for the Jews in Palestine, where they would exist side by side with the native population in a binational state. Some advocated the creation of a Jewish state, created by the Jews for the Jews. Others saw Zionism as leading to spiritual renewal, the position attributed to the cultural Zionism of Ahad Ha'am. The Zionists in America were closer to the cultural than to the political camp, and many leading Zionists imagined a Jewish homeland that would serve as both a place of refuge for Jews who otherwise had nowhere to go and a site of cultural renewal for Jews all over the world. Their nationalism differed in an important way from the type that dominated world politics—it did not require political sovereignty. Not coincidentally, a nationalism without political sovereignty had the clear advantage of not raising uncomfortable questions regarding the loyalties of American Jews.

Louis Brandeis, the distinguished jurist, progressive leader, and first Jewish US Supreme Court justice, is rightly credited with assembling and promoting this image of Zionism and thus making Zionism safe for American Jews. Brandeis was an American success story before he became an American Jewish success story and a leader of the American Zionist movement. Born in 1856 in Kentucky, Brandeis became a prominent lawyer who took up causes of injustice, like his contemporary, Louis Marshall. But unlike Marshall whose commitment to Jewish welfare informed his dedication to civil and political liberties, Brandeis's progressive politics led him to Zionism. Although raised Jewish, there was little in his childhood or early adult years to suggest that he would become a leader of the American Jewish community. He did not identify with Jewish causes, favor Jewish charities, belong to a synagogue, or see his Jewish heritage as an important source of meaning. In fact, when he spoke to Jews on the subject of America, he urged them to put aside any ethnic or religious distractions and concentrate on becoming good Americans. In a speech in 1905 celebrating the 250th anniversary of the landing of the first Jews in New Amsterdam (New York), he lectured his audience on the need to forget the past and become immersed in an America that had no room for "hyphenated Americans." Americans would warm to Jewish immigrants, he predicted, once the newcomers accepted their American identity. This transition should not be too onerous, he argued, because Jewish and American values were one and the same.

Within a few years, though, the very same Brandeis who had railed against hyphenated Americans, displayed little interest in Jewish affairs, and preached that American Jews should embrace their American identity to the exclusion of all others, became the leader of American Zionism. According to most accounts, his epiphany occurred in 1910 when he became involved in a labor strike of nearly 60,000 garment workers, most of them Jewish immigrants. At the request of the progressive department store owner A. Lincoln Filene, Brandeis agreed to try and mediate the strike. Although he did not end the labor dispute (ironically, the anti-Zionist Louis Marshall succeeded where Brandeis failed), the workers made a lasting impression on him. He was profoundly moved by these recent arrivals, who were enduring long hours and miserable working conditions to better the lives of their children, but were not so quick to get ahead that they forgot the importance of economic justice. This encounter apparently stirred in him a greater interest in American Jewish politics. By 1913 he had familiarized himself with Zionism and internal Zionist politics, and the following year, on the eve of World War I in August 1914, he became the leader of the Zionist movement.

Why he chose not simply to join but to lead the American Zionist movement is a matter of considerable debate—some cynically suggest that he was trying to impress the powerbrokers in Washington, while others claim he had reunited with his Jewish identity.[13] According to Brandeis, however, it was neither opportunism nor sentimentalism but rather a reconsideration of the relationship between American identity and nationalism. As he put it in a 1915 address to the Conference of the Eastern Council of Reform Rabbis, American Jews needed to cohere their Jewish and American identities:

For us the Jewish Problem means this: How can we secure for Jews, wherever they may live, the same rights and opportunities enjoyed by non-Jews? How can we secure for the world the full contribution which Jews can make, if unhampered by artificial limitations? The problem has two aspects: That of the individual Jew, and that of Jews collectively. The individual must be allowed to develop as is his want, but we develop as individuals within a group of which he is a part.[14]

American Jews need Zionism.

His Zionism had a four-part intellectual foundation. It began with an assessment of liberalism. Liberalism, he cautioned, was something of a poisoned chalice. It emancipated Jews, allowing them to be citizens in public and Jews at home. Yet it came at a steep price, leading them to abandon their heritage, culture, and history. Although Brandeis, himself a thoroughly assimilated Jew, might have been expected to be indifferent to this news, he worried that without a strong sense of self, individuals would become lost and unwilling to contribute to the betterment of society.

Second, Brandeis concluded that while liberalism solves the Jewish Problem because it secures the rights of Jews as individuals, it does not solve the Jewish Question, because it does not address how Jews will situate themselves in and make positive contributions to society. As he stated in one address,

> We must protect America and ourselves from demoralization, which has to some extent already set in among American Jews. The cause of this demoralization is clear. It results in large part from the fact that in our land of liberty all the restraints by which the Jews were protected in their Ghettos were removed and a new generation left without necessary moral and spiritual support.[15]

Jews could recover their sense of self through Jewish nationalism. Nationalism, he argued, had "infused whole peoples with hope, manhood, and self-respect. It has ennobled and made purposeful millions of lives. It offered them a future, and in doing so revived and capitalized all that was valuable in the past."[16] While some forms of nationalism were dangerous and vile, Jewish nationalism built healthy Jewish souls who had a progressive spirit. For instance, many of the

Jewish leaders of the garment workers' strike were committed Zionists, but they had no interest in moving to Palestine and instead were fighting for decency, freedom, and equality in America. For Brandeis, then, Zionism was a catalyst for the creation of self-confident Jews whose communal identity would better all of humanity. Importantly, Brandeis embraced Zionism not only because of his concern for Europe's Jews, but also because of his love for America. For Brandeis, Zionism could protect Jews who lived in illiberal lands such as Russia *and* empower Jews who lived in liberal lands such as the United States.

The third pillar was the claim that it was possible to be both American and Zionist. The reform movement and other Jewish anti-Zionists had characterized Americanism and Zionism as diametrically opposed. This was wrongheaded, according to Brandeis. He reassured them: "Let no American imagine that Zionism is inconsistent with Patriotism. Multiple loyalties are objectionable only if they are inconsistent. . . . There is no inconsistency between loyalty to America and loyalty to Jewry."[17] If Zionism was going to gain traction among American Jews, then American Jews had to feel they could be Zionist without calling into question their loyalty to their new homeland. Brandeis was a man who could be trusted, so if he believed it was safe, then it probably was.

Fourth, and related, not only could Jews be Americans and Zionists, but by being Zionists they would also be better Jews and Americans. In contrast to the "old" Brandeis, the "new" Brandeis now saw hyphenated Americans not as a point of weakness but rather as a point of strength. The following refrain became a stock line in his addresses: "To be good Americans, we must be better Jews, and to be better Jews, we must become Zionists!" In his speech at the 1915 Zionist convention in Boston, Brandeis proclaimed: "The highest Jewish ideals are essentially American in a very important particular way. It is Democracy that Zionism represents. It is Social Justice which Zionism represents, and every bit of that is the American ideals of the twentieth century." Jews, Brandeis suggested at another moment, had been accumulating centuries' worth of values that encapsulated American ideals, enabling Jews to teach Americans how to become better Americans.

The Jewish spirit, the product of our religion and experiences, is essentially modern and essentially American. . . . America's fundamental law seeks to make real brotherhood of man. That brotherhood became the fundamental Jewish law more than twenty-five hundred years ago. America's insistent demand in the twentieth century is for social justice. That also has been the Jews' striving for ages. Their affliction as well as their religion has prepared the Jews for effective democracy. Persecution broadened their sympathies. It trained them in patent endurance, in self-control, and in sacrifice. It make them think as well as suffer. It deepened the passion for righteousness. Indeed loyalty to America demands rather that each American Jew become a Zionist. . . . The Jewish spirit, so long preserved, the character developed by so many centuries of sacrifice, should be preserved and developed further, so that in America as elsewhere the sons of the race may in the future live lives and do deeds worthy of their ancestors.[18]

In general, Brandeis warned America's Jews that stripping themselves of their Jewish identity would leave them impoverished and unfit for American citizenship, and that by embracing Zionism they would become better Jews and better Americans.

Brandeis's ideas crystallized with the help of Horace Kallen, an American Jewish sociologist at the University of Wisconsin who went on to have a very distinguished academic career.[19] A student at Harvard of the renowned philosopher and theologian William James, Kallen had been struggling over the relationship between communal identity, on the one hand, and the universalizing ideologies such as liberalism, on the other. He was a founding member of the Harvard Menorah Society, a group dedicated to Jewish humanism; the Harvard Menorah Society later expanded and became the Menorah Association, with branches across college campuses in the United States, and published the *Menorah Journal*, a leading outlet for debating central controversies of American Jewish life. In 1915 Kallen published an immensely influential essay in *The Nation* that became the basis for his later development of the concept of "cultural pluralism."

The essay and the notion of cultural pluralism denounced the rival image of America as a melting pot. Popularized by another Jew, Israel

Zangweil, the idea was that newcomers to the United States shed their old selves as they became Americans. Kallen objected to this observation for empirical and normative reasons. There was no evidence that immigrant communities had or would rid themselves of the past. Nor was there any reason why they should. Asking immigrants to become "Americans" was just a code word for demanding that they adopt the manners, habits, and characteristics of the dominant culture, which was white, Anglo-Saxon, and Protestant. Why should Jews, Slavs, and Chinese become WASPs? Part of the reason that images like the melting pot were so seductive to many Americans, he argued, was because of the fear that diversity threatened American society. But this was an artificial fear. Not only could America tolerate diversity—this was its great strength. It was the existence of multiple identities that accounted for America's vibrancy and progress. Individuals can have multiple national identities, these national identities can reinforce one another. Foreshadowing contemporary versions of multiculturism, Kallen claimed that Jews could and should retain their communal identity.[20] However, he rejected religiously based anchors such as chosenness, believing it and associated concepts were "attractive to our vanity" and products of "colossal egotism."[21] The only thing that made Jews distinct, he asserted, was that they thought they were distinct, and insofar as they were content to live a life of distinction without a sense of superiority, then no harm was done. But if Jews were distinct for completely self-manufactured and arbitrary reasons, then it was not clear why Jews should remain as a group. Zionism, he believed, would enable the Jews to retain their communal identity in a liberal community. Other communities were able to maintain their sense of self by identifying with the homeland, and Zionism was the Jews' nationalism.[22]

Kallen's ideas not only influenced Brandeis but also were heavily debated by other leading thinkers of the time, including Raymond Bourne and John Dewey. Raymond Bourne, a student of Dewey and important leftist writer of the period, used Kallen's thesis to inform his influential essays "Trans-National America" and "The Jew and Trans-National America." According to Bourne, individuals can navigate an increasingly multicultural society if they use the Jews' methods of navigation as a model.[23] He criticized the melting pot metaphor

for several reasons: it would transform a vibrant "American population into a colorless, tasteless, homogeneous mass of WASPS," and
it would create a nationalism that the elite could easily manipulate
into dangerous military adventures, such as the nationalism-fueled
war currently engulfing Europe. A hyphenated America would not
only guard against blandness but would also provide a check against
nationalist militarism. "If America is to be nationalistic without
being chauvinistic," it needed a new concept of the "state, of nationality, of citizenship, and of allegiance."[24] He credited the modern Jew with managing to retain an identity that is transnational
and does not need "the external props of territorial sovereignty and
a political machine."[25] Able to maintain a cultural allegiance without requiring a political allegiance, the modern Jew is a role model.
The "modern world, and above all America, needs these Zionist
conceptions."[26]

A defining feature of the Zionism of Brandeis, Kallen, and many
other American Zionists was its rejection of tribalism and embrace
of the prophetic tradition, which allied them with Mordecai Kaplan's
idea that Jews are a civilization.[27] An eminent theologian and rabbi,
and founder of the Reconstruction movement, Kaplan was born in
Lithuania in 1881 and moved with his family to America in 1889.
Steeped in the old world and the new, a devout Jew who nevertheless
was drawn to contemporary life and Enlightenment ideas, Kaplan became one of America's greatest and most influential Jewish thinkers,
in large measure because of his dedicated and sophisticated effort to
find a space between the particular and the universal in the American context and the world. According to him, Jews are a civilization
because the density of their interactions, connection to a homeland,
cultural attributes, and religious folkways have created bonds of
common identity, history, memory, and fate. These defining attributes of the civilization, moreover, are fluid; as a consequence of internal dialogue and interaction with the world outside, the definition
and boundaries of the civilization can change. Judaism, though, helps
Jews stay Jews—the function of the Jewish religion, in other words, is
to help provide continuity to the Jews as a people. One reason Kaplan
preferred to see the Jews as a civilization rather than a nation is because the prevailing definition of nation required a state; in contrast,

Kaplan argued, Jews are a transnational and diasporic people whose sense of peoplehood does not require a state. In short, Kaplan opted for the language of civilization over nationalism because he wanted to highlight the transnational character of Jews and avoid the stigma of being a "nation."

Civilizations also have a purpose—hardly the first time a political community made such a claim. Kaplan argued that a distinguishing characteristic of a civilization was its contribution to its immediate surroundings and world history. American Jews, as part of the Jewish civilization, have a well-defined mission: "to promulgate a concept of American democracy and ethical nationhood" based on Kaplan's "vision of the Jewish paradigm of collective identity."[28] Similar to Brandeis, Kaplan warned that American democracy faced two dangers. Liberalism threatened to strip individuals of their culture and history, to reduce them to abstract rights and responsibilities. However, individuals could only be truly human when they carried tradition with them into a changing future. There also was the opposite problem of religious nationalism, particularly an America that defined the nation as Christian. Kaplan, in other words, jousted with the prevailing characterization of America as a melting pot, with the presumption that Jews and other minorities were expected to surrender their identity and become (white) Protestants. Such forced conformity threatened democracy and removed the diversity that is the source of progress. America is much better off because of its Jews.

So, too, is the world. In Kaplan's view Jews were a civilization that embodies "ethical nationhood." In contrast to a nationalism that insists on its political sovereignty and its superiority, ethical nationhood allows for an "internationalism which, admitting a high degree of autonomy to each nation, advocates the submission of each nation to a sovereignty higher than its own and representative of a group of nations but preferably of all nations."[29] Kaplan offered a cosmopolitan vision of a world in which separate peoples are not only tolerated but also are genuinely welcomed and viewed as a potential source of moral progress. Jewish civilization contributes to universal integration; the particular inspires the universal.

Many leading Jewish intellectuals and theologians were offering important interventions into political theology that prepared the ground for Zionism, but Brandeis deserves considerable credit for putting it on the American scene and altering the landscape of American Jewish politics. Much of his impact owes to the fact that he was the right messenger with the right message. This defender of Zionism was one of the best known, beloved, and respected Jews in America, whose patriotism was beyond reproach and whose commitment to the public good was unimpeachable. In short, he made it safe for American Jews to be Zionists. He also brought his incredible organizational talents to the cause. He successfully (if momentarily) challenged Zionists to set aside their petty quarrels and hair-splitting differences for the greater good. He helped to forge the Zionist Organization of America in 1918, transforming the Zionist movement from a collection of ramshackle, disconnected parlor societies into a bona fide organization. Under Brandeis's leadership the Zionist movement grew spectacularly, from 12,000 members in 1914 to more than 176,000 members in 1919. And because these were dues-paying members, its budget swelled from $15,000 in 1914 to more than $3 million in 1918. This messenger also advanced a set of views that successfully appealed to American Jews who wanted to be both particular and universal, and who were prepared to accept a Zionism so long as it did not threaten their American identity.

In the process of lifting Zionism's popularity, Brandeis also challenged the existing American Jewish establishment in general and the American Jewish Committee in particular. The AJC opposed both Zionism and any sort of public gathering that might put Zionism to a vote. Its opposition to the democratization of American Jewish politics owed to the fear that it would lose a referendum and the rise of the great mass of uncultured Jews would embarrass the Jewish community. Brandeis and others sympathetic to Zionism insisted that a more democratic body of Jews should meet at a congress to decide on issues of significance to all American Jews. In fact, Brandeis argued that because of the AJC's antidemocratic character, the Zionist movement was the true partner of American democracy. The first American Jewish Congress convened in late March 1916. Just prior to being nominated to the US Supreme Court, Brandies delivered a fiery and passionate defense of Zionism and the democratization of American Jewish politics.

Brandeis helped make Zionism safe for American Jews, and then Britain made it even more difficult to resist. On November 2, 1917, British foreign secretary James Balfour sent a letter to Baron Walter Rothschild, a leader of the British Jewish community, pledging Britain's support for a Jewish homeland in Palestine. This was a watershed moment in the history of Zionism—for the first time a Great Power backed the idea of a Jewish homeland. Although Britain was mildly sympathetic to Zionism, at least if it was understood as a homeland or perhaps part of a future British commonwealth, Britain's decision was motivated by concerns for its own fate and not the fate of the Jews. British officials had been busily corresponding with the leaders of different communities during the war, promising a variety of rewards if they would either outright support the British side or, at least, not help the German-Ottoman alliance. In 1915 British officials exchanged a series of letters with Hussein bin Ali, sharif of Mecca, promising independence for the Arabs in much of the region (though not specifically Palestine) if he opened a front against the Ottoman Empire (promises Britain later broke).

Two years later and under more desperate circumstances, Britain made a similar promise to the Jews. Britain did not expect the Jews to open a second front, but it hoped that by showing sympathy to Zionism it would shore up support with American Jews who had powerful friends. Americans Louis Brandeis and Felix Frankfurter were ardent Zionists and close friends of President Woodrow Wilson, and part of Britain's calculation was that its support for Zionism might prod Washington to formally back London. It was also thought that some of the most important banking houses, many of them owned by Jewish families, would be pleased. Once Britain issued the Balfour Declaration, Zionism and the idea of a homeland for the Jews became tied to the war, and Palestine was bound to be included in the postwar discussions.

The British calculated correctly, at least insofar as the declaration tilted the support of American Jews toward Britain.[30] Until that point, Jews were probably more pro-German than pro-Allies.[31] Many leading American Jewish families were from Germany. The hundreds of thousands of immigrants from Eastern Europe and Russia, whose memories of their homeland were filled with persecution and whose families back home continued to suffer from anti-Semitism, had little love for the czar. Consequently, American Jews were faintly pro-German, anti-Russian, and largely agnostic toward Britain and France, which placed them in a slightly awkward position vis-à-vis American policy, which was formally neutral but clearly supported the British-French-Russian alliance. American Jews understood that cold-calculating interests, and not heartfelt sentimentality, drove Britain's public support for a Jewish homeland. And even though the lack of Great Power support had not affected Zionism's favorability among American Jews, Britain's pledge made the idea of a Jewish homeland more realistic, which, in turn, convinced many who were previously undecided to reassess their existing belief that Zionism was pure fantasy.

Yet a remaining, highly vocal anti-Zionist constituency was unimpressed by the declaration. "While most American Jews applauded the news [of the Balfour Declaration], die-hard anti-Zionists, especially in the Reform camp, were outraged."[32] They opposed Zionism for reasons that had nothing to do with whether or not it was popular with the Great Powers, so they had little reason to feel differently now that Great Britain endorsed it. And even though the carefully worded Balfour Declaration did not promise a state for the Jews or that Palestine might be the only homeland for the Jews, the very hint that the Jews were a nation sent the anti-Zionists into convulsions. In fact, the Balfour Declaration seemed to realize their fear that Jewish nationalism would trigger anti-Semitism. In Eastern Europe and elsewhere, anti-Semites used the Balfour Declaration as further proof that Jews were a separate nation and offered to help these aliens pack their bags for Palestine. An editorial from the Saint Louis–based *Modern View* condemned the declaration in the following terms: "American citizens of Jewish faith who are thoroughly American neither approve nor counsel political Zionism. It fosters the thought and spirit of a divided allegiance, as indicated in pictures printed in the daily press, which shows some Zionist Legion volunteers under the caption, '*Going home* to Palestine.' "[33]

The Balfour Declaration placed enormous pressure on the AJC.[34] It needed to respond, but it was not exactly sure what to say. The AJC's executive committee was of two minds, with some believing that the time had come for the AJC to moderate its opposition and others insisting that Britain's blessing did not change wrong to right. As a consequence of this internal debate and uncertainty, it took the AJC until late April 1918, a full six months, to issue a statement—and a fairly compromised statement at that. It acknowledged the growing support for Zionism among American Jews and gave a qualified endorsement. But, fearful that Zionism might call into question the loyalty of American Jews, it proclaimed: "Let Palestine be one of the many homes where Jews may live in peace and happiness . . . and nothing must be done which may prejudice the rights and political status enjoyed by Jews in any other country."[35]

And in an effort to emphasize its unqualified support for liberalism and the rights of minority populations, the AJC insisted that the Jewish immigration to Palestine should not harm the interests of Palestine's current occupants: "nothing shall be done which may prejudice the civil and religious rights of existing non-Jewish communities in Palestine, or the rights and political status enjoyed by Jews in another country." There was no reason why Jews should not be allowed to settle in Palestine, but, then again, there was no reason why Jews should be forbidden from settling wherever they wanted, within reason. And if they did go to Palestine, they should live by the same principles that Jews enjoyed in America. American Jews were cautiously becoming part of the Zionist camp—but not the part that advocated a separate sovereign state. Theirs was a Zionism that saw a Jewish identity as residing in a cosmopolitan field.

AMERICAN JEWS IN PARIS

The end of the war did not end the violence against the Jews. In the chaotic postwar environment, anti-Semitic agitation and violence flourished, often under the cover of nationalist campaigns, which were being whipped into a chauvinistic frenzy with the end of the war and the fight for independence in the aftermath of the fall of the Ottoman, Russian, and Austro-Hungarian empires. Precisely how many Jews died during and after the war is unknown—tens of thousands to be sure. Although widely covered at the time but now forgotten, places like Lemberg (Lvov) experienced horrendous anti-Semitic violence. The violence continued even during the peace negotiations in Paris, when nationalist groups were petitioning the Great Powers to accept their case for independence and Jewish groups were pleading to be protected from these candidates for statehood. Eastern Europe provided daily reminders that the Jewish Problem required immediate attention at the highest levels.

The Jewish Problem had been a frequent agenda item at multilateral gatherings for a century.[36] It was discussed at the Congress of Vienna in 1815. It reappeared at the London Congress of 1830, which had recognized an independent Greece that guaranteed equal treatment for minority groups in its constitution. Meetings in Paris in 1856 and 1858, and in Berlin in 1878, discussed the Jewish Problem, and so, too, did the Bucharest Conference in 1913. And here they were, once again, addressing the Jewish Problem. But the Jewish Problem was part of a larger minority problem, which was not only a humanitarian matter but also a peace-and-security issue.[37] How states treated their minorities had caused considerable friction between governments, and, in some cases, triggered conflict. Something had to be done.

The Jewish delegations arrived in Paris with various suggestions, but there were two main proposals. One focused on Palestine. But what Palestine would become was a matter of debate. Some recommended the establishment of a Jewish state; the Jews were a nation and deserved a nation-state. Others set their sights not on sovereignty but instead on a homeland, a designated safe haven for Jews.[38] Another proposal looked to solve the Jewish Problem in Europe, and here the divisions were even greater. Some wanted the Jews to be recognized as a separate nation and to be granted national rights in their existing countries. Advocates for categorizing the Jews as a nation with group rights had various ideas of what those rights might be.[39] Others went so far as to suggest that Jewish national minorities should be granted special recognition and autonomy—thus carving out states within states.

Yet the Jewish delegates were not so naive as to believe that Jews would be safer once they had a new political status and legal protections. Why would anti-Semitic governments and majority populations

Figure 3.2. Jewish Delegations at Paris, 1919. Courtesy of The Jacob Rader Marcus Center of the American Jewish Archives, Cincinnati, Ohio. americanjewisharchives.org

now feel or act any differently toward Jews? Accordingly, the Jewish delegations envisioned a major role for the future League of Nations. But what would that mean? Once again, numerous possibilities were discussed. One proposal was to grant these new Jewish national communities international representation. A gathering of Zionist organizations in Copenhagen passed a plank favoring a homeland in Palestine, equal rights including national autonomy for Jewish minorities, and "Admission of the Jewish People to the League of Nations."[40] But because the Jewish national communities could be expected to have different interests, other delegates advocated that each should have its own voice, suggesting one Jewish delegation per country.

In addition to representation, others urged the league to monitor and enforce provisions to protect minorities. But this opened another Pandora's box of complications and debates. How active should the league be and when should it get involved? And, if it carved out a role for itself in these states, how would these instruments exist alongside sovereignty and the principle of noninterference? Were the victors really prepared to create new international mechanisms that ran roughshod over the principles of sovereignty in favor of the emerging principles of minority rights? Were they prepared to limit this unprecedented move to the new national states, essentially making them second-class citizens in the international community? Or would they subject all states to these conditions? Were France and England prepared to submit themselves to such scrutiny?

The American Jewish delegation was no more unified than any other.[41] In order to prepare for Paris, American Jewish leaders met in Philadelphia at an American Jewish Congress and passed two declarations: in support of Zionism, though a Zionism defined as a homeland and not a state, and in support of minority protection, which was centered on a Jewish bill of rights for the new national states of Eastern Europe.[42] Not trusting the welfare of the Jews to these new national states, the congress further recommended that the future League of Nations have the authority to impose constitutional guarantees and to monitor and enforce its provisions. By calling for an international bill of rights they were projecting the American constitution onto the world. Their bill of rights, moreover, was couched in terms of the rights of individuals and minorities—not nations. Jews deserved rights not because they were a separate nation but rather because they were citizens of national states, and as such they had both rights and responsibilities. And by proposing that these rights become integrated into international institutions, the Jewish delegations were imagining a new relationship between the international community and individuals. The congress elected a group of Jews representative of the entire political and religious spectrum to go to Paris: the AJC's Judge Julian Mack, Louis Marshall, and Cyrus Adler; Colonel Harry Cutler of the Jewish Welfare Board; Bernard Levinthal, an Orthodox rabbi; Rabbi Stephen Wise, one of the most prominent Jews in America and a well-known Zionist; Joseph Barondess, a labor leader and political figure from New York's Lower East Side; Jacob de Haus; Leopold Benedict; and Dr. Nahman Syrkin, a leader of the Socialist Zionists.

Many prominent American Jewish leaders rejected the American Jewish Congress's recommendation for a Jewish homeland in Palestine and the underlying insinuation that the Jews were a "nation." One very public statement of opposition appeared on March 19, 1919, in the *New York Times*. Organized by US representative Julius Kahn, a Republican from California, the petition was signed by nearly three hundred prominent Jews from thirty-one cities; it is likely that it had even greater support, but many Jews who were otherwise sympathetic to the petition did not want to publicly associate themselves with it at such a sensitive time. Titled "A Statement to the Peace Conference," the petition urged President Wilson to oppose Zionism and the creation of a Jewish state in Palestine on various grounds. It wrongly assumed that Jews needed to be segregated from the rest of the world. Jews are not a nation that wants to be segregated, it continued, but rather are a people bound by a common religion who want to be integrated. Consequently, being tagged a nation would harm the Jews' campaign for their "full citizenship and human rights in all lands in which those rights are not secure." Moreover, it would stir accusations of dual loyalty at the very moment that Jews had proven themselves to be patriots in the Great War. Palestine's territorial boundaries were fuzzy. A Jewish state in Palestine would harm the rights of the existing population and undermine democracy, which is "an avowed purpose of the World's Peace Conference." Zionism, in short, was antidemocratic in practice. If the local population could not determine the future of Palestine, then Palestine should be internationalized, but there were no grounds to sanction an exclusive Jewish homeland.[43] Although slightly more measured, Morris Rafael Cohen, a legendary professor of philosophy at City College, made similar points in a widely circulated article he published at the time of the Versailles conference titled "Zionism: Tribalism or Liberalism?"[44]

The various divisions on how to solve the Jewish Problem were evident both across and within the Jewish delegations in Paris, making it difficult to forge the unity they required to advance the cause of Jewish security, welfare, and rights.[45] Enduring long days of sometimes bitter and highly personalized exchanges, they converged on two broad positions: Zionism and minority rights. And this was the conclusion of the peace negotiations. Incorporating the Balfour Declaration, the idea of a Jewish national home now became a fixture of international politics. In retrospect it is easy to minimize the significance of the event; however, only a few years earlier, Zionism had seemed to be a hopeless cause supported by a minority of a minority. Now that they had an international commitment, Zionists had to turn to the difficult task of turning principles into reality.

The other solution was minority rights. This fascinating chapter in the history of international human rights has been told in considerable detail, and rather than retracing the months of intricate and delicate negotiations, I want to draw attention to six critical features.[46] First, Jews were frightened by the prospect of self-determination for these new states. Life had been hard enough when they were one minority in a large empire, but the idea of being a highly visible and disliked minority in a small state worried them. Marshall and others emphasized that the need for minority rights was not an abstract or hypothetical right but rather critical for survival. Violence was an everyday occurrence, providing evidence and urgency. For instance, in a letter to President Wilson dated May 23, 1919, Louis Marshall recited only the most recent attacks on Jews in Eastern Europe and noted that millions of Jews were at risk if the Great Powers did not provide security guarantees and impose rights-based language into the constitutions of the new states.[47] And the numbers at risk were astounding. In Poland there were nearly three million Jews, comprising nearly 10 percent of the population; in Romania 750,000 equaling 4.2 percent; and in Hungary a half million, amounting to 5.1 percent.

Second, Jews were hardly alone in pressing for minority rights, but they had a prominent voice. One reason for their visibility was that many like-minded governments and peoples were not present to make their case because they had not been invited to the conference.[48] Indeed, in a bit of historical irony, the German government depended on the Jews to forward the cause of minority rights, an issue with which it was deeply concerned because of the prominence of the German minority in many of the new national states.[49]

Third, although the Jewish delegations were primarily interested in protecting Jewish minorities, they understood that for principled and strategic reasons it was best to bundle Jewish rights with the rights of all minorities. The Jews were fighting for an important principle, not asking for special treatment. Jewish lives were important, but no more important than the lives of other minority populations. In a 1921 letter reflecting on Paris, Marshall emphasized that "we were not asking for any rights for the Jews that we were not anxious to have accorded to other minorities. We were dealing with minorities, not with our people. The only reference to the Jews in the treaties was with regard to the subject of Sabbath observance, as to which limited rights were conferred and which are entirely free from reasonable objection."[50] Furthermore, the focus on rights necessitated more universalizing language.[51] Upon his return to the United States after the conference, Louis Marshall exclaimed that the American delegation was hoping that "justice might be attained not only for the Jews, but for all people who, like the Jews, are minority peoples. Whatever the American Jewish Congress has achieved, it has achieved not for Jews solely or chiefly, but for the sacred cause of justice and for the emancipation of men of every race and language and every faith who in the past have anywhere been denied equality of right."[52]

Fourth, the Jewish delegations were fiercely divided over whether Jewish minorities should be referred to as a nation or some other grouping. The question of minority rights, in other words, was entangled with the issue of "who" are the Jews? Eastern delegations routinely used the language of the nation. For them, the discourse of nation was empowering; Jews were just like all others, no longer a second-rate people. And given that the language of nationalism dominated the political scene in Eastern Europe, it was difficult to think in other terms. The eastern delegations, in short, imagined themselves fighting for the national rights of Jews and Jewish communities. Jewish delegations from the West preferred alternatives to the language of the nation because they feared that if the Jews were labeled a "nation" it would undermine their integration into their countries, suggest that they were permanent outsiders, and expose them to charges of dual loyalty.[53] In a letter to Louis Marshall, Cyrus Adler wrote: "We must see to it that nothing is done by us in America, even for the purpose of helping the Jews in Poland, which would injure the Jews in America."[54] Marshall was so fearful of fraternizing with the "nation" that he refused to meet the other Jewish delegations at the Zionist headquarters in Paris and asked for the more neutral setting of the Great Synagogue on the Rue de la Victoire.

If they weren't a nation, then what were the Jews? Identical to their presentation at home, Western Jews often referred to themselves as a religious community or as a generic minority group. Some even thought in terms of individual rights, foreshadowing the future discourse of human rights; Jews should petition for their rights not as Jews but rather as human beings. Regardless of whether they were a religious community, a minority, or humans, the underlying premise was that Jews did not deserve special treatment because of their identity. And then there were Jewish delegates (from both the West and the East) who believed that the language of minority and national rights was the mistake of the bourgeoisie, and that Jews should see themselves in class terms and fight for socialism. Workers, not Jews, of the world unite.

The Western delegations had a powerful ally in President Woodrow Wilson, who also opposed labeling the Jews as a nation. President Wilson had a steadfast commitment to the principle of self-determination and presumed that "self" equaled "nation," and that individual nationalities deserved their own nation-state. One problem was that different nationalities were often mixed in the same neighborhood, city, and territory. The search for exclusive national states, consequently, could mean that one nation's self-determination might lead to conflict between competing nations. The challenge in Paris, then, was to address the fact that many candidates for national independence and statehood had significant minority populations in their midst. Some nationalist groups were happy to solve this problem by creating ethnically homogenous states, through violence if needed. Drawing from a charitable reading of their history, the Great Powers recommended liberalism and the rule of law to handle the challenge of diversity.

Fifth, in order to secure Jewish lives, they had to think in terms of short-term protection and long-term prevention. Immediate protection would require the willingness of major powers, working alongside the League of Nations and its enforcement mechanisms, to intervene on behalf of Jews under threat. Because the major powers could not be counted on to act of their own accord, the Jewish delegations expected that they would have to make noise and publicize what was occurring at the highest diplomatic levels, hoping that international awareness would reduce the persecution. These were stopgap solutions until anti-semitism could be doused by the rule of law, a culture of tolerance, and the injection of liberal principles into constitutions and laws. They fully understood this was a long-term project.

Sixth, discussions in Paris became a struggle between untrammeled sovereignty and a sovereignty dependent on how states treated their national populations—and the right of the international community to have a say. The Jewish delegations were hardly naive about the utility of rhetorical pledges of support and paper declarations of the rights of the Jews. They knew that these treaties were only as credible as the states that backed them up. They also understood that states had never shown much interest in sacrificing their interests for Jews. Consequently, they initially proposed that the League of Nations have the authority to take independent action and punish those states that violated their treaty obligations. However, they refrained from aggressively advocating this position for three reasons: If they presented their position as all or nothing, they might go home empty-handed. If these protections were too intrusive they might cause a backlash; there was possibly no better way to play into the idea that Jews were an alien nation than to suggest that minorities deserved special rights and protections. And they also could not imagine that the Great Powers, regardless of their sympathy for the plight of Jews and other minorities, would establish the principle and precedent that international institutions have the authority to intervene directly in the affairs of sovereign states.

After months of debate, the Great Powers and the new national states reached a compromise formula, which included some protections for linguistic, racial, and religious minorities. The minorities treaties were a first in the history of international human rights. How governments treated their minority populations was now subject to oversight and comment by an international institution, giving legitimacy to the idea of human rights and encouraging other organizations, individuals, and groups to mobilize around the cause. On June 28, 1919, Poland became the first state to formally accept minority provisions, followed by other Eastern European states.

Paris delivered not one but two milestones—Palestine and minority rights—and, at least on paper, the international community had established unprecedented measures for addressing the Jewish Problem. But it did not require a student of Jewish history or an astute analyst of international affairs to react cynically to these breakthroughs. After all, the defining subtext of their discussions was the simple recognition that states had a hard time treating Jews as equals and probably would not do so in the future. Also, they departed Paris only committed to principles, deferring the details to be worked out at some unspecified meeting in the future, and failed to give the international community significant powers to help them do so or fulfill their oaths. As Horace Kallen bitterly concluded a few years later, "The outcome of the Paris Peace Conference was a vindication that the West still was not sure how to handle the Jewish Question: On the one hand, it insisted on principles of minority rights and religious liberty in all the new countries, suggesting that the Jews should not have to go anywhere. On the other hand, it also backed the idea of a Jewish national aspiration, which was a recognition that the world could not back up its promises to the Jews."[55] Ultimately, Jews were still dependent on the international community aligning its collective interests with Jewish interests.

The minorities treaties, like many international treaties and statements that are long on universalizing principles but disconnected from the interests of states, failed when they were most needed. At the next postwar conference in a few decades, the world would once again address the Jewish Problem, but this time without the European Jewish delegations because European Jewry would no longer exist.

RING OF FIRE

Europe descended into dark times and became gripped by a feverish anti-Semitism scarcely imaginable. The Jews of Europe were, quite literally, trapped. There were no easily identifiable solutions. Germany and much of Eastern Europe decided that they would deal with the Jewish Problem once and for all, and the League of Nations did not utter a peep. The League of Nations had few if any options to punish bad behavior, and if it was not going to punish the Germans for breaking various pledges that threatened states' immediate security, there was no reason to expect that it would draw the line at the Jews. For all the good they did, the international minorities treaties that American Jews had fought so hard to create might never have existed. They had no teeth and, it turns out, the Jewish minorities were reluctant to ask for international assistance for fear of being accused of treachery by their governments. Moreover, because the United States had refused to join the League of Nations, American Jews had almost zero influence there.

Although the League of Nations had formally approved the idea of Palestine as a national home for the Jews, Jews were not much more welcome there than they were elsewhere. Pointing to its responsibilities to protect the interests of the local inhabitants and wanting to avoid at all costs a civil war in Palestine for fear of jeopardizing its strategic and wartime goals, the British essentially decided that while Palestine was a home for the Jews, it was not a home at this time for these Jews. Few countries of any importance objected to Britain's handling of its mandatory responsibilities.

Nor were Jews able to flee for safety. After World War I the international community began to stitch together a regime to protect refugees, but the Evian Conference of July 1938 and its failure to address Jewish flight provided further evidence that Jews were on their own. These protections for refugees were meaningless if states refused to open their doors. But almost all remained shut, including their preferred destination, the United States.

Because of fears that these immigrants were bringing radical communism to American shores, growing nativism, and hard economic times, the United States started erecting walls around its borders. In 1917 Congress overrode President Wilson's veto and imposed a literacy test for all immigrants. Then in 1921 Congress approved a temporary quota system that discriminated against eastern and southern Europeans, which then became anchored in 1924 with the Johnson Act, affecting Jews and Catholics more than any other religious minority. In fact, during this period more Jews were entitled to visas than were granted them by the US administration.[56] Speaking on this issue on July 21, 1922, Louis Marshall warned that Congress was increasingly convinced that "America is being made the dumping ground for European refugees," and was beginning to blame European Jewish organizations for "passing the buck" to the United States and "burdening the labor market here with dangerous competitors in spite of a serious condition of non-employment under which American labor is struggling."[57] It was fanciful if not ludicrous to imagine that Congress would suddenly welcome hundreds of thousands of impoverished Jews during a depression. Perhaps in the period immediately prior to the war and during the war years American Jews might have been able to convince Congress to save more Jews, but I will leave that debate to historians.[58]

Additionally, American Jews were worried about their own security and feared that if they made too much noise they might draw unwanted attention to themselves. After decades of steady acceptance, World War I reversed this trend as anti-Semitism resurfaced.[59] The Russian Revolution and the communist threat led to fears of "Judeo-bolshevism" and accusations that Jews were radical troublemakers wherever they went. Anti-Semitic rhetoric became increasingly common in public debate and congressional politics. Partly in response to the growing acceptance of Zionism among American Jews, it was not unusual to hear well-respected figures question openly the loyalties of American Jews. At the American Society of International Law, Philip Marshall Brown, an American diplomat and law professor at Princeton University, warned that Jews would never be able to pledge allegiance to any land.[60] Harvard and other educational institutions began imposing quotas on Jews, which Jews saw as a dire threat because of their belief that education was the path to respectability and acceptance.

Matters worsened with the Great Crash of 1929 and the Great Depression of the 1930s, as Jews became singled out as a principal cause and beneficiary of the hard economic times. Jews voted heavily in favor of Franklin Roosevelt for president, and his policies and record-breaking appointment of Jewish advisers led critics of the New Deal to call it the "Jew Deal." The auto magnate Henry Ford exercised his power and wealth to whip up anti-Semitism, using the *Dearborn Independent* as his personal mouthpiece and helping to underwrite the publication and distribution of the slanderous *Protocols of the Elders of Zion*. Using *Protocols* as a source, in late May 1933 Pennsylvania congressman L. T. McFadden took to the House floor to expose the Jewish plot to bring down America. In the 1930s Father Coughlin's populist nativism railed against Jews, Catholics, and other minorities. Although these anti-Semitic stirrings were hardly a shock—after all, America still harbored its fair share of hatred, and most of the immigrants had arrived from places where restrictions on, and violence against, Jews were familiar—they were particularly jarring given America's reputation for being more welcoming than any other land. Moreover, Jews had tried to make themselves presentable, watering down their Judaism to the point that it was nearly indistinguishable from Unitarianism and scrubbing away all remnants of the shtetl so that they looked, acted, and dressed like Americans. Yet it still was not enough.

For American Jews worried about how to save their friends and family, Zionism became the default option, the choice of the desperate. After decades of opposition, silence, and backhanded acceptance, Zionism had a celebratory moment on May 25, 1920, when the Jewish community held a parade down Fifth Avenue in New York to fete the idea of Palestine.[61] Yet this enthusiasm did not last very long. Membership in Zionist organizations peaked at 200,000 in mid-1919, and while there is no agreement on the exact number, membership dropped to less than 65,000 by the end of the 1920s. Moreover, 45,000 were only members of the all-women's organization Hadassah, which did not help American Zionism because men who discounted the opinions of women ran the major Jewish organizations.[62]

The rise of anti-Semitism in Europe predictably made the Zionist option more attractive to American Jews, but arguably not with nearly the kind of fervor that might be expected given the circumstances.[63] Reform Jewry split between an ascendant accommodationist and an increasingly ostracized anti-Zionist camp. Those who were prepared to make their peace with Zionism also remained highly sensitive that it might overstep its boundaries. Some continued to insist that the Jews needed a homeland, not a state of their own. When the World Zionist Organization proposed to work with local Jewish agencies to help develop Jewish and Hebrew culture, reform leaders rose in opposition on the grounds that it encouraged "diaspora nationalism" and insinuated that American Jews had a loyalty to the Jewish nation above and beyond the American nation.[64] The cosmopolitan sensibilities of American Jews colored their Zionism, giving it a much softer pigment than the Zionism coming from Eastern Europe.

It took a Holocaust to get American Jews to embrace not just Zionism but the necessity of a territorial state. Their steady and cautious embrace of Zionism during these years is charted by three major events in the history of American Zionism: the 1922 congressional hearings into the idea of a Jewish homeland; the 1935 Pittsburgh Declaration by Reform Jewry; and the 1942 Biltmore Declaration.

While the US delegation to Paris had supported the cause of Zionism, the US government had yet to adopt any sort of formal statement or resolution in its favor. Part of the reason for the hesitation was because many prominent Jews still opposed Zionism in the most strident terms. Although somewhat extreme in his views, Henry Morgenthau became a most outspoken opponent. The former American ambassador to Turkey, who had distinguished himself as one of the few who called attention to the Armenian genocide and had helped channel relief to the Jews in Palestine during World War I, was a bitter foe of Zionism. He, along with hundreds of other Jews, had signed the petition circulated by Representative Julius Kahn imploring President Wilson to oppose Zionism. Despite Zionism's growing acceptance at home, Morgenthau lost none of his conviction regarding its errors.

His animosity boiled over on the occasion of the 1920 American Zionist conference in Cleveland, which split between the Brandeis camp, which saw Zionism as a spiritual project and homeland for the Jews, and Chaim Weizmann, the world-famous chemist who had become the leader of the world Zionist movement and supporter of a state for the Jews. This divisive meeting led to the ouster of many of the most esteemed and patrician members of the American Jewish community and more moderate understandings of Zionism.[65] Writing with disgust in a Jewish weekly, Morgenthau's diatribe was prominently covered by the anti-Zionist *New York Times*. He had lots of choice words for Zionism. It was the "most stupendous fallacy in Jewish history. . . . Zionism is a surrender, not a solution. It is a retrogression into the blackest error, and not progress toward the light." He accused Zionism of being an "East European proposal" that could potentially jeopardize the safety of American Jews. It was utopian and naive. Palestine would never be economically viable. The British, who controlled the mandate, would never allow the Jews to have real independence; British imperialism would see to it that the Jews were subordinate to their empire. Zionism was not all bad,

Morgenthau added, but only if Zionism is detached from any sort of territorial project and limited to food for the Jewish "soul." His parting words, though, were perhaps the most spirited and confrontational: "The Jews of France have found France to be their Zion. The Jews of Britain have found Britain to be their Zion. The Jews of America have found America to be their Zion. I am not a Zionist. I am an American."[66]

At the request of several Jewish leaders, in spring 1922 both houses of Congress held hearings, led by Senator Henry Cabot Lodge and Representative Hamilton Fish, on the idea of a Jewish homeland.[67] Because of a split between the anti-Zionist State Department and the White House, the US government had never publicly endorsed the Balfour Declaration. The hearings were intended to rectify that omission. But rather than being an occasion for American Jewry to speak with a single voice in favor of a Jewish state in Palestine, the hearings showcased the continuing divisions in the American Jewish leadership and even the retrospective cautiousness of many of Zionism's biggest advocates. The split among American Jews was now showcased on Capitol Hill. Although Fish hoped to have only witnesses in favor of the Balfour Declaration testify, all manner of opinions were aired. Anti-Zionist Jews recited the standard arguments against Zionism, from concern for the native inhabitants to the indignation that Jews were being considered a nation. When Congress endorsed the Balfour Declaration, the *New York Times* accused the resolution's congressional supporters of caring more about their reelection than their principles.[68]

The second scene is the gathering of reform Jewish leaders in Columbus in 1937. When the reform leaders met in Pittsburgh in 1885 to discuss and draft their principles of commitment and action, they did not mince words regarding their strong antipathy toward Zionism. A lot had happened in the ensuing fifty years, in the world and at home, and the reform movement's statement on Zionism looked hopelessly out of date. Personifying this about-face was Rabbi Abba Hillel Silver, once a stalwart opponent of Zionism but now a cautious advocate. At the turn of the century it was understandable to have a hope that things were getting better for the Jews and to cast aside the particularistic elements of Judaism in favor of a more universalizing ethic of prophetic ideals and social justice; but that was then, this was now.[69] Rescinding the 1885 platform's belittling dismissal of the idea of a Jewish return to Palestine, the Columbus platform made its peace: "We affirm the obligation of all Jewry to aid in its upbuilding as a Jewish homeland by endeavoring to make it not only a haven of refuge for the oppressed but also a center of Jewish culture and spiritual life." Not that different from the sentiments of the Balfour Declaration. While the Pittsburgh platform insisted that exile had a positive meaning, the Columbus platform now referred to Judaism as the soul and Israel as the body. Israel would not only be a place where abandoned Jews could go, but it would also be the site of a cultural renewal.

Another wing, though, continued to rail against Zionism. And while this wing shrunk in size as the 1930s wore on, it was remarkably difficult for some leaders of the reform movement to let go of their hostility toward Zionism. For instance, in October 1934 Julian Morgenstern, a former head of the Hebrew Union College, a well-respected authority in biblical studies, and a staunch opponent of Zionism, delivered the annual lecture to inaugurate the academic year. Hitler had come to power in March 1933 and over the subsequent eighteen months had advertised his hatred of the Jews, which increased Zionism's popularity among the Jews. Given these developments, Morgenstern might have toned down his anti-Zionist position. But he did not. Instead, he asserted that Zionism equaled Nazism in terms of its threat to Jewish survival. Just like Hitler, Zionists were emphasizing that the Jews were a separate nation and advocating their exclusion from society. By one account, his audience was sympathetic to his position on Zionism, unsettled by his caustic comparison of Zionism to Nazism, and in general agreement with his commitment to universalism, belief that Jews had a contribution to make to world civilization, and antagonism to anything that smacked of particularism.[70]

At the upscale Biltmore Hotel in New York City in May 1942, leading Zionists of the world gathered in favor of a transformation of Palestine into a "Jewish commonwealth."[71] In hindsight this looks like something between a natural progression in the Zionist position and a "what took so long?" moment. Until that point the general Zionist position was to put aside any question regarding the final status of Palestine in favor of the more practical issue of gathering Jewish refugees, settling the land, creating an economy, and building institutions. This position was something of a compromise between the American Zionists and world Zionist leaders; while the latter kept stressing statehood, the former had their doubts regarding its necessity and practicality, and, thus, in the interest of keeping the peace, the umbrella movement adopted a more practical rather than political and legal agenda.

Although the Zionists were able to compromise among themselves, in many respects what mattered was not what the Zionists wanted but rather what the British mandatory authorities would permit. And what the Zionists saw as practical the British saw as likely to create greater conflict between the Palestinians and the Jews. Accordingly, the British often opposed many of the Zionist demands, including the one that was becoming increasingly urgent—Jewish immigration. In 1939 the British issued a White Paper that nearly ended Jewish immigration. Now that the most urgent demand was deemed to be the least "practical" by the British, there was a growing insistence among the Zionists for a state of their own whose borders they could control. The growing demand for a Jewish State also undercut support (largely among American Zionists) for a binational state, whose more famous advocates included Judas Magnes, the president of Hebrew University of Jerusalem, and Henrietta Szold, the founder of Hadassah. American Jews did not quite resemble Irving Kristol's famous definition of a neoconservative—a liberal who is mugged by a reality—but the fight for survival had a sobering effect on these prophets.

CHAPTER FOUR

THE COSMOPOLITAN
AND THE NATIONAL

From the standpoint of how the world dealt with the Jewish Problem, World War II changed everything and nothing. The world had fiddled while European Jewry was destroyed. Six million Jews murdered, nearly one-third of the world's Jewish population. Centuries of Jewish life reduced to ashes. *Shtetlach*, settlements, and quarters emptied of Jews, and in many cases the buildings either torched or wiped clean of any signs of their previous residents. Once vibrant town squares and schoolyards filled with children's voices became transit centers for death camps. Religious artifacts carted away by the Nazis to display in a future museum for the remains of an extinct people. When Allied forces liberated the labor, concentration, and death camps, there were millions fewer among the living.

Yet the world was still at a loss regarding what to do with the Jews. In many cases the survivors had traded one camp for another; whereas before they were in concentration camps knowing that there was little hope of escape, now they were in displaced-persons camps waiting to leave once the authorities decided when and where they would go. Understandably, the survivors did not want to return to their countries of origin, and the allies were reluctant to force them, especially where their countries were now part of the Soviet bloc. Many wanted to be united with their families in the United States and other Western countries, but these governments refused them entry.

Figure 4.1. Jews at a Displaced Persons Camp. Photo by Chris Butler. Reprinted courtesy of *Stars and Stripes* © 1947.

Palestine remained a designated homeland for the Jews, but for all practical purposes it remained a distant country, as Britain continued to restrict Jewish immigration. Six million dead Jews later, the international community was having the same debate about the Jewish Problem.

There was, however, a noticeable change in the debate in the international community about the postwar arrangements and the balance between internationalism and nationalism. The previous thirty years had delivered soul-crushing reminders of the destructive power of nationalism. For civilization and humanity to have a fighting chance, nationalism had to be tamed. Such sentiments did not mean that states were ready to surrender their sovereignty. Western states had not become idealists. The global South was in the throes of decolonization, and nearly all the states that had been fighting for independence could not imagine surrendering their hard-won sovereignty to a higher power. But just because states were not going to sponsor their own demise did not mean they were averse to the idea of accepting some restraints on their actions in order to further their long-term interests. States created a United Nations Charter that retained their exclusive prerogative yet also acknowledged that genuine security is premised on mutual security, enlightened self-interest, and limits on the use of force. With two world wars as a reminder, the European states would soon begin an experiment in international cooperation that was intended to move Europe from old-style nationalism to new-style internationalism.

In addition to an internationalism intended to protect the mutual survival of states, the United Nations also recognized that it was responsible for the survival of another constituency: people. Sovereignty needed to share space with humanity. In response to a decade in which tens of millions of innocents around the world had been murdered, herded, stripped of their makeshift rights by their governments, and treated like human waste, all because they were seen as other than human, a coalition of states, pushed by nongovernmental organizations, fought to create international mechanisms to safeguard the basic rights of all people. The desolation caused by World War II became the foundation for a new humanity. The UN Charter poured the foundation for international human rights and then states built the scaffolding with the creation of the Genocide Convention, the United Nations Declaration of Human Rights, and the International Refugee Convention. Outside the United Nations system, but a piece of this movement, states also extended the Geneva Conventions to give more protection to civilians. And at Nuremberg and Tokyo the victors initiated an experiment in international criminal justice, putting the killers on trial.

Jews played a prominent role in these postwar discussions and the development of various human rights mechanisms. Often of European descent and motivated not just by the Holocaust but also by their long-standing commitment to liberalism, Jews made seminal contributions to the emerging vision of a cosmopolitan order. René Cassin, a French Jew with a distinguished background in law who would subsequently become president of the AIU, worked alongside Eleanor Roosevelt and the Lebanese Charles Malik to draft the Universal Declaration of Human Rights.[1] Hersch Lauterpacht, a German Jewish refugee who taught international law at Columbia University, wrote *An International Bill of the Rights of Man*, which became a central text in the debate.[2] Ralph Lemkin, the Polish Jewish refugee, was the force behind the Genocide Convention.[3] Hannah Arendt, another German Jewish refugee, delivered a series of searing observations regarding the question of postwar justice, the need for noncitizens such as refugees to obtain rights, and the equivocal victory that comes from having the right to have rights.[4] In many respects, Jewish intellectuals were acting like their nineteenth-century counterparts—using the Jewish experience to point to the failure of a world of nation-states to protect minorities, aliens, and the unwashed. Jewish voices were influencing how the world thought and talked about its future.

The Jewish experience also hovered over the debate on the postwar order. A word of caution, though: The Holocaust left its mark, but it was not nearly as consequential as some would like to remember; more often than not, the Jewish experience became another example of the barbarism and inhumanity even the most "civilized" groups were capable of.[5] Arguably, the Holocaust's greatest impact was on the beginnings of international criminal justice at Nuremberg. The inability of the Jews to escape Nazi Germany, and their current holding pattern in displaced-persons camps, also influenced discussions on the rights of refugees. But the destruction of the Jews was among the many atrocities routinely cited to justify the need for a new system of human rights, and the burst of humanitarianism and desire to relieve the suffering of distant strangers pointed to the Jews and millions of others.

Throughout this period the international community used the discourse of humanity and referred to cosmopolitanism as a great leveler of power and protector of the vulnerable, yet this was a cosmopolitanism that retained strong elements of inequality. This common humanity had been forged by inhumanity. World Wars I and II had collectively challenged the West's civilized self-image. How could the West rescue the myth of its superiority and its civilization? It had to renounce the narcissism of nationalism and embrace the expanded duties of humanity. Those in the West would continue to care about their own, but also others, and especially those harmed by conflict and circumstances not of their making.

This humanitarian relationship, though, was built on a clear asymmetry of power, identity, and suffering: The world was now divided between victims and their rescuers. The victims, being victims, were powerless, vulnerable, and incapable of helping themselves because they had neither the resources nor the aptitude. The rescuers, being rescuers, often saw themselves and their acts of compassion as signs of their own goodness and moral authority. This was a cosmopolitanism of suffering, not solidarity. The rescuers acted, and rarely if ever asked questions. The victims were expected to be grateful recipients. Those with and without means did not sit down in a condition of mutual respect to explore their dreams and determine how they might have shared identities, interests, and fates. A cosmopolitanism made by suffering had produced a politics of pity.

After World War II the Jews became a beneficiary of this cosmopolitanism of suffering.[6] Prior to World War II the Jewish association with cosmopolitanism was a source of suspicion and after World War II and in places like the Soviet Union, Jews were reminded that cosmopolitanism could be a crime and a code word for Jews. Yet overall, Jews largely benefited from this postwar fit of cosmopolitanism. Why? Cosmopolitanism was increasingly seen as an antidote to nationalism. Jews had certainly suffered as much as any people from nationalism's chauvinism and xenophobia. However, Jews did not become the beneficiary of this cosmopolitanism of suffering because they had suffered more than other peoples over the centuries and in the recent past. The Jews, reduced to a miserable skeletal existence by the Germans, were not any more lovable now than before. Their elevated status owed instead to the fact that the world had just waged a war against the Nazis, and the Nazis had waged a war against the Jews. Simply put, because the Nazis, the personification of radical evil, had made the Jews their enemy, any society that claimed to be civilized had to care for the Jews.[7]

The Jews became a test of the humanity of the West. If the West did not treat the Jews any better than had the Germans, then how could the West claim to be morally superior? Writing in *The Nation*, the American theologian Reinhold Niebuhr, one of the twentieth century's most influential religious figures, observed: "The problem of what is to become of the Jews in the post-war world ought to engage all of us, not only because a suffering people has a claim upon our compassion, but because the very quality of our civilization is involved in the solution."[8] Writing in the *Manchester Guardian* in 1944, Lord Davies reflected:

> In this tragic conflict we must be for or against the Jews: there can be no neutrality. Our attitude towards them becomes the test of our professions and the sincerity of our war aims. It strikes at

the root of our morale, and if we abandon the Jews we abandon everything, because Hitler has chosen to make them his special target. Whether we like it or not, and however inconvenient it may be, the Jewish people have become the personification of the issues involved in the world struggle between right and wrong, between good and evil. If we desert the Jews it may result in our losing the war, because it is a betrayal of our avowed war aims. Surely it is the height of folly to repudiate our principles and to cold-shoulder our friends in order to curry favor with neutrals or potential enemies.[9]

Horace Kallen similarly observed that the Jews had become "the symbol of this faith's victories in the Christian world." According to Victor Klemperer, a survivor and memoirist of the Holocaust, "A critical register of the general health of civilization is the status of 'the Jewish Question.'"[10] Whereas once the association with cosmopolitanism had been a curse, now Jews became the world's light meter—signaling whether it was trending toward dawn or night.[11]

The West was now associating the Jews with cosmopolitanism and the fate of humanity at a time that the Jews had decided that they were a nation that needed a state of its own. The lesson of World War II drawn by the West was that the world needed a little more cosmopolitanism and a lot less nationalism, but the Jews drew the opposite lesson that nationalism and not cosmopolitanism was their best bet for protection and security. After centuries of anti-Semitism and inability to solve the Jewish Problem, the West was hardly in a position to deny the Jews the opportunity to try their luck at a project that they found laced with the potential for self-destruction. Along these lines, Isaac Deutscher wrote:

> The decay of bourgeois Europe has compelled the Jew to embrace the nation-state. This is the paradoxical consummation of the Jewish tragedy. It is paradoxical, because we live in an age when the nation-state is fast becoming an anachronism. . . . The world has compelled the Jew to embrace the nation-state and to make of it his pride and hope when there is little or no hope left in

it. You cannot blame the Jew for this; you must blame the world. But Jews should at least be aware of the paradox and realize that the intense enthusiasm for 'national sovereignty' is historically belated.[12]

The Jews seemed to be the last people closely identified with the "West" who believed that nationalism could be their savior. Yet perhaps this ancient people might accomplish what had eluded other nations. While postwar Europe and North America were still reeling from a modernity that turned upon itself, in the years immediately following its creation, Israel became "everyone's fantasy of youthful vigor, joyful labor, human authenticity, and just retribution. It was the only place where European Civilization seemed to possess a moral certainty, the only place where violence was virtuous."[13] Just as the prophets hoped, Israel was taking its place as a light unto nations.

Mirroring the times, American Jews also attempted to rebalance the national and the cosmopolitan as they reflected on the Jewish Problem and the Jewish Question. Their opinions mattered now like never before, because they had become the single largest Jewish community in the world and bore the burden of leading the response to the Jewish Problem in a world that had plenty of problems.[14] Devastated by and guilt-ridden over the destruction of the European Jews, they threw their energies behind the creation of a Jewish state. But the American Jewish leadership had not completely forsaken the prophetic tradition. In addition to hoping that Israel would be more than just another "normal" state, it also renewed its plea for international institutions, law, and human rights. American Jews, in short, had struck upon a new balance between the national and the cosmopolitan. In many respects, this convergence was not only intellectual but also temporal. The year 1948 proved to be monumental for the national and the cosmopolitan. The Jewish national quest found its victory in the establishment of the State of Israel. This also was the year, though, that saw the creation of the Universal Declaration of Human Rights. In both cases, American Jews played a part.

THE GOLDEN AGE IN AMERICA

If American Jews had responded to the Holocaust by turning inward, it would have been understandable.[15] But they did not, and one reason was because America became more accepting of its Jews, making them feel more at home and a valued member of the American family. For this reason, this early postwar period is often referred to as the "golden era"—Jews were invited to be both Jewish and American.[16] Perhaps the gateway to this golden era occurred on September 8, 1945, when Bess Myerson was crowned Miss America, the first Jew ever to hold the title. And she was not an example of a fully assimilated Jew, for her parents were part of the New York Jewish immigrant working class, spoke Yiddish in the home, and briefly sent her to a socialist Yiddish school.[17] Her coronation was hardly uncontroversial. During the competition she was advised to change her name to something less Jewish. The judges received threatening calls, warning them to not vote for a Jew. She did not receive any of the same commercial attention as previous winners. But a Jewish woman had won (the first and only time), America had survived, and the sense among American Jews was that her victory was their victory.

Doors everywhere began to open to Jews. Barriers to Jews in housing, private clubs, schools, and private associations began eroding. Universities began removing their quotas. The movies, stage, and literary crowd began turning to Jews for inspiration. Jewish authors dominated the literary scene, among them J. D. Salinger, Norman Mailer, Arthur Miller, and Allen Ginsberg. Phillip Roth and Saul Bellow, who explicitly drew on Jewish themes to comment on American life, were finding sizable audiences and critical attention. Jews began running for public office in greater numbers, and not only from districts that were heavily Jewish. And perhaps most remarkably, only a few years after the US Supreme Court in 1931 had declared the United States a "Christian nation," Americans began referring to the United States as a "Judeo-Christian" civilization. Jews became elevated to the status of a defining people, becoming closely identified with the promise of America and the vibrancy of its democracy.[18]

American Jews owed their newfound acceptance to many immediate and longer-term developments. The immediate was the Holocaust. It was no longer as acceptable to be anti-Semitic, not after the United States had fought a war against the Nazis in the name of civilization, and the Nazis had targeted the Jews for special hatred. A deeper reason is because America had developed a more inclusive political culture, which owed partly to the effort by American elites to respond to their interwar and wartime fear of a fragmenting American society by creating a more pluralistic and tolerant "vision" of America.[19] Jews were one of many cosponsors.

The Depression at home and the rise of fascism and communism abroad led to a growing fear that American society was becoming dangerously fractured. The Great Crash followed by the Great Depression challenged capitalism's cachet in American society and created the climate for President Roosevelt's New Deal and theme of economic security. In response to this assault on the sanctity of the private sector and the authority of the business community, the country's economic elites responded by substituting "private sector" with "free enterprise" and argued that it was a foundation of American society and central to civil and religious rights. If "free enterprise" went, they argued, so went American values and the American way of life.

The 1930s also showed signs of a growing kulturkampf. America's elites believed the American identity was as Protestant and white as they were. The previous decades, though, had produced two great migrations that upset their color scheme. Millions of immigrants came to the United States, but these were not Germans, English, or Swedes; instead they were Slavs, Poles, Jews, and Russians, populations that were neither white nor Protestant. After a generation of toiling in sweatshops and slaughterhouses and being treated like second-class citizens, they were clamoring for acceptance by the 1930s. They swarmed to Franklin Roosevelt, and Roosevelt returned the favor by appointing a record number of minorities to political office. The other migration was by black Americans from the south to the large urban centers in the north after World War I, which led to new demands for accommodation, equal treatment, and acceptance. This darkening of America's complexion led to the development of right-wing and reactionary movements that warned that (white) America was under attack.

The country seemed to be fraying, and in response America's cultural elite and opinion makers argued that enforced homogeneity is a sign of totalitarianism and that diversity is a defining feature of democracy.[20] The challenge, therefore, was to get Americans to accept that diversity was an essential part of the American experience and to discover common values that would create a climate of inclusion. One answer to the challenge was to emphasize interfaith unity and religious pluralism, which had the dual effect of deadening anti-Catholicism and anti-Semitism and locating shared values. The 1930s also heightened the fear of fascism and communism, and the American elite worried that these ideologies would unleash a "divide and conquer" strategy to weaken the United States from within and expose it to left-wing and right-wing ideologies. In short, the American elite responded to the grave ideological challenges of the 1930s by emphasizing the themes of equality and civility, and how pluralism and individual rights took precedence over economic concerns and class conflict.[21]

The threats anti-Semitism posed, alongside these new opportunities opened up by the search for cultural consensus, led American Jews to actively make their case, defend their rights, and craft a more inclusive narrative of American society. Various Jewish organizations, including the American Jewish Committee, strategized endlessly and labored tirelessly to confront anti-Semitism. Much as they had when they emphasized the importance of minority rights after World War I, Jewish organizations embedded their campaign against anti-Semitism within a broader movement to end all forms of prejudice and to portray prejudice as anti-American and sympathetic to Nazism. In 1943, for instance, the AJC's Public Relations Committee declared as its long-range goal: "To increase public appreciation for the fact that Americanism means diversity rather than goose-step uniformity—the idea that the very strength of America lies in the variety of its people, the richness of its heritage, rather than in any stereotyped homogeneity."[22] Jewish and Christian organizations joined forces to promote religious harmony, the most famous being the National Conference of Christian and Jews (NCCJ), which hammered on the theme that Protestants, Catholics, and Jews share the same God and believe in the one principle that underpins democracy—religious freedom.[23] Jewish values are American values, Jewish leaders asserted, and Jews are interpreters and custodians of American values.[24] In general, while the interwar years were a searing reminder that Jewish life was vulnerable and cheap, after World War II America's Jews encountered an unprecedented period of acceptance and prosperity.

Although the barriers were coming down, this golden age was not entirely carefree, and American Jews were occasionally reminded, or remembered, that progress could be erased with a careless misstep. One particular problem was the Jewish association with the radical left, which became a growing burden with the rise of the Cold War and new kinds of political conservatism.[25] The infamous case of Julius and Ethel Rosenberg put on trial not just two suspected spies but American Jewry's anxieties and dreams. The Rosenbergs were arrested on July 17, 1950, on charges of passing nuclear secrets to the Soviet Union; they were convicted and then executed on June 19, 1953. At the Rosenberg trial the defendants, lawyers, and judge were all Jews; it was not only the Cold War that was on display, or whether Jews could be trusted, but also the different visions American Jews had of themselves. The second generation's reigning ideology, prominent throughout the New Deal, was that Jewish and American ideals coincided and that "Jewishness meant pursuing the goals of left-wing liberalism."[26] Although Jews always had a fear of being accused of dual loyalty, here the concern was that their left-wing sympathies threatened to harm their beloved United States.[27] In response, many American Jewish organizations attempted to remove the hints of radicalism. Even the Rosenbergs' death, according to the historian Hasia Diner, "represented a symbolic atonement demanded to signify the loyalty of American Jews to the United States and its ideals."[28] In partial response to the trial, the growing linkage between the Soviet Union and Hitler's Germany through the language of totalitarianism, the Soviet Union's anti-Semitism as evidenced by the "Doctor's Plot," and desire to burnish their patriotism, American Jews, or at least their major organizations, became solidly anti-Soviet.[29]

Although the American Jewish community accepted the invitation to integrate into American society, it also was experiencing a period of renewal and revival.[30] American Jews were participating more fully in associational life, and they began building ever more synagogues, day and religious schools. Now that Americans were more accepting of Jews, Jews were less inhibited in their public display of Judaism. The Holocaust also meant that the world's largest surviving and active Jewish population felt a special responsibility to preserve the Jewish people. The creation of the State of Israel encouraged American Jews to take greater pride in their Judaism and to work with Israel to contribute to the revival of the Jewish community. As one leader put it, while Israel might help with a sense of renewal, American Jews could not be parasites but rather had to make their own way and develop their own internal strengths.[31] The eminent historian of the Jews, Salo Baron, wrote in the inaugural issue of *Commentary*: "American Jewry more and more must stand wholly on its feet."[32] For decades American Jewry could attend to its needs at home because of the existence of an older, more mature, and more established European Jewry. No longer.

Another reason for the revival was that the Jewish community was on the move like never before. Rather than being sheltered in shtetl-like enclaves in the city, Jews were migrating to the suburbs.[33] Accordingly, remaining Jewish became much more active and intentional. Jews needed to be reminded and taught why they were Jews and why they should remain Jews. Their assimilated parents, though, needed help answering the basic questions, so they began to outsource Jewish education to newly established Jewish institutions. In the suburbs they were intermingling with non-Jews in new ways, and such interactions often led to a greater need to retain their Jewish identity. Jews started building and attending synagogues in record numbers. Whether this burst of institution-building represented a new Potemkin village, a renewed Jewish ethnicity, or a new feeling of religiosity became a matter of debate.[34]

The Jews were acting just like other Americans, for a religious resurgence was sweeping all of America. During the Eisenhower years the US Congress added "under God" to the pledge of allegiance and made "In God We Trust" the motto of the United States. If Jews were going to synagogues, attending services, and sending their children to religious schools, they were not only acting just like their Christian neighbors but were also showing the outward signs of decency and respectability.[35] And by acting just like their Christian neighbors, they were contributing to the very idea of a Judeo-Christian culture.[36]

The Jewish renewal also included a newfound desire to reach out to non-Jews and to become concerned with social justice. American Jews had always been willing to demonstrate that they were responsible citizens who cared about all Americans, but this sort of voluntary service now became a more routinized and central feature of organized Jewish life.[37] In a survey in Chicago in the late 1950s, most Jews said that to be a good Jew was to support humanitarian causes and promote civil betterment and helping the needy.[38] The Union of American Hebrew Congregations published a manifesto for Jewish social action, explicitly tying the prophetic tradition to a range of issues, including fair housing, civil rights, immigration, and support for the United Nations.[39] Prophetic Judaism's landmark statement of the time is *Justice and Judaism*, which had various cosmopolitan-sounding pronouncements, such as the following: "A synagogue that isolates itself from the fundamental issues of social justice confronting the community and the nation is false to the deepest traditions and values of the Jewish heritage."[40]

Several factors explain this widening circle of compassion and obligation. Because Jews were more settled and affluent, they no longer had to focus exclusively on the needs of their own community. There also were more opportunities for Jews to work outside of their community. Barriers to Jewish participation were crumbling, which meant they could be on the Board of Trustees of the local art museum and patrons of the symphony. Some of this outreach occurred through interfaith programs, which many Jews particularly enjoyed because they savored this symbol of acceptance that only a few years before had been unavailable. Also, such work allowed Jews to show how their Judaism led them to be concerned with social justice for all, and not just social justice for the Jews. Social action through identifiably Jewish institutions, in other words, became another opportunity for Jews to show Christians that they were full and equal members of American society. Social justice and civil rights as the stuff of Judaism.[41]

Finally, in areas such as human and civil rights, expanding their concern from the rights of Jews to the rights of others was a natural and fitting extension of their political theology.[42] American Jewry's involvement in the civil rights movement is often, and justly, cited at such moments.[43] Jews were highly visible in the struggle, playing important leadership roles. When Louis Marshall was not busy defending Jews around the world, he was aiding the cause of civil rights. American Jews participated in the movement in numbers that exceeded their percentage of the population. Two of the three civil rights workers killed during the 1964 Freedom Summer were Jews, Michael Schwerner and Andrew Goodman, and their tragic deaths were a source of outrage and pride in the Jewish community. The beloved scholar of Prophetic Judaism Rabbi Abraham Joshua Heschel was a highly visible participant in the civil rights movement. During these years the *American Jewish Year Book* often gave more prominence to the civil rights movement than to Israel.[44]

American Jewry's involvement in human and civil rights owes to many factors. The decline in anti-Semitism at home meant that Jews, who felt more secure, could turn their attention to the struggle for the human rights of oppressed minorities elsewhere.[45] It was consistent with their view that their rights were intertwined with the rights of others. The American Jewish Committee, for instance, became a leading organization in the struggle for civil rights, and among the reasons for its involvement was the belief that Jews had a responsibility to others and that minority survival should be a concern of all minorities.[46] By joining the struggle of others, American Jews would help affirm the principle of equality that was instrumental for their survival. Jews felt a further connection to the civil rights struggle because the African American community looked to Jewish history as inspiration.[47] In one civil rights march, African Americans wore yarmulkes, which they called "freedom caps." Moved by the gesture, Jewish supporters shipped cases of yarmulkes to civil rights organizations.

Their decision to become so deeply identified with such a polarizing issue, though, was not without its risks. Jews were beginning to feel more accepted than ever, and to immediately turn their attention to the civil rights movement risked a backlash. And, from time to time it sparked one, especially because those who defended segregation also often had uncharitable feelings about Jews. But they accepted the gamble in many cases because they believed it was the right thing to do and, as an oppressed minority, they had special obligations to others who were fighting for freedom and equality.

THE COSMOPOLITAN

The prophetic tradition continued to resonate for American Jews, not just domestically but also internationally. World War II and the Holocaust could have knocked the stuffing out of prophetic Judaism, but it had not. And, American Jews remained as, if not more, thankful that they lived in America and enjoyed the protection afforded by its principles. Consequently, as they looked globally, they used their prophetic and liberal values to imagine the postwar arrangements. By attempting to create a more safe, sound, and secure postwar order built around these principles, American Jews believed that they had the opportunity to enhance their own reputation at home, extend American values around the world, and help lay the foundations for the protection of Jews and other vulnerable peoples.[48] There is no better illustration of these enduring elements of the foreign policies of American Jews than their discussions of the future role of international human rights.[49]

The combination of the demise of the international minorities treaties and the destruction of the European Jews might have caused American Jews to give up on human rights, but they didn't. "The Jewish experience demanded otherwise," reflected a long-serving member of the American Jewish and human rights communities. "After the Holocaust, Jews had to believe that the world could get better, and human rights provided that tangible and intangible salvation. Throughout we emphasized rights."[50] But the recent experiences proved that rights needed more than rhetoric; they also needed strong institutions.[51] And so the American Jewish community, led by the American Jewish Committee, became deeply involved in providing the intellectual material for thinking about the place of human rights in the postwar order. The AJC financed Hersch Lauterpacht's scholarship—which influenced how the United Nations and Eleanor Roosevelt conceptualized human rights—and the form and content of the Universal

Declaration of Human Rights. It assisted the immensely influential Commission to Study the Organization of Peace led by James Shotwell and the Carnegie Endowment for International Peace. And the AJC established its own research arm, the Research Institute on Peace and Postwar Problems. Involving some of America's most important intellectuals, legal minds, and scholars, the institute held a series of meetings and published a set of reports that crafted a coherent account of what had gone awry with the human rights mechanisms after World War I and proposed remedies to ensure that history did not repeat itself.[52]

The institute made several key observations as it built the case for a more robust human rights machinery to protect the lives of Jews and other vulnerable populations in the world. Post–World War II international peace depended on human rights.[53] Human rights were not a luxury; they were essential. If the world was going to enjoy a long peace, it had to begin by acknowledging the centrality of human rights, individual freedoms, and liberal values. The implication, therefore, was that the ultimate security and welfare of the Jews and other minorities depended not on external security guarantees but rather on a political culture of tolerance, rights, and respect. Real security was dependent on acceptance. The obvious problem, though, was that many societies were years, if not decades, away from a culture of tolerance. Until then, the international community would have to become actively involved.

What kind of role should the international community play? The history of the international minorities treaties was a good place to start to identify the possible and impossible. It had failed for predictable and unpredictable reasons. The treaties would only be as strong as the League of Nations, and it was a bust. Many of the reasons for its failure were no surprise—its advocates had had the same concerns at the time of its founding. They predicted that the League of Nations would have difficulty operating without the participation of the United States, the world's emerging Great Power. Yet even if the United States had joined, its ability to protect minorities at risk would have been limited because states placed severe restraints on the league's ability to investigate and punish violations. The proponents of the minorities treaties understood this at the time, which was why they pushed so hard to give the league independent monitoring and enforcement powers.

The treaties also produced some unintended consequences. The very idea of minority treaties was premised on the recognition that every country has its majority and its minorities. In effect, it resulted in governments and societies seeing their countries as divided into two groups: the majorities were true patriots, while minorities were malcontents and aliens. As the AJC's Morris Waldman wrote in the *New York Times*, "the well-intentioned doctrine of national self-determination did not break down tensions between racial and cultural groups but nurtured them."[54] It not only created two classes of groups within countries, it also created two classes of states in world affairs: states that could be trusted to protect their minorities and for whom no signature or pledge was required, and states that could not be trusted and that were expected to sign on the line and subject themselves to intrusive invasions. Governments forced to sign the minorities treaties did not appreciate being on a "watch list." Such experiences led Waldman to conclude that human rights, and not Jewish or minority rights, was in the best interests of the Jews.[55]

The very operation of the minorities treaties also inflamed existing mistrust and resentment. The League of Nations was not expected to actively identify cases of discrimination and persecution; instead, it would wait for minorities to come for help. What was the likely response by the league? The League of Nations, like all international organizations, was something of a coalition of cronies interested in protecting their privileges and avoiding situations that might cause them to sacrifice their interests on the altar of principles. The league, then, might investigate the claims, but it was highly unlikely to undertake costly action. The consequence was that the only thing a minority could expect from petitioning the league was more persecution and punishment from its government and neighbors. Given this predicted scenario, the best thing for the Jews and other minorities to do was to go along to get along.[56] And by and large, this is what they did. The fact that minorities were not availing themselves of the league's mechanisms was not an indication of their sense of security, but evidence instead that they had well-developed survival instincts.

The AJC's conclusion was that the international community needed to rid itself of the majority-minority lens and develop a real human rights machinery that would put sovereignty in its place. Toward that end, it imagined five innovations. First, states would recognize the importance of individual, as opposed to national and minority, rights. Individuals, not nations and groups, needed protection and should be the building blocks of the postwar order.[57] This did not mean that all American Jews or everyone in the AJC had completely abandoned the language of group rights; in fact, some die-hard nationalists recommended that the Jews should represent themselves at the new United Nations (this would be in addition to any seat for a future Jewish state). However, even those who had staked their reputations on minority rights concluded that they had bet wrong.[58]

Second, the language of rights became attached to the "human."[59] Such thoughts had been floating around the AJC (and elsewhere) for more than a decade. In 1932 the American Jewish Committee considered establishing a Committee for the Protection of Human Rights, which would be open to all liberal-minded human beings and would, it was hoped, include perhaps a majority of non-Jews.[60] In April 1944 the AJC's German Advisory Group rejected the language of "Jewish rights" because it would lead to "endless complications" and recommended shifting to a "new concept of international rights and of the position of the individual . . . which would embody the general protection of human rights."[61] "Ceasing to talk about minority rights or group rights, from now on the AJC would refer to human rights, individual rights, and freedoms."

American Jews were not alone in souring on the discourse of minority rights—nearly everyone had. One reason for its nearly universal decline was because the German government had appropriated the language of minority rights as one of its many excuses for war. Specifically, the Nazi government argued that it had a right to protect its German populations living abroad. Once the Nazi regime had appropriated the language of minority rights to justify its racist stance, the term *minority rights* was forever polluted. In part because of the stigma attached to the league and the language of minority rights, Roosevelt and Churchill deliberately chose *human*, as opposed to *minority*, rights when issuing the Atlantic Charter in 1941. And their own attraction to the language of human rights, as opposed to minority rights, owed to the fact that it worked effortlessly with liberal political thought and the war against totalitarianism. The Americans and the British also felt that human rights had the advantage over minority rights because it would do a better job of protecting them from critics: the United States had its own minority problem and the British had a colonial policy that did as well. And the governments of Eastern Europe also made clear that they had no interest in protecting minority rights, which they associated with their being branded inferior states after World War I.

Third, if Jews were truly interested in the human rights of all, and not just for Jews, then they had to dedicate themselves to the cause of everyone's human rights. Citing Hillel's injunction, "If I am not for myself, who will be? But if I am for myself alone, who am I? And if not now, when?" the first installment of the course on the study of Jewish postwar problems proclaimed that "as a duty both to ourselves and our fellow-men, and in the firm belief that nothing which collective Jewish thought and conscience would evolve, can be contrary to the ideals and interests of civilized mankind."[62] In an internal memorandum, the AJC urged, "as a matter of enlightened self-interest, to interest ourselves in situations involving other minorities, even though Jews are not primarily affected."[63]

Fourth, the AJC wanted an international document to codify individual rights, ideally something akin to an international bill of rights, and it devoted considerable energy to the cause. Modeled after the United States' Bill of Rights, the idea was to universalize and internationalize the various kinds of principles embodied in this revolutionary document. Columbia University's Hersch Lauterpacht drafted such a bill. As Waldman wrote, "The nations of the world must accept an international Bill of Rights as a substitute for minorities rights."[64] The AJC got 1,326 "distinguished Americans" from all faiths and walks of life to back a six-point international bill of rights in December 1944. Although the title never stuck, the idea did, and eventually influenced the American-accented Universal Declaration of Human Rights in 1948.

But as everyone knew and had learned the hard way after World War I, such declarations, covenants, and documents were meaningless if states could hide behind sovereignty.[65] Consequently, and this was the fifth innovation, the United Nations needed to build a human rights machinery that could intervene in the domestic affairs of states. How much of an overhaul was required?

One ambitious option suggested almost doing away with sovereignty in favor of global federalism. There are lots of different federal arrangements, but what they have in common is that political sovereignty is nested within a supranational authority such as the United Nations. There was much to recommend it. It would be consistent with the "prophetic ideal of world brotherhood, so deeply ingrained in Judaism."[66] Jews and other minorities have always fared better in larger political and economic units. Also the "problem of Jewish group rights would be essentially a cultural one," favoring cultural pluralism. And "Palestine could be more easily solved if it were a unit in a federation than if it were a sovereign state." In fact, the "question of political loyalty or the charge of 'dual allegiance,' sometimes raised against the Jews who advocate that Palestine be established as a sovereign Jewish state would disappear." The report might have had fantasies of world federalism, but its authors were grounded enough in reality to know that some private thoughts should be kept private.

A Bill of Rights enforced by a new international organization was much more imaginable. International organizations should have the power to unilaterally bring human rights violations to the attention of the world, to declare the existence of a "troubled zone," and even to be "empowered to enforce decisions, either through general sanctions by member-states against the culprit nation, or through some other simple, direct, and effective means."[67] The AJC could not be fairly accused of naïveté after World War I, nor could it now.[68] It mourned the absence of enforcement mechanisms but hoped that any movement might establish an important precedent that could take on a life of its own. It wrote:

> Even if an international bill of human rights is at first a little more than a pious expression of noble sentiments, something will be gained by putting the nations solemnly on record. In the short run it may lead to the observance of a less ambitious but more concrete informal minimal standard of human rights, since states

would tend to avoid any gross violation of the formal bill of rights. This would be a practical gain. . . . In the long-run the degree of its observance may increase with the time until the document is very widely held in respect and there is close obedience to its provisions.[69]

The AJC campaigned for human rights at various gatherings that were intended to build the future international arrangements. In March 1944, just before his death, President Roosevelt met with the AJC at Dumbarton Oaks, where the first concrete discussions regarding the postwar order took place, and the Soviet Union, Britain, and the United States agreed that human rights would become part of the future United Nations. However, by the time they reached San Francisco, Britain and the Soviet Union had rights remorse, and the issue of human rights was low on the United States' list of priorities. Learning that the Allies were backtracking on human rights, the NGOs rose in vocal opposition.[70] Working closely with other American NGOs, the AJC circulated a petition urging the United States to show some backbone.[71] In a hurriedly arranged midnight meeting, the AJC and a small number of consultants appealed to Secretary of State Edward Stettinius to reconsider and even pushed him to add human rights as a "purpose of the world organization; to demand that all member states oblige themselves to guarantee specific human rights; and to ensure that a 'human rights commission' would be mentioned by name in the Charter."[72] According to first-hand accounts, the AJC's Joseph Proskauer was particularly persuasive, perhaps the person most responsible for restoring human rights to the UN. To build a world body without human rights in the aftermath of Hitler and facism, he asserted, would condemn the UN to the same fate as the League of Nations.[73]

The AJC's commitment to the cause of international human rights owed to several considerations.[74] There were other agendas to consider and some narrow organizational interests to protect. The discourse of rights also had the advantage of isolating that other movement the AJC had always found frightening: nationalism.[75] According to the historian James Loeffler, this is what truly motivated Proskauer and the AJC. Neither wanted to see Zionism become too powerful. Human rights became their antidote—it was a way of "twinning American and Jewish political aspirations so as to achieve a palpable yet positive Jewish influence in American foreign policy without the stigma of dual loyalties."[76] And, the AJC was involved in a competition not only of ideas but also with rival Jewish organizations. The AJC had moved from being anti-Zionists to non-Zionists, but now with World War II and the coming postwar period it had to put forward its own foreign policy vision, "authentically Jewish yet untainted by any hint of nationalism or ethnic parochialism. Such a vision would allow the Committee to assert its claims to leadership in national and international Jewish affairs, lest its rivals 'steal the leadership for activities outside of Palestine.' "[77] Yet the AJC was not a newcomer to the cause of international human rights—in fact, it could claim to be an original member of the movement.

The destruction of the European Jews might have sworn American Jews off human rights, and the fact that it did not was testament to its centrality to American Jews' identity and interests. Human rights flowed from their commitment to liberalism, rights, and equality, commitments that were viewed as intrinsic to their political theology of prophetic Judaism and their belief that the security of Jews depended on their integration into the broader society. Human rights would be good for the Jews, and all other peoples; and by furthering the cause of humanity they could also further their own survival. By advocating for human rights, American Jews were not asking for any special favor but rather for rights that would cover Jews and others.[78] Human rights also could help address the crisis of Western civilization and humanity caused by Nazi Germany, fascism, and totalitarianism. It could help restore a loss of faith. It was not enough, though, to pronounce the words "human rights." It also was necessary to create a working human rights machinery. The AJC's sober assessment of the failure of international human rights between the wars led it to insist on human and not group rights, and to strenuously advocate for strong, binding enforcement mechanisms to support these high-minded ideals. For many American Jews, and for organizations such as the American Jewish Committee,

Figure 4.2. The AJC's Jacob Blaustein and Joseph Proskauer, and UN Secretary-General Dag Hammarskjöld examining the United Declaration of Human Rights. Reprinted with permission. New York: American Jewish Committee, ©1956. www.AJC.org. All rights reserved.

the fate of the Jews and humanity depended on transforming human rights from rhetoric into reality.

THE NATIONAL

Most accounts of this period, understandably, contrast the Holocaust with the creation of a Jewish state. Each event was unimaginable on its own terms, and together they were otherworldly, one from hell and the other heaven, creating a singular moment in Jewish history that belonged alongside the other stories of destruction and redemption that populated the Bible. But unlike the Bible, whose stories many Jews perceived as something between tall tales and mythology, there were eyewitness accounts of this living, tangible hell followed by a miracle. Given the twinning of these exceptional events, it was inevitable that Israel would become saturated with hopes, expectations, and meanings. Israel represented the eternal wish of the Jewish people to return to their homeland after centuries in exile, a home for the survivors of the Holocaust and all future Jewish communities that found themselves persecuted and threatened with physical destruction, and the ultimate mark of the Jewish people's refusal to die, their symbol of resistance. Israel meant *"the triumph of life over death."*[79]

Although American Jews had once been half-hearted Zionists, no more. A gathering of intense emotions became channeled toward the campaign to create a Jewish state. American Jews felt tremendous guilt. There was survivor's guilt. There was guilt that they had never fully grasped what was happening in Europe until it was too late. There was guilt that they had never found the right words, or tried harder, to convince their relatives to flee while it was still possible. There was guilt that they had equivocated on Zionism. There was guilt that they were still not doing enough for the survivors. And there was guilt that, once again, they were living comfortable lives in America while Jews were fighting and dying an ocean away.

In addition to guilt, American Jews felt pride. Watching the Zionists take a stand in Palestine, smuggle survivors, and fight for Jewish independence became a moment of expiation and redemption. The image of emaciated bodies being bulldozed into nameless pits was now being replaced by uplifting pictures of muscular Jews fighting for their land. They were proud, and thankful, that these Zionists showed the world a different side of the Jew. And such pride also restored a measure of dignity. As a minority population who lived in chronic fear and often suffered sticks, stones, and smears, it was reassuring to know that they could stand on their own. Juxtaposing the Holocaust with the Jewish fight for independence, Hannah Arendt observed: "Gone, probably forever, is that chief concern of the Jewish people for centuries: survival at any price. Instead, we find something else essentially new among Jews, the desire for dignity at any price."[80]

The creation of Israel was a revolutionary moment in Jewish history, and American Jews, once hesitant, were eager to become part of history.[81] In the months before Israeli independence American Jews did everything they could to get the power of the United States behind the cause of Jewish sovereignty, playing a key role in convincing President Harry Truman to recognize the Jewish state and to overcome the forceful objections of the State Department and many of his foreign policy advisers.[82] Public opinion polls showed that an overwhelming percentage of American Jews were either "very pro-Israel" or "pro-Israel." Once Israel was created, American Jews reported that its presence or absence either did or would greatly affect their lives. After dropping during the interwar years, membership in Zionist organizations rose to nearly 250,000, and thousands of more Jews called themselves Zionists but were not dues-paying members. American Jews began giving in record amounts to Israel. Giving had been on the rise since the late 1930s; in 1946 it broke the $100 million mark, with a fair bit being earmarked for Holocaust survivors; and then within two years it reached nearly $200 million. When David Ben-Gurion declared Israel's independence on May 14, 1948, American Jews threw parties, held parades, and waved the new Israeli flag, which they now put alongside the American flag in Jewish institutions. Some American Jews who had received military training during World War II volunteered for battle in Israel, making critical contributions to Israel's small, ramshackle, but important air force. Other American Jews went on a clandestine shopping spree in Europe, buying surplus military equipment for Israel.

These stories, frequently repeated in texts and speeches about American Jewry's contribution to Israel's creation, capture a changing attitude among American Jews toward Israel—but at the risk of exaggerating its magnitude. American Jews exhibited a burst of Jewish nationalism, but it is better understood as an outburst rather than a "new normal." Although American Jews unambiguously supported the cause of independence, their support did not translate into action.[83] Indeed, once Israel was relatively safe and secure after 1950,

American Jewry's interest in Israel waned considerably. Zionist membership declined almost 75 percent between 1948 and 1956, from 250,000 to 100,000. American Jews reduced their financial support to Israel 40 percent between 1948 and 1953. Not only were American Jews less generous, but they were also replacing their grants and cash donations with Israeli bonds. And even though there was now a Jewish state, some American Jewish leaders did not see it as the answer to the Jewish problem. For instance, when the Jewish communities of North Africa were threatened after the creation of Israel, *Commentary* magazine stressed that integration and not emigration was the best solution to the Jewish Problem.[84] Old habits die hard.

Israel remained on the margins of American Judaism in the 1950s and 1960s.[85] In his study of the Jews of Lakeville in the 1950s, the sociologist Marshall Sklare found that Israel meant rather little. Lakeville's Jews were certainly supportive and appreciative of the Jewish state, but they were passively, not actively, engaged.[86] Lakeville was no different from other Jewish communities. In some years, the *American Jewish Year Book* gave more attention to Germany than it did to Israel.[87] Although American Jewish dignitaries visited Israel, most American Jews showed little interest in making a pilgrimage to their ancient homeland. As one commentator perceptively put it, "Here [is] a bewildering thing: out of five million American Jews not five hundred were inspired to throw in their lot with this miracle of the ages, the reborn Jewish state."[88] This lack of interest did not go unnoticed by American Jewish and Israeli leaders, who feared it was a prelude to estrangement.[89] Reflecting on this puzzling lack of interest, Sidney Hook observed, "We were sensitive to the national aspirations of all other persecuted people, were positively empathetic with them. Yet when it came to our kinfolk, we leaped into a proud universalism."[90]

If American Jews appeared slightly reserved in their embrace of Israel, it was partly because its existence raised many uncomfortable questions that they preferred not to ask. Some of these were questions Jews were now having to ask of themselves, and others were questions that Gentiles might ask of them.[91] For decades American Jews had worried that Zionism and the creation of a Jewish state would cause their fellow Americans to question their allegiances, and they worried that they might now be asked to take such loyalty tests.[92] To minimize the possibility that their support for Israel might undermine their position at home, some American Jewish leaders argued that American Jews should become actively involved in shaping Israel, and in a direction that was consistent with their values and views. This was the position of the highly influential Rabbi Abba Silver. Others, such as Rabbi Stephen Wise, recommended a policy of non-interference.

American Jewry's security also was dependent on how Israel envisioned its role. As a sovereign state it clearly represented its citizens, but as the state of the Jewish people it also might claim to represent the core values and interests of the entire Jewish nation, that is, Jews everywhere. If Israel began acting and speaking as if it represented the entire Jewish nation, including American Jews, then this could potentially jeopardize the security of Jews because it would raise the charge of dual loyalty. Consequently, many American Jewish organizations and leaders used the occasion of Israel's independence to communicate their pride but also the importance of Israeli leaders recognizing that they represented the Israeli state and not the Jewish nation. Consider the American Jewish Committee, which had spent most of its forty years opposing Jewish nationalism. At Israel's birth, the AJC put out a statement that recognized Israel's "historic significance" but also reminded the Israeli government that the "citizens of the United States are Americans and citizens of Israel are Israelis," and that it looked forward to helping Israel "build up" the state in the "framework of national interests." The *national* in national interests *did not* refer to the Jewish nation.

This question of the relationship between American Jewry and Israel also tapped into a broader subject of how their values related to Israel's. Many American Jews did not worry about the question about Israel's values because Jewish lives were at stake. Other prominent American Jews, though, worried that Israel did not represent their values. Israel was the Jewish people's nationalism, and some American Jews believed that Jews were better than nationalism and its primordial and provincial sentiments. Jews should invest in humanity rather than nationality. As one author wrote: "It is peculiarly ironic and unfortunate to find Zionism—at a moment when the very preservation of civilization seems to depend increasingly on humanity's ability to rise above nationalistic ideologies—fostering a worldwide movement of the more intensely nationalistic character. . . . If history has any logic, no group in the world has been so obviously chosen to be the protagonist to fight against nationalism as have the Jews, whom nationalism singled out for destruction. By now it should be obvious even to the most blind that in fighting nationalism wherever they see it, Jews will serve not only the interests of mankind at large, but their own interests as well."[93] Will Herberg, who would later write the classic *Protestant-Catholic-Jew*, observed that "the Jewish people's uniqueness has grown from the fact that at certain climactic points it has chosen to place its hopes for survival elsewhere, almost eccentrically elsewhere, than where other peoples have customarily placed them."[94]

Another prominent strand of American Jewish opinion either assumed or hoped that Israel's values would resemble their own. For most American Zionists, Jews could have their nation and their (American) values, too. After all, ever since Brandeis, American Jews had become accustomed to linking Zionism with basic liberal and democratic principles. Consequently, the presumption and aspiration was that Israel would develop a civic nationalism, not an ethnic nationalism. One sure test of which nationalism might emerge was its treatment of the Arab minority and whether it would develop a national identity that could include them.[95]

The question of whether the values of American Jews and Israel aligned also connected to the broader question of what the new Israeli state would stand for. On the eve of Israeli independence, the AJC's Joseph Proskauer commented that aid from American Jewry was given with the hope that the new state would "become a truly democratic state . . . the idea of a state where Jews did not dominate Arabs and Arabs did not dominate Jews. It is in the field of morality that Judaism has made its greater contribution to the world. Let us work to the end that this new state will be reared upon that morality." And in a bit of clever editing, Proskauer then proceeded to merge the choice words from the Declaration of Independence with the Old Testament.[96]

This issue of what Israel would become was the subject of a fascinating exchange between Rabbi Simon Dolgin and the new Israeli Prime Minister David Ben-Gurion. Dolgin had written to Ben-Gurion to ask about the purpose of the Jewish state. Certainly the survival of the Jewish people, but was survival enough? Would survival lead to a meaningful existence? If Israel stood only for survival, Dolgin wondered, would that impress American Jews?[97] Answering his own question, he said, "In America, we Jews have an objective—similar in quality—which we call 'survival.' Our American Jewish educators, rabbis, and leaders all flaunt 'survival' as the great Jewish task. This, I believe, is a betrayal of our weakness. Healthy individuals, groups, and nations do not worry about 'survival.' They are concerned about living and creating *now*, not surviving in the future. The person or society on the deathbed is anxious about 'survival.' Healthy living carries with it, as an accrued dividend, subconsciously, survival."[98] Israel, he pleaded, has to stand for something.

Ben-Gurion did not disagree, but his mind was on creating a state. Drawing from prophetic theology, Ben-Gurion was fond of saying that Israel was attempting to normalize the Jewish people but also be a light unto the nations. When Ben-Gurion presented his first government to the Israeli Knesset, in words echoing Israel's Declaration of Independence, he declared, "Our activities and policies are guided . . . by a political and social vision that we have inherited from our Prophets."[99] In his response to Dolgin, he wrote, "Two basic aspirations underlie all our work in this country: to be like all nations, and to be different from all nations," and Israel should be a "state that has *profound Jewish dedication* with universal human overtones."[100] That said, Ben-Gurion the realist and nation-builder stressed that the fundamental goal of all nations is survival. Accordingly, Israel might not be anything special. He wrote: "I accept your bewilderment and fear at the idea that the State of Israel might be merely a state. I am, in truth, prepared to accept the State of Israel as a state, and am prepared to offer my life for it, even if this state does not excel in anything special." Better to be run of the mill, though, than religious. A religious state, the secular Ben-Gurion prophesied, "will definitely estrange our grandchildren as would 'anarchy.' "[101] It would not be the last time that an Israeli prime minister equated religion with lawlessness and the usurpation of a vibrant civil society.

Ben-Gurion had a low opinion of religion, and an even lower one of Diaspora Jewry—and, as the prime minister of the new Jewish state, he felt at liberty to tell them so and speak for them.[102] Israel is the homeland for the Jewish people, and as the representative of the Jewish homeland, he believed it had the authority to speak on behalf of all Jews anywhere in the world. Ben-Gurion suggested that Israel's role as the agent of world Jewry was not only a matter of principle, it also was warranted, because the *galuth* Jews could not be trusted to take care of themselves.

Such attitudes were straight from Zionism's derogatory and dismissive view of *galuth* Jews.[103] Two thousand years of exile had created a Jew who was physically and emotionally weak, feeble, and slavish in his deference to non-Jews. Jews have not only been forced to play the victim, they have also developed the survival skills of the victim: they have become a cowering, cowardly passive, and obsequious people. They have gladly accepted the most disgusting and parasitic occupations, acting as moneylenders, middlemen, and merchants, living off other people's labor. Yet traits that might be useful for survival in one situation could be a fatal flaw in another. When the leaders of the Yishuv (Jewish community in Palestine) learned about the Holocaust and heard that Jews were obediently going to their deaths, they believed the rumors because it matched their view of Diaspora Jews.[104] Yitzhak Rabin recalled that as a child he learned to see the Diaspora Jew as a "bent-over Jew possessed of meager bodily strength and immense mental powers."[105] Referring to Shakespeare's infamous Jewish character, David Ben-Gurion observed:

> I do not despise Shylock for making his living from usury. He had no other choice in the place of his exile. . . . Each of us stands in awe and deep admiration before the tremendous emotional power revealed by the Jews in their wanderings and sufferings in the diaspora. . . . I will admire any man who is sick and in pain and who struggles for his survival, who does not bow to his bitter fate, but I will not consider his to be an ideal condition.[106]

Zionists were not surprised that non-Jews did not respect Jews—they were not worthy of respect and they would not be until they earned it. In one survey of Israelis, nearly one-third of the respondents believed that the main cause of anti-Semitism was the characteristics of Jews in the diaspora.[107]

Zionism was a twelve-step program that would transform the "old Jew" into the "new Jew."[108] In the Zionist imagination, *galuth* Jews and Zionist Jews were polar opposites. Diaspora Jews were *nebishes*, bent-over, pasty, and effeminate, while Israelis were the muscular, bronze-skinned Ari Ben-Canaan as played by Paul Newman in *Exodus*. Pre-dating Frantz Fanon's arguments that the colonized people needed to deploy violence in order to erase the emasculating effects of coloni-alism, the Revisionist leader Vladimir (Zvi) Jabotinsky saw violence as cathartic, healing, and empowering. When Masada was originally proposed as possible source material for the Yishuv's collective iden-tity, Ben-Gurion reportedly answered that he did not believe that a story that ended with the decision to commit suicide rather than fight was consistent with the Zionist image.[109] The acquisition of political and military power in a framework of sovereignty would purge the stereotype of the "submissible cowardly Jew."[110]

Because American Jews were so crippled, Israeli Jews often pre-sumed that they can and should speak for world Jewry. Israeli leaders and intellectuals repeatedly and contemptuously dismissed American Jews. American Jews might be members of the most successful Jewish community in the history of the Jewish people, but they could not buy their way out of a *galuth* mentality. As far as Ben-Gurion and other Israeli leaders were concerned, American Jews would always be second-class American citizens and third-rate Jews.[111] Ben-Gurion enjoyed reciting the following line from the Talmud: "Whosoever lives outside the land of Israel is considered as if he had no God."[112] If they wanted to be real Jews, then they had to make aliyah. American Jews who visited Israel during this period recount how Israelis would constantly ask them when they were going to leave their comfortable, bourgeois, and ultimately soulless lives in America and develop genu-ine, authentic, and meaningful Jewish lives in Israel. Insult intended, insult taken.

Given American Jewry's ambivalence toward Israel and Zionism's arrogant attitude toward *galuth* Jews, it was inevitable that their re-lationship would need work.[113] After several years of dust-ups, often provoked by yet another of Ben-Gurion's anti-*galuth* outbursts, Ben-Gurion and the AJC's Jacob Blaustein exchanged a set of let-ters that constituted something of a contract outlining rules, rights, and responsibilities.[114] Ben-Gurion, finally, publicly acknowledged that American Jews could be first-rate Jews and pledged that Israel would respect them and their contributions to Israel. He stated:

> The Jews of the United States, as a community and as individuals, have only one political attachment and that is to the United States of America. They owe no political allegiance to Israel . . . In the first statement with the representative of Israel made before the United Nations after her admission to that international organization, he clearly stated, without any reservation, that the State of Israel represents and speaks only on behalf of its own citizens and in no way presumes to represent or speak in the name of the Jews who are citizens of any other country. We, the people of Israel, have no desire and no intention to interfere in any way with the internal affairs of Jewish communities abroad.

Ben-Gurion conceded that the "ingathering of exiles" did not apply to American Jews, acknowledged that American Jews have their primary loyalty to the United States, and vowed to respect the independence of Jewish communities around the world.

This principle of noninterference was a two-way street. When the Israeli government was insinuating that it represented world Jewry, it was only natural that world Jewry would expect to be consulted before Israel made important decisions. Now that Israel and American Jewry had an exchange of recognition, Israelis believed that American Jews should mind their own business. American Jews, in short, were expected to provide diplomatic and financial support with almost no questions asked. In return, Israel would be a proud symbol of the Jewish people and a center for Jewish renewal.[115]

Both sides had difficulty sticking to their agreements. Over the years Israeli officials, including Ben-Gurion, would say something unkind about American Jews, American Jews would protest, and Israeli officials and Ben-Gurion would apologize or claim that the remarks had been taken out of context.[116] The AJC and the American Jewish community could pledge not to interfere in the internal affairs of Israel, but the assumption that Israel's behavior reflected on them meant that they felt the urge to do so. What if Israel started behaving in ways that left American Jews ashamed or vulnerable to anti-Semitism? Did American Jewry have a responsibility or right to intervene? Most took the position that they should provide economic and political support but not involve themselves in internal politics or matters of security. American Jews largely kept their opinions to themselves, but it became increasingly difficult to do so after the 1967 war, the occupation, and the development of the settlements.

There is one last bit of evidence that American Jews were hardly fixated on Israel. In August 1966, *Commentary* magazine asked leading rabbis, Jewish intellectuals, and scholars to comment on the nature of American Jewishness, Jewish identity, and what distinguishes Jews from others.[117] The thirty-eight respondents represented a cross-section of American Jews along religious and political lines. There was lots of commentary on the Jews as a chosen people, with most accepting formulations that were consistent with humanistic interpretations and that denied the implication that they saw themselves as superior.

One feature of these responses passed without much notice at the time but later became evidence of the massive change among American Jews: Israel and the Holocaust were scarcely mentioned. When asked to comment on the sources of Jewish identity, these leading thinkers overlooked the two events that would soon define American Jewish life. The Holocaust received comparatively little attention. The return of the Jews to the homeland, after a nearly 2,000-year exile, also passed without much comment. Israel had been in existence for eighteen years, fought a war for its independence, fought a second war in 1956, and had been gathering Jews from around the world. Israeli leaders had been clamoring that Israel represented the future of the Jewish people. Not so, according to these leaders of American Jewry. Israel was important, but it was not central to the American Jewish identity. American Jews supported Israel, but they were not so attached or so closely identified that it ranked in the top echelon of factors affecting their Jewish identity. However much nationalism and particularism might have settled into the American Jewish consciousness, American Jews still felt most comfortable stressing the forces that connected them to Gentiles, not kept them apart.

CHAPTER FIVE

THE NEW TRIBALISM

COSMOPOLITANISM'S LEAD OVER TRIBALISM HAD BEEN SLIPPING over the decades. Until the early 1900s American Jews pledged their allegiance to American liberalism and universalism and disowned Jewish nationalism. They grew more comfortable with Zionism beginning with World War I, but always with the caveat that America was their promised land and Palestine was a homeland for *other* Jews. The Holocaust won over most of the holdouts, and then the birth of Israel thinned the opposition to a radical fringe. Yet despite the enormity of world wars and the Holocaust, these events had remarkably little impact on how American Jews saw themselves and the world. The Holocaust and the creation of Israel realized every single fantasy, both phantasmic and redemptive, that Jews had privately held and publicly shared for centuries—and now they fused into a single moment. If American Jews had responded to this rapid-fire sequence of destruction and creation by becoming mistrustful, reconsidering the permanence of the American promise and buying real estate in Israel, it would have been understandable. In fact, they did just the opposite. Instead of moving to Israel, they moved from the cities to the suburbs and unreservedly accepted America's warm embrace. They were living their dream. The other dream of a Jewish return to Palestine had never been their dream. They had certainly helped the dream become a reality, and had done their part in the days before and after the creation of the State of Israel, but then they returned to the comfortable role of armchair advocate.

After decades of emphasizing the American half of their Jewish American identity, in the mid-1960s they began exploring their other half.[1] This turn could be a sign of the Jewish community's maturation and confidence. Before they could casually talk about their differences, they needed to feel accepted and secure.[2] However, Jews were not the only minority group talking about self-empowerment and auto-emancipation; new social and cultural movements were bursting onto the scene. The African American community was fighting for respect and power, the women's liberation movement was shaking the gendered pecking order, and other minorities, including Native Americans and Latinos, were asking for equal time and recognition on their own terms. Multiculturalism became the new watchword in American society and across college campuses. Identity politics had become fashionable. Jews were acting just like others.

Although American Jews contributed to, and were affected by, this period of identity politics, their self-assertions of difference appeared to be driven by the sorts of fears associated with nationalism and tribalism, not the cultural pluralism of Horace Kallen or multiculturalism.[3] American Jewish leaders and organizations began pointing to a new set of threats to Jewish survival. After decades of seeking America's acceptance, they now worried that too much of a good thing was becoming fatal. American Jews were disappearing into America's secular fold. Jews were identifying as ethnic rather than religious and were better able to recite lines from a Woody Allen movie than basic religious prayers. There were dire predictions that if trends continued, the American Jewish population would dwindle in significance.

The other, much more conventional threat to their survival was anti-Semitism. How could American Jews be at risk from both assimilation *and* anti-Semitism? It was no longer acceptable to express outright anti-Semitism, so it had gone underground and become masked and shrouded in code words. And there were times when the surface serenity became disturbed by either offensive insensitivity or outright hostility, including from those they thought were their friends and with whom they were in solidarity. And while anti-Semitism had become dormant in America, it was quite active in the rest of the world. The Soviet Union targeted its Jews for special treatment and circulated the sort of slander that was commonplace in late nineteenth-century Russia. After centuries of treating the Jews with a combination of tolerance and leniency, the Arab and Islamic worlds began exhibiting a virulent anti-Semitism that blended traditional European and home-grown Islamic-inspired varieties. Countries like Poland showed that it was possible to be anti-Semitic without having Jews. Israel was still fighting for its survival and legitimacy, increasingly lonely and ostracized at international gatherings. Much of the criticism of Israel could be explained without reference to anti-Semitism, but many anti-Semites used Israel as an avatar for their prejudices.[4]

Yet there was something quite odd about the timing of this heightened concern for Jewish survival. If American Jews were becoming more fearful, then the logical presumption was that their world had become more ominous. But objectively speaking, life had never been better.[5] Anti-Semitism still existed, but nothing like before. Intermarriage had increased between 1970 and 1980, but the Jewish population was relatively stable. Jews were more accepted, integrated, and successful than ever, highly visible in all walks of life, and their presence at once-exclusive settings was no longer a source of scandal or surprise. Israel was the region's major military power, possessed nuclear weapons, and was moving from austerity to prosperity. "It was a curious moment in the history of ideas. Twenty years earlier, Jews had responded to the Nazi Holocaust by plunging headlong into a politics of trust and optimism. Their answer to the Second World War was a vow to create a world where such terrible things could not happen to anyone. Now . . . Jews were . . . retreating into a politics of fear and suspicion."[6] And such fears seemed to narrow the horizons of American Jews. American Jews, of course, had always looked after their own and worried about their disappearance, but they had done so with the belief that their fates were tied to those of others. In other words, they practiced enlightened self-interest. Now, in many quarters Jews were expressing a narrow-minded form of self-interest.[7] Jews were going it alone, and at the very moment that they seemed to be safer than ever.

What happened to invert Heine's law? Why were American Jews becoming distressed at precisely the moment when the present and future seemed brighter than ever? One school of thought points to Jewish neuroses. If things seem too good to be true, they probably are. Just ask the Jews of Germany. As the Israeli statesman Abba Eban once joked, "Jews are amazing in their inability to take 'Yes' as an answer."[8]

Another argument is that Jews were trying to dissipate the dangers of assimilation by reminding one another of threats past, present, and future. A time-honored strategy for tightening the ranks is to remind the members of the community that wolves surround them.

A related possibility suggests that the pendulum was swinging back from the universal to the tribal. By the early 1960s American Jewry's enthusiastic embrace of liberal universalism was generating the beginning of what would become a countermovement. Some of this was a response to the simple fact that American Jews had achieved so much success that they now risked assimilation; consequently, there was an effort to preserve some element of particularism.[9]

Yet according to some critics, American Jewry and its romance with Prophetic Judaism bore some of the blame. American Jews, once again, were mistaking social action for "authentic" Judaism.[10] The great Jewish theologian and scholar Emil Fackenheim asserted that liberal Jews were a walking dilemma: wanting to be Jewish but also divorcing themselves from their heritage; wanting to cite their heritage as a source of their values but also refusing to become learned in Judaism; wanting to assert their particularism while also referencing a universalism that denies their separation.[11] In 1963 Rabbi Arthur Hertzberg warned that American Jews were becoming too intimately connected to the rest of society; they needed to keep their distance and engage in Jewish learning.[12] Critics of the AJC accused it of caring more about civil rights than Jewish education, of ceasing to be a Jewish organization with a civil rights program and becoming a civil rights organization whose members are Jewish.[13] Daniel Bell delivered a jeremiad against "ethical Judaism," calling it "superficial rationalism" that has "taken some disturbing profundities of the Old Testament and transformed them into glossy moral platitudes."[14] Lucy Dawidowicz, who would soon achieve considerable fame with her book *The War against the Jews, 1933–1945*, argued that there is nothing fundamental about Judaism that demands an interest in social justice. Instead, American Jewry's long-lasting identification owes to the belief that liberalism, democracy, and rights are good for Jewish self-preservation.[15] These dissident voices and pleas for particularism would discover a much more receptive audience after 1967.[16]

The more widely accepted explanation for this renewed fear points to the 1967 Six-Day War. Just as there is before and after 1967 for understanding the Arab-Israeli conflict, there is before and after 1967 for understanding American Jewry's outlook on the world. Of course, all turning points and transformations have a history, and, in many respects, the 1967 war was less of a cause than a consolidator and conductor of forces at home and abroad that compelled American Jews to turn inward.[17] Yet the 1967 war *was* a shock to the system. What was it about the war that was so disturbing? This was not Israel's first war, but the third in less than twenty years. Israel won, not lost, and it did not just win on points, it delivered a first-round knockout. Moreover, while wars frequently create a greater community spirit, such solidarity does not always translate into a climate of fear. To understand why the events of the 1967 war had the impact they did requires recognizing that there were two phases to the war—the prelude in the month of May and the actual war in early June, and May left a bigger impression than June.

Beginning in spring 1967 Syria and Israel began engaging in a series of border skirmishes, most of them aerial dogfights above the Golan Heights, almost always ending with another demonstration of Israel's prowess. Feeling as if he needed to move from the sidelines to the front lines in order to maintain his image as leader of the Arab world, Egypt's President Nasser evicted the UN observer force and began predicting the coming destruction of Israel. The Arab states kept tightening the noose throughout May, and Israel's allies were doing little to loosen it. Israel's closest military ally, France, abandoned it in its hour of need. The United States, mired in its own war in Vietnam, was unwilling to commit itself to anything more than diplomacy and, when that failed, essentially wished Israel good luck. The United Nations, whose charter forbids war except in the act of self-defense, did remarkably little to stop the Arab states from launching an unprovoked attack on a member.

It was not only Israel that felt abandoned—so, too, did American Jewry. Over the years American Jews had developed close ties with various emancipatory movements, especially those from the political left. This was a strategy born of principle and survival. As a persecuted minority, American Jews could sympathize with the fight for equality. As a small minority, American Jews believed that if it came to the defense of others in their time of need, these groups would reciprocate when American Jews felt threatened. During the month of May, American Jews kept expecting their friends to raise their voices in support of Israel, but that never happened. American Jews were watching Jews in Israel threatened with annihilation, and their non-Jewish comrades did not seem very concerned; some even made anti-Israeli comments that bordered on anti-Semitism.[18] This disappointment and sense of abandonment was acutely felt with regard to the African-American community. Although relations between the two communities were already showing signs of strain, American Jews saw themselves as friends with African Americans and thought that African Americans felt the same way. However, when the crisis hit and American Jews expected support, their friends were nowhere to be found. Equally unexpected, political conservatives and military hawks, circles that American Jews did not frequent, voiced their support.[19]

American Jewry gazed upon these events with a frightful sense of déjà vu. Just as before, murderous anti-Semitic forces were gathering and advertising their intentions, and the world was shrugging its collective shoulders. The world had learned nothing from the Holocaust. Indeed, its indifference was even more egregious now than before: the West had never made any promises to protect the security of the Jews of Germany, but in the intervening decades the West had made pledges of "never again" and had given strong assurances of support to Israel. It was not just the United States and the West that were failing to come to Israel's defense; the United Nations was equally useless. Once again the world was abandoning the Jews, and there was little that a wealthier, more secure, and politically connected American Jewry could do. There was, though, one important difference between then and now: the Jews had an army. Surprising itself and the rest of the world, in six days the Israel Defense Forces destroyed three Arab armies, captured Jerusalem, the West Bank, the Golan Heights, and the Sinai Peninsula, and demoralized the entire Arab world.

The 1967 war transformed the map of the Middle East—and the attitudes of American Jews toward Israel. Surprising not just others but also themselves, American Jews erupted with an outpouring of

Figure 5.1. American Jews at Victory Celebration at Lafayette Park, across from the White House, in June 1967. Courtesy of the Jewish Historical Society of Greater Washington. Photograph by Ida Jervis.

emotion. Even the young Jewish Left, perhaps the segment of the American Jewish population least connected to Israel, discovered that Israel's fate meant more to them than they had ever imagined. "The immediate reaction of American Jewry to the crisis," wrote Rabbi Arthur Hertzberg, "was far more intense and widespread than anyone could have foreseen. Many Jews would never have believed that the grave danger to Israel would dominate their thoughts and emotions to the exclusion of all else."[20] Twenty years of respectful but hardly rapturous affection for Israel was now replaced by near hero-worship. American Jews spoke of Israel with awe, and treated Israelis as if they were a separate and superior Jewish race. American Jews not only collapsed with relief and in disbelief at the outcome of the war, they also rose to pay respects and rushed to make up for lost time.

Several factors explain this entirely unexpected reaction by American Jews. Experiencing their own version of post-traumatic stress, American Jews relived the Holocaust as they watched events unfold in the Middle East. Returning to Lakeville to examine the war's impact on the Jewish community, Marshall Sklare wrote that the "response . . . was not a response to Israel in the conventional sense but rather a response to the events of Jewish history from the 1930s onwards."[21] They also were discovering that their existence depended on Israel's existence in ways previously unimagined. American Jews reflected how Israel's survival was bound up with their spiritual existence, and how Israel's destruction would have been their destruction. In response to the question of whether the Six-Day War changed him, Elie Wiesel said:

> Has the Six Day War produced a change in my weltanschauung? I would go even further and say that the change was total, for it involved my very being as both a person and as a Jew. . . . To destroy Israel . . . to let it be destroyed, would have meant the end of an affirmation, the end of hope, the end of our history which we shaped as both Jews and human beings. . . . The end of Israel would mean to me the end of man.[22]

With comparable anguish and surprise at the depth of emotions aroused by the threat to Israel's survival, another American Jew commented:

> Our support of Israel is intimately connected with our desire to preserve a feeling of our worth as human beings. . . . Furthermore, we support Israel to protect our sense of meaning. Israel created meaning, for it meant that out of the destruction of the holocaust something new, clean, and good was born. . . . Israel's destruction, then, would involve the destruction of meaning. . . . By upsetting

our sense of meaning, a new holocaust would have plunged American Jewry into a total anomie. From this perspective, Israel *had* to be supported as never before. Her destruction would have meant our end as an American Jewry, for we could not survive such a complete loss of meaning.[23]

Once believing themselves to be satisfied and content, American Jews were shocked to discover how close they were to "a deep emotional abyss."[24]

The 1967 war not only gave American Jews a glimpse of life without Israel, its victory also instilled in them a self-respect they never knew they had been missing. Jews were an American success story, but they still felt tolerated and not truly respected. Israel's battlefield exploits infused American Jews with a new sense of self-respect. Jews were not just clever; they were warriors, too. Jews did not need to depend on the charity and pity of others; they could take care of themselves. Jews no longer had to suffer in silence or turn the other cheek because they had no other alternatives; they could hit back. Israel's accomplishments were not its alone, for they belonged to all Jews. American Jews started carrying themselves a little differently, a little more erect, and with more confidence and an air of resolve.[25] Jews who previously shrouded their heritage now began wearing Israeli military paraphernalia.[26] American Jews who might never have considered volunteering for the US military began fantasizing about serving in the Israeli army. American Jews might not have fought on the battlefield, but they contributed in their own way. Israel had F-15s, America had the American Israel Public Affairs Committee (AIPAC), and it was because of AIPAC that Israel had the F-15s. Israel and American Jews made a great team. At times, American Jews seemed to mistake Israel's military feats for their own.

American Jews began to identify with Israel like never before.[27] They were attending rallies in record numbers. On May 28, 1967, nearly 150,000 Jews marched in support of Israel. Nearly unprecedented at the time, Jewish leaders expressed disappointment if the next rally was not bigger than the last. American Jews were giving money in record amounts. In 1966 the American Jewish community donated $64 million and bought $76 million in Israeli bonds, but in 1967 it contributed $432 million, unprecedented in terms of the speed and scale.[28] Although the amount of giving declined after 1967, it remained at levels far beyond anything seen before then. Young American Jews started visiting Israel, volunteering on kibbutzim, and treating a pilgrimage to Israel as a rite of passage, nearly comparable to the Bar or Bat Mitzvah. By the end of 1967, 10,000 American Jews had visited, and thousands more followed. Even more astounding, they began immigrating to Israel. In 1966 the total number of Americans Jews living in Israel was somewhere between 12,000 and 15,000; between 1967 and 1971 around 22,000 made aliyah. In other words, nearly twice as many American Jews moved to Israel in the four years after the war as the previous twenty. Although it was not quite the deluge that Ben-Gurion prophesied in 1948, it was far beyond anything previously seen.

Israel also was becoming increasingly central to the American Jewish identity.[29] Perhaps the surest sign of this change was that it was becoming nearly impossible to be an accepted member of the Jewish community without saying the right things about Israel.[30] An American Jew could be an atheist, never set foot in a temple, and fail miserably at lip-syncing Hebrew prayers, but as long as he said the right things about Israel he could be a self-respecting Jew and a solid member of the Jewish community. Conversely, an American Jew could be deeply observant, a fixture at the synagogue, and give generously to the local Jewish community, but could be accused of being a self-hating Jew if he said the wrong things about Israel. AIPAC, once a relatively unknown lobbying group in Washington, became revered among American Jews, its growing prominence an immediate product of an American Jewish community that was forming its identity through Israel. AIPAC, in other words, was not just a pro-Israel lobby, it became a bellwether of one's Jewish identity. The AIPAC annual conference became something akin to High Holiday services for the Jewish political elite. In general, the American Jewish community, and its rising leadership, moved from a theme of assimilation to one of survivalism.[31]

The 1973 Arab-Israeli War replayed and reinforced these themes. Egypt and Syria launched a surprise attack on Yom Kippur, the holiest day of the Jewish calendar, which symbolized and strengthened the connection between their own Jewish identity and Israel. As they had six years before, American Jews looked around for domestic support, only to find the political left shockingly unsympathetic and conservatives rushing to Israel's defense. And even though Egypt and Syria had violated the UN Charter prohibiting the use of force outside of self-defense, the international community acted as if Israel was in the wrong. Part of the explanation for the world's response owed to the Arab oil embargo. The Arab oil-exporting countries announced that they would not sell oil to any country that supported Israel, and many states quickly capitulated without exhibiting much inner turmoil. In the United States energy and gas prices rose dramatically, and cars began forming long lines at gas stations. A few of those cars had bumper stickers that announced who they blamed: the Jews. It was nearly impossible to read "Burn Jews, not oil" without thinking of the Holocaust.

The 1967 and 1973 wars reinforced the time-honored adage that Israel and the Jews could not count on anyone but themselves, which corresponded with the primary cautionary tale of the other major event of this period: the "discovery" of the Holocaust. There is a widespread impression that American Jews ignored the Holocaust prior to the 1960s. However, they were not nearly as inattentive to the Holocaust as they are often rumored to have been.[32] Many public ceremonies and events commemorated the tragedy and raised awareness. *The Diary of Anne Frank* became a cultural phenomenon in the United States in the late 1950s, first as a Broadway play and then as a major motion picture. In 1961 Israel kidnapped Adolph Eichmann, an architect of the Holocaust, from his hiding place in Buenos Aires and charged him with crimes against humanity and the Jewish people. His trial in Jerusalem was widely covered in the press, and the testimony by survivors put faces and stories to the Holocaust, transforming it from an abstraction into a sentient event.[33] That said, American Jews felt ambivalent about how closely they wanted the Holocaust to symbolize them. In fact, when a proposal for a Holocaust Memorial in New York City came before representatives of the leading Jewish organizations in the late 1940s, they unanimously rejected the idea. It would, they feared, give currency to the image of Jews as "helpless victims, an idea they wished to repudiate."[34]

Beginning in the late 1960s the Holocaust became a defining symbol and source of identity. Its prominence in American and global life would never have occurred without the collective effort of well-placed individuals and organizations—and especially Jewish leaders and organizations—who determined it must become more central to Jewish and global consciousness. Why now? Some commentators sympathetically portray Jewish leaders in America, Israel, and around the world as belatedly correcting a gross historical oversight, giving the Holocaust its proper due and forcing the world to recognize the enormity of the event. Others accuse Jewish leaders of cynical manipulation and ulterior motives, of wanting to cultivate the world's guilt at a moment when the world was becoming less sympathetic to Israel and to put the fear of Gentiles into American Jews who were too easily tempted by assimilation.[35] Closer to the mark, the increased emphasis on the "Holocaust" resulted from accidental and intentional activity, sincere and strategic action, and the conjunction of forces beyond anyone's control.[36]

The creation of the US Holocaust Memorial Museum (USHMM) captures both the emerging centrality of the Holocaust in American life and the enduring tensions between the particular and the universal for American Jews.[37] In the early 1970s Jewish communities around the country were organizing events on, raising awareness for, and planning to build local memorials and museums to commemorate the Holocaust. In addition to a sincere desire to firmly root the Holocaust in the public memory, American Jews also hoped that elevating the Holocaust in the American consciousness would help maintain the bonds of the Jewish people and bolster American support for Israel. It was all well and good that cities and communities around the country were taking the initiative at the local level, but several leading American Jews began to advocate for a national project. Motivated partly by a desire to salvage his relations with the American Jewish community, in 1978 President Jimmy Carter announced the formation of a Holocaust Commission on the occasion of Israel's thirtieth birthday, consecrating the political value of the Holocaust and tethering it to Israel.

The commission issued various recommendations, the most famous and lasting being the creation of what would become the USHMM. The idea that there should be a museum and memorial to the Holocaust

was widely applauded, but there was considerable debate about its lo-
cation. The decision to build the USHMM on the National Mall, where
it would become sanctified as part of the American experience, stirred
considerable controversy. Those who favored the idea of building a
national memorial were not persuaded that it merited a place at the
symbolic center of America. Some Jews were embarrassed that they
would be obtaining a memorial on the Mall for an event that occurred
in Europe—and before America had properly recognized its responsibility for its crimes against Native Americans or African Americans.
Others worried that by locating it on the Mall, the Holocaust would
cease to be a Jewish story and become an American story; the Holocaust, just like the American Jews, would become Americanized to
the point that it lost its Jewishness.

Regardless of whether the USHMM was on the Mall or in a suburb
of Washington, the commission still had to address how the Holocaust was an American tale.[38] At a minimum, "the story had to be
told in such a way that it would resonate not only with the survivor
in New York and his children in Houston or San Francisco, but with
the black leader from Atlanta, a Midwestern farmer, or a northeastern
industrialist."[39] It was not enough to describe and display the Holocaust in all its evil—it was equally important to offer an explanation
for how such evil could happen and connect that explanation to
the American experience. One tie-in was that genocides and crimes
against humanity occur in countries where minorities are stripped
of their rights, persecuted, and demonized. Yet how did this model
of tolerance square with America's indifference to Jewish suffering
during the Holocaust? Some prophesied that by placing a memorial
on the Mall, future policy makers would be reminded of the words
"never again" and be forced onto the moral ground. For some American Jews the Americanization and universalization of the Holocaust
was a welcome development in the spirit of the prophetic tradition.
For others, it meant that Jews no longer had sole ownership of an
event they claimed as their own. Once again, American Jews found
themselves caught between the particular and the universal.

The wars of the Middle East and the sanctification of the Holocaust bonded to form a single experience for American Jews.[40] By the
mid-1970s it became nearly impossible to think about Israel without

also conjuring up the Holocaust, and vice versa. The Holocaust was an immediate reminder that Jews are never safe and can never rely on others for their existence, and a self-reliant, strong Jewish state is the only guarantor of the Jewish people. Israel is a Jewish state dedicated to ensuring the survival of the Jews, in the here and now, in the future, in Israel, and in the diaspora. The Holocaust reminded Jews that forces would rise, from time to time, to destroy the Jewish people, and Israel reminded them that Jews would persevere. Israel and the Holocaust became central to American Jewish identity—to the point that some Jewish leaders worried that all this talk of destruction was smothering Jewish religious life.[41] Perhaps, but the issue for many Jewish leaders was not the religiosity of American Jews but rather their sense of peoplehood, and American Jews came together in response to fear and not to light the Shabbat candles. Suffering and survival became increasingly prominent themes in the making and maintenance of the collective identity of Jewish peoplehood.[42]

The growing centrality of these events in the American Jewish collective memory altered how American Jews saw and presented themselves. For more than a century American Jews had been telling their fellow Americans that they were just like everyone else—to the point that Jewish leaders had to expend energy reminding American Jews that they were not just Americans but also Jews. The Holocaust and Israel became reminders that Jews were a separate people, that they would never be fully accepted, and that Gentiles would always see the Jews as different. Jews needed to spend less time thinking about how to ingratiate themselves with their hosts and more time working on their continued existence. The Holocaust and the Israeli-Arab wars provided an answer to the question of why Jews should remain Jews—because non-Jews hated them.[43] Survival became reason enough to stay Jewish. In 1968 the theologian and Holocaust survivor Emil Fackenheim issued his well-known proclamation that the 613 commandments needed another: "Jews are forbidden to give Hitler a posthumous victory. They are commanded to survive as Jews, lest the Jewish people perish. They are forbidden to despair of God and Israel lest Judaism perish."[44] Jews must survive because others want them dead, and there is no reason to get bogged down on bigger questions about the meaning and purpose of the Jewish people.

Stories of destruction and survival cannot exist without corresponding accounts of suffering and victims, and an immediate consequence of the twinning of the Holocaust and Israel was an acute sensitivity among Jews about their history of suffering and a growing identification with the role of victim. Jews, of course, are not the only people to invest suffering with meaning; many religious communities and nations do. Yet suffering is a defining theme in Judaism and central to the historical memory of the Jews.[45] The Torah tells how the Jews began to suffer as a people even before they saw themselves as a distinct tribe. One of the most famous stories of the Bible is the Book of Job, in which a righteous man who has lived a good and virtuous life is subjected to a series of seemingly random trials that test his devotion and faith. After the Romans destroyed the Second Temple in Jerusalem and expelled the Jews from their homeland in 70 CE, Jewish history became defined by a never-ending series of persecutions. Holidays, stories, fables, and religious references remind Jews of their constant persecution.[46] Purim is a festival when children dress up in costume, play games, and eat sweet desserts, but the holiday commemorates an occasion when Jews outwitted their genocidal enemies. At the Passover seder Jews recite, "in every generation, our enemies rise up to destroy us." The Israeli diplomat Abba Eban once observed that "the essence of Jewish history can be summed up in a single phrase: the few against the many. Thus it was in the past, so it is today."[47] Similarly, the revered Israeli author Aharon Appelfeld said, "Jewish history is a series of holocausts, with only some improvement of technique."[48] Themes of suffering are so pronounced that, according to some, they form the backbone of Jewish humor. In a signature line by Tevye in *Fiddler on the Roof*: "I know, I know. We're your Chosen People. But, once in a while, can't You choose someone else?"

Suffering is so central to the Jewish historical narrative that it possibly distorts everything else. According to the eminent historian of Jewish history Salo Baron, Jews are such a long-suffering people that they possess a "lachrymose" view of their history.[49] David Biale's *Power and Powerlessness in Jewish History* became an instant classic because it wrote against this tradition and examined the occasional and limited power of otherwise supposedly powerless Jews.[50] Born a Polish Jew, Lewis Namier, the esteemed historian of England, responded in the following way when asked why he wrote English and not Jewish history: "There *is* no modern Jewish history. There is only Jewish martyrology, and that is not enough for me." Isaiah Berlin tells this story in such a way that he indicates both pity for the Jews and sympathy for Namier's dismissive attitude toward the study of Jewish history.[51] In his essay "Israel: The Ever Dying People," Simon Rawidowicz warned that using tragedy to mark history can leave the Jews with a distorted view of themselves and the world.[52] Jewish history becomes reduced to a series of cataclysms, obscuring periods when Jews were safe in exile, demonstrated considerable diplomatic acumen, and shaped their own destiny.[53] How a people narrate their history tells us much about how they see themselves.[54]

Once a people perceives itself in a particular way, its members can become committed to that persona. "Jews," write Liebman and Cohen, "often have a deep emotional investment in preserving their image as a uniquely long-suffering minority."[55] A people that becomes consumed by its own suffering and survival can adopt the identity of the victim; and once its members become accustomed to being the victim, they can develop the unflattering qualities associated with victimhood, such as self-absorption, cowardice, obsequiousness, and passivity. This is precisely the highly unflattering and nearly anti-Semitic view Zionist political thought holds of Diaspora Jews.

According to Zionist leaders, Israel and Jewish sovereignty would help rid Jews of their victim mentality, but after 1967 they, too, learned the joys of suffering. What happened? Some suggest that they were cynically playing the victim card to cultivate support for Israel, and because they were relying more heavily on Jewish suffering to legitimate their policies at a time when Jews and Israel were doing relatively well, they had to try harder and issue more frequent and audible reminders of Jewish suffering.[56] There is no clear answer to whether the growing reliance on victimhood was cynical or sincere, but, as with American Jews, the timing points to the role of the Holocaust and the 1967 and 1973 wars. According to Yael Zerubavel, the 1973 war, more than any other event, transformed Israel's attitude toward victimhood; it showed the Israelis that they could also live with a false sense of security. Israel increasingly identified not just with the Holocaust but also its status as a victim.[57] Timing is everything. The Holocaust and Israel's security elevated the role of victem in Jewish consciousness.

This darker and gloomier worldview of American Jews had two important effects. There was a conscious recalculation of the political strategy of creating alliances with similarly excluded populations. In the past, American Jews had hooked their wagons to liberalism and coalitions of the oppressed, believing that there was strength in numbers and minority groups could form a mutual aid society.[58] Yet during the 1967 crisis, and then in the ensuing years of trying to generate support for Israel, their friends were nowhere to be found. Because of this experience, American Jews began to rethink their political alliances. In the process, they began to doubt the efficacy of these fundamental liberal values. "The values that for so long had characterized American Judaism—equality, tolerance, and social justice—became suspect in New Jewish leadership circles. A new set of basic values came to replace them: loyalty to the Jewish people, commitment to its survival, and hostility toward its enemies."[59] Their circle of obligation was shrinking and American Jews were reappraising their reservations regarding particularism and fondness for universalism.

Also, the ground underneath Prophetic Judaism began to crumble. It is important to not exaggerate the extent of this development. Social justice and voluntary service continued to rank high on the list of elements of Jewish identity. By the 1980s some American Jews were beginning to use the language of tikkun olam.[60] A 1988 *Los Angeles Times* survey of American Jews reported a stronger interest in social justice, world peace, and equality than in religion and Israel.[61] Yet on the surface there was grumbling that Prophetic Judaism had not earned the Jews any points and that its values represented a possible threat to Jewish interests. The chain went as follows: Prophetic Judaism is connected to liberal values; liberal values are not helping and might be hurting Jewish interests; therefore, Prophetic Judaism is a possible threat to Jewish interests.[62] To reverse this trend, they became more attentive to the needs of the Jewish community to the commensurate neglect of the needs of others. Jewish philanthropy began allocating more of its resources to mainly Jewish causes.[63] In general, by the "end of the 1960s, Jewish spokespersons who had championed a theology of social responsibility faced inexorable pressures to reconsider those values."[64] American Jews were gazing differently at themselves and the world.

PROFILES IN TRIBALISM

The shifting balance between particularism and universalism affected the foreign policies of American Jews. Just like they had less interest in other people's problems at home, they had less interest in problems of the world if they did not immediately affect Jews. "Was it good or bad for the Jews?" became an oft-heard refrain. Just as they had begun to fear the political left at home and to reconsider their natural coalition allies, American Jews began reassessing progressive politics abroad and associating with Cold War politics. Just as they had been retreating from universalism and inching toward particularism at home, they were doing the same abroad, becoming less enamored of multilateralism and international human rights.

American Jewry's revitalized relationship with Israel encapsulated this new thinking. The 1967 war changed the map of the Middle East, the American Jewish relationship with Israel, and the US-Israel relationship. Prior to 1967, the so-called special relationship was not so special. The United States was friendly to Israel, but not overly so, at least not if friendship is measured in terms of dollars and tanks. Although American officials constantly reminded Jewish audiences that the United States was the first country to recognize Israel, it always conveniently omitted how it retreated to the sidelines during Israel's war for independence and even supported an arms embargo on the front-line states, which put Israel at a distinct military disadvantage because the Arab states could easily procure weapons from their Arab allies (at least in theory—practice was another matter). In the 1950s the United States kept Israel at arm's length because of the belief that any association would interfere with its Soviet containment policy and a stable oil supply. In fact, in the mid-1950s Secretary of State John Foster Dulles, in the hopes of winning Egyptian President Nasser's support, asked Israeli Prime Minister David Ben-Gurion about the possibility of Israel's ceding part of the Negev to create a land bridge between Egypt and Jordan.[65] In response to the 1956 surprise attack by Israel, Britain, and France on Egypt, President Eisenhower forced Israel to withdraw under the threat of massive sanctions. Relations improved with President Kennedy, and he authorized the first shipment of weapons to Israel. When Lyndon Johnson became president he offered to open the pipeline a little more, but with the expectation that American Jews would return the favor by supporting his policies on Vietnam (or at least stop leading the protests). And while President Johnson offered comforting words of support to Israel in May 1967, he refused to provide security guarantees. Israel and the United States did not have an alliance, much less a special relationship.

Various factors led the United States to change Israel's status from problem child to invaluable strategic ally. Israel was now unquestionably the most powerful country in the region. America had attempted to court the Arab world for two decades, and with what result? Egypt and Syria were more firmly aligned than ever with the Soviet Union. The Arab world was becoming radicalized, led by an insurgent Palestine Liberation Organization, which looked centrist when compared to the more radical wings of Palestinian politics. After 1973 the belief that the United States had to choose between Israel and the Arab world became questioned. Not only did America's alliance with Israel not negatively affect its relationship with the oil-exporting states, but also after 1973 Egyptian President Anwar Sadat jumped from the Soviet to the American ship. These changing geostrategic factors meant that it became easier for American policy makers to tout how their friendship was based on their Judeo-Christian heritage and commitment to democracy, human rights, and liberal values.[66] In other words, these sentiments had always existed, but only after 1967 did the heart and the head align. All this was good news for American Jews, who now could more convincingly and emphatically claim that it was in America's national interest to safeguard Israeli security. Moreover, unlike when AIPAC first began lobbying, American Jews no longer worried about accusations of dual loyalty—the United States and Israel were now on the same team.[67]

In addition to mobilizing for Israel, American Jews started a movement for Soviet Jewry. The Soviet persecution of the Jews began long before there was a Soviet Union. Under the czars, Jews faced constant hardship, occasional violence, restrictions on where they could live, and limited interactions with the non-Jewish world. A renewed round of violence erupted in the early twentieth century, and World War I created new opportunities to target Jewish populations. Life improved somewhat for Jews after the 1917 revolution—or, at least, the government no longer actively stoked anti-Semitism, and Jews could count themselves no worse off than any other minority. In the early 1950s life became much more unnerving, climaxing in 1952 when the Kremlin accused these "rootless cosmopolitans" of a "doctor's plot" on Stalin's life. Things got slightly easier after Stalin's death in 1953, but the two million Soviet Jews faced constant hardship, especially those who wanted to practice their faith. Implementing a zero-tolerance policy, the Soviets began closing down synagogues, publishing anti-Semitic tracts, and running political cartoons that portrayed Israel as Nazi Germany.

As soon as American Jews started mobilizing to protect their brethren abroad, the Russian Jews came to their attention. The 1881 assassination of Alexander I triggered an outburst of anti-Semitic violence, and various prominent American Jewish leaders petitioned Washington to pressure Russia to end it. Two decades later a series of pogroms led to renewed protection efforts, including the formation of the American Jewish Committee in 1907. Over the next several years it continued to monitor closely the situation in Russia, and in 1913 the AJC led a remarkable campaign to abrogate a several-decades-old commercial treaty between Russia and the United States on the grounds that it discriminated against American Jews. During and after the war, American Jews sent millions of dollars in emergency relief to Russian and Eastern European Jews. For the next fifty years, though, the condition of Russian Jews fell out of view, in part because of other, more pressing issues, such as the extermination of the European Jews and then the creation and protection of Israel.

Beginning in the early 1960s, American Jews slowly began to turn their attention to Soviet Jews. Motivated in part by the inaction of American Jews during the Holocaust, Lou Rosenblum and Herb Caron established the first committee to mobilize on behalf of Soviet Jews.[68] The cause of Soviet Jewry got a burst of publicity when Supreme Court justice Arthur Goldberg and senators Abraham Ribicoff and Jacob Javitz, the Senate's two lone Jewish members, announced their involvement. Yet the cause remained peripheral to the American Jewish community. In late November 1963 Goldberg and Ribicoff approached the Conference of Major American Jewish Organizations with the idea of raising the visibility of the issue by holding a conference, but it declined for various reasons, including the desire to stick with quiet diplomacy for a cause that still barely registered on its radar screen.[69] In 1965 a relatively unknown Holocaust survivor, Elie Wiesel, published *Night*, a memoir that would transform him into a spokesperson for Holocaust survivors and humanity. That same year Wiesel traveled to the Soviet Union and subsequently wrote a book, *The Jews of Silence*. His account not only lifted the curtain on the hardships Jews endured—it pointed an accusatory finger at American Jews for, once again, staying silent as millions suffered.[70] Although the historical analogy between the Holocaust and Soviet Jewry was hardly perfect—in the Holocaust, at stake was the physical survival of the Jews, and in the Soviet Union it was their cultural survival—they shared the common factor of an American Jewry that was passive in the face of persecution.

After 1967 the condition of Soviet Jewry began to deteriorate. Like the American Jews, Soviet Jews responded to the news of Israel's victory with considerable pride and began demanding basic religious rights and permission to visit Israel. But unlike the American Jews, who could exhibit their emotions in a liberal democracy and a country that was an ally of Israel, Soviet Jews were registering their feelings in a closed society that backed the Arabs. In response to growing activism at home, the Soviets unleashed a new round of repression, including harassing, arresting, and imprisoning Soviet Jewish leaders. Not only was it difficult to leave, but also the very process of applying for an exit visa invited harassment from Soviet authorities; these "traitors" did not deserve to have a job or have their children in elite schools, and they could expect unexpected visits by the Soviet authorities and perhaps even a spell in a Soviet prison. In August 1972 the Soviets announced a "diploma tax," requiring all Soviet Jews wanting to emigrate to first repay the cost of their education; given the fees charged, one would have thought the Soviet Jews had gone to very expensive private schools.

The cause of Soviet Jewry became something of a coming-out party for an American Jewry that was more self-confident, assertive, and prepared to defend its interests.[71] Under the slogan "let them be free or let them go," American Jews began building a movement at home and around the world to force the Soviet Union to allow its Jews to emigrate. Toward that end, American Jews began to organize mass rallies, lobby Congress and the White House to demand that the Soviet authorities provide the names of imprisoned Soviet Jews, hold vigils outside the Soviet embassy in Washington, picket Soviet cultural events, and smuggle Bibles and other Jewish religious objects to underground synagogues in the Soviet Union.

American Jews were fighting for the religious and movement rights of Soviet Jews, but were they also fighting for broader human rights principles? Some accounts make the case that the campaign to free Soviet Jewry should be placed in the pantheon of international human rights.[72] The climax of the campaign for Soviet Jewry, the passage of the Jackson-Vanik amendment, immediately preceded the Helsinki Act, which is routinely credited with triggering post–World War II international human rights advocacy. The sequence is not coincidental but causal. American Jews had a history of embedding their concerns for Jewish security and safety within a broader discourse of rights. At the time, some American Jewish leaders noted how movement was a human right, established in the Universal Declaration of Human Rights and reiterated in many other human rights documents.

My view is that the campaign for Soviet Jewry is best understood as an outgrowth of the new tribalism and not as part of a longer history of cosmopolitanism. The focus was on the Soviet Jews. There was little attention among American Jews to the desire by other Soviet ethnic and minority groups to emigrate, by other religious communities to practice their faith, and by other rights-oriented activists to create a more open society. According to Elliott Abrams, who has an intimate knowledge of this history, aligns himself with human rights, and advocates for a strong Israel, "The Jewish argument wasn't about liberalizing Russia; it was about the right to immigrate. . . . It was limited to Jews, and wasn't extended to non-Jews."[73]

Figure 5.2. March to Free Soviet Jewry in Chicago. Undated. Courtesy of The Jacob Rader Marcus Center of the American Jewish Archives, Cincinnati, Ohio. americanjewisharchives.org

The most vivid example of this tribalism was the entry of a new, powerful, and more extreme Jewish voice—Meir Kahane's Jewish Defense League. Rabble-rouser, agitator, and friend of violent resistance, Kahane's fiery rhetoric and tactics did not please the American Jewish establishment, but there was no denying that his "take-no-shit" Jewish nationalism appealed to a younger generation of Jews who were influenced by the protests against the Vietnam War and their parents' presumed passivity during the Holocaust. After one of the first big marches in Washington for Soviet Jewry on March 21, 1971, Kahane's pride that Jews were turning inward filled the pages of his journal entry: "Instead of being arrested for Vietnam, Angola, Chicanos, Blacks, Indians, or Eskimos, for the first time, huge numbers of young Jews were beginning to look at themselves not with self-hate or disinterest but with pride and self-respect. From a period of time when young Jews looked at themselves and asked, 'Who am I?' and answered either: 'I don't know,' or worse, 'I don't care,' . . .

thousands of young Jews [were] marching off to jail after looking at themselves in the mirror and saying 'I am a Jew and I am beautiful. I am a Jew and Jewish is beautiful. I am a Jew and I give a Jewish damn.'"[74]

If American Jews had seen their campaign as part of the broader human rights movement, they might have worked with the United Nations and other international human rights organizations, but they didn't. To some extent, this was not necessarily of their choosing. The United Nations, for all intents and purposes, was a closed door. American Jews had supported the creation of the United Nations and its human rights instruments for precisely these moments, but it was either indifferent or hostile to the Jewish cause. In 1968 Rita Hauser, a prominent attorney associated with the American Jewish Committee, was appointed to the UN Human Rights Commission. She quickly concluded that the only thing the commission had to do with human rights was the name, and that it had no interest in the rights of Jews. She warned, additionally, that the moment this was brought to its attention, the Arab delegates would respond by saying, "occupied territories."[75] On August 6, 1969, eighteen Georgian families wrote a letter to the UN Human Rights Commission to plead for their right to emigrate, perhaps the first time Soviet Jews publicly appealed to an international body.[76] No one answered.

Not only did the Soviet Jewry movement *not* go out of its way to link up with the broader human rights discourse, it also actively attempted to maintain its distance. While the Soviet Jews were lobbying to leave, a small but highly visible dissident community was fighting for reform at home. In other words, the Soviet Jews and the dissidents had very different reactions to Soviet oppression—with the Jews wanting to flee and the dissidents wanting to reform Soviet society. Although they occasionally cooperated, there developed something of a mutual understanding that they were better off on their own than together. By many accounts the Soviet dissidents had little interest in allying with the Soviet Jews, in part because the Soviet Jews showed little interest in them and in part because they did not believe that being associated with a group that wanted to leave rather than fight would strengthen their cause.

The Soviet Jews kept their distance from the dissident movement for various reasons, including the political calculation that no good would come from a closer association.[77] As Zionists they were interested in leaving the country, not making it better. In this regard, they were following the advice to the Zionists of Zvi Jabotinsky, the founder of the Revisionist movement in Israel, the forerunner to the Likud Party: be single-minded and not distracted by broader movements that intend to improve the condition of the world. Indeed, as Soviet Jews looked back into history, they recalled that those Jews who had joined the Bolshevik movement soon found themselves in league with many anti-Semites.[78] Soviet Jews needed to be equally careful. Not all dissidents or critics of the Soviet Union were their friends.

American Jews also showed little interest in tying their campaign to the dissident movement. They were certainly sympathetic to the cause, but their goal was to free the Soviet Jews, not the Soviet people; theirs was an emigration and not a human rights issue. For all intents and purposes, the American Jewry movement might have been prepared to abandon the likes of Andrei Sakharov, the eminent Soviet nuclear physicist who won the Nobel Peace Prize for his work in the Soviet Union, if the Soviets capitulated on freedom for Soviet Jews.[79]

Robert Bernstein's first encounter with human rights advocacy illustrates how the Soviet Jews and the dissidents sat at different tables.[80] A founder of Human Rights Watch, Bernstein's long and storied involvement with the international human rights movement formed in the early 1970s when, as Chairman and President of Random House, he became involved in the campaign for freedom of expression in the Soviet Union. From there he became active in the human rights section of the Helsinki Act.

Although the cause of freedom in the Soviet Union led to his broader involvement in human rights, he remained largely separate from the Soviet Jewry movement, a product of both his own commitments and the nature of the dissident and Soviet Jewry movements. Although he identified as Jewish, he was most attracted to the broader causes of freedom of thought and expression; these freedoms, in his view, were primary. Soviet Jews were fighting for their right to leave, but the Soviet dissidents were fighting for freedom of expression, which was proximate to his own principles. And there was little encouragement to take a greater interest in the Soviet Jewry movement, he insists, because the two movements ran along parallel paths.

Perhaps one reason why the Soviet Jewry movement did not make a more concerted effort to connect to international human rights was because it had something much better than justice on its side—the power of the United States. The ability to look to US power was made possible by several developments. American Jews had access to Congress like never before, in part because there were more Jewish representatives and in part because they were better organized. This is also a moment when the symbol of the "Jew" was shifted from global cosmopolitanism to more traditional power politics. As we saw, after World War II the Jew came to represent the condition of the world; it was impossible to imagine saving the world without also saving the remnants of global Jewry. However, the association between the fate of the Jews and the fate of humanity began to loosen as Israel came into its own. Then, after the 1967 war and the creation of the "special relationship" between Israel and the United States that was forged by the Cold War, Jews became more closely associated with geopolitics than with cosmopolitics. As American Jews began to mobilize on behalf of Soviet Jewry, they could remind their American audience of how Israel was inimical to the US's containment strategy and how Soviet Jews were prisoners in the Soviet Union.

Soviet Jews became entangled in cold war politics and the fight over détente. Neither the Soviet Union nor the Nixon administration was happy about the insertion of Soviet Jews into their relationship. The Kremlin's reasons are obvious. The White House's ire owed to the possibility that this marginal issue might interfere with its policy of détente and high-level negotiations on Vietnam, arms control, and trade. There was a lot at stake, and the Jews were getting in the way. Responding to Nixon's frustration that American Jews were injecting the issue of Soviet Jews where it did not belong, the German Jewish refugee and devotee of realpolitik Henry Kissinger replied: "Let's face it: The emigration of Jews from the Soviet Union is not an objective of American foreign policy. And if they put Jews into gas chambers in the Soviet Union, it is not an American concern. It may be a humanitarian concern."[81]

With a White House hostile to the cause of Soviet Jewry, the action shifted to Capitol Hill, where the issue got a much warmer reception. The forces that wanted to do something for the Soviet Jews now joined with the forces that wanted to halt détente—and they were married in the office of Senator Henry "Scoop" Jackson. A devoted cold warrior, he wanted to derail détente. So, too, did his young aide, Richard Perle, who would later become known as the Vulcan of the neoconservatives. Perle assembled a close-knit group comprised largely of other Jewish aides to prominent senators and representatives and began operating from what he described as a "bunker." Although Perle was primarily motivated by anticommunism, the other Jewish staffers in his group persuaded him to help his fellow Jews in the process of writing a bill.[82] Recalling the motives of those who put together the bill, Morris Amitay, who was born in Israel and became the foreign policy adviser to Senator Ribicoff, said: "There are now a lot of guys at the working level up here who happen to be Jewish, who are willing to make a little bit of extra effort and to look at certain issues in terms of their Jewishness, and this is what has made this thing go very effectively in the last couple of years."[83] In any event, the alliance with Scoop Jackson, in the words of Elliott Abrams, helped to "kosherize" the Soviet Jewry movement, mainstreaming it into traditional politics.[84]

Working with several American Jewish organizations, those gathering in the "bunker" decided to link the diploma tax and other restrictions on Soviet Jewish emigration to any possible "most favored nation" status for the Soviet Union, which would enhance its ability to buy American goods, obtain American credit, and enjoy other economic dividends of détente. When Senator Jackson introduced the bill, he insisted that it was intended to help not just Jews but all Soviet citizens; however, this was not how its architects or supporters saw it, and they rarely used it for anyone but the Soviet Jews. And American Jews, who generally supported détente, threw their weight behind legislation that was designed to kill it. The Jackson-Vanik amendment passed with bipartisan support on October 19, 1974, and President Ford signed it into law on January 3, 1975.

The awarding of the 1974 Nobel Peace Prize to Andrei Sakharov and the beginning of the Helsinki process brought more attention to the dissidents and the broader human rights movement, which in turn led the Soviet Jewry movement to seek a closer association. The Helsinki Final Act, signed in 1975 by the United States, the Soviet Union, and thirty-five other states, was an accidental boost to the human rights movement.[85] In the spirit of détente, the two blocs built three "baskets" of agreements containing security (Basket One), trade (Basket Two), and humanitarian aims (Basket Three). The third and least noticed basket, though, quietly had a far-reaching impact on the Soviet Union. Specifically, Basket Three established a set of basic human rights that all signatories should respect. The realist Henry Kissinger had bothered with an issue he considered marginal to détente because he wanted to show his critics at home that he was not without a heart; however, he intended to let this basket disappear. The Soviets also believed that human rights would be a soon-forgotten part of their agreements.

Although the Soviets and Americans thought that Basket Three would languish and die, the dissidents, the Soviet Jewry movement, and human rights activists used it as a new platform to promote their causes. Representative Millicent Fenwick (R-NJ) wrote legislation to form a Helsinki Commission to follow up on the pledges made in the Helsinki Final Act.[86] In 1976 Jimmy Carter was elected president, and he brought greater vigor and attention to human rights. His relationship with the Soviet Jewry movement, though, was complicated. At the time of his election the movement was largely a cudgel against the Soviets and part of the Cold War. Carter, on the other hand, was sympathetic to Kissinger's policy of détente and had little interest in needlessly provoking the Soviet Union. So here was a cause that had all the trappings of a human rights movement but nevertheless was tightly associated with Cold War politics.[87]

Recognizing an opportunity when they saw it, Soviet and American Jews began to tie their campaign to Helsinki and the broader rights movement.[88] Looking for any sort of tool that might help them leave, three weeks after the signing of Helsinki, Jewish applicants for emigration visas appealed to Helsinki and its language of reuniting families.[89] Then a young refusenik named Natan Sharansky attempted to be a bridge between these two movements. For him, unlike many other Soviet Jewish activists, there was no contradiction between being committed to reform at home and Soviet Jewish emigration. Human rights and Jewish rights coincided.[90] In March 1976 Sharansky, working with another Soviet Jew, Yuri Orlov, proposed that citizens form committees to monitor their government's compliance with the Helsinki Final Act. These committees, in turn, would collect and share information on human rights violations. This was a bold move, one that could easily land them in jail, or worse. Their idea soon became Moscow Helsinki Watch, and the brilliance of the idea was its simplicity. By using this one document to assess the human rights situation in their country, they could solidify and centralize their efforts in ways that resonated with the West.[91] Moscow Helsinki Watch quickly became the focal point for human rights activists in the Soviet Union.[92]

American Jews had been coordinating with Israel in the campaign, all the while assuming that they were fighting for Jewish interests, but soon discovered that they and the Israeli government interpreted them differently. The first wave of Soviet Jews who emigrated had ideological motives and headed to Israel. But in time most of the Zionist-oriented Soviet Jews had left and a growing percentage of emigrants had economic and political motives and preferred the West.[93] Increasingly upset by their choices, Israel wanted to force Soviet Jews to make Israel their first stop. Israel was also prepared to do more than encourage—it wanted to cut aid to Soviet Jews who did not go to Israel. The suggestion, was that the principle of freedom of movement was good only as long as Soviet Jews were in the Soviet Union; the moment they stepped outside its borders, they would find that freedom severely curtailed. For American Jews, this was beyond hypocrisy to the point of heresy. Soviet Jews should be free to choose among those countries that would have them, they insisted. The *noshrim* war (noshrim is Hebrew for drop-outs) was resolved in ways that gave Soviet Jews the freedom to choose.

American Jewry's failure to link the Soviet Jewry movement to human rights was not only because of tribalism or failure of imagination—it also owed to its growing suspicion of human rights. Beginning in the 1960s American Jews and international human rights began going their separate ways, representing a break of near historic proportions. American Jews had been forceful advocates of, and tied their own fates to, the discourse of rights even before rights became a household word. An article of faith among many American Jewish organizations was that Jewish lives could be best protected through the acceptance of human rights and the creation of international organizations such as the League of Nations and the United Nations and its human rights machinery. In his 1963 Dag Hammarskjöld Memorial lecture, the AJC's Jacob Blaustein gave a spirited address on the enduring potential of human rights and proposed the establishment of a United Nations High Commissioner for Human Rights.[94] It is unimaginable that a leader of an American Jewish organization would make a similar appeal a decade later.

Although American Jewish support for human rights had begun eroding prior to 1967, the 1967 war, according to Roberta Cohen, a veteran of the international human rights community, was the moment that the relationship turned chilly.[95] Writing of this period, Louis Henkin, an eminent professor at Columbia University and one of the world's foremost authorities on human rights, observed that whereas Jews once were in the "vanguard of those advocating additional human rights laws of general applicability and stronger measures of enforcement," they had entered into a profound period of disquiet.

> Disappointment in the international human rights program has been strongest perhaps among Jews and Jewish organizations. Some Jewish organizations have cut back their programs; some Jews have abandoned the field. Leaders in the effort to promote human rights, they have felt most keenly the lack of progress and, even more, its political abuses, particularly as a weapon with which to beat the State of Israel and to attack the Jewish non-governmental organizations. In the United States, domestic issues tending to range Jews in competition with less advantaged minorities have spilled over to trouble human rights activities, including international human-rights programs.[96]

The separation was nearly as swift as it was complete.[97] In the view of the distinguished human rights activist Aryeh Neier, "I really see Jewish organizations as having withdrawn from international human rights."[98]

Similar to all accounts of divorce, this is a story of initial infatuation followed by growing bitterness and feelings of betrayal, hard

feelings, and nearly irreconcilable perspectives. The simplest explanation for why American Jews lost interest in human rights is that
it no longer served their interests. Jews had flocked to rights because they had few alternatives. No longer all that weak and beginning to enjoy a period of unprecedented political and economic
power, American Jews were given the traditional tools of influence
of the rich and powerful. Even better, American Jews were exercis-
ing influence in the world's most powerful country. Who needed
rights when they had power? In a 1966 address to the World Jewish
Congress, Nahum Goldmann, the organization's reigning president,
warned that all this success was causing Jews to lose their way.
He observed: "In the past, especially in the nineteenth century, the
Jewish people was in the ideological and active forefront of all the
great progressive movements." Jews had abandoned that tradition, he
observed, because they had focused on "consolidating the homeland" and because of "economic development." A pity, warned Goldmann, because it is "essential that we resume our position among
the seekers of peace, social justice, and equality for all humanity."[99]
American Jews were more secure, had less need for human rights,
and were not going to continue their support because of some mis-
placed sense of loyalty.[100]

Also, Jews were increasingly living in democratic countries. American Jews had tried to build a human rights machinery not for their
survival but rather to protect Jews in illiberal lands, imagining them
as stopgap measures until the day that Jews could enjoy protection
from their own societies. That blessed day had come, though because
of tragic circumstances rather than natural causes. In their search for
security and acceptance in the late nineteenth and early twentieth
centuries, Jews left the East and headed West. Hitler did not live long
enough to see his plan of a Europe emptied of Jews nearly succeed—
because of a combination of mass murder and mass exodus, the Jewish population in Europe plunged. Arab states chased out their Jews—
most went to Israel, and some went to other liberal democracies such
as France. Jews began emptying out of the former Soviet Union the
first chance they got. Israel was not only a haven for Jews, but also
a liberal democracy. In some instances, Jews stayed where they were
and democracy came to them. Regardless of whether it was because

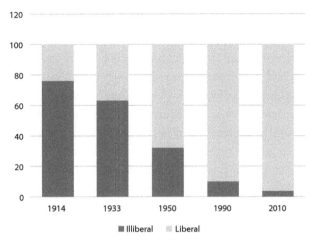

Figure 5.3. Global Distribution of Jews by Illiberal and Liberal Countries

of forced or unforced migration, or because of natural or unnatural causes, Jews were increasingly enjoying the protections afforded by liberal democracy—which is exactly what the AJC had always believed would solve the Jewish Problem. Figure 5.3 illustrates this monumental change. In 1914, 76 percent of all Jews lived in illiberal lands and 24 percent in liberal lands; in 1933 the divide was 63 percent and 37 percent; in 1950 it was 32 percent and 68 percent; in 1990, and as a consequence of the great flight of Jews from the Soviet Union, the distribution was 9.78 percent and 90.12 percent; in 2010 a miniscule 3.5 percent live in authoritarian countries and 96.5 percent live in liberal democracies. Now that Jews were enjoying the equality and security provided by liberal democracy, there was less reason to spend their time and resources on international human rights.

In addition to no longer having the same need for human rights, American Jews could hardly be despondent because human rights had never really been effective. The hard-won minorities treaties had been reduced to kindling for the Nazis. To compound the indignities done in the name of minorities treaties, Nazi Germany had bellowed the language of minority rights as its tanks rolled into its neighboring countries with the pretext of protecting German minorities. The nascent refugee regime provided almost no refuge for European Jews before, during, or after World War II. Human rights, international institutions, and international law were vacuous at best, and misleadingly dangerous at worst. And even though the Universal Declaration of Human Rights and Israel were born the same year, they became quickly separated at birth.

In addition to being ineffective, the international human rights institutions were drifting away from Jewish interests. Beginning in the 1950s decolonization and the democratization of the United Nations reordered the human rights agenda: it lost interest in the rights of minorities in the West as it focused on the more urgent and demanding fight for self-determination and independence of the colonized. Jewish organizations remained a part of human rights discussions, and occasionally they lobbied the United Nations to look into anti-Semitism, but it almost always declined, either because of a lack of interest or the presence of more compelling issues.[101] The Jewish Problem might still be a problem in some parts of the world, but not as great as it once was or in comparison to others.

The declining urgency of the Jewish Problem was the tip of a broader sea change: the relationship of Jews to the cosmopolitanism of suffering. After World War II the Jews, and by extension Israel, symbolized the world's victims, worthy of sympathy and support. Not only were the needs of Jews as great as those of any other people, but their security had become a sign of the international community's health. With the passing decades, however, Jewish circumstances radically improved, and Israel, which was designed to solve a minority problem in Europe, developed its own minority problem with its Arab inhabitants. And then, after 1967, Israel became one of those states that ruled over another people; from a human rights calculus, Israel was to the Palestinians what the colonial powers were to the colonized. American Jewish and Israeli officials increasingly reminded the world of the long history of Jewish suffering and that Israel had not started the 1967 war, but from the perspective of the present, there was no objective reason why the international community should privilege Jewish (and Israeli) suffering.[102]

The difficulty of making the case for the Jews was compounded by the universalization of the Holocaust. The Holocaust remained a Jewish event, but it also belonged to the world. "Never again" no longer meant "never again will the world stand by and allow the Jews to be killed" but rather "never again will the world ignore the genocide of any people." Jews were losing their place in the pecking order of the cosmopolitanism of suffering as they were rising to prominence as a symbol of the Cold War.[103]

Yet the story is more complicated than two old friends growing apart. In their telling of the break-up, many American Jews accuse the very institutions that they helped build to further their own security of becoming a source of their insecurity. In short, American Jews did not abandon international human rights and the United Nations—it turned on them. The United Nations' human rights mechanisms had become politicized, and this politicization transformed the Jews from being among the abused to being among the abusers.[104] To illustrate this point, Roberta Cohen tells a personal story of a job interview at the United Nations in 1974. While working for an international human rights organization, she was approached to work for the United Nations on women's issues. She goes to the job interview, which is supposed to be something of a formality. The only thing the Peruvian-born UN official wants to know about, though, is her Jewish background, her personal feelings about Israel, and whether she has ever engaged in pro-Zionist activities. She didn't get the job.

At the very moment that American Jews were identifying with Israel and expressing their pride through Zionism, the anti-Israel coalition contorted every gathering of the United Nations and other international bodies into an occasion for placing Israel before a kangaroo court.[105] A meeting on women's rights could quickly become sidelined by discussions of Israel's treatment of Palestinian women. A discussion on the rights of children could become focused on the condition of Palestinian youth in the occupied territories. In early efforts to delegitimize the State of Israel, the Arab states organized to suspend Israel's membership in, or expel it from, the United Nations. Many of those who were genuinely dedicated to human rights were unhappy to see the cause of the Palestinians drown out discussion of everything else, but from the American Jewish perspective what mattered was not what some in the international human rights community wanted but rather how human rights was being used as a weapon against Israel and the Jews.[106] And while American Jews had demonstrated decades before that it was possible to be anti-Zionist without also being anti-Semitic, the line between the two could be blurry on both the giving and the receiving ends.

There are several well-known reasons why the United Nations and swaths of the international community treated Israel as the "usual suspect." Zionism ceased to be defined as a national liberation movement of the Jews, and Israel was no longer an expression of the Jewish people's right of self-determination. Instead, Zionism and Israel became the oppressor. Given the climate of the times, any country ruling over another people would feel considerable heat. But the fact that Israel was ruling over the Palestinians, whose fate was of keen interest to the Arab world and the increasingly powerful Arab oil-exporting states, meant that Israel would get special attention. Little matter that the world was stuffed with violators of human rights, and some of the most egregious of them were leveling accusations at Israel from the perch of the UN human rights bodies.[107] To observe that a chunk of the human rights movement had an Israel problem is not to say that Israel did not have a human rights problem. Both can be true, a possibility often lost in the polemics.

The climactic point of no return for American Jewry's attitude toward the United Nations arrived on November 10, 1975, when the General Assembly passed the infamous "Zionism is Racism" resolution.[108] In many ways it would be unfair to see this resolution as part of the history of international human rights. But in many ways it was: the resolution was passed at a time when the world community in general, and the human rights movement in particular, was focused on group rights and national self-determination, and Zionism was explicitly labeled as a violator of human rights. Israel's very right to exist seemed up for debate. The national movement of the Jewish people was being singled out and accused of something that is true of nearly all nationalist movements—discrimination in one form or another against those who are not defined as part of the nation. And it was not clear how Zionism was racist, except for the fact that racism was a particularly inflammatory charge at a moment when the world was trying to dismantle apartheid in South Africa. The United Nations, and the "international community" by association, became seen by Jews around the world as not only irrationally anti-Israel but also (faintly) anti-Semitic. In an act that made him

Figure 5.4. UN, Human Rights, and Israel. © 2001 Kevin Siers (Best and Wittiest) North America Syndicate, Inc.

a hero to the Jewish community, Daniel Patrick Moynihan, the US ambassador to the United Nations, famously warned before the vote that, "(t)he United Nations is about to make anti-Semitism international law." Although the resolution did not have the same impact on the American Jewish community as the 1967 war, its effects should not be underestimated. There was fair and unfair criticism of Israel, and there was no debating where this resolution stood. When the United Nations rescinded the resolution in 1991, it was too little, too late for many American Jews.[109] American Jews had once looked to the international community to help with the Jewish Problem, and now the international community was on record as seeing Israel, and by extension the Jews, as the problem.

The tightening link between human rights and anti-Zionism meant that American Jewish organizations that had a human rights orientation would have to placate two, increasingly antagonistic, constituencies. The AJC was the proverbial canary.[110] Its founding mission was to protect Jews in the diaspora. In its first decades of existence, it opposed Zionism on the grounds that it would potentially threaten the safety of Jewish communities around the world; Jews needed to place their hopes in the civilizing forces of internationalism and rights.[111] Eventually it reconciled itself to Zionism and then Israel, but during the first few decades of Israel's existence the AJC focused on building human rights at home and abroad and left Israel to other Jewish organizations.

After 1967, though, the AJC was forced to juggle its commitments to Israel and human rights. As an occupying power, Israel was receiving more attention from the human rights community. Although it agreed with the standard exclamation by American Jewish organizations that much of this criticism was politically motivated, and, at times, anti-Semitic, it did not reflexively dismiss the accusations. Whether the charges were fair or unfair, the charges against Israel were hurting the AJC's ability to protect Jews in other parts of the world. There was the possibility that Israel's behavior might be both cause and pretext for more acts of anti-Semitism, but much more tangible and immediately felt was the ability of the AJC to work with others in the human rights community to protect Jewish communities. Many human rights organizations were increasingly reluctant to partner with an organization that seemed to be an apologist for an Israel that was on the world's watch list and that had close commercial, military, and political ties to a racist South Africa. Improving Israel's human rights record would be beneficial to Jews around the world, and Israel, too.[112]

Believing it had no choice but to try and improve Israel's human rights record, but also not wanting to be too visibly or heavily involved, the AJC decided that the best route was to help develop a human rights community in Israel that could independently investigate, discuss and defend, and improve Israel's human rights record. Israel, in short, needed to become more like other Western countries. Toward that end, the AJC helped create Israel's first human rights organization of any substance, the Association for Civil Rights in Israel (ACRI). In general, the AJC saw itself as helping to anchor Israel in the West, playing both role model and sponsor.

If American Jews no longer relied on the language of rights, it was partly because they now enjoyed something much more effective: power.[113] They had become an important political and economic group, freely moving about the corridors of the world's most powerful country.

If American Jews wanted to protect Israel and Jewish communities around the world, why use principles when interests were much more effective? American policy-makers were treating Israel as a best friend and strategic linchpin, which made it a lot easier for American Jews to say, without hesitation, that what was good for Israel was good for the United States. American Jews argued that the defense of Israel and Jewish communities was part of the panoply of American values, but even better, they were able to more persuasively argue that it was consistent with American interests. If what was good for the United States was also good for Israel, then American Jews no longer had to worry about charges of dual loyalty. American Jews were sounding a lot like the nineteenth-century French Jewish community, which also tied the language of French national interests to Jewish interests.

The shift from enlightened to narrow self-interest, and from rights to power, had the consequence of creating greater tension between American Jews' traditional liberal values and their feelings about Israel. Liberal values could be linked to the defense of Israel, as Jewish progressives and liberals had effectively demonstrated over the decades. But this connection became increasingly difficult because of changes at home and in Israel. The political left was increasingly hostile to an Israel that it saw as a better representative of conservative than liberal values.[114] Israeli leaders often boasted of a principle of two eyes for an eye, which violated international humanitarian law's principle of proportionality, and their iron-fisted actions sat uneasily alongside the more peace-oriented policies associated with the American Jewish left. American Jews defended Israel and the rights of Jews to enjoy self-determination, but it was difficult to ignore how Israel's right came at the expense of the rights of Palestinians.[115]

These changes encouraged American Jews to begin circulating with a different political crowd. After spending most of their lives ensconced in liberal and Democratic Party circles, American Jews were increasingly associating with middle-of-the-road and right-of-center groups and even part of the Christian Right. Some of this owed to the economic ascendance of the Jews; as Jews became wealthier and more established they became more sympathetic to some Republican positions. And American Jewry's growing sense that the world is a dark and menacing place and that civilization can be undone in a heartbeat fit better with the ideologies of the political right than the political left.[116] Yet, unquestionably, this was a union made over Israel. Israel and the goal of survival coaxed American Jews rightward on the political map.[117]

This blend of political conservatism and national interests became a calling card of the neoconservative movement. It is important not to exaggerate the influence of American Jews on its rise, but it also is impossible to ignore. Jews led the movement at the moment of creation, founded by a relatively small group of New York Jewish intellectuals and academics who had tired of Leftist politics. Many of its most famous fellow-travelers were not just progressives but had spent their youths debating the relative virtues of Leninism and Trotskyism. But over the years they had developed doubts about the legitimacy and workability of the Left agenda. Some wear-and-tear had been caused by international events: the so-called socialist revolutions in the Soviet Union and China were associated with unbelievable suffering and the denial of basic human freedoms; there were growing challenges to fundamental democratic values around the world; and the political Left was spewing anti-Israel rhetoric. They also had become disgruntled by the growth of the welfare state, which they believed had been the accidental cause, and not remedy for the decay of the cities, a permanent class of poor, and a growing culture of dependency and complacency in American society. They also wanted an activist foreign policy, including the promotion of human rights, democracy, and American values—liberal internationalism on steroids.[118]

They could have just been plain old conservatives, but the "neo" was necessary for several reasons.[119] Traditional conservatives, now called paleoconservatives, were not exactly trusting of the neoconservatives who looked different, sounded different, and had very different backgrounds. They were not just Jews, but New York Jews, which distinguished them from the William Buckleys, the members of the Mayflower Club, and the Daughters of the American Revolution. They had none of the paleos' reverence for the past; the past had not been very good to the Jews or other minorities, and they had no interest in turning back the clock. They also had spent their formative years in left-wing politics. Although conservatives were always happy to see liberals confess their sins and see the light, that did not mean they were unreservedly trusted. Finally, the paleoconservatives had doubts that it was in the US national interest to support Israel. Leading conservative voices, such as Pat Buchanan, trafficked in rumors that the Jews had captured US foreign policy and that American Jews took their marching orders from Israel.[120] The neos and the paleos were not soul mates.

After several years of preaching to American Jews that their interests were better represented by conservatives than by liberals, *Commentary* magazine, which had become a platform for neoconservative thought, surveyed fifty-two leading American Jewish thinkers, doers, scholars, and theologians on the relationship between Jews and liberalism. Citing a string of recent events that supposedly signaled the hostility of liberalism to Israel and the Jews (though most references were to Israel rather than to American Jews per se), in late 1979 the editors asked if the marriage between liberalism and Jews was nearing the end, and whether the Republican Party would have a feast in the November 1980 elections. The responses revealed more than that Jews know a leading question when they read one—they also intimated that American Jews had not changed all that much. American Jews were still searching for a way to maintain their group survival without becoming overly particularistic, and while they had their doubts that either party adequately represented their orientations, the Democratic Party seemed to be a better match. American Jews remained concerned about Jewish survival and Israel's security, but they had plenty of other global concerns.[121] It would take a lot more to dislodge Jews from liberalism and Prophetic Judaism.

For the next decade, whenever a Jewish figure opined that it was time for Jews to mature with the times, there was an Arthur Hertzberg, a former president of the American Jewish Congress, to remind them that to drift right meant to abandon their Jewish soul and their commitment to justice, democracy, and fundamental rights.[122] Jews consistently defied the experts who predicted that Jews would eventually become just like other voters who voted in line with their economic interests and not to advance the cause of justice.[123] Milton Himmelfarb is credited with delivering the most memorable line on this "problem": "Jews earn like Episcopalians, and vote like Puerto Ricans."

CHAPTER SIX

BACK TO THE FUTURE?

READING AMERICAN JEWISH HISTORY THROUGH THE LENS OF NA-
tionalism and cosmopolitanism suggests a narrative in which, from
the nineteenth century until the late twentieth century, the former
steadily but decisively came to dominate the instincts and interests of
American Jews. At the beginning of the twentieth century, American
Jews viewed Jewish nationalism as a possible threat to the values of
inclusion that they believed were essential to their security and welfare in America. After World War I American Jews began to accept the
possibility that they could be Americans and Zionists, too, but only if
it was a Zionism that looked like the civic nationalism they enjoyed at
home. An implication of their desire to have a Jewish nationalism that
was consistent with their own place in American society was that they
were not too eager to see an exclusive Jewish state; after all, there was
a large Arab population that had to be accommodated. The shock of the
Holocaust and the urgency of the moment led American Jews to worry
a lot less about what happened to the non-Jewish inhabitants. For
the next two decades, American Jews supported Israel and praised its
democratic values, but exhibited remarkably little interest. After 1967,
though, Israel became central to their identity, expressed through
words, deeds, and dollars. They were proud of Israel and Israel made
them proud. American Jews seemed to be much less ambivalent about
Jewish nationalism. And all this love for Israel seemed to be coming
at the expense of cosmopolitan sentiments among American Jews.

Beginning in the 1980s, though, the relationship between nationalism
and cosmopolitanism seemed to be entering into a more complicated

chapter, driven in part by growing doubts about Israeli policies.[1] The 1982 Israeli invasion of Lebanon, Israel's first "war of choice," led to unprecedented dissent in Israel and unease among American Jews. Israeli soldiers were openly protesting their government's military decisions. The nightly news featured horrific scenes of Israel's army pummeling Beirut. Maronite forces, aided and abetted by Israel, massacred somewhere between eight hundred and three thousand Palestinians at the refugee camps of Sabra and Shatila. Then in 1987 the first intifada erupted, shredding the convenient myth among American Jews that Israel ran a benign occupation; it was hard to see the occupation the same way after watching footage of Israeli soldiers breaking the bones of rock-throwing Palestinian youth. The beginning of the Oslo peace process in 1993 offered a glimmer of hope, but the subsequent years of failed negotiations and cycles of conflict transformed the "peace process" from tragedy into farce. Although Jews remained highly supportive of Israel, they were less so of its policies, most notably its occupation of the territories and expansion of the settlements. Each violent encounter, whether minor or major, brief or extended, seemed to increase the ambivalence toward Israel.[2]

Alongside this reconsideration of their relationship to Israel, American Jews began to demonstrate renewed enthusiasm for universalism. This latest turn to cosmopolitanism had many familiar elements. There were explicit references to the prophetic tradition. There were statements regarding how the Jewish identity is best expressed and understood in and through humanity. Jews would help "repair the world." There were suggestions that at stake was not only identity but also interest, and that by repairing the world American Jews also would be strengthening the security of Jews, both at home and abroad. The rise of tikkun olam and resurgence of cosmopolitanism did not have to come at the expense of Israel or particularistic sentiments. Nationalism and cosmopolitanism are not necessarily hostile to each other. As the history of American Jewry (and postwar international relations) clearly demonstrates, the two have a much more complex, and, at times, compatible relationship. That said, the more Israel became perceived by American Jews to have an ethnic nationalist and tribal character, the more difficult it would be for them to accommodate their attachment to Israel with their cosmopolitanism.

This chapter tells the story of the resurgence of cosmopolitanism among American Jews beginning in the late twentieth century. There are two important dimensions to this story. The first is the growing ambivalence of American Jews toward Israel. Whether or not American Jews are becoming increasingly "distant" from Israel is a major source of debate, and while the evidence is not clear cut one way or the other, my view is that it is happening. One reason why the evidence does not point firmly in one direction is that American Jewish attitudes are much more complicated than "for" or "against" Israel. As I have stressed, they are defined by ambivalence, which cannot be necessarily reflected in standard surveys and polls. Alongside this question of whether growing ambivalence is occurring, there is the matter of why. There are lots of reasons, many of them home-grown, but Israel also plays a part. Does this rising ambivalence have anything to do with the rise of tikkun olam? Once again the evidence is not clear cut. The growing popularity of tikkun olam could be read as nothing more than a natural countermovement to the previous period's pronounced tribalism; American Jews have always swung between tribalism and cosmopolitanism, and whenever they have moved too far in one direction in one period, they tend to reverse course in the next. Yet there are several ways in which their growing ambivalence with Israel might have encouraged them to reunite with cosmopolitanism, especially if Israel is seen as an expression of particularism that runs against the grain of their universalism. Whereas the cosmopolitanism of much of the world is laden with the discourse of human rights, American Jews remained averse to it and had to find an alternative formulation. It is in this context that the language of "justice" and "humanitarianism" became much more pronounced among American Jews; it was not only more in keeping with Jewish ethics but also had none of the baggage of human rights.

Figure 6.1. National Solidarity Rally for Israel in Washington, D.C. on April 15, 2002.
(AP Photo/J. Scott Applewhite)

AMBIVALENT NATIONALISTS

At first it was just a rumor circulating in the early 1980s: American Jews were losing their love for Israel.[3] By the turn of the century, this rumor had become accepted wisdom. I have talked to experts and lay people, scholars and theologians, believers and nonbelievers, Orthodox and non-Orthodox, American and Israeli officials, doves and hawks, Democrats and Republicans, students and senior citizens—and the widespread assumption is that relations between American Jews and Israel have become more distant and complicated. They refer not only to their friends and families as examples, but also themselves. They talk about not only what they think they know but also what they feel. But do their personal feelings and experiences support their conclusions? I have pored over the data, and in my judgment the evidence does not firmly support their confidence. I want to be clear. It does not necessarily challenge their observations. It is just that the data we would like to have is not available. Still, there are reasons, as I suggest below, why I think it can be cautiously sustained.

Much of the debate about distancing is waged through survey data.[4] If you want to know how American Jews feel about Israel, ask them. But it is not so easy. What you learn from surveys depends on their specifics. When is it taken? It matters whether the survey is conducted during peacetime or wartime. What do you ask? It matters whether questions are asked about verbal support for Israel or tangible support such as writing their elected officials, giving money, or marching in a demonstration. Whom do you ask? It matters whether the person polled belongs to a synagogue or identifies as a "cultural" Jew. What is the order of the questions? Asking respondents straight out if they support Israel will elicit different responses than if the question is asked after a series of questions that possibly trigger negative feelings about Israeli policies, such as settlement expansion.

Furthermore, most surveys provide a snapshot, but it is when a series of snapshots are arranged in a sequence that it becomes possible to tell a story. What story we tell depends on when the first picture is taken. In part because these surveys were not asked on a systematic basis until after 1967, most stories about distancing begin after 1967, at a moment widely assumed to be the high-water mark of American Jewry's support for Israel. Consequently, it is almost impossible to tell any story other than distancing because there was no other place to go but down. Conversely, if the first pictures had been taken in 1950 and not 1970, the conclusion might be that Jews are just as attached as ever, and the post-1967 spike was just a moment in time. We can alter the moral of the story depending on when we begin the telling.

Perhaps we should care less about what American Jews say and more about what they do. Money can be a proxy for attachment. From 1950 to 1967, American Jews gave generously to lots of causes—but not to Israel. After 1967, however, American Jews began giving in record amounts, a clear reflection of their greater affections and concerns, and the amount of giving doubled between 1994 and 2007, from around $1 billion to $2 billion.[5] Although this rise might be interpreted as growing attachment, the authors of an authoritative report note that it probably reflects that these fund-raising organizations are better at what they do.[6] Moreover, a large and increasing chunk of these funds are directed at religious education and the settlements, suggesting that those in the Jewish diaspora are acting in ways comparable to those in other diasporas, where more conservative and nationalist forces are more easily mobilized.

Perhaps as significant as a change in the amount of giving is the source of the giving.[7] The American Jewish philanthropic sector's relationship with Israel has undergone considerable shift over the last several decades, and it is unclear what it all means in terms of attachment to Israel. A generation ago Jewish children would bring their spare change to Sunday school to plant trees, help resettle refugees, and feed the hungry in Israel. Today they still bring their change, but it goes to causes other than Israel. Much of this money, moreover, was channeled through large Jewish organizations such as the United Jewish Appeal (UJA), which accounted for 80 percent of all giving from 1948 through the early 1970s. By 2007, though, 90 percent of the nearly $2 billion given by American Jews went outside the UJA and through dozens of new entities.[8] A large chunk of this support, moreover, is coming from a few very large donors. The Ronald Lauders. The Sheldon Adelsons.[9] In this way, the current profile of American Jewish philanthropy looks more like the distribution of giving at the turn of last century, when a few wealthy benefactors like the Rothschilds and the Warburgs accounted for most. And if we were to come to the same conclusions as before, we would surmise that Zionism's support was narrow and not wide. Yet alongside some degree of concentration in giving, there are more American Jewish organizations than ever before. To some extent, this proliferation represents the fragmentation of views among American Jews, yet it also reflects the development of the third sector in Israel, making it easier for American Jews to target their assistance.

American Jews also show their feelings through political action. In the "mobilization" model, evidence of American Jewish support for Israel is reflected in how American Jews vote, the issues that get their attention, and how quickly and passionately they rally for Israel.[10] If judged on these terms, then there is probably a growing divide between what American Jews say they feel and what they are politically prepared to do. Jews are not single-issue voters, at least not if the issue is Israel, and according to some surveys, Israel has slid down their list of concerns.[11] Anecdotal evidence is that American Jews, young and old, do not turn out in the ways they once did for rallies, and that pro-Israel organizations have to spend more energy and resources for the same result. I have spoken to people with Hillel, the Jewish student organization on American college campuses, who tell me that programs about Israel no longer grab the attention of Jewish students the way they once did; consequently, they have shifted their events, not because Hillel staffers have necessarily changed but rather because American Jewish youth have changed, and Hillel wants to give them what they want in order to keep them coming through the doors. Some of this inattention owes to alienation, but there also is evidence of indifference.

One reason it is difficult to get a fix on the attachment of American Jews to Israel is that the instruments used treat the attitudes, feelings, and emotions as if they reside on a sliding scale, with apathy or antipathy on one end and adulation on the other. Yet ambivalence cuts across these dimensions. Our measures are straightforward but our emotions are messy, and the emotions of American Jews toward Israel, historically speaking, have always been and continue to be complicated. As Paul Wilkes put it, "Israel, to Jews around the world, is both holy object and graven image. It is a loving father and an incorrigible brother; a beam of religious integrity and the harsh light of hate and retribution; a precursor of universal Judaic observance and a bellwether of blatant secularity; a holy land of milk, honey, and bloodshed."[12]

Small group discussions pick up more of this complexity. One researcher conducted a series of focus groups in which Jewish youths were asked to talk about the sources of their Jewish identity. Israel hardly came up—until they were directly asked to talk about it. He concluded that, at least for these participants, Israel does not inform their core Jewish identity.[13] When I listen to small groups of American Jews talk about their feelings about Israel, a rich, textured, and paradoxical conversation comes pouring out. In Fall 2013 I attended a workshop at Washington, DC's "Sixth and I" synagogue on how American Jews might handle their dysfunctional feelings about Israel. Attended primarily by former participants of Birthright, a program that brings young adult diaspora Jews to Israel for the first time, there was a subtlety and nuance not easily captured by surveys. As one person who had visited Israel on several occasions memorably put it, "I cannot wait to go to Israel, and then I cannot wait to leave." Although some public opinion polls indicate that the 2014 Israeli invasion of Gaza had either no impact whatsoever or perhaps even increased American Jewish support for Israel, the conveners of a series of meetings around the United States found just the opposite in their wide-ranging and open-ended discussions.[14]

Assuming American Jews are feeling more ambivalent toward, and less dependent on, Israel for their Jewish identity, then why? History instructs us to look first at the home front. America has changed in ways that have coaxed American Jews from their rendezvous with tribalism to return to a more familiar position of cosmopolitanism. To begin, anti-Semitism has virtually disappeared in the United States. The number of anti-Semitic incidents has declined, historically speaking, and American Jews have noticed. According to the Anti-Defamation League, an organization unlikely to soften the numbers, in 2013 "the total number of anti-Semitic incidents in the United States fell by 19 percent . . . continuing a decade-long downward slide and marking one of the lowest levels of incidents reported by the Anti-Defamation League since it started keeping records in 1979."[15] In a poll of American Jews in 2006, those under forty were half as likely as Jews over forty to see anti-Semitism as a "serious problem."[16] Arguably, it is far easier to be Jewish than to be a member of any other minority in American society. American Jews have broken virtually every glass ceiling imaginable. They are visible in arts and letters, entertainment, journalism, education, politics, high-earning professions, and finance. If American Jews are less tribal, a reasonable explanation is that they feel safer and more accepted. Heine's law returns.

Attachment to Israel is also associated with a strong Jewish identity, and its fraying or changing character is having an impact. Intermarriage is on the rise, and while many non-Jewish spouses convert, the love for Judaism does not necessarily translate into a love for Israel. Formal Jewish organizations are weakening, no longer playing the role they once did in American Jewish life. Sixty years ago Jewish institutions had a decisive influence on where Jews lived, whom they socialized with, which clubs they belonged to, where they played basketball, and where they volunteered. No more. And because the synagogue, the Jewish Community Center, Sisterhood, and Hadassah invariably delivered a clear pro-Israel message, their declining centrality means that American Jews no longer receive a party line. Furthermore, and similar to the pattern in American society, the American Jewish identity has become more fluid and personal.[17] No longer bottled up by a single identity or content to live their lives in a pluralistic bubble, Jews are comfortable splicing, merging, and importing other traditions into Judaism and experimenting with multiple and hybrid identities, a pattern observed among all Americans.[18] American Jews appear to be moving in a more religious and spiritual direction, trends that might be affected by the view that "Israel has been judged and found wanting."[19] In short, this generation is less likely than the previous one to find meaning through Israel and the Holocaust.

Although these developments are leading to a change in the American Jewish identity and weakening identification with Israel, they might be temporary or reversed. One possibility rests with the increasing percentage of American Jews who identify as Orthodox. Orthodox Jews do not fit this pattern because they practice a traditional form of Judaism, live in Jewish enclaves and within walking distance to synagogues, are more likely to work and socialize with other Jews, and do not intermarry at the same rates. If Orthodox Jews become a larger percentage of the American Jewish population, which some studies predict, then it might cancel out the changes happening in the non-Orthodox community. At the very least, we are likely to see two worlds of American Jewry, with Orthodox Jews showing greater identification than non-Orthodox Jews. Yet the Orthodox community is not a homogeneous group. There are strands of Orthodox Judaism that treat Israel as a sacrilege. Modern Orthodox Jews are less tribal than other branches, and there is a small but identifiable movement to encourage religious Jews to leave their cocoons and engage with the world.[20]

Another possibility is that these patterns of fragmentation might be truer of the younger generation, and as the younger generation ages it might resemble the older generation of today. This is known as the "life-cycle" argument. In other words, just wait—the wild-eyed, rebellious, innocent youth of today will develop diabetes, middle-aged spread, a greater sense of kinship, and a fear of anti-Semitism. Much of the evidence for the life-cycle argument hinges on survey data, which can be interpreted in several ways. Some read the surveys and find signs that the young eventually turn into their parents and grandparents. Others disagree and interpret the data as showing that each generation is becoming less attached than the previous one. This downward trend is even more pronounced among the growing percentage of Jews who identify as cultural or ethnic.[21]

The unstated assumption of the life-cycle hypothesis is that as we age our political attitudes and behavior change in highly predictable ways—we become more conservative, clannish, and concerned with our immediate (and primordial) community. But such deterministic projections overlook that while political attitudes often change over a lifetime, they change within a historical context. Consequently, even if individuals become more conservative and insular over time, this does not necessarily mean this generation of American Jews will express such changes by clinging to Israel. After all, earlier generations of Jews grew old without becoming Zionists. There might be something particular about the generation of Jews that came of age in the historical circumstances after 1967 that made them more likely to become attached to Israel. Specifically, it mattered that this generation was living in the immediate shadows of the Holocaust and watched helplessly as Israel was in mortal danger from unsheathed aggression and the world, once again, looked away. However, today's millennials have been raised in an America that has been as welcoming to Jews as any generation in American history, were born a half century after the Holocaust, are more likely to see Israel as a Goliath than as a David surrounded by Goliaths, and have found other avenues to express their Jewish identity.[22] Under such conditions, how likely is it that this generation will become their grandparents? Might they not respond, for instance, to rising anti-Semitism in Europe by attempting to convince European Jews to resettle in America rather than Israel, just as Amercian Jews did in the decades before the Holocaust?

Much depends on how the current and future generations of American Jews respond to Israeli policies and judge Israel's character. American Jewry has had complicated feelings toward Jewish nationalism. They expected Zionism and Israel to answer the Jewish Question and the Jewish Problem in ways that were consistent with their own and reflect favorably on them. They expected Jewish sovereignty to deliver more than survival. Israel's character mattered. They wanted an Israel that was liberal and democratic and fulfilled a prophetic role. Conversely, American Jews have been wary of Jewish nationalism and Zionism to the extent that they were perceived to be inconsistent with their own American-inspired values. When the first generation of American Zionists made the case for a Jewish homeland (or state) in Palestine, they stressed that it would help solve the Jewish Problem in a way that was consistent with their cosmopolitan approach to the Jewish Question.

The core issue, then and now, is: What kind of state is Israel? Is it a Jewish state or is it a state for the Jews? Is it a place where the majority of the population happens to be Jewish or a state that is constituted by the Jewish identity? If it is a Jewish state, it will have an ethnonational and religious character infused by Judaism, but how much? Will it privilege Jewish citizens, and will its purpose be to give expression to one people—the Jews?[23] Non-Jews are certainly allowed to live in Israel, have rights, and hold Israeli citizenship, but none of these allowances mean they will be truly equal in law, politics, or culture. If, on the other hand, Israel is a state for the Jews, then Jews and non-Jews can expect to have equal rights, responsibilities, and duties. In this spirit, all Israeli leaders have insisted, in the tradition of liberalism, that all citizens have the same legal, political, and human rights, and, in the tradition of democracy, all are enfranchised and able to participate in free and fair elections. Yet historically, Israel has preferred not to choose between the two but rather to tiptoe along the tensions. As Shafir and Peled observe, "For some time, Israel's main political and moral dilemma has been described as the need to choose between the two cardinal principles of its political culture: the particularistic commitment to being a Jewish State and the universalist commitment to being a Western-style democracy."[24] Whether

Israel is one or the other, should be one or the other, or is in danger of becoming too much of one or the other is an enduring source of controversy among Israelis.

What concerns me is not what Israelis think or even whether Israel qualifies, according to some metric, as a liberal democracy.[25] Instead, it is whether American Jews perceive Israel to be a liberal democracy and care whether it is. In other words, the fundamental question is: do American Jews think that Israel shares their basic values, and if not, does it affect their attachment? The evidence is that American Jews do care about Israel's values, want them to resemble their own, and are disturbed by the differences. One survey found that the most frequently cited reason for their alienation from Israel was "the political aspect of the State of Israel," the runner-up was "religious coercion," and garnering an honorable mention was the feeling of Jewish peoplehood that "opposed the global/modern spirit."[26] Relatedly, the younger generation of American Jewish leaders is much more inclined toward universalism, not particularism, and inclusivity, not exclusivity—and less disposed toward a politics of protection.[27] This shift translates into a "more nuanced and complicated relationship . . . with Israel."[28] Israel no longer automatically commands the sympathies and loyalties of American Jews, and they are less able or willing to separate their liberal orientation from their support for Israel. In contrast to their parents who lived more easily with a double standard, finding reasons to excuse behavior by Israel that they would never extend to another country, these younger American Jews are less likely to do so.[29] To the extent that American Jews want Israel to share their fundamental values and believe that it does not, the more difficult it will be to integrate Israel into their Jewish identity.[30]

Three aspects—religion, the rule of law, and democracy—are at the heart of this debate. Secularism, the rules governing whether and how religion should be involved in public life, operates differently in the United States and Israel—and most American Jews have a clear preference for the version of secularism in the United States to that in Israel. Secularism in the United States translates into various foundational arrangements such as precluding the state from favoring one religion over another, honoring the principle of religious liberty, and creating the conditions for religious pluralism. As a religious minority, American Jews are most comfortable where religion is private and the state is precluded from allowing public spaces to become public displays of religion and from favoring one religion over another. Consequently, American Jews have been opposed to various reforms that might alter the status quo, including school prayer and government funding for religious institutions. If the government gets into the business of "supporting" religion in public life, American Jews fear that a country where Christians are the overwhelming majority will decide that America needs to act like the Christian nation it is.

Israel defines itself as a Jewish state. The relationship between Judaism and the state has been a matter of central dispute since Israel's creation. Israel's founding fathers and mothers were card-carrying socialists who had little affection for religion, but they did not want to start a culture war in Israel when they had other wars to fight. Because of the assumption that the Jewish state was Jewish and because of the compact between secularism and religion, religious authorities accumulated more power, perks, and preferential treatment than they enjoyed in most other liberal democracies.[31] The consequence is that while the majority of Jewish Israelis consistently define themselves as secular or non-observant, religion maintains a privileged position in the national identity and political institutions.[32] Israel has a chief rabbi, a largely ceremonial position that comes with a bully pulpit. Israeli laws allow religious authorities to determine various kinds of civil and personal integrity rights. Consequently, Orthodox religious institutions and authorities get to define "who is a Jew," who has the authority to perform conversions and religious ceremonies, whether Jews can get married, divorced, and remarried, and whether women are allowed to lead religious services at sites such as the Western Wall.

Also, because they are able to put their stamp on religious life in Israel, they also have the power to clip the wings of their rivals, which means that Israel does not have the same tradition of religious pluralism as does America. The Orthodox use the power of the state to squelch forms of Judaism, including Reform. As a result, Israel ranks relatively low on metrics of religious freedom. According to a 2014 Pew Forum study, Israel's scores place it closer to Turkey, Sudan, and

Chad than to the United States.[33] In this respect, it has much more in common with many of its neighbors in the Middle East than it does with Western democracies such as the United States.[34] The power of the Orthodox extends beyond religion to include using their political perch to secure a disproportionate share of the state's welfare transfers, to exempt themselves from many basic responsibilities expected of other Israeli citizens, including military service, and to create ever-expanding religious enclaves in Jerusalem and elsewhere.

How do secular Israeli Jews feel about the place of religion in Israeli society? By most accounts they are most troubled not by the arrangement but rather by its abuse. In other words, they generally concede that because Israel is a Jewish state, religion will, and probably should, play a greater role than in other secularized societies, and the Orthodox community can have a large say. However, there are limits, and for many secular-minded Israeli Jews, the Orthodox community has exceeded them. The Orthodox community defends itself as serving the Jewish people and keeping the Jewish state Jewish. If Israel is a Jewish state, then the "Jewish" must have a religious content. And who better than the Orthodox, the true keepers of the faith, to decide what is and is not Judaism? Religious pluralism might very well mean the dissolution of Judaism.[35] Orthodox Jews have little desire to see Israel's Judaism resemble what they perceive to be the Christianized Judaism that exists in America.

The power of the religious community in Israel might be tolerable to Israeli Jews, but it is intolerable to American Jews because it violates the sacred principle of religious pluralism.[36] American Jews live in a secular society that forbids the state from favoring one religion over another, cherishes religious liberty, and permits considerable religious experimentation and competition. American Jews have a long history of mixing different ingredients and subtle shades of religious institutions to accommodate the diversity. Because of the power of the Orthodox authorities, American Jews often have difficulty practicing their version of Judaism in Israel. American Jews not only feel put upon, but they also resent the assumption that their Judaism is phony and they are second-rate Jews.[37]

American Jews and Israeli Jews also live under very different kinds of nationalism. American Jews live in a land of civic nationalism,

whereas Israeli Jews live in a land of ethnic and religious nationalism. From the very beginning of the Zionist movement, American
Jews have worried that a Jewish state might develop a form of nationalism that violated their values. Early American Zionists, however,
dismissed the fear that Zionism would acquire such illiberal characteristics, insisting that it would honor cultural pluralism, with many
even imagining some form of a binational state where Jews and Arabs
contributed equally to national life. At the time of Israel's creation,
some American Jews predicted that Israel would be less than liberal
and be haunted by own its minorities problem, often drawing a direct
historical analogy to the conditions of the Jewish minority in Eastern
Europe prior to the 1930s. Whereas such concerns were once a staple
of anti-Zionist thought, they faded because of the exigencies of the
war, the fear that the Arab minority might be a fifth column, and the
fact that a growing percentage of Israel's population was Jewish.

Yet Israeli nationalism has a defining ethnic quality. Israel extends
citizenship and legal protections to Jews and non-Jews alike, but Jews
in Israel have always had a dominant position. It is nearly categor-
ically impossible for an Israeli Muslim or Christian to be an Israeli
nationalist. The very fact that only Jews (with the exception of the
Druze) can serve in the Israeli army speaks to the segregation. From
time to time a bill makes its way through the Knesset that threatens to transform Israel's Jewish character from implicit to explicit,
with the possibility that Israel's non-Jewish population will be closer
to a legal status of second-class citizens. In 2014 the Israeli Supreme
Court ruled on whether "Israeli" was a nationality. It responded "no"
because the concept of Israeli did not sufficiently capture the Jewish
dimension of Israel. In short, Jewish and Arab Israelis "share a common citizenship. . . . But they are not members of the same nation."[38]

The quality of Israeli democracy has become a growing concern
since the 1967 war and the occupation. American Jews identify Judaism with democracy. They are proud of Israel's democratic characteristics, almost to the point that it is virtually impossible for them to
imagine a Jewish state that is not democratic. They understand that
Israel is not the United States, that as a Jewish state it will have Jewish elements woven into citizenship, that as a state surrounded by hostile neighbors Israel will not be able to live up to its ideals. However,

they know that they would not want to live in a democracy whose national identity was defined by a religion. As a minority themselves, they know what it means to be treated without equal status, rights, and standing. They also do not operate with a single understanding of what it means to be either Jewish or democratic. But American Jews are emphatic on a single point: they want Israel to be Jewish and democratic. American Jews can accommodate the various contradictions that are embedded in a democracy that has a religious identity—until the point that Jews are a minority.[39] For most of Israel's history, this has been a hypothetical because Jews have been a firm majority and might have to resort to illiberal means to maintain their power.

The hypothetical is becoming the probable. Specifically, according to many forecasts, in the very near future Palestinians and Arab Israelis will become the majority of the population between the Jordan River and the Mediterranean Sea. If Israel continues with the status quo and the occupation, then it will cease to be a democracy, and instead will be an illiberal democracy, an apartheid state, or some other authoritarian alternative. At this moment, American Jews will have two very unpleasant choices given their liberal values: either withdraw their support from Israel, or live with a double standard, in which they apply one set of values for Israel and another for America and the rest of the world.

There are many reasons why American Jews might be distancing themselves from Israel. America keeps getting better and better for American Jews, which has weakened the Jewish identity and association with Israel. Yet it would be counterintuitive, and historically odd, if somehow Israel's character and policies did not play a role. American Jews always wanted an Israel that not only helped address the Jewish Problem but did so in a way that made them proud and was consistent with their values. In the early days of Zionism American Jews opposed Jewish nationalism for various reasons, including the fear that the very idea of a Jewish state might reflect badly on them. Early Zionist leaders quelled such fears by insisting that a Jewish homeland or state would be a place where Jews could be both safe and a light unto nations. After the Holocaust, American Jews became die-hard Zionists, but all along saw Israel as more than a sanctuary for unwanted Jews. And even after the 1967 war, when their tribalism increased, they justified Israel's existence and attempted to maintain the United States' strong support of Israel by referring to its liberal and democratic values. If American Jews no longer believe that they and Israel share the same values, it is almost inevitable that this will increase their ambivalence. The fact is that the Jewish Problem and the Jewish Question have been equally influential in shaping American Jewry's attitude toward Israel.

Whether or not American Jews are distancing themselves from Israel, American Jewish (and Israeli) leaders believe them to be and are attempting to reverse the trend through three courses of action. The first is to emphasize the continuing threats to Israel and world Jewry. Simply put, American Jews should worry a little less about the quality of Israel's civic life and a little more about the very survival of Israel and world Jewry. The emphasis on the existence of external threats, whether sincerely felt or strategically embellished, is a technique many groups use to maintain internal cohesion and combat complacency. And in order to reduce the possibility that American Jews might be accused of dual loyalty, this response often emphasizes that support for Israel is consistent with support for American interests and values.

These scare tactics do not seem to be working, or at least they are not as effective as they once were and not with the younger generation. Surveys of young American Jews suggest that they feel very secure and "scoff at what they regard as a 'circle-the-wagons' approach to Jewish life."[40] In their eyes, the world has changed and largely for the better.[41] Accordingly, a growing percentage of American Jews, and especially the younger generation, reject the view that the "whole world is against us."

In part because of the ineffectiveness of this narrative, the Union for Reform Judaism, founded in 1873 by Rabbi Isaac Mayer Wise and now representing more than nine hundred synagogues in the United States and beyond, recently launched an Israel Engagement Initiative. According to its promotional materials, this initiative is a response to the dominant narrative of suffering of the Jewish People. The goal of the iEngage Project is to respond to growing feelings of disenchantment and disinterest toward Israel among an ever-increasing number of Jews worldwide by creating a new narrative regarding the significance of Israel for Jewish life. This narrative will serve as a foundation for a new covenant between Israel and world Jewry, elevating the existing discourse from one with a crisis-based focus to one rooted in Jewish values and ideas.

> The core feature of the "traditional" Israel narrative was the precariousness of Jewish survival. In this narrative, Jewish existence, both in Israel and around the world, was viewed as threatened by inevitable and often imminent danger. One of the long-lasting effects of the Holocaust generation and that following it was the shaping of a consciousness deeply suspicious and fearful of the world. This inspired the creation of a Jewish identity in which the survival and perpetuation of the Jewish people and the defense of Jews in danger became central values.[42]

To counter this narrative, iEngage intends to give greater attention to the accomplishments of the Jewish people. Replacing themes of survival with success will help give "meaning to Jewish statehood and sovereignty." The articulation of "a vision of Israel that lives up to the highest standard of Jewish values, morality, and democracy can form the basis for a new covenant for Jews around the world."[43]

A second response is to guide Israel in a more congenial—that is, liberal-democratic—direction. Instead of "distancing" themselves from Israel, some American Jews aspire to change those policies they find contrary to their fundamental values.[44] From this perspective, American Jews should care about Israel's character for many reasons. They have a special responsibility to Israel, which includes not only defending it against its enemies but also binding it to Jewish ethics, values, and standards of justice. "For Jews who espouse liberal principles," writes Peter Beinart, "indifference to whether the Jewish state remains a democracy constitutes as deep a betrayal of the bonds of peoplehood as indifference to whether there remains a Jewish state at all."[45] Moreover, American Jews should care about Israel's character, if only out of self-interest. American Jews have staked their case for American support for Israel on its democratic and liberal character; if Israel no longer has those values, then the case for Israel becomes reduced to its Jewish identity, an argument unlikely to have wide appeal. Also, Israel presents itself as a Jewish state and Israeli prime ministers often present themselves as speaking on behalf of all Jews, which means that what Israel says and does potentially affects what Gentiles think of Jews. American Jews, in other words, can try and distance themselves all they want, but as Jews they are forever closely associated with the Jewish state.

Over the last several decades American Jews have attempted to implant, nurture, and defend liberal values in Israel. The American Jewish Committee helped create the human rights organization Association for Civil Rights in Israel in the 1970s, and American Jews continue to be major supporters of Israeli human rights organizations such as B'Tselem. Perhaps the best known of these American Jewish organizations is the New Israel Fund. Established in 1979 in reaction to Likud's victory and the fear that Israel was becoming more nationalist and rightist, it aims to advance Israel's commitment to social justice, democracy, human rights, religious pluralism, women's empowerment, and the rights and welfare of the Arab minorities and the Palestinians.[46] Its engagement owes not to a sense of guilt or the belief that the Palestinians and other minorities are owed this assistance as reparations, but rather because these goals are consistent with Jewish and Israeli values. And, apparently, its general orientation has tapped into American Jewish values: in its early years it raised about a quarter of a million dollars annually; by 1999 its annual collections had risen to $19 million, and in 2013 it raised roughly $28 million—nearly half of AIPAC's reported annual revenue of $60 million. In general, there has been a growth of progressive American Jewish organizations that are interested in aligning Israel's values with their own.[47]

The desire by American Jews to keep Israel on a liberal track can take an unexpected twist. By the turn of this century, American Jewry's giving to Israel was in decline, tensions between Israel and the Palestinian authorities were increasing, and Palestinian organizations were attempting to strengthen Palestinian national consciousness and fortify ties among Palestinians in Israel and the occupied territories.[48] Yet transnational Jewish giving to Palestinian civil society organizations was on the rise, amounting to nearly $3 million by 2005. As a percentage of total American Jewish giving to Israel it is not an impressive figure, but American Jewish organizations ranked among the top donors to Palestinian organizations, providing anywhere from 20 to 30 percent of their total grants. And a fair bit of these funds was coming from fairly large foundations, such as the New Israel Fund. Why would transnational Jewish organizations that are committed to Israel's future give to Palestinian solidarity and civil society organizations? In keeping with their pluralist and liberal worldview, they believe that Israel's long-term security is dependent on recognizing the legitimate national rights of the Palestinians and on a Palestinian state committed to liberal democracy. To fund and support a liberal and democratic Palestine is good politics, especially if the alternative is radicalization and extremism.[49]

A third response by the American Jewish community is to encourage young American Jews to get to know Israel, which means programming, and lots of it. Perhaps the most famous, expensive, and ambitious of these initiatives is Taglit Birthright, which gives American (and other Diaspora) Jews who are eighteen or older, and who have not yet been, a ten-day trip to Israel. Launched in 2000, as of 2014 the program had brought more than 500,000 Jews from sixty-six countries to Israel.

Although it is widely understood as an effort to instill a greater love for Israel among young Diaspora Jews, its primary inspiration was to strengthen Jewish peoplehood. American Jews have always feared that they were living on borrowed time and that eventually the seductions of assimilation would win, but a 1990 report by the National Jewish Population Survey contained the alarming statistic that 52 percent of all American Jews intermarry. Although the accuracy of the number was endlessly debated, a group of wealthy North American Jews decided to take matters into its own hands. It could have acted within existing channels, but it believed that one reason for the frighteningly high assimilation rate was because the existing Jewish organizations were nothing short of inept.[50] Ultimately it decided that the best way to instill a Jewish identity was by making sure that all Jews had the opportunity to visit Israel. Zionism and Israel, once again, would save American Jews from themselves.

When these benefactors pitched the idea to the Israeli government, they found a highly receptive audience. Many prominent Israeli intellectuals and politicians were increasingly worried that American Jews were becoming detached from Israel and believed that this drift might be countered by giving young Diaspora Jews the opportunity to experience Israel for themselves. This was hardly a novel thought. Since 1948 Israeli leaders had imagined that if American Jews visited, they would stay for a lifetime. After decades of disappointment, though, they scaled back their ambitions and hoped that a visit would nurture a Zionist gene as they entered into an era of transnationalism and globalization.[51]

What has been Birthright's impact after fifteen years of existence and hundreds of thousands of visits? The evidence is that it has strengthened the connection between young American Jews and Israel, that these effects are not fleeting but rather are long-lasting, and that American Jews who have been on Birthright are more likely to identify with Israel than are Jews who have not.[52] One explanation for this result is that these impressionable youths are being brainwashed by parties at night and a party line on the tour bus. This is simplistic. Drawn from across the ideological spectrum, the tour operators do not operate from a single script; it is not unusual for the guides and the bus drivers to argue over the presentation of material, airing Israel's lively political discourse. The Diaspora Jews also come from across the political spectrum. And because eligibility for Birthright is dependent on not having previously visited Israel, they are possibly less attached to Israel than the Jewish population—which, of course, is the program's target population. In other words, the guides are hardly preaching to the converted. And the participants are not sponges, but often combative, challenging, well-informed, and ready to rebel against any hint at "re-education." If the participants are eventually "converted," it is not because of dogma but rather because their visit seems to have awakened sentiments once dormant.

Recall, though, that Birthright's original rationale was not to improve Israel's favorability scores among American Jews but rather to strengthen their Jewish identity. What does that mean? The organizers operate with a "big tent" view of the Jewish people in the broadest possible sense. There is no right or wrong way to be Jewish. The benefactors themselves come from an array of traditions, united only in the hope that this generation will carry forward the Jewish people. In fact, there is a noticeable lack of religiosity in the program or among many of the participants (partly because many American Jews with a strong ethnic and religious identity have already visited Israel by the time they are eighteen). The participants are not expected to participate in religious study, keep kosher, or even observe the Sabbath. Indeed, the most popular way to express their Judaism is to shop—they buy kiddush cups, yarmulkes, mezuzahs, and other Jewish artifacts. In other words, they express themselves in the ways expected of anyone who was raised in a consumer culture. But even if identity is learned through shopping rather than praying, these seemingly superficial acts can make the participants more aware of their Jewishness—even as the collectibles gather dust at home.

By working from this lowest common denominator, the hope is not only to strengthen the Jewish identity but also to build a transnational Jewish community. "If the tours can be said to be Zionist in any classical sense of the term, it is in an Ahad Ha'am way that envisions the state not as a means of dismantling diaspora but as a spiritual center that can help sustain Jewish life around the world."[53] Birthright, in other words, is not a standard nation-building project. It does not expect Diaspora Jews to identify with Israel at the expense of their existing national identity. Nor does it expect American Jews to make aliyah. Instead, it intends to use "Israel to sustain the diaspora, not to eliminate it."[54] The alternative to the diaspora, after all, is not mass migration to Israel but rather mass assimilation. In short, this "nation-building" exercise is intended to give Jews a home in multiple places and spaces, to maintain simultaneous connections to fellow citizens, Israel, and the Jewish people. In this way, it attempts to give Jews a way of living with the tensions between the particular and the universal.

Assuming that American Jews maintain their prophetic theology and continue to favor the universal over the particular, then the urgent and at times painful question becomes: where does Israel fit? At the turn of the twentieth century the dominant view of the American Jewish leadership was that Zionism was a disruptive force—American Jews could not be American and Zionist. Circumstances at home and abroad, though, lowered the resistance and, eventually, convinced American Jews that they could have their Americanism and their Zionism, too. America became more tolerant of hyphenated identities, American Jews became less worried that the golden land was about to become fool's gold, American Jews increasingly saw Israel as a country that stood shoulder to shoulder with American interests and values, and the American Jewish community increasingly saw Israel not as a threat to its existence but as helping to fend off forces of assimilation.

The post-1967 period simultaneously reinforced and undermined such thinking, as American Jews increasingly defined their Jewish identity through an Israel that, at times, did not always live up to the values that they cherished. American Jews responded to tension between their traditional prophetic values and Israel's character and policies in various ways. Some began to demonstrate evidence of cognitive dissonance, especially when they used one set of standards to defend Israel and another set to judge other countries. Others began to exhibit greater evidence of an emotionally charged ambivalence. And then there were those who began searching for new ways to enact their cosmopolitan commitments. Israel was an acceptable outlet for those looking to accentuate their particularism, but it was often a dead end for those wanting to express their universalism.[55] If Israel is distant from, and perhaps even challenges, their cosmopolitanism, then where will American Jews turn?

REPAIRING JEWS?

Although the spike in Jewish nationalism after 1967 might have made it appear as if American Jews no longer had time for other peoples' problems, it only looked that way. Obscured by a sea of blue and white, American Jews continued to volunteer, join social justice campaigns, and do service work in disproportionate numbers relative to the American population as a whole. Beginning in the 1990s, however, social justice became increasingly prominent. Articles began populating Jewish newspapers and magazines. Books began filling shelves at bookstores and the libraries at synagogues.[56] Rabbi Jonathan Sacks, the former chief rabbi of Britain, began enjoying considerable fame with his tikkun olam–laced version of Judaism and call for Jews to become more ethically engaged in the world.[57] More and more Jewish organizations were founded to promote social justice. Even more novel, existing American Jewish aid organizations, such as the Joint Distribution Committee, and newly established agencies, such as the American Jewish World Service (AJWS), began to target non-Jewish populations around the world. In 1999 AJWS and Hillel created alternative spring breaks for college students.[58] Reflecting the growing supply of organizations and demand by American Jews for volunteer opportunities, in 2009 several Jewish social justice organizations created "Repair the World" to be a clearinghouse for Jewish service learning and volunteer efforts. The tenets of Prophetic Judaism seemed to be enjoying a revival. For many American Jews, their identity is best expressed not through their love of Israel but rather their love of humanity.

Much of this activity has occurred under the banner of tikkun olam, loosely and commonly translated as "repairing the world." Tikkun olam was largely unknown before the 1960s. A search of the archives of major American Jewish newspapers turned up a few mentions before 1960 and only two during the 1960s.[59] In the 1970s the phrase began to circulate in a movement of American conservative youth, and then as part of the left-oriented New Jewish Agenda. In the 1980s it inspired the title of Michael Lerner's progressive journal, *Tikkun*. In 1988 Conservative Judaism incorporated tikkun olam into its statement of principles.[60] By the 1990s tikkun olam was becoming a household word (at least in Jewish households).[61]

Although the concept is quite ancient, its current meaning is, historically speaking, a recent invention and far from the original. The first usage occurred in the second-century *Mishnah* and in the context of establishing legal arrangements governing divorce.[62] Later it became part of an *Aleynu* (a prayer recited during prayer services in relationship to the Torah), but it referred less to repairing the world than it did to restoring the world to its rightful place under the direction of God. The concept's current meaning owes its origins to the sixteenth-century Lurianic branch of the Kabbalah. Rabbi Luria's mystical vision is that God is both infinite and provides room for the world because "God contracted into himself to leave a space in the world. . . . Only when God is hidden can the world exist."[63] *Olam* is

Figure 6.2. American high school students with the American Jewish World Service in Winneba, Ghana, August 2012, where they volunteered for Challenging Heights School. Photo courtesy of Maya Barnett

the idea of the universe. Yet when God made the world, he could not remove all evidence of his presence and therefore, sent out rays of light in containers. The rays, though, broke through the vessels, "scattering fragments of light throughout the world. It is our task to gather these fragments, wherever they are, and restore them to their proper place."[64] This is the meaning of *tikkun*, to repair. Luria had in mind religious acts, not social action. Still, Luria's rendering proved compelling to modern Jews because of its emphasis on how the Jewish people must help make the world whole once again. The emphasis on religious acts broadened, grounded, and graphed onto the universalizing tenets of post-Enlightenment Judaism.

To some extent the rising popularity of tikkun olam can be explained by the faddishness of the expression itself. If the phrase did not exist, Jews might have used synonyms such as *tzedakah* (justice), *chesed* (caring), and *gemilut chasadim* (acts of loving kindness). However, where these other terms are often associated with giving to one's own, tikkun olam is generally assumed to mean giving to non-Jews.[65] It also has become a covert way for Jews to tie their traditional liberal values to Judaism. References to tikkun olam are rarely attached to right-of-center causes such as ending entitlements, downsizing the state, lowering taxes, or defending the right to bear arms. Most references instead connect it to green politics, ending hunger, gay rights, reproductive rights, development, universal health care, and other causes usually associated with progressive politics. As pointedly observed by an American rabbi, "It is no coincidence that our Jewish program looks pretty much like that of the ACLU or the Democratic Party. . . . God seems to require of us no more and no less than a vote for Al Gore or saving the whale."[66] Taken to the extreme, tikkun olam threatens to reduce Judaism to Do-It-Yourself Judaism, platitudes, and being good to others, the same complaint registered a century ago by critics of America Jewry's perceived penchant for social action over religion.[67] In the spirit of sarcasm, Jack Wertheimer summarized the ten commandments of contemporary American Jewry as follows:

I.   I am the Lord your God, Who took you out of Egypt to "repair the world."
II.   You shall not be judgmental.
III. You shall be pluralistic.
IV.   You shall personalize your Judaism.
V.   Meaning, meaning shall you pursue.
VI.   You shall create caring communities.
VII. You shall encourage the airing of all views.
VIII. You shall not be tribal. (We shouldn't give preference to our own people, but acknowledge that we are part of a cosmopolitan world.)
IX.   You shall celebrate your Jewishness.
X.   You shall hold the Jewish Conversation in Public.[68]

For every movement there is a countermovement.

However easy it is to poke fun at tikkun olam, its popularity owes to more than faddishness or political camouflage—it reflects the demise of the "survival" mentality and the enduring connection between the American Jewish identity and cosmopolitanism.[69] Surveys of American Jews consistently tap into such sentiments. When asked about the qualities that were most important to their identity, nearly half said social equality, double the number who cited support for Israel or religious observance.[70] Twice as many believed that a commitment to social equality was more important than religious observance and more than three times as important as Israel to their Jewish identity.[71] A 2011 survey reported that the vast majority of young Jews sampled had performed some sort of service within the year of the survey.[72] Although most young Jews see service as independent of their Jewish identity, a large percentage sees it as connected. And a stunning 94–96 percent stated that they were proud when Jewish organizations performed service work.

American Jews continue to see themselves as part of the world—not apart from it. Jews like to volunteer and give, but to volunteer and give as individuals who are concerned with the circumstances of others, and not necessarily to volunteer and give as Jews. They are more likely to give universal rather than Jewish reasons for volunteering.[73] They prefer to work through nonsectarian, not Jewish, organizations and for nonsectarian rather than exclusively Jewish causes. Their list of concerns reflects this outlook—at the top are domestic issues such as welfare to the poor, health care, and education; second are global issues such as development, human rights, and emergency relief; and trailing far behind is Israel.[74] This ranking holds across political ideologies, though political conservatives are relatively more concerned with Jewish issues, including Israel. When young Jewish concerns are broken down by ideology, the general percentages hold, though Israel drops to second from the bottom among those who identify as liberals and progressives. Service to the Jewish community also ranks toward the bottom of driving concerns, except among politically conservative Jews, who place it in the middle of the pack.[75] In general, Jews enjoy volunteering, don't care whom they volunteer with, have surprisingly little interest in working on Israel-related issues or for exclusively Jewish concerns, and when they volunteer are less likely to do so with religious organizations than are their Christian counterparts. If Jewish organizations want to capture this interest, then they should be a little less Jewish.[76] All of this is very consistent with a political theology of Prophetic Judaism.

The political theology of Prophetic Judaism is an enduring aspect of American Jewry and explains the long-standing interest in social justice, but constants cannot explain change, and certainly not the ascendance of tikkun olam. What has happened in America and the world to account for the rising voluntarism and interest in social justice among American Jews? In many ways, Jews are just like everyone else. The rise in Jewish humanitarianism is consistent with the ascendance of faith-based humanitarianism in the rest of American society and around the world, so if we want to understand the particular we should start with the general.[77] Explanations for the rise of Christian and Islamic humanitarianism often cite the worldwide religious revival, sparked in part by a search for meaning. This religious resurgence, moreover, is intersecting with discourses of humanity and universal ethics, generating a greater desire for global justice. To be religious is to help the poor, needy, and vulnerable. And once religious organizations improve their capacity, this supply can create its own demand, encouraging the devout to give more. Not only are religious agencies giving more, but they are also giving to more kinds of people. Decades ago they tended to give to their own, practicing principles of partiality. Christian organizations (though less so, Islamic organizations) are much more likely to exhibit impartiality and give on the basis of need.

American Jews exhibit similar trends and effects. American Jews are showing a renewed religiosity and search for meaning, which includes a connection to universal ethics. Jews are doing better than ever, materially and existentially secure. There is a perceptible generational shift in the Jewish identity "from religious to secular, ethical to cultural, community-oriented to individualist and universal."[78] Their prophetic theology always inclined them toward universalism, but their focus on the Jewish Problem meant that they were more inclined to practice principles of partiality. Now that Jews are doing better, they are expanding their universe of compassion. "The classical Jewish civil religion, while liberal in political orientation . . . was almost exclusively concerned with Jewish defense and advancement. Many younger Jews found this too confusing. They want to express their Jewishness through social justice work globally."[79]

Conversely, their universalism makes it much harder to privilege Jewish suffering, and the improved welfare of Jews makes it less excusable to do so. Previously, when American Jews worked globally they focused on the needs of Jews, in the spirit of the Talmudic saying, *aniye ircha kodmim*—"the poor of your town comes first." Although they proclaimed a prophetic spirit, they often justified their favoritism on the grounds that they had special responsibilities to Jewish communities in trouble, especially since these communities would be abandoned if not helped by able-bodied Jews from abroad. But as previously discussed and captured in figure 5.3, the vast majority of the world's Jews now live in liberal democracies. World Jewry is doing better than ever, and this is especially true of American Jewry. Consequently, contemporary American Jews are less likely to "play favorites." In many ways, they are becoming increasingly reminiscent of Rosa Luxemburg's response to the accusation that she was insensitive to the plight of Russian Jews:

> Why do you come with your particular Jewish sorrows? I feel equally close to the wretched victims of the rubber plantations in Putumayo, or to the Negroes in Africa with whose bodies the Europeans are playing catch-ball. . . . I have not a separate corner in my heart for the ghetto: I feel at home in the entire world wherever there are clouds and birds and human tears.[80]

Luxemburg sounded particularly cold-hearted because she was speaking at a time when Jews were arguably as much in need as any group, and she might have shown a little sympathy without doing much damage to her Marxist credentials. But American Jews have even less reason to privilege Jewish suffering because Jews around the world are, historically speaking, doing better than ever. American Jews can continue to give preferential treatment to their brethren, but doing so will not enhance their cosmopolitan credentials.[81]

A new generation of American Jewish service organizations is attempting to meet the growing interest in social action by American Jews, and Israel figures into the demand-and-supply in subtle but significant ways. Jewish organizations, like all organizations, have an interest in the survival of the organization and accomplishing their mandates, which, in the case of Jewish organizations, are related to the survival and well-being of the Jewish community. Thirty years ago American Jewish organizations attempted to further these twin interests by offering programming on Israel or the Holocaust. In other words, by giving Jews what they wanted, Jewish organizations could retain and attract members and, in the process, help cultivate and maintain the bonds of Jewish peoplehood. At the risk of sounding overly instrumental, one might say that Israel and the Holocaust were useful marketing devices. Although three decades ago they were the workhorses of Jewish identity, they no longer have the same pull—and especially when compared to social justice. As various reports on the future of American Jewry and social action note, if Jewish organizations are interested in their own survival and the survival of the Jewish people, then they should offer programming and themes that appeal to this younger generation of Jews, which are voluntarism, social action, and tikkun olam. Do not ask what tikkun olam can do for others; ask what it can do for Jewish peoplehood.

This shifting emphasis from Israel and the Holocaust to social action belies a shared theme: the instrumentalization of suffering. Suffering is certainly not the only way to maintain a communal identity, but historically it has played a prominent role, and not only for Jews. The possible appropriation of the suffering of one's own people, however, does not raise the same moral concerns as when other people's suffering is appropriated. The Holocaust and Israel are "our" suffering, and therefore "we" are entitled to use it as "we" want. But what about the appropriation of the suffering of another people for the purpose of maintaining one's own communal identity? If Jewish organizations are doing this, they are acting just like other faith-based organizations. My research on Christian-based aid agencies finds that they do want to help vulnerable populations, but they also hope that such missions will lead their participants to return home as better Christians and congregants.

Yet there is a fine line between second-order benefits and first-order exploitation, and many faith-based agencies struggle over the proper balance. So, too, do Jewish organizations. Rabbi David Rosenn, the founder of AVODAH, the Jewish Service Corps, has worried that the goal of Jewish continuity might overshadow Jewish social justice goals.[82] The AJWS's Ruth Messinger similarly cautioned that, "(s)ervice programs that exist and are being created will be successful if, first and foremost, they are about service to others and not strengthening ourselves."[83] Indeed, the AJWS's fear that its short-term volunteer trips crossed the line of good taste factored into its decision to suspend this highly popular program. Still, nearly every single commissioned study, founding document, and prospective pitch for greater attention to social justice that I have read emphasizes how it will help attract Jews to Judaism.

Another soft-spoken reason why Jewish leaders are keen to develop social justice organizations is that they believe it will help improve Jewish favorability scores with Gentiles and reduce anti-Semitism in the world. This calculation has a long pedigree. Since the founding of the United States, American Jews have seen charitable and philanthropic activity as a way to convince their neighbors that they are just like them, are not the clannish and self-absorbed people they are rumored to be, and care about the world. In the listed contributions of the American Jewish World Service, Ruth Messinger concluded on the following note: "perhaps most importantly, it will also deter anti-Semitism by demonstrating that Jews work to provide social justice and dignity for all people regardless of race, religion, or ethnicity."[84] I have heard other Jewish leaders offer similar thoughts.

This leads me to the last, but hardly least, possible Jewish-specific reason for the rise of tikkun olam: Israel. I began my research with a hunch that there was a connection between the rumored distancing of American Jews from Israel and the rise of tikkun olam. There is the distinct possibility that there is no relationship and that independent factors account for each. Even if there is a connection, there is a debate regarding which comes first, distancing or tikkun olam. Tikkun olam could come prior to distancing. One possibility is that as American Jews became more attracted to the prophetic tradition and involved in social justice they more closely scrutinized Israel's values, found them wanting, and consequently became more distant.

The alternative sequence is that growing ambivalence toward Israel comes prior to the rise of tikkun olam. Simply put, American Jews, who are increasingly uneasy with Israel, are turning to tikkun olam to enact their Jewish identity in the world. Thirty years ago American Jews were comfortable expressing their identity through Israel, but no longer.[85] Israel raises all kinds of questions that do not get triggered, for instance, when building schools in Ghana. There also is the more subtle possibility that American Jews have a choice regarding how to express their identity in the world—and Israel no longer looks as attractive in comparison to social justice. It might be that Israel has too many negatives, but it also could be that Jews, perhaps wanting to be like everyone else, are increasingly turning to social justice in this era of cosmopolitanism and globalization. Nearly everyone I spoke with working in a Jewish social justice agency emphatically agreed that there was a connection between the two; yet the only evidence they could provide me was their firsthand experiences and intuition. I cannot do any better in terms of hard data, but the scattered evidence from the contemporary period, conversations with staff and volunteers, and the historical patterns provide support for the following narrative.

American Jews are steeped in the prophetic tradition, and historical and contemporary trends affirm that they are inclined toward cosmopolitanism and skittish about tribalism. The post-1967 period is the clear exception to this trend, as American Jews became, first, more assertive of their Jewish identity because of permissive changes in American politics, and, second, more connected to Israel. In other words, forces in America, Israel, and the world were bringing out the particularism in American Jews. Yet since the 1980s there have been changes in America, Israel, and the world that are particularly likely to cause American Jews to taper any tribalism and reunite with cosmopolitanism. American Jews no longer fear anti-Semitism, globalization is causing American Jews to rekindle their prophetic political theology and to imagine what unites and not what separates them from others, and an Israel that increasingly acts like an ethnonational state is not the best outlet for such cosmopolitan longings.

American Jews have always been concerned with how they are viewed by Gentiles and have hoped that their voluntarism would help counter the stereotype of clannishness. My conversations with volunteers and staff of social justice organizations, though, suggests a twist on this long-standing hope that social action will reflect well on the Jews—it also helps counteract the negative impressions left by Israel and its policies. So, American Jews might be turning from Israel to tikkun olam in order to improve the image of the Jewish people—

especially compared with an Israel that does not reflect their values.[86] I once had a conversation with an aid worker from Islamic Relief who said that one reason he chose to work for an identifiably Islamic organization was because he wanted to show the world that Muslims were more than terrorists. I have spoken with many American Jews who have offered very similar confessions. American Jews and Muslims might have something in common—a concern that their Middle Eastern namesakes are making life hard for them at home.

The impact of the ambivalence of American Jews toward Israel is felt among Jewish social justice organizations, as the following event illustrates. In April 2012 the Jewish Agency in Jerusalem convened a meeting of Israeli and American-based Jewish social justice organizations to examine their future collaboration.[87] Although it might seem as if Israel and American Jewish organizations should have no difficulty finding a common interest, there was a large unmentionable in the room that forced them apart and first had to be addressed: Israel. American Jewish organizations roamed the world but skipped over the Middle East and Israel. As one Israeli participant probed, "Why doesn't Israel feature more prominently in discussions about justice in the North American Jewish community?"

A long list of reasons came pouring out. One person diplomatically explained that it was not personal; they wanted to avoid mission creep. Although plausible, bear in mind that all Jewish organizations have expanded their operations over the years, and if they have not expanded toward Israel, it is probably intentional and not accidental. Other participants said that they preferred to keep their distance from Israel because it is a polarized and polarizing issue that leaves little room for nuance. To work on Israel is to have a gate-keeping organization such as AIPAC decide which side you are on, and its loyalty tests do not leave much room for subtlety. And to be found "against us" can imply not just a difference of views but rather latent anti-Semitism on the part of the dissenter. Also, if these justice-oriented organizations started working in and with Israel, they would probably feel compelled to include Israeli Arabs and Palestinians in their activities; to do otherwise would be downright hypocritical. Better to avoid the situation altogether than be hypocritical and risk tearing the organization apart. Israel's particularism, moreover, runs counter to its universalism. As one participant put it, "Israeli understandings of social justice don't always resonate with Americans', due to differences in the historical and sociological realities between North America and Israel." Furthermore, a reason why these justice organizations exist is to allow North American Jews to avoid having to deal with Israel. Not only is Israel possibly an unhealthy distraction, it might also cause difficulties with their members and supporters. If these justice organizations were to become more involved in Israeli politics, then they would immediately leave the morally calm world of tikkun olam and become exposed to the morally uneven and rough-and-tumble world of Israeli politics. There are, in short, principal and practical deterrents.

Tikkun olam organizations are not only uncomfortable engaging Israel, they also want to keep their distance from human rights. This suspicion of human rights distinguishes them from other agencies in the relief and development sectors, which have mainstreamed rights since the end of the Cold War. American Jewish justice organizations, however, have distanced themselves from its increasingly hegemonic discourse. Some agency officials explain its absence by suggesting that Jews prefer to speak in terms of justice, which focuses on duties and obligations to others, while Christians prefer to speak in terms of rights, which emphasizes entitlements. In other words, Jewish organizations are adopting language that resonates with the Jewish tradition. My reading of the record, though, is that American Jewish organizations have avoided a language that has been immensely popular with others in the sector because there is something about human rights they find either troubling or troublemaking.

The discussions among the Israeli and American Jewish social justice organizations provide numerous examples of the forces of hesitation and opposition. So, too, do the background papers for the 1992 Task Force on World Jewry and Human Rights of the National Jewish Community Relations.[88] Historically, American Jews have focused on Jewish needs, but if they are going to use the language of rights, then they are probably going to have to devote resources to other peoples' problems. The issue was not simply whether Jewish organizations had the disposable resources. Instead, it was whether an American Jewish community would be able to even look beyond the Jewish world. To illustrate this point, one paper cited Philip Roth's short story, "The Conversion of the Jews." The character of Mrs. Freedman takes little notice of a plane crash that killed fifty-eight people until she realizes that eight were Jews. At this point she calls it a "tragedy." If American Jews are prepared to move beyond their own needs, what triage system should they use? The challenge of selectivity and prioritizing confronts all rights, development, and relief agencies—after all, there is more suffering than there is available assistance, and all must decide whose suffering matters most. One proposal suggested that American Jewish organizations should target those Gentile populations where Jews might be affected either directly or indirectly; for instance, they could address those places where an improved human rights situation might immediately benefit the local Jewish community, or avoid those circumstances where involvement might compromise the safety of the local Jewish community or bring unwanted attention to Israel.

Several other papers worried that if American Jewish organizations started adopting the language of rights, then they would be forced to address the uncomfortable question of human rights in Israel. "The fact is that it is difficult to explain how we can speak out on a wide range of human rights issues and develop chronic laryngitis with respect to Israel's own record." The American Jewish community, another observed, is expert in the art of self-censorship and even shies "away from keeping with human rights organizations like Amnesty International or Humanitas partly because of the Israel factor." Despite these dangers and risks, there is one immediate payoff: Because of its "moral clarity," young Jews are attracted to human rights, with the implication that by engaging human rights young Jews might become more attracted to the Jewish community. These observations were offered more than two decades ago, and developments since have only aggravated these worries.

There are other, Israel-related reasons why American Jewish organizations have retreated from the human rights movement.[89] American Jews worry that if they criticize other governments, and especially their own, for human rights violations, then Israel will become vulnerable. American Jewish organizations were noticeably silent on questions of US torture at Guantanamo and other sites where "enemy combatants" were detained, in part because they did not want to draw attention to Israel's record on torture. The United States was fighting an asymmetric war against Arab and Muslim foes, and American Jewish groups were reluctant to criticize these invasions and occupations because the parallels with the Israeli situation in the territories were too close for comfort.[90] Also, many organizations continue to see the United Nations and international human rights as highly politicized, harboring a vendetta against Israel, and often laced with anti-Semitic statements; the UN's meeting on racism in Durban, South Africa, in 2001 was such an occasion. Israelis are credited with popularizing the term "lawfare," which concerns the instrumental use of human rights norms and laws by radical organizations such as Hamas to further their own political and military goals.

To better appreciate the difficulty of combining human rights and Israel, talk to individuals who try to do so. Rabbi Jill Jacobs is the executive director of T'ruah, the Rabbinic Call for Human Rights (formerly Rabbis for Human Rights—North America). She became politically aware beginning in the 1980s and can still remember issues such as the movement for Soviet Jewry when the relationship between Jewish interests and human rights was not so tense. She says that while she considers Judaism and human rights to be bedfellows, there is little doubt that American Jews are suspicious of human rights organizations and the United Nations. In her experience, the moment she tells American Jews and Jewish organizations that she works on behalf of human rights in Israel, she immediately has to explain that she does not necessarily keep company with organizations that want to single out or focus excessively on Israel.

It is not much easier for those who are members of the human rights movement and want to defend Israel's record. In 2009 Robert Bernstein, who founded Human Rights Watch in 1978 and chaired it for the next two decades, used the opinion page of the *New York Times* to accuse his own organization of "helping those who wish to turn Israel into a pariah state."[91] Under his tenure Human Rights Watch became one of the world's premier human rights organizations, and like many rights organizations, was focusing attention on Israel. The more it did so, the more a few board members, including Bernstein, became uncomfortable, eventually concluding that its staff had an unhealthy obsession with Israel. Bernstein emphasizes that the issue is not that Israel is immune from criticism; he acknowledges that there are issues to criticize. Instead, it is that "the human rights judgments on the issues of war and the devastation it causes are often not credible and rather extremely subjective," and that the root of the Palestinians' plight is the failure of Arab governments to recognize Israel's right to exist.[92] Aryeh Neier, a Holocaust survivor, supporter of Israel, cofounder of Human Rights Watch, and longtime colleague of Bernstein, disagrees, arguing that the core issue is that as a democratic country involved in more conflicts than other countries in the region, it is natural that Israel will get more attention than other countries.[93] Regardless of the reasons, they agree that Israel comes under a harsh glare, which does not make life easy for American Jews.

If American Jewish organizations want to show their commitment to universal values, but are uncomfortable doing so in the language of human rights, then how? Through humanitarianism, emergency relief, and social justice programs. Humanitarianism has become cosmopolitanism's defining symbol, articulating discourses of impartiality, neutrality, and humanity, and operating in a depoliticized space. This is a universalizing mission that American Jews can get behind. Two organizations, one old and one new, reflect different elements of this braided relationship among American Jews, the tensions between particularism and universalism, the strain with human rights, and the search for an alternative discourse. The old is the American Jewish Joint Distribution Committee (Joint) and the new is the American Jewish World Service (AJWS).

The Joint was founded in 1915 to provide relief to Jewish victims of World War I. The Jewish Problem only got bigger over the next several decades, and the Joint got bigger with it, expanding to new parts of the world and providing all manner of relief. Until the 1970s nearly all of its beneficiaries were Jews. It made the occasional exceptions, though. It sometimes provided assistance if it believed the relief effort would also help Jews, especially if it was unable to get access to Jewish populations in need. For instance, in 1921 it gave $4 million, a very healthy sum for those days, to the American Relief Administration for its work in Russia and Eastern Europe, but with the expectation that it would work in areas where there were significant Jewish populations. And when it provided direct assistance, it served anyone who came through its doors.[94]

After sixty years of single-minded focus on Jewish needs, the Joint began to widen its horizons. In the early 1970s it accepted an invitation from Catholic Relief Services to join in an interfaith campaign to combat world hunger. A more significant turning point, though, came in 1978 with the Cambodian genocide. American Jews, feeling a responsibility to victims of genocide, wanted to act.[95] They could, quite obviously, donate through the many UN agencies and nongovernmental organizations that were operating in the area, but many wanted to give through a Jewish agency. The North American Jewish Federation, a major donor, approached the Joint. Initially the Joint rejected the request on the grounds that it would detract from its primary responsibilities, but it eventually acceded and began accepting donations that were in excess of existing pledges. For the very first time the Joint was providing relief to an area that had no Jewish presence, and its experiment was an unqualified success.[96] It fulfilled the desires of its constituents, gained favorable publicity, and did not have to worry that a nonsectarian dimension would subtract from its primary responsibility to Jews in need.[97] The precedent was firmly established, and whenever there was a major, publicity-saturated, disaster, the Joint established an "open-mailbox" campaign to allow donors to earmark their contributions.[98] In late 1986 it further elevated the profile and importance of nonsectarian aid by creating the International Development Program.[99]

Nonsectarian aid, however, did not mean need-based aid. Instead, it meant broadening the understanding of what it meant to help Jews in need and how it might do so. There was a belief that in the process of helping non-Jews the Joint could also help Jews. Its aid might give it access to Jewish communities that otherwise were out of reach. For instance, during the Ethiopian famine in the mid-1980s, the Ethiopian government would only give it access to the Falasha Jewish communities if it agreed to serve everyone. The Joint also might be able to use its assistance activities to make life easier for the local Jewish community. One staff person I spoke with pointed to its operations in Morocco, where it believes its work with Muslim communities benefits the once large but now fairly small Jewish community.

The Joint's expansion from sectarian to nonsectarian relief, according to staff members I interviewed, was a response to changes taking place in the American Jewish community.[100] American Jewry and world Jewry were doing better. Like everyone else, advances in information technology increased their awareness, and the history of Jewish suffering made them particularly sensitive to the plight of others. American Christian relief and development agencies had moved from partiality to impartiality, and the Joint had a more difficult time explaining why it continued to focus only on Jewish needs. Furthermore, American Jews wanted the opportunity to act as Jews in the support of universal causes, and this was especially so for the younger generation that wanted to look beyond its own. By moving into nonsectarian relief, moreover, the Joint had the opportunity to bring Jews closer to humanitarian action, the Jewish world, and the Joint. Reflecting on the push into nonsectarian relief following the 1994 genocide in Rwanda, one official from the Joint said,

> The nonsectarian programs speak to a segment of our Jewish world that tends to have limited affiliation with—let's call it the system [Jewish organizations]. They are not part of—they are not interested in the system . . . I think that in some ways the system has missed out on that segment of the population. And I felt JDC had a unique opportunity to bring some of those people closer to the system in a broader sense. . . . I think disaster relief was a particularly important way to focus public attention on the Jewish world's commitment to the wider world.[101]

And if the Joint chose not to provide the opportunity for American Jews to work through a Jewish organization for the benefit of humanity, beginning in 1985 there was a new kid on the block that would: the American Jewish World Service. Its creation not only provided a fresh alternative, it also was another piece of evidence that American Jewry was changing. The Joint could either adapt or become an anachronism.

The Joint's growing nonsectarian profile was both a consequence and a cause of further reconsideration of the relationship between the particular and the universal. It was a Jewish organization, but if it began to operate according to needs-based principles, it would probably no longer be serving Jewish communities and instead be working primarily in Gentile communities. As posed by one high-ranking official, "Do we help just Jews or everyone?" What principles of discrimination could it use? Speaking personally, but providing an answer I have heard from other staff in other nonsectarian-oriented Jewish aid organizations, one staff member said that he operated through a "Jewish lens." It begins with the needs of Jewish communities, widens to include those communities where Jews might benefit directly (for instance, Ethiopia) or indirectly (for instance, Morocco), and then continues on to help all those in need. Its journey from partiality to humanity occurred, though, without a concept that has figured centrally in the broader humanitarian world—human rights. Part of the reason, this official explained, is because the Joint wants to avoid anything that smacks of "politics." And, he further hinted, it would help them avoid getting dragged into the debates about Israel.

The American Jewish World Service, the best-known American Jewish aid and development agency established during this period, also reflects this broader movement in cosmopolitanism among American Jews. In the early 1980s several justice-oriented American Jews, including some who worked in other relief, development, and rights organizations, decided it was time for the American Jewish community to have something that all other religious communities had: a nonsectarian aid organization of its very own. Catholics had the Catholic Relief Service. Evangelicals had many organizations, including World Vision International and Samaritan's Purse. Lutherans had Lutheran World Relief. And Quakers had the American Friends Service Committee. The Joint existed, but unlike these other organizations, it operated on principles of partiality and focused almost exclusively on Jewish needs. American Jews, they thought, needed a Jewish organization that served the world. And so in 1985 they created the American Jewish World Service.

By creating an aid organization that worked in the best tradition
of humanitarianism, cosmopolitanism, and universalism, they intended AJWS to both respond to and anticipate the emerging zeitgeist
in the American Jewish community in several ways.[102] To begin, AJWS
would operate in the prophetic tradition and in the cosmopolitan
spirit of the global times. The founding document is sprinkled with
references familiar to prophetic theology, including the Talmudic expression "Whoever saves one life, it is considered as if he saved an entire world." [103] And, subsequent literature and teaching manuals made
generous references to the demand for Jews to help Jews balance the
particular and the universal in ways that are consistent with the prophetic tradition.[104] Moreover, AJWS would respond to the current demand by American Jews to donate to global causes. Furthermore, the
founders imagined that the new organization would do more than
meet an untapped demand—its very existence also would create demand. Specifically, they hoped that with the creation of a Jewish-based
agency, American Jews would become more active on global justice issues. American Jews donated generously to existing nonsectarian organizations such as Oxfam, CARE, and Doctors without Borders, and
perhaps they would give even more through a Jewish organization. If
all proceeded as planned, "AJWS will help create a cohort of 'global
rabbis.'"[105] Not only would American Jews be changed by their experiences, but it would also shape how the rest of the world views the
Jews, and for the better. As observed in one founding document, "Our
own organization . . . will allow us, as Jews, to exert a visible presence
in the developing nations, thus sowing the seeds of good will for our
own people while acting on our deepest moral obligations."[106]

AJWS resembled other aid agencies not only in its broad principles but also in its activities. Yet there were two areas of notable exception, one of no responsibility and the other of special responsibility. The area of no responsibility has been Israel and the Middle East.
It has a strict policy of avoiding all things Israel. Some staff members
have suggested that this refusal owes to the fact that there are lots of
other Jewish organizations that cover Israel and the region; therefore
it would prefer to focus its energies on places where it can make a
difference and Jewish organizations are not already present. Perhaps.
But with "Jewish" in its name it cannot easily work in Arab or Islamic

societies. Also, Israel is an unwanted distraction. The moment it steps into Israel and the territories it will become swept into the nasty politics of the region and the American Jewish community. Not only would it consume a tremendous amount of time, but it also would undermine one of the rationales for AJWS: to give American Jews an opportunity to give to the world.

Owing to the Holocaust and the history of the Jewish people, AJWS also claimed a special responsibility to respond to genocide. Darfur was an example of this commitment. The advocacy and aid community was already quite involved in Sudan by the early 2000s, though most of the activity was focused on southern Sudan. As the killings in Darfur began to intensify and the international community continued to ignore the situation, AJWS decided it had to do something. It was not the first or only Jewish face in the mobilization effort. An American Jew is credited with putting into place the very first advocacy campaign. Sam Bell, the grandson of four Holocaust survivors, was told by his mother that he was being raised to lead the Warsaw ghetto, if needed. He is credited with getting the ball rolling, including fund-raising for the African Union's peacekeeping capacity, while he was a senior at Swarthmore.[107] In 2004 the movement entered a more organized and visible stage as a consequence of an event at the US Holocaust Memorial Museum attended primarily by Jews and Jewish organizations. Because of the Jewish community's sensitivity to the international community's indifference to genocide, this was "not a hard sell," according to Ruth Messinger.[108] Eventually, American Jews made up one-third of the leadership and are rightly credited with turning the attention from southern Sudan, where the evangelicals were busy, to Darfur, where the mass killings were occurring.[109]

What moved the American Jewish community? Some have argued that it was the fact that Sudan was a Muslim country. While that might have been a (subconscious) motive for some, much more present was Darfur's equation with the Holocaust and the tenth anniversary of the Rwandan genocide, when the world watched as 800,000 Tutsis were slaughtered.[110] In her comprehensive and balanced account of the coalition, Rebecca Hamilton insists that "Save Darfur was not a Zionist conspiracy. While some advocates say it 'didn't hurt'

Figure 6.3. Photograph by Arzinda Jalil. Photograph provided by the Jewish Vegetarians of North America. Photo taken during the 2006 rally on the Mall for Darfur, organized by the Save Darfur Coalition.

that Darfur provided a counternarrative to Arab victimization in the Arab-Israeli context, Jewish organizations were drawn to Darfur because of the connection that had been made to Rwanda, which spoke to a particular guilt among some segments of the Jewish community about not having acted to stop the 1994 genocide."[111] One of the original leaders, David Rubenstein, insists, "The Jewish community really was moved to respond by the term 'genocide' and that was an enormous part of the effectiveness of the Save Darfur movement."[112]

As an advocacy campaign, the coalition had to do more than simply recite "Never Again"—it also was expected to come up with some solutions, which was much easier said than done. Bell had wanted to raise money for the severely underfunded African Union peacekeeping force in Darfur, but that ran into legal and political hurdles. Others insisted on military action, with some recommending a protection force and others hinting that any intervention should be prepared to march all the way to Khartoum. Because it was difficult to find countries that would put their troops on the ground and in the middle of a war, another proposal was to impose a no-fly zone—giving the United Nations the legal authority to shoot down any Sudanese aircraft that approached civilian populations. However, most of the killing was being done not from the air but from the ground; consequently, it would probably do little more than provide an aerial view of the killing. Although states were unwilling to go to the vulnerable populations, they were prepared to receive those refugees that could make it to the safety of the camps.

There was one other active option that unnerved the Jewish organizations, including AJWS—the International Criminal Court (ICC). Established by the Rome Statute in 1998, the ICC was created to give the world the opportunity to bring to justice those individuals accused of war crimes, crimes against humanity, and genocide. The ICC, it was hoped, would end impunity, help deliver justice to the victims and the international community, and perhaps even deter future perpetrators because of the threat of punishment. Although the Nuremberg prosecutions after World War II, which put on trial many of the leading Nazis, was a direct predecessor of the ICC, the Jewish community was ambivalent, if not downright nervous, about its existence. Several countries, including the United States and Israel, refused to accede, in part because they believed that they would be the targets of politically motivated prosecutions. Consequently, referring Darfur to the ICC might strengthen it, and what was good news for the ICC was potentially bad news for Israel. When the ICC hinted at its readiness to indict those involved in Darfur, the Jewish groups that were part of the Darfur coalition were "uncomfortable taking any position indicating support for the court."[113] They had several fears: the ICC would move directly from Darfur to Israel, they would look anti-Israel because of the Israeli opposition to the ICC, and once they stated the case for prosecutions in Darfur they would have to address why Israeli crimes should not be considered as well. The coalition decided that rather than support ICC action and risk its splintering, it would call generically for accountability.

AJWS's avoidance of Israel and hesitation about involving the ICC in Darfur also connects to its broader caution toward human rights. There are remarkably few mentions of human rights in AJWS's documents through the early 2000s, which, again is particularly striking given the rush to rights in the broader aid world during this time. I have talked to some in the agency who have suggested it owes to the fact that, as a Jewish organization, it is more attracted to the language of justice than rights. Perhaps, but it also is consistent with the general inclination of Jewish organizations to keep their distance from the human rights community and discourse.[114] If it used the language of human rights, then observers and supporters might interpret this as a sign that the organization has taken a position on the Arab-Israeli conflict and supports a two-state solution. As an organization dedicated to impartial relief and wanting to stay away from the quagmire of Israeli politics, better to avoid the inflammatory and politicized language.

Beginning this century, though, AJWS slowly warmed up to human rights. At a certain point, given the widespread acceptance of human rights in the relief and development community, its distance began to look odd. Contemporary global campaigns against hunger, poverty, and disease are nearly always connected to rights and tied to the Universal Declaration of Human Rights. Their partner organizations on the ground and their beneficiaries had been linking development to rights, and AJWS had to spend more time explaining why it didn't.[115] It has become nearly impossible to do development and relief work without using rights discourse, which means those who do not do so draw attention to themselves. Accordingly, and despite the concern that if they adopted the language of rights they become singed by the politics of the Middle East, AJWS began to couple human rights to its traditional association with tikkun olam. When its board members increasingly saw references to rights in AJWS's materials and worried that it was an indication that the agency was either becoming anti-Israel or associating with known anti-Israel organizations, Messinger brought the issue to the board. She ultimately convinced it that AJWS would be able to refer to rights without becoming mired in the politics of Israel.[116]

AJWS owes its origins and impressive expansion to the enduring desire by American Jews to connect with the universal. But the AJWS has had to answer the fundamental question that bedevils all Jewish organizations that orbit around universal values: what is the "Jewish" in American Jewish World Service. Because of its commitment to principles of impartiality and desire to steer clear of Israeli politics, Jews are not the intended beneficiaries. There is no "Jewish" way to dig a well, inoculate children, or provide women's empowerment. There is no attempt whatsoever to proselytize or even advertise their Jewish assignation. Jews and Gentiles are part of the organization.

So what exactly is Jewish about AJWS? The Jews on its staff will mention how their Jewish background and theological training influenced their decision to work on global development and justice issues. Its fund-raising efforts directly appeal to the cosmopolitan spirit of American Jews. Its educational materials also emphasize how the AJWS helps Jews think through the relationship between the particular and the universal, with the hope that Jews can discover how one nourishes the other. In other words, the AJWS would not only be about American Jews doing world service but also would help American Jews stay Jewish. AJWS and other justice-oriented organizations hope that tikkun olam will help Jews remain Jews by creating a strong link between their identity as Jews, Judaism, and social justice. The Jewish in AJWS is intended to ensure that Jews stand alongside America and world service.

I briefly accompanied one of the AJWS's young Jewish leaders' volunteer trips to Ciudad Romero, El Salvador, in the summer of 2012. I had contacted the AJWS two years before because my intuition was that if any organization in the American Jewish community was seeing a possible connection between distancing from Israel and tikkun olam, it would be the AJWS. Said otherwise, if this connections was not occurring in and around AJWS, it probably would not be happening anywhere. The leaders agreed that a major reason for the AJWS's rise is that, in many ways, it was the right Jewish organization at the right time—tapping into a strong desire by American Jews to connect to concerns beyond the Jewish community. Unfortunately, like a lot of individuals I have interviewed who were certain that there was a connection between distancing from Israel and the rise of tikkun olam, they had only their experiences and no hard data.

The staff at the AJWS suggested that I should see for myself how they and their volunteers wrestle with the particular and the universal, which is how I came to be in Ciudad Romero. Specifically, the AJWS ran a program that brought young rabbis, rabbinical students, and future Jewish community leaders to this extremely impoverished village in western El Salvador to experience for themselves how the other half lives and to wrestle with their own responsibilities, as Jews, to global justice. During the day they would do manual labor, working in the fields, digging irrigation ditches, and the like, talk to individuals about their struggles, and meet with community organizations and recipients of AJWS grants. The evening was dedicated to discussion and study. The materials were much as I expected and have already described elsewhere, with lots of references to the prophetic tradition.

The discussions and readings, though, did not give me a clearer understanding of the "Jewish" in AJWS, except that questions of global justice were filtered through a (prophetic) Jewish lens. But it did leave me with a much better appreciation of the complicated relationship between the particular and the universal for those American Jews with a strong Jewish identity. Those who were already inclined toward the universal kept wanting to locate the "Jewish." And those who were inclined toward the particular, which included almost everyone in the group because they had made a lifetime commitment to the Jewish community, were keen to find a connection to the universal.

And if I was looking for a sign that there was an interest in global justice because of disenchantment with Israel, I was at the wrong place—nearly all had studied and lived in Israel for a time, and almost all were making their first trip to the global South. There was not a chance that a visit to Ciudad Romero was going to dislodge their attachment to Israel. However, quite a few did openly wonder how they might apply the principles they were learning in Ciudad Romero to

Israel. They had not thought actively about justice issues in Israel, but now that they were asking the questions, they intimated that their own thoughts about Israel were becoming more complicated. This was not necessarily the AJWS's intention, but it was a direct consequence of moving the lens of social justice from El Salvador to Israel.

CHAPTER SEVEN

THE FOREIGN POLICIES OF AN UNCERTAIN PEOPLE

THE JEWS, HISTORICALLY SPEAKING, ARE AN UNCERTAIN PEOPLE. They have been uncertain about what kind of people they are. They have been uncertain about their physical and existential existence. The American Jewish community's certainty of its own survival is arguably greater than any others because of its fairly nurturing environment. But uncertainty remains, especially with regard to the Jewish Question. American Jews continue to try and find a stable position between the particular and the universal—but the dilemma is that each represents something of a poisoned chalice. And as in all dilemmas, there is no solution, just temporary fixes that constantly push and pull in opposite directions. To move toward the universal is to unleash fears of disappearing through assimilation and of nostalgic longings for the comfort of the communal. To move toward the particular is to unleash fears that they will appear grandiose, clannish, unto themselves, and will become detached from history and humanity.

American Jews are betwixt and between also in their sense of place in the world. They are part of three different communities—and don't feel completely at home in any of them. American Jews are part of world Jewry—*Am Yisrael*, the people of Israel. Jewish communities are scattered across the world but they are unified by a common history, a sense of collective fate, and a historical memory that references the same joys and sorrows. They feel a special responsibility to one another and form a mutual aid society. They feel a close attachment to the Jewish people's spiritual home, Israel, and Israel, in turn, sustains their attachment to the Jewish people. Jews might believe that each generation might be the last, but this ever-dying people has harbored such thoughts for centuries.

Yet the Jewish identity of American Jews is not totalizing. Many American Jews want to be Jewish, but not too Jewish. Jewish people-hood is not what it once was. Polling numbers suggest that this generation of American Jews feels less responsible for the welfare of other Jews.[1] Younger Jewish adults are much less likely than older Jewish adults to agree with such statements as "Jews in the United States and Jews around the world share a common destiny" or that "when people are in distress, American Jews have a greater responsibility to rescue Jews than non-Jews."[2] American Jews are attached to and ambivalent about Israel. To draw any closer to Israel or to further develop a sense of peoplehood might force American Jews to sharpen the distinctions between themselves and their fellow Americans, which American Jews are loath to do.[3] A little space can be a good thing.

American Jews are Americans, and proudly so. By nearly any measure they are an American success story, often seeing their achievements as a sign of America's greatness. They arrived in this Christian nation an impoverished, persecuted minority and, in a few generations, achieved political, economic, and cultural success in a country that now claims to have a "Judeo-Christian" heritage. Anti-Semitism has declined dramatically, and when it occurs, it is mainly hurtful and not harmful; it is far better to be Jewish than almost any other minority in the United States. And even when anti-Semitism has been the most threatening, American Jews did not panic, turn to Zionism, or consider leaving for Palestine or Israel; instead, they doubled down on America. The gamble paid off, not only for the Jews but also for America. American Jews are proud of their personal accomplishments, and especially proud of their contributions to American life. Jews have written some of the most patriotic and beloved songs in the American songbook, including the cherished Christmas holiday song "White Christmas." Yiddish expressions have become part of everyday English. Jewish humor has profoundly shaped American comedy, and the American comedian hall of fame includes Jews such as Jack

Benny, Milton Berle, Lenny Bruce, Rodney Dangerfield, Larry David, Jerry Seinfeld, and Jon Stewart. A disproportionate share of America's Nobel Prize winners are Jewish. Over the last century Jews have been among America's most influential opinion-makers and public intellectuals, including Walter Lippmann, and Thomas Friedman. Jews helped build and lead many of America's most prominent civil rights and civil society institutions. As soon as the American public was prepared to elect and follow leaders of Jewish heritage, Jews swarmed to public service.

Notwithstanding all their prosperity and achievements, American Jews can still feel as if they are outsiders, in danger of overstaying their welcome. They proudly point to their security and acceptance, but, privately, many American Jews worry that their amazing run of luck will end. Events occur from time to time that release these anxieties. In 1985 Jonathan Pollard, a US Navy intelligence officer, was arrested on charges of leaking classified material to the Israeli government; the fact that he was being managed by the Israeli embassy in Washington only made matters worse. The occasion rekindled worries among many American Jews that they would be accused of dual loyalty. Other Jews believed that such possibilities were grossly exaggerated and only revealed an irrational fear that another Holocaust was around the corner. During the Great Recession, many Jews secretly feared that if America counted the number of Jewish names associated with high finance and economic policy-making, it would stir doubts about whether Jews were taking care of themselves at the expense of "real" Americans. Wall Street once again might be called Jew Street. The "Israel Lobby," often referred to as the "Jewish Lobby," might be viewed not just as any other interest group but rather as an interest group representing a nation that undermines the American national interest. Yet however much Jews want to be accepted, they also want to retain their separateness and are highly conscious of their distinctiveness. In general, as Jews they will never be quintessential Americans, and as Americans they will never be quintessential Jews.[4] There is a reason why alienation is a major theme in the reflections, writings, and art of American Jews.

American Jews also see themselves as part of a common humanity. As transnational, diasporic people that have wandered the earth,

Jews have been compelled to engage the universal. Exile, in short, necessitates that Jews be constantly looking skyward. Separatism is not a viable, long-term strategy for survival.[5] Yet they have lived this diasporic life and engaged the universal without losing a sense of themselves. In the context of an ongoing debate with the Zionists, the Russian Jewish activist and scholar Simon Dubnow wrote a century ago that it is a sign of the strength of the Jewish people that they have managed to develop even though they have no state and have been scattered and fragmented.[6]

Jews have done more than survive—they have shown the possibility of possessing simultaneously a strong communal identity and a shared humanity. Even hardheaded and hard-nosed realists such as Hans Morgenthau (who, in full disclosure, was Jewish) congratulated the Jews for their contributions to humanity: "It is an historic fact that there exists within the Jewish tradition a moral and religious loyalty which transcends the boundaries of any particular nation."[7] By constantly gazing toward the horizon and back again, Jews perform the sacred task of creating a common humanity. And they also provide a role model of how to become globally minded without losing a sense of self.[8] The Jewish Question is an enduring feature of Jewish politics—and a central feature of these global times. You don't have to be Jewish to experience the Jewish Question, and everyone can learn from the Jewish experience.

This uncertain people has adopted foreign policy beliefs that are more cosmopolitan than tribal, and their uncertainty and alienation provide reasons why. Before suggesting how their liminality possibly lays the foundation for cosmopolitanism, I want to mention briefly the two archetypical alternatives. The first draws a straight line between religious values, orientation, and action. There are various statements that the Jews possess this or that set of values, as if these were hardwired at Mount Sinai. If Jews are universalists, then it is because Judaism and Jewish values are universalist in essence. To make this claim, however, demands selective reading and considerable historical amnesia. Anyone familiar with Judaism's texts knows they are crowded with sayings and lessons that, by today's standards, are shockingly backward and immoral. I vividly recall sitting around a table at a yeshiva in Jerusalem during the 1982 Israeli invasion of

Lebanon, and having a rabbi tell us that the Talmud permits the slaughter of the enemies of the Jewish people. Public opinion polls indicate that Reform Jews are more committed to values of equality and inclusion than are Orthodox Jews, and I doubt it is because the former have a better understanding of the Torah. There are rabbis and Jewish scholars who forcefully argue that liberalism and Judaism are not compatible for the simple reason that liberalism believes that law derives from humans and Judaism believes it comes from the divine. Judaism matters to the story, but which version of Judaism gets adopted depends on historical circumstances.

The second view is that foreign policy beliefs derive from narrow self-interest. This interpretation is closely identified with realism: because states cannot rely on anyone else for their survival, their national interest revolves around protecting and maximizing their security. The tools that are used depend on where one sits in the pecking order. Great Powers can rely on muscle and have little need for norms, laws, and values. Weak powers, on the other hand, must depend on their wiles, bandwagon with more powerful states, and appeal to universal norms. Jewish foreign policy resembles the foreign policy of all weak states—being highly attentive to their survival, relying on some combination of allying with more powerful actors, placating and appeasing their enemies, framing their interests as the interests of the broader community, and appealing to universal norms. If Jews have seemingly adopted a more "moral" foreign policy than other peoples, it is not because they are more virtuous but because it better serves their interest in security and survival. Simply put, cosmopolitanism is an ideology, and like all ideologies it is designed to serve ulterior motives and fundamental interests; there is always the possibility that a people might believe its own public relations, but onlookers should not be so gullible.

There is something to this argument. Beginning with the Enlightenment and emancipation, Jews (and other minorities) learned the language of humanity. They would not have been so infatuated with it, however, if they had power. Yet no people want to believe that their actions are the product of narrow self-interest or that they have a relationship of convenience with ethics, and so they often comfort themselves by finding principles and values in their history that can fit the times. Fast-forward several decades to the 1960s, and American Jews begin to fall out of love with human rights and exhibit doubts about cosmopolitanism, which, not coincidentally, is also the time when they become more secure and powerful at home and better connected to a Washington that was a global superpower. The right circumstances can unleash anyone's inner tribalism.

A version of this argument is linked to a strategy of security through acceptance. One way that minorities attempt to reduce their insecurity is by convincing the majority population that they are not that different; this often means attempting to mimic those with power, to demonstrate that their characteristics overlap with those of the majority. In this scenario, the majority people do not change how they see themselves; instead, the minority people try to change how the majority sees them. In an alternative scenario, the minority population might try and create a more expansive and shared identity for both the majority and minority populations. This is one of the histories of contemporary nationalism. A little-known aspect in the rise of nationalism is the role minority populations play. In the Arab world, for instance, Christian minorities were at the forefront of Arab nationalism, and one reason why Christians had a vested interest in nationalism is because it possibly checked the Islamic rival. Jewish minorities in parts of Europe took a very similar position, and American Jewish populations worked hard to try and create a more inclusive version of the American nation. A survival streak by a minority, in short, can lead its members to try and establish a more inclusive, cosmopolitan, collective identity.

Yet values cannot always or easily be reduced to self-interest. Not all minority groups have shown the same affection for liberalism. "Although it is true that Jews were prompted to join the liberals because of such motivations, it is still a remarkable fact that they could do so without finding insurmountable impediments in their traditions or inhibitions in their mentality."[9] American Jews, and Jews in general, have a long history of working on behalf of global justice, making up a greater percentage of many of these movements than their actual numbers or even a heavy dose of instrumentalism could predict.[10] Moreover, values once adopted because of self-interest can take on a life of their own and become part of one's identity. Indeed, American

Jews often might be seen as acting against their true interests. Once American Jews achieved a level of security and equality after World War II, they were not going to earn many points with the American power elite by marching alongside Martin Luther King Jr. and joining the campaign for civil rights. American Jews keep voting Democratic even though their economic interests suggest that they should vote Republican.[11] After we answer "What is the matter with Kansas?"—Tom Frank's inquiry into why the poor and middle class in Kansas vote Republican despite the fact that Democrats are closer to their economic interests—we can ask, "What's the matter with New York?"

A third, less conventional reason for American Jews' cosmopolitanism is their liminality and state of alienation.[12] The argument is as follows. Regardless of how much of their identity they abandon and how hard they try to fit in, they will always be outsiders. Gentiles will never fully accept them. Jews, Daniel Bell observed, grow up "casually accepting or ardently seeking cultural assimilation. They find themselves, however, rejected by the dominant culture because of its historical fear of the Jew."[13] The Gentiles, however, are not completely at fault. Jews also want to keep their distance and maintain their distinctiveness. This mutually choreographed dance of approach/avoidance is encapsulated by Woody Allen's famous joke (stolen from another famous American Jew, Groucho Marx, who supposedly paraphrased a famous Austrian Jew, Sigmund Freud): "I do not want to be part of any club that would have someone like me as a member." This assertion of difference rekindles rumors that Jews cannot be trusted.[14] Stranded between two different worlds, Jews experience alienation from others and from themselves, sometimes leading to self-hatred. Moreover, there is a spatial dimension to this story. Alienation is not simply a state of mind, it is also a state of place—or rather the absence of a place. "This otherness, for us, is a special role," writes Daniel Bell. "It cannot exist within a territorial demarcation. It can exist . . . only as the attitude of an eternal stranger in a foreign land." The American Jew is constantly constructing and deconstructing connections to other Jews, other Americans, and the world.

An effect of this liminal standing is that Jews adopt a more critical perspective toward the world.[15] Jews are permanent critics. In the nineteenth century Rabbi Isaac Wise proudly observed that wherever they went, Jews could never leave well enough alone, were constantly doubting and questioning, and their skepticism was constantly stirring up trouble. In the early twentieth century the sociologist Thorstein Veblen observed that the Jew is a "disturber of the intellectual peace [and] an intellectual wayfaring man, a wanderer in the intellectual no-man's land, seeking another place to rest, farther along the road, somewhere over the horizon. They are neither a complaisant nor a contented lot, these aliens of uneasy feet."[16] In his 1926 address to the B'nai B'rith in Vienna, Sigmund Freud credited his Jewish background with enabling him to approach the world with an ability to "join the Opposition."[17] Three decades later Daniel Bell wrote that Jews wear a "double set of glasses, each blending their perspectives into one."[18]

Anyone can be a critic, but not just anyone can transform a critical stance into a new way of seeing—and uniting—the world. Jews, the story continues, are able to perform this magic because they wander between, and exist at the edges of, civilizations. According to Mordecai Kaplan, the Jews' remarkable contribution to global intellectual and spiritual growth owes to their alienation and insider/outsider status.[19] The eminent sociologist Irving Horowitz argued that Jews can only reside in a partial world and on the "marginal interstices of society," and, as a result, Judaism "has the capacity for universalism without demanding an exclusivism in ideology."[20] Isaac Deutscher credited the ability of "non-Jewish Jews" such as Spinoza, Heine, Marx, Trotsky, and Freud to offer truly mind-bending ways of seeing the world to their transnational liminality.[21] Veblen offered a similar account for the Jews' supersized contribution to civilization. They possess a natural intelligence, but their talents remained dormant and were not unleashed until they were forced to "crossbreed" and intermingle with Gentiles. He writes:

> It appears to be only when the gifted Jew escapes from the cultural environment created and fed by the particular genius of his own people, only when he falls into alien lines of gentile inquiry and becomes a naturalized, though hyphenated, citizen in the gentile

republic of learning, that he comes into his own as a creative leader in the world's intellectual enterprise. It is by loss of allegiance, or at the best by force of a divided allegiance to the people of his origin, that he finds himself in the vanguard of modern inquiry.

Because of their liminality, Jews are the world's human growth hormone.

This parable of Jewish alienation and human progress has an additional feature worthy of attention: what is bad for the Jews is good for humanity. The world is better off with Jews being stateless and anxious. Conversely, anything that makes them feel permanently settled and content should be opposed. Veblen explained that his objection to Zionism had nothing to do with what was good or best for the Jews, but rather what was best for civilization. He conceded that the Jews have a rightful claim to a nation-state and are as deserving as any people of security and peace of mind. But what would happen if they received their just desert? If all went according to the Zionist plan, they would become "normal." And, he speculated, once the Jews became a normal people they would no longer feel alienated, and would cease to make a sizable contribution to civilization. God help humanity if Jews find peace and a homeland.

American Jewry's cosmopolitan leanings are a product of how the American context blended the religious, the self-interest, and the sociological. It begins with a religious minority seeking survival through a strategy of acceptance. American Jews attempted to convince their new hosts that they would fit in and not be misfits. Although they might have completely assimilated, they wanted to remain Jews. Accordingly, they reformed their rituals and handpicked and picked over centuries of writing, texts, and interpretations to find a usable past, which they found in the prophets. The political theology of Prophetic Judaism allowed Jews to maintain their group identity in a manner that created a virtuous, friction-retardant cycle between the particular and the universal. The simultaneous presence of the particular and the universal, however, means that there can be no stable solution, only fixes that are more or less satisfactory at a historical moment. To think otherwise is to chase a holy grail. Yet perhaps some quests are not meant to be abandoned. A long line of Jewish religious and political thought suggests that the process is the purpose. Ever since the beginning, Jews have struggled with the central question of their relationship between the particular and the universal, and this struggle represents one of their contributions to the world. For American Jews, though, better to err on the side of the universal.

BROTHERS FROM DIFFERENT PLANETS

The relationship between American Jews and Israel is the object of considerable attention, much of it deserved. They are the two largest Jewish communities in the world, and their relationship will determine the future health and vitality of world Jewry. Both the American Jewish and Israeli Jewish communities feel a heavy responsibility for the future of world Jewry and for each other, and they depend on each other for their identity and sense of well-being. American Jews credit Israel with giving them meaning and reflect that its disappearance would send them into an abyss.

To understate the matter, Israeli Jews are not nearly as sentimental about American Jews or as reliant on them for their emotional needs. "Indeed, Israeli Jews exhibit very little interest in contemporary Diaspora Jewishness or Judaism. For over 60 years, no Israeli curriculum has included a unit on Diaspora Jews. Diaspora Jews are mentioned, if at all, only in connection with the dangers of assimilation and anti-Semitism."[22] Leading Israeli intellectuals will occasionally remind American Jews that they are second-rate Jews, as the Israeli author A. B. Yehoshua did in 2012 when he called American Jews "partial," something of a half-breed. With remarkable regularity, the Israeli government gets into trouble by reminding American Jews just how little Israelis think about them, or even worse, suggesting that they are the enemy. In 2011 the Israeli Ministry of Absorption launched a campaign warning Israeli Jews of the poisonous seductions of American Jewish life.[23] Yet however much they might deny it, Israeli Jews are dependent on American Jews. Israeli Jews like to believe they are the spiritual core of the Jewish people, but such conviction will become increasingly difficult to sustain if American Jews distance themselves from Israel. A conventional wisdom is that American Jews are responsible for a US foreign policy that heavily favors Israel; assuming American Jews help tilt the United States' Middle East policy toward Israel, then their distancing would probably cause American policy-makers to rethink their policies for the region.

The relationship between American Jews and Israel is central to each and to the future of the Jewish people, which is why the relationship is endlessly monitored for signs of trouble.[24] American Jews and Israeli Jews have intense feelings about each other, both good and bad, which is quite normal for any family. Yet they exhibit not just sibling rivalry but also very real personality differences. These are brothers from different planets. They were born under very different signs and under very different circumstances; they matured in very different environments; they live in very different kinds of societies with different political cultures, and, importantly, in one society they are the minority and in the other the majority.

One way to measure the distance between American and Israeli Jews is to imagine how each would score on a test of universalism, where one is particular and ten is universal. Undoubtedly, American Jews would score closer to universalism than would Israeli Jews. American Jews imagine themselves as intimately connected to the world. Israeli Jews less so. In the context of discussing the biblical passage that Jews are a people that dwells alone, Menachem Begin is reported to have closed the evening's conversation by reading the following excerpt from Yaacov Herzog's *A People That Dwells Alone*: "The theory of classic Zionism was national normalization. What was wrong with the theory? It was the belief that the idea of a 'people that dwells alone' is an abnormal concept, when actually a 'people that dwells alone' is the natural concept of the Jewish people."[25] As I have done my research over the last several years, I have imagined giving the following Rorschach test to a sample of American and Israeli Jews: Which is the correct wording of the famous proverb by the first-century scholar Hillel:

(1)   If I am only for myself, who will be for me?
(2)   If I am not for myself who will be for me? If I am only for myself, what am I?

(3)   If I am not for myself who will be for me? If I am only for
        myself, what am I? If not now, when?

The correct answer is (3). However, I have heard many Israeli and tribally oriented American Jews choose (1). At the 2013 J Street annual
conference, a representative from the center-right spectrum of the
Israeli political system jokingly said that Israeli Prime Minister Benjamin Netanyahu assumed it to be "If I am not for myself, who will
be for me?" The audience of progressive Jews, who exuded prophetic
characteristics and would have gotten the proverb right, laughed at
the inside joke.

Another test that does not require knowledge of the Talmud compares each community's feelings about liberalism. American Jews live
and breathe liberalism in ways that Israeli Jews do not. In a statement
that is two decades old but remains as resonant as ever, if not more so,
Liebman and Cohen write:

> These two concepts [universalism and political liberalism] are
> central to American Jewish formulations and essentially meaning-
> less to the Israeli . . . Each group has in effect chosen to attribute
> Judaic values to its own environment. For Israelis this means Jew-
> ish people, land, and state; for American Jews it perforce includes
> not just Jews but the larger society of non-Jews as well. . . . At the
> heart of American Jewish liberalism lies the belief that life among
> Gentiles serves some essential Jewish purpose, and that the kind
> of relationships Jews establish with Gentiles are based not only on
> strategies of survival but on principles of Judaism.[26]

In contrast to a United States that is committed to civic nationalism,
Israel's purpose is to be a Jewish state.[27] The difference also is a product of their different historical circumstances. America has made good
on its promise, and America has the Jews it deserves. The promised
land of Israel, however, did not turn out as dreamy. In one of the most
famous predictions ever made about Israel, Hannah Arendt warned:
"The newly created state of Israel would be a land 'quite other than
the dream of world Jewry, Zionist and non-Zionist'—an armed and
introverted society, in which 'political thought would centre around

military strategy,' degenerating into 'one of those small warrior tribes about whose possibilities and importance history has amply informed us since the days of Sparta,' leaving the Arabs 'homeless exiles' and the Arab problem as 'the only real moral and political issue of Israeli politics.' "[28]

American politics provide additional Rorschach tests of where each community stands on the balance of universalism and particularism. American Jews have been strong supporters of President Barack Obama. In 2008 he received a stunning 78 percent of the American Jewish vote, despite the efforts by various American Jews to throw their considerable political and financial weight behind Republican candidate John McCain, frequently warning that Obama was no friend of the Jews or Israel. Four years later, even after several high-profile rifts between Obama and Prime Minister Netanyahu, American Jews overwhelmingly preferred Obama to Republican candidate Mitt Romney. American Jewry's strong and consistent support for Obama is often explained by the standard reasons American Jews vote Democratic, and then some: undoubtedly many can identify with his multiculturalism and acceptance of diversity. And if his occasional flare-ups with Israel do not cost him too much with Jewish supporters, it might be because they largely agree with him on the need to stop settlement expansion and the urgency of a two-state solution or because a candidate's stance on Israel no longer determines how they vote. In contrast, Israeli Jews have a deep distrust of Obama. Their views often veer away from reasoned policy differences to the kinds of accusations that are familiar in Tea Party circles—Obama was not born in America, he is a Muslim and is anti-Semitic, and he freely associates with radical voices that deny Israel's right to exist. And these views are not necessarily part of the fringe of Israeli politics. Michael Oren, the American-born former Israeli ambassador to the United States, attempted to explain why Obama has so little sympathy for Israel: because he has "daddy issues"—abandoned by two Muslim father figures, he strives to be accepted in the Islamic world.

Why would American Jews be so naive? Why would they have such a distorted view of reality and back political views clearly designed to hurt Israel and the Jewish people? Israeli Jews often draw from the same material that was used to explain the problem with *galuth* Jews. American Jews, like all Diaspora Jews, have led overly charmed lives, operate with a false sense of security, are hypersensitive about how they are viewed by the Gentiles, and want to get along by going along. In this tradition, Michael Oren explained the self-destructive behavior of American Jews in the following way: "I could not help questioning whether American Jews really felt as secure as they claimed. Perhaps persistent fears of anti-Semitism impelled them to distance themselves from Israel and its often controversial policies. Maybe that was why so many of them supported Obama, with his preference for soft power, his universalist White House seders, and aversion to tribes."[29] American Jews are dangerously gullible.

Their different values also are evident in their foreign policy beliefs. In stylized fashion, American Jews want a Jewish identity heavily laced with the prophetic tradition and the belief that Jews are a nation among nations; Israeli Jews tend toward tribalism. American Jews would like to make the world a better place; Israeli Jews are too consumed with building and defending an ethnonational state to worry about much else. American Jews have been highly sympathetic to a value-driven foreign policy; Israeli Jews are more inclined toward the standard tools of realpolitik.[30] American Jews think in the moral categories associated with a minority people; Israeli Jews think in terms of political categories and with the pragmatism and expediency expected from a people with power. American Jews have had a long-standing interest in social justice at home and abroad; it is of secondary importance to Israeli Jews, and some see it as a threat.

These differences shape not only American Jews' and Israel's foreign policy beliefs but also their bilateral relations.[31] Because they care dearly about their relationship and are committed to its future, American Jews and Israel have a *ketubah,* a marriage contract, which includes a set of rights and responsibilities. Several factors influenced the nature and content of their initial contract. They did not marry under the easiest of circumstances—in many ways, it was an arranged marriage.[32] The wedding was cause for celebration, but there was not much of a honeymoon. Each one came into the marriage with its own expectations, needs, and suspicions of the other. American Jews were committed to Israel's survival and welfare, not only because they cared about their fellow Jews but also because Israel's existence was essential to their own well-being and Jewish identity. Zionism and Israel made it easier for them to be Jews. Israel now became their homeland, replacing Lithuania, Poland, and other countries of origin that provided unpleasant memories. Israel, in this way, would allow American Jews to be like other ethnic groups in the United States.[33] They now had a homeland they can visit, a language they can speak, and even an army they can salute. Still, they worried about what kind of state Israel would become and whether Israel's existence would complicate their own.

Israel saw itself as being charged with the historic mission of saving the Jews in body and soul. Israelis expected Diaspora Jews to leave their soulless existence and make aliyah to the new Jewish state. American Jews did move, but to the suburbs, not to kibbutzim and development towns in Israel. If American Jews did not have the wisdom and wherewithal to return to their homeland, then they needed to know their place: providing financial, political, and diplomatic support for Israel and entrée into the corridors of power in Washington, and with no questions asked. And Israeli leaders had a responsibility and moral obligation to speak on behalf of world Jewry, including American Jewry. American Jews were, at best, a junior partner, the wife in a traditional marriage. Although Israeli leaders would repeatedly say that they had tremendous respect for American Jews, at times their "real feelings" of contemptuousness of these "second-rate" Jews would slip out. Their differences surfaced immediately following Israel's declaration of independence. Within a few years the American Jewish community and Israel worked out a modus vivendi of rights and responsibilities, and dos and don'ts, which became formalized in an exchange of letters between Prime Minister Ben-Gurion and the AJC's Jacob Blaustein. They had a contract, both largely kept their promises, and peace prevailed in the marriage for decades.

That was then—what about now? The contract was a reflection of the times, but much has changed over the decades, and these changes appear to be weakening the "symbiotic relationship between the Golden Land [America] and the Promised Land [Israel]."[34] The world has changed, and in ways that are weakening the Jewish identity. Contemporary globalization, a scaled-up version of the Enlightenment and modernization, is rumored to be the culprit. According to one report, the greatest challenge facing the Jewish people is the "difficulty of preserving, developing, and furthering a unique Jewish identity in an open and universally-minded global environment."[35] Contemporary globalization contains cosmopolitan ideologies that elevate principles of humanity over particularism, and the "emergence of a global village and with it, massive exposure to a huge diversity of identities and cultures," is encouraging Jews to see themselves not as a separate people but rather as part of an integrated community.[36] Yet in the same way that different national experiences shaped the Jewish response to modernity, the reactions by American and Israeli Jewish communities to globalization reflect their national histories. American Jews, given their prophetic theology, individualism, and relative affluence, are more likely to be enticed by the affective charms of globalization than are tribally minded Israelis.[37] Quite possibly, globalization is drawing American Jews closer to the world and further from Israel.

Also, American Jews and Israel no longer appear to need each other in the same way.[38] American Jews still feel connected to Israel but don't register the same pride, are often unsettled and embarrassed by Israel's conduct, are no longer as dependent on Israel for their search for meaning, and do not have the same inferiority complex or the same guilt about staying put. These changing attitudes are said to be causing American Jews to be less financially generous, less easily mobilized for Israel, and less willing to accept the perceived "love-it-or-leave-it" attitude of AIPAC and other established Jewish organizations.[39] In fact, while American Jews are not as supportive as they once were, Christian Zionists in the United States are far more numerous, politically powerful, and much less likely to ask uncomfortable questions.

Israeli Jews have more respect for American Jews than they once did, but because the former are more economically and strategically secure, are less reliant. Yet Israel remains dependent on American Jewry's approval, in part because its possible withdrawal would discredit Israel's moral purpose to be a state for the Jewish people. The consequence is that Israeli Jews are more willing than ever to factor the opinions of American Jews into religious life.[40]

These recent and projected changes are central to why relations between American Jews and Israeli Jews are becoming more complicated. Yet there remains an underlying commitment to, and dependence on, each other. Divorce is not an option. They will stay together for the sake of the children and because a separation would be too painful and too destructive to each partner's sense of self. American Jews, for the foreseeable future, will likely see Israel as an important source of their Jewish identity and counterweight to their assimilation. Israelis will certainly continue to want a strong relationship with American Jews, not only for instrumental reasons but also because Israel sees itself as representing the Jewish people, and it is difficult to do so if the second largest Jewish community in the world keeps its distance. Consequently, the future could be like the present—a mixture of affection and ambivalence. Or, the future could be an extreme version of the present, characterized by a growing distance as American Jews heal the world and Israeli Jews fortify the walls of an ethnonational state. In such circumstances, their relationship might be best described as a loveless marriage.

But could American Jews and Israeli Jews become closer? One way to imagine this possibility is to ask what would have to happen for them to achieve similar scores on my measures of particularism/universalism. There are two scenarios that might move American Jews closer to the current Israeli position. One possibility is that a growing percentage of American Jews becomes Orthodox and more inclined to see the Jews as a people apart. It is possible. However, if so it will be a very slow-moving demographic trend. Moreover, it assumes that modern Orthodoxy in an American context is incapable of incorporating a universalistic dimension. The other scenario is a catastrophic surge in anti-Semitism. The various attacks on Jews in Europe over the last few years, often by Muslims, have given rise to a concern for a "new" anti-Semitism and renewed questions about the future of European Jewry. Is the United States immune from such happenings? If American Jews cannot be certain, then they better think about what they will do, just in case. This is the premise of Philip Roth's *The Plot against America*, in which Charles Lindbergh rallies America against the Jews, and in turn, the Jews are driven into the arms of a Jewish state.

American Jews and Israelis might possibly now be sharing a narrative of Jews as victims, but not all victims see their suffering in exactly the same way. Many American Jews have interpreted their suffering through the filter of Prophetic Judaism and concluded that the Jews are uniquely qualified to be a light unto nations.[41] Israeli Jews wear the victim identity in ways that lead to a different stand toward the world. Because it brilliantly encapsulates and explains this possible difference, it is worth quoting in full a lengthy passage from Ehud Luz's *Wrestling with an Angel*:

> There is a decisive difference between the way the victim image functions for a powerless minority struggling against an oppressive majority—like the Jewish people in exile—and the way it functions in a sovereign polity possessed of military power. In the former case, the narrative of victimization serves as an ideological weapon, a source of comfort and solace to a defenseless group. But in the latter case it can serve to legitimate and encourage indiscriminate violence. The victimized community can gradually be transformed from the persecuted party to the persecuting one. Having assumed for itself a monopoly on suffering, the victim-community becomes indifferent to the suffering of the other. Furthermore, it expects the world to sympathize entirely with its position, as a way of repaying a moral debt and atoning for its wrongs done it in the past. It refuses to consider at face value any accusation made by others, seeing in such accusations merely another line in the chain of hatred, suffering, and degradation that is its exclusive inheritance. Being in constant danger, it also rejects all demands from inside for self-criticism and moral accounting with the claim that they are likely to weaken its resolve to stand fast. Moral criticism is taken as a sign of weakness or lack of faith in the rightness of the struggle, and it is thus branded as hypocrisy or falsification. In this way, the community may gradually lose not only its moral sensitivity but also its awareness of the limits of its power.[42]

American Jews and Israeli Jews might each see themselves as victims, but they will act very differently depending on whether they are in or out of power.[43]

Alternatively, American and Israeli Jews might align if the latter became more universalistic and cosmopolitan, finding their own prophetic tradition. For those American Jews and Israelis who contemplate and work for such an outcome, tikkun olam figures prominently. One reason why some Israeli Jews place great hopes in tikkun olam is because the traditional, unifying causes that involved saving Jews from harm no longer exist. The Soviet Jews do not exist anymore— because there is no Soviet Union and because the Jews who wanted to leave have left. The last remaining Jewish community in Ethiopia was airlifted to Israel in August 2013. Most of the other large pockets of Jewish communities outside of Israel reside in countries that are friendly to Jews. The one ominous exception is the growing anti-Semitism among Muslims, especially in Europe. Still, in the absence of an immediate and direct threat, American and Israeli Jews have more reason to put their hopes on joint action for cosmopolitanism.

A small but growing number of Israelis are developing Israel's capacity for global volunteer work, hoping to nurture Israel's sense of universalism and commitment to tikkun olam, and perhaps even groom it for a leadership position.[44] There is the Global Gabriel Project, which brings together Israeli and Diaspora Jews to work on literacy projects with the local Indian Jewish community in New Delhi. Tevel B'Tzedek has been slowly but impressively expanding its ability to help Israelis volunteer on short- and long-term stays in more parts of the world. The centerpiece of these developments, though, is the Tikkun Empowerment Network, known by its acronym TEN (which means "give" in Hebrew). Sponsored by the Jewish Agency, it brings together Israelis and Diaspora Jews to work in various sites, including Kiryat Shmona, Israel; Hyderabad, India; Gondar, Ethiopia; and Oaxaca, Mexico; and the hope is to expand to other sites in the near future. Part of the motive for the initiative is not only to meet existing demand among Israeli Jews but also to make it relatively easy for young Israelis to engage in social action while they are abroad. After they do their military service, many Israelis travel the world, often heading to remote, less-traveled, and impoverished locales. Since they are already there, the logic goes, why not provide them with volunteer opportunities? And why not do it with American and other Diaspora Jews, with the hope that it will encourage Israelis to become a little more outward-looking and create a sense of Jewish peoplehood?

Israelis who champion tikkun olam point to various reasons why its time has come and why it might help cure what ails Israel. It represents the logical next step for an Israel whose mission is to help build up the Jewish people. The Jewish Agency has played a central role in this mission, and it describes tikkun olam as the third stage of a natural evolution.[45] In stage one the immediate challenge was to create the physical infrastructure necessary for Israel to become a modern nation-state. Check. In stage two it addressed the complex challenge of resettling Jews from around the world and creating a modern Jewish nation. Check. Now that it has completed the task of state and nation building, it is ready for stage three: to strengthen the collective identity of the Jewish people. Tikkun olam figures centrally in its plans.

There are other reasons why Israelis might be becoming more open to Jewish humanitarianism. Left-leaning Jews, who have soured on the peace process, want to find another way to work for peace and justice. In this respect, they sound like many progressive American Jews who have decided that tikkun olam, instead of Israel, is a less complicated way to express their Jewish identity. Now that Zionism has exhausted itself, Israelis are involved in their own search for meaning. Tikkun olam is important for Israel because it runs counter to its self-absorbed zeitgeist. Consumed by their own needs, mistrusting of others, and often seeing themselves as permanent victims, Israelis might learn that their problems are relatively minor compared to those of many others.[46]

Not only are the conditions right for a tikkun olam revolution, but also the rewards will reinforce this movement. An Israel committed to tikkun olam would become immediately more attractive to other Jews and the world. It would certainly appeal to American Jews.[47] Israel is judged according to whether it lives up to the international community's highest values, and tikkun olam might help restore its legitimacy.[48] In other words, by becoming committed to global justice, Israel would develop a kinder, gentler reputation. Not only might others feel better about Israel, but they might also be more easily persuaded by what it has to say—that is, it would acquire soft power.[49] In general, if Israeli and American Jews worked together, it would represent a Jewish multiplier. In rousing words, one report stated that "an initiative encouraging Tikkun Olam activities under the leadership of the State of Israel and the Jewish people could reposition the State of

Israel and the Jewish people as a leading force in contributing to the whole of humanity, in the spirit of the vision of the Prophets."[50]

Israel, though, is relatively immune to tikkun olam fever. One Israeli I interviewed communicated this indifference through the following joke: "What did the Israeli Jew say to the American Jew? How do you say tikkun olam in Hebrew?" Israel was never outwardly oriented, and today it is less so. At the time of the state's founding, when it was fighting for survival and consumed by the challenge of nation-building, it nevertheless identified with a prophetic ideology. The first generation of Israeli officials proudly offered their young state as a role model for other developing countries, citing the accomplishments of the kibbutzim and agricultural development, and had an official program that sent Israelis to provide technical assistance. Those days are long gone. In 2010 Israeli foreign assistance as a percentage of its gross national income was 0.07 percent compared to the average of 0.32 percent among the developed economies. Israel ranked even below Italy, the last on the list at 0.15 percent. And this figure looks even less impressive when it is recognized that Israel's definition of foreign assistance includes immigrant absorption, defense, homeland security, and the Water Authority budget.[51]

A recent story dramatizes the situation. In Fall 2013 world leaders gathered in South Africa to pay their respects to Nelson Mandela, to both the man and the ideals he stood for. One of the few countries not to send high-level representation, Israel was on the outside looking in. According to official Israeli sources, Israel was unable to attend because of the expense. This nearly *Onion*-worthy explanation only drew attention to the real reason: Israel had close intelligence, political, economic, and military ties with the racist government that had imprisoned Mandela for a quarter century. All transitions have winners and losers, and when the apartheid regime was finally dismantled, Israel lost. Unintentionally punctuating this point, during the week of events surrounding Mandela's funeral the Israeli newspaper *Ha'aretz* ran a story recalling that the South African air force helped "rescue" the Israeli air force with a large purchase of advanced fighters. At the same time that some Israelis were suggesting that it was fine to be on the wrong side of history if it helped Israeli national interests, American Jews were mourning Mandela's passing, referring to him as a modern-day Moses who liberated his people, and calling on Jews to honor his legacy by working for the betterment of humanity.

Israeli nationalism, similar to many nationalisms, tends to leave little space for the needs of others. An advisor to former President Shimon Peres, who worked directly on these issues observed that because Judaism is universal and cosmopolitan, it remains just at the surface ready to bloom in Israel. Still, he acknowledged, contemporary Israel is not the ideal climate for such a venture.[52] Others looking for evidence of Israel's cosmopolitanism often go to extraordinary lengths. Referring to Darfur, one Israeli journalist pronounced: "Israel cares. . . . The response of Israeli society shows that both the Israeli public and the Jewish diaspora share common beliefs, concerns, and values, factors that tie them together as one people. These principles of social justice, tikkun olam, fixing the world, can form the basis for common action between Israel and the Diaspora, independent of the government."[53] Yet there was scant evidence provided that Israel cared what was happening in the Sudan. Indeed, Israel made African refugees feel quite unwelcome.

If Israelis evidence little affection for tikkun olam, it might be because they don't need it. As the Israeli journalist Shmuel Rosen commented, "American Jews use tikkun olam to turn away from the tribal identity. . . . But Jewish Israelis do not need tikkun olam to build identity. It is tribal and nationalistic, unapologetically."[54] Many Israelis have told me that their lack of Jewish humanitarianism is a sign of their emotional health. American Jews use tikkun olam to convince themselves and the Gentiles that they are just like everyone else. Israeli Jews, on the other hand, do not labor under such anxieties and therefore do not need to accessorize their identity in this way.

A final reason for the lack of popularity of tikkun olam in Israel is that some Israelis see it not only as an unnecessary extravagance but also as an outright threat. Israelis are not the only ones who think so. Even American Jews who are sympathetic to the prophetic tradition and a universalist orientation believe that too much of a good thing might be fatal. Ever since American Jewry began toning down rituals and turning up ethics, critics have warned that a Judaism defined by ethics is not only no substitute for an authentic

Judaism but also might have a blanching effect.[55] For instance, Daniel Bell cautioned that a Jewish community that reduces Judaism to ethics and superficial rationalism, taking the Torah and transforming it into "glossy moral platitudes," provides "no deep feeling for being Jewish. . . . Theologically, there is no more justification for a special Jewish ethic than for a Unitarian one . . . or for any non-ritualistic creed."[56] For similar reasons, and with greater passion, religious Jews in Israel have a disdainful attitude toward American Jewry and see tikkun olam as toxic. For right-leaning Israelis tikkun olam poses a threat not just to Judaism but also to Israel. They often treat human rights as a potential threat to Israel's security. Accordingly, they have established various organizations such as NGO Monitor to report on their activities and have passed laws to control them under the guise that they contribute to the de-legitimation of Israel and harm its security.[57] These watchdog organizations though, do not seem as concerned with the (Christian and Jewish) religious organizations in the United States that help fund settlement activity.

Is there anything that American Jews can do to help support tikkun olam in Israel? Some have proposed that American Jews could be something of a spiritual guide. From the early days of Zionism many American Zionists believed that they might help nurture the right kind of Zionism—often implicitly and explicitly contrasting their vision with Labor Zionism's more nationalist and socialist interpretation. At the time of Israel's birth, many American Jews argued that they could do more than give money and support—they could help the new state fight the understandable temptation to cut moral corners in the name of national security. Since then American Jewish organizations, including the American Jewish Committee and the New Israel Fund, have supported Israeli organizations that champion principles of diversity in religion and ethnicity. Peter Beinart has been delivering jeremiads on the need for American Jews to save Israel from itself by helping it reunite with its liberal side.

It is not only American Jews who see themselves as playing the role of spiritual guide. In 1950 Robert Weltsch suggested that American Jewry could help Israel avoid an excess of tribalism. Born in Prague in 1891, from 1919 to 1938 he was the chief editor of the highly respected Berlin-based Zionist newspaper *Juedische Rundschau* and was well known for his advocacy of a binational state in Palestine. He fled to Palestine in 1938 and then ran the Leo Baeck Institute. Having experienced firsthand the violent excesses of nationalism, he feared that Israel might develop similarly unflattering characteristics. Writing from Jerusalem soon after Israeli independence, he suggested that American Jews could perform an important service and save Israel from provincialism. It can link Israel with the

> larger civilized world and transmit to her what is best in the human traditions of the great free countries outside. The view that external influence may be needed to keep Israel within the orbit of Jewish ethical tradition may seem exaggerated at the present moment—while European educated Jews are still predominant in Israel—but it can soon become a matter of bitter reality. . . . Just as the Diaspora needs the national cultural values that may be created in Israel, so Israel needs a compensating spiritual influence to check any tendencies to an excessively isolationist nationalism. For it will be a miracle if young Israelis now growing up in an atmosphere of permanent watchfulness and semi-military preparedness do not fall prey to nationalist narrow-mindedness which inclines to underestimate, even scorn, universal and supranational values.[58]

American Jews do not have to make aliyah to contribute to a vibrant Israel.

American Jews and Israeli Jews are separate peoples, formed by distinct national experiences, differently situated in relationship to the national and the cosmopolitan, and have taken separate journeys to find their home in the world. Israel and the United States offer two different ways for Jews to be in the world. Israel offers a solution born of nineteenth-century European nationalism that ultimately found its answer to the Jewish Problem with the creation of a Jewish homeland. This history has shaped how Israeli Jews understand the Jewish Question. They now have a state, territory, and land of their own. They have a military whose mission is to protect the Jewish people. They are unapologetic nationalists and do not need to make excuses for their concern about the needs of their (Jewish) citizens and the Jewish people.

America has provided a different set of conditions and possible responses to being Jewish in the world. As a country that celebrates principles of equality, liberty, and autonomy, and imagines the possibility of a diversity within a unity, it nurtured the prophetic theology and the idea that the particular and the universal were equally nourishing. Jews did not have to choose between their communal identity and their universal aspirations; they could have both. And they would not be only passive recipients or the sole beneficiaries of this more forgiving environment, for they would help create a world that benefited all. This condition of rooted cosmopolitanism is the best of both worlds. It has allowed American Jews to feel grounded. Yet it also has enabled Jews to venture far and wide.

WHAT IS THE FUTURE OF THE FOREIGN POLICIES OF AMERICAN JEWS?

The future foreign policies of American Jews depend on the future of American Jews, their identity, how they imagine themselves in relation to the particular and the universal, and how such projections connect to contemporary practices of tribalism and cosmopolitanism, especially as they relate to the Jewish Problem and the Jewish Question. To get a sense of the rich array of possible futures we only need revisit how Jews around the world have imagined their relationship to the national and the cosmopolitan for more than a century. As in the past, some scenarios are more likely than others because they are more firmly rooted in American circumstances and trends among American Jews. As in the past, as well, otherwise seemingly durable trends might be disrupted by a "bolt from the blue." There is no predicting these black swans except that they are likely to exist, and, if the future is like the past, they will originate outside the United States. In the past the Holocaust and the 1967 war had such an impact. In the future it might be a Europe that abandoned its Jews to the new anti-Semitism, an Israel that became surrounded by radical Islamic forces actively attempting to destroy it, or an Israel that made the Arabs second-class citizens or attempted to cleanse the territories of non-Jews.

Still, two scenarios—one that veers toward tribalism and the other toward cosmopolitanism—are most likely because they represent a combination of the past and the present. For simplicity's sake, though, I want to treat them separately rather than thinking through how they might mix. Before sketching these two alternatives, I want to acknowledge one highly unlikely possibility that ignites the fears of American Jews: American Jews will cease to articulate a Jewish foreign policy because American Jews will cease to exist. In other words, this ever-dying people, at least in the United States, will become extinct in spirit if not in corporeality. When American Jews speculate about the demise of Jewish communities around the world, they imagine that the cause is anti-Semitism. When they speculate about their own demise, they imagine the cause is assisted suicide through assimilation. With little compelling reason to stay Jewish, intermarriage on the rise, and an Israel that no longer serves as a force multiplier for Jewish identity but rather as a force subduction, American Jews will assimilate to the point that Jewishness is reduced to bagels and the occasional Yiddish slang word. Often these fears are inflamed by a report or study that charts the projected decline of American Jewry; the most recent alarm was sounded by the 2013 survey by the Pew Research Center, which, depending on how you read the report, fell somewhere between bad and horrible news for the future of American Jewry.[59] If American Jews cease to exist, the Jewish Problem or the Jewish Question will no longer bother these former members of the tribe.

One future is defined by tribalism and the overshadowing of the Jewish Question by the Jewish Problem. As in the past, this tribally oriented future can have roots in both religious and secular Judaism. My history of the foreign policies of American Jews has neglected Orthodox Jewry largely because it has had little impact on the matter, but that could change, especially if Orthodox Jewry becomes more prominent in American Jewish life. Indeed, Orthodox Jews have a well-deserved reputation for being more attentive and sensitive, compared to non-Orthodox Jews, to the welfare of the Jewish people. In those areas such as parts of New York where they compose an important voting bloc, they are much more likely, relative to other Jews, to be single-issue voters when it comes to Israel. However, the Orthodox

community is not monolithic and is divided among different interpretations, including modern Orthodoxy, and some of these offshoots
show a growing interest in the Jewish Question and express obligations to the world beyond the Jews. Tribalism also can be fueled by
the non-Orthodox, though for reasons having less to do with theology
and more with ethnicity. Indeed, for many non-Orthodox Jews, identity is formed less around Judaism than around Israel and broader
fears of anti-Semitism. Although many Jews who actively support
Israel also give to non-Jewish causes, the tribally minded more unapologetically privilege Jewish needs.

Even if they are a minority among American Jews, the tribally
oriented might dominate American Jewish political life and thus
have a decisive influence on the foreign policies of American Jews,
because they will control the major American Jewish organizations
for several reasons. They most clearly and closely identify with Jewish interests and thus are most easily mobilized; as a consequence,
they are likely to become more involved and take leadership roles in
the major Jewish organizations. They also might be less bothered by
cognitive dissonance than prophetically minded Jews. In other words,
they have an easier time reconciling their defense of an Israel that
does not comply with the same values that they enjoy and defend
in the United States. According to some observers, this world has
already arrived. Most famously, Peter Beinart observes that there is
an "American Jewish Establishment" that represents the passions of a
well-connected and highly committed minority.[60] Left behind, he argues, is a silent majority. Some, including Beinart, claim that the reason for their silence is because they have been locked out of the major
Jewish organizations. Yet they also might be silent because they no
longer care enough to make their voices heard. This possibility leads
to the second alternative.

The alternative to the tribal is the cosmopolitan, which treats the
Jewish Question as relatively more important than the Jewish Problem, wants to see a Jewish people that is connected to humanity, and
expresses greater ambivalence toward a more nationalistic Israel. In
this vein, many Jewish leaders in the United States and elsewhere
are using the term *Jewish peoplehood*, which might not render Israel
invisible but certainly downsizes and decenters it. And similar to the

past, this development is likely to be fueled by a combination of identity and interests.

There are the traditional prophetic sources of a more cosmopolitan-oriented American Jewry. In addition, there is talk of American Jews developing a "postethnic" identity.[61] Postethnicity does not have a single meaning. For some it can be little more than identity as fashion accessory and an opportunity to surround oneself with more items, food, and music from more parts of the world. For others it is an invitation to integrate different traditions, practices, and rituals into one's life, creating something of a fluid, do-it-yourself cultural stew. In either and any case, it means that distinctions no longer make a difference, at least not politically. Conversations about the postethnic possibilities for American Jews typically paint a multiculturalism that includes a Judaism that is less about religion and more about spirituality. In the same way that the line between Jew and non-Jew becomes hazy in a postethnic world, the Jewish in Jewish Problem and Jewish Question fade into the background. There might still be a Jewish Problem. But there are lots of problems. There are GLBT Problems. Muslim Problems. Gender Problems. And on and on. In this way, they are twenty-first-century versions of Rosa Luxemburg's conclusion that there is no human reason to elevate Jewish suffering over the suffering of others. Although some postethnic Jews might still make a case that they have a special responsibility to Jews, such justifications will have to be seen as reasoned exceptions to the fundamental principles of humanity and impartiality. Not only will the Jewish Problem no longer occupy the politics of postethnic Jews, but Israel might become a "normal" state and no longer be a place of significance. To get a sense of this world, recall features of pre-twentieth-century Jewish life in America.[62]

Yet if cosmopolitanism has a future in American Jewry, it also will have to be connected to the interests of American Jews as they define them. There are the traditional motives, such as attempting to fit into an American society that is becoming more multicultural, respond positively to a world that is becoming more globalized and internationalized, and connect to broader humanistic trends in domestic and world politics. Additionally, Israel might encourage American Jews to turn to cosmopolitanism for various reasons. Israel's nationalism might make cosmopolitanism more attractive to American Jews. In the nineteenth century many European Jews attempted to put as much distance between themselves and the insular, cloistered world of shtetl and ghetto life by joining socialist and secular-humanist movements. Perhaps in this century the more American Jews perceive Israel to be insular, nationalistic, and tribal, the more likely they will be to seek a cosmopolitan politics to counterbalance the tribalism of Israel. Relatedly, if Jews are looking for a source for Jewish peoplehood, it looks less and less likely that Israel will play that unifying role. Israel once unified the Jews and helped forge a sense of a broader Jewish community among the diaspora, but no more. Israel no longer unifies the way it once did, and in fact often divides. Consequently, if American Jews are looking for a sense of Jewish peoplehood, they might do best to look beyond Israel. Also, Israel unwittingly fans the flames of anti-Semitism, just as Zionism did a century ago, which will further encourage Diaspora Jews to seek their Jewish identity elsewhere. Of course, there are liberal Zionist voices who argue that the proper response to an Israel losing its way is to help it rediscover its true democratic spirit by removing Israel from the territories and by safeguarding the rule of law. But assuming there is no withdrawal, it will become increasingly difficult to connect Israel's values to their own.

As an alternative to Israel in this age of globalization, many of those who want to retain and develop a sense of Jewish peoplehood have resurrected the idea of diaspora nationalism. Diaspora nationalism's roots were in the late nineteenth century and the struggle by European Jews to maintain their communal identity while living in a world of nation-states. It accommodated itself to the states system because it accepted that Jews would become citizens of their countries. Yet it also wanted to see the development of transnational political and cultural ties among Diaspora Jews. Many versions of diaspora nationalism also saw no need for a sovereign state for the Jews. A homeland would serve the function of providing a space for Jewish belonging and cultural renaissance. Those advocating diaspora nationalism a century ago made their case not only on what was pragmatic but also on what was principled. The Jews' historic mission could only be performed while they were scattered around the world. Not having a state was not a sign of weakness but rather a sign of strength. As the early twentieth-century Jewish writer and activist Simon Dubnow wrote, "State, territory, army, the external attributes of national power, are for you superfluous luxury. Go out into the world to prove that a people can continue to live without these attributes, solely and alone through strength of spirit."[63] Conversely, he and others argued, the Jews will lose their purpose if they get their own state.

Diaspora nationalism is enjoying a twenty-first-century reconsideration for some very familiar reasons.[64] There are those who argue that it answers the challenges posed by this moment in the states system. Whereas in the nineteenth century diaspora nationalism was a functional response to the rise of the nation-state, now it is a useful answer to its decline. With globalization eroding the world's territorial boundaries and unleashing new forms of transnationalism and transnational identities, it is perfect for the age.[65] Other arguments in support of diaspora nationalism also suggest that Israel became something of a false promise. Although Zionism aspired to turn Jews into a "normal people," perhaps normality is not so desirable. Jews might be no better cut out for political sovereignty than any other people. The Jewish experiment with political power might not have been conducted at the best time or under the most opportune circumstances, but it provides one more piece of evidence in favor of the diasporic option. Maybe the Jews were at their best when they were a prophetic people living in the diaspora.[66]

I doubt that diaspora nationalism will become any more accepted in the future than it was a century ago, but its prophetic foundations are likely to remain as attractive as ever to American Jews. Yet however attractive the prophetic tradition has been and will continue to be, it always confronted two limits, both imposed by a basic desire of the Jewish people to survive in body and soul. To recognize this nearly primordial imperative, I want to turn not to a Jewish voice but rather to the Christian theologian and Judeophile Reinhold Niebuhr. He offered the following remarks on the occasion of writing the introduction to a book by Waldo Frank, a well-known progressive in the American Jewish community in the mid-twentieth century. In this collection of essays published in 1944, Frank was concerned that World War II, flashes of anti-Semitism on American soil, and the

Holocaust would cause American Jews to turn inward and forsake their prophetic calling. He wanted American Jews to stay the prophetic course, and apparently thought that Niebuhr would support him.

Niebuhr used the opportunity not to praise Frank's vision but rather to challenge the prophetic tradition. In one particularly telling passage, Niebuhr asks: "How can the 'particular' be a servant of the universal, if the life of the particular has no security? It is of course possible for individuals, in the highest reaches of ethical freedom, to sacrifice their lives for a cause greater than they. But is that possible for a nation?"[67] It is impossible, Niebuhr answers. Nations, including the Jews, cannot be expected to take universalism to its logical conclusion because it would entail their erasure and extinction, which, of course, runs against their survival instinct. Also, Niebuhr cynically adds, groups can be expected to draw from their own history and survival imperative to offer their distinct version of the universal. There can be no "pure" universalism because all are corruptions and artifacts of a "will to power" and "will to survive." So, according to Niebuhr, we are left with an unresolvable tension between the needs of a people and the demands of transcendence. The Jews, at least those who follow the prophetic tradition to its end, have been trying to do the impossible. "A nation cannot be a church," he insisted. However, he added, "it must be gratefully recorded that the Jews have come closer to accomplishing this impossible task than any other people."[68]

NOTES

INTRODUCTION

1. Messinger, "Jewish Service: A Vision for 21st Century American Judaism."
2. Oz, "Discreet Charm of Zionism," 107–8, cited from Dowty, "Israeli Foreign Policy and the Jewish Question."
3. Cited from Young, "Emma Lazarus and Her Jewish Problem," 291.
4. Cited from Mendelsohn, *On Modern Jewish Politics*, 37.
5. Karl Emil Franzos, "Every Country Has the Jews It Deserves," 1877; cited from Mendes-Flohr and Reinharz, *Jew in the Modern World*, 253–54.
6. Liebman and Cohen, *Two Worlds of Judaism*, 96.

CHAPTER ONE: HEINE'S LAW AND JEWISH FOREIGN POLICIES

1. Martin Buber, "The Jew in the Modern World," in Buber, *Israel and the World*, 167.
2. Ibid. For a related thesis, see Marx, *The People in Between*.
3. Hammerschlag, *Figural Jew*, 7.
4. Buber, "Jew in the Modern World," 167, 168.
5. Ibid., 170.
6. Ibid., 169.
7. For various statements on the tension between the universalism and particularism in Jewish religious and political thought, see Fine, "Two Faces of Universalism"; Prell, "Against the Cultural Grain"; Borowitz, "Dialects of Jewish Particularity"; Hollander and Kaminsky, "Introduction: 'A Covenant to the People, A Light to the Nations' "; Hammerschlag, *Figural Jew*; Talmon, "Uniqueness and Universality of Jewish History"; Cohen, "A Preface to Modern Jewish Political Thought"; and Sorkin, "Between Messianism and Survival." For a fascinating exchange involving former Israeli Prime Minister Menachem Begin on the contemporary relevance of the biblical passage on the Jewish people's dwelling alone among the nations, see Avner, *The Prime Ministers*, 395–99.
8. Berlin, *Against the Current*, 257.

9. Katz, *Out of the Ghetto*; Kallen, *Zionism and World Politics*, 37–38; Mahler, *Jewish Emancipation*.

10. Levitt, "Impossible Assimilations, American Liberalism, and Jewish Difference."

11. Kallen, "Judaism as Disaster," 48.

12. Miller and Ury, "Cosmopolitanism: The End of Jewishness?"; Trevor-Roper, "Jewish and Other Nationalisms."

13. Naraniecki, "Karl Popper on Jewish Nationalism and Cosmopolitanism.".

14. Marx, "On the Jewish Question."

15. Birnbaum, *Geography of Hope*; Vromen, "Hannah Arendt's Jewish Identity"; Bernstein, *Hannah Arendt and the Jewish Question*; Naraniecki, "Karl Popper on Jewish Nationalism and Cosmopolitanism"; Tamir, "A Strange Alliance"; Hacohen, "Dilemmas of Cosmopolitanism"; Dubnov, *Isaiah Berlin: The Journey of a Jewish Liberal*; Dubnov, "Anti-Cosmopolitan Liberalism"; Dubnov, "A Tale of Trees and Crooked Timbers"; Knepper, "Polanyi, 'Jewish Problems,' and Zionism."

16. Dubnov, "Anti-Cosmopolitan Liberalism."

17. Mendelsohn, *On Modern Jewish Politics*, 98–100.

18. Horowitz, *Israeli Ecstasies / Jewish Agonies*, 203.

19. Katznelson and Birnbaum, *Paths of Emancipation*; Podhoretz, *Why Are Jews Liberals?*

20. Katz, "Post-Emancipation Development and Rights: Liberalism and Universalism," 284.

21. Buber, *For the Sake of Heaven*.

22. Leff, *Sacred Bonds of Solidarity*, 2; Slezkine, *The Jewish Century*, 62.

23. Cited in Fein, *Where Are We?*, 233.

24. Crane, "Why Rights? Why Me?"; Katz, "Post-Emancipation Development and Rights: Liberalism and Universalism," 294; Slezkine, *The Jewish Century*, 62.

25. The literature on nationalism has the (mis)fortune to be blessed with a rich menu of typologies, many of which are built around, or refer explicitly to, the Jewish nation. See, for instance, Kohn, *Idea of Nationalism*; Gans, *Limits of Nationalism*; Roshwald, *Endurance of Nationalism*.

26. Ignatieff, *Blood and Belonging*, 3–5.

27. Ibid., 6.

28. Gottlieb, "Interview with Michael Walzer," 10. Quoted from Pianko, "'Make Room for Us': Jewish Collective Solidarity in Contemporary Political Thought." On a similar note, see Batnitzky, *How Judaism Became a Religion*, 169–79; Trevor-Roper, "Jewish and Other Nationalisms."

29. French National Assembly, "Debate on the Eligibility of Jews for Citizenship"; cited from Mendes-Flohr and Reinharz, *Jew in the Modern World*, 114–16.

30. Wistrich, "Zionism and Its Jewish 'Assimilationist' Critics"; Batnitzky, *How Judaism Became a Religion*; Meyer, *Jewish Identity in the Modern World*, 61.

31. Penslar, "An Unlikely Internationalism."

32. Nordau, *Jewish Return to Palestine*.

33. Katznelson and Birnbaum, *Paths of Emancipation*; Conforti, "East and West in Jewish Nationalism."

34. Sarna, introduction to *American Jewish Experience*, xvi. Also see Dollinger, *Quest for Inclusion*.

35. Howe, "New York Intellectuals," 31. Cited from Imhof, "Between Home and Homeland," 29.

36. There is a voluminous literature on the tight relationship between liberalism and American Jews. For a sampling, see Liebman and Cohen, *Two Worlds of Judaism*, chap. 5; Hertzberg, *Being Jewish in America*; "Liberalism and American Jews," special issue of *Journal of Modern Jewish Studies*; Dollinger, "American Jewish Liberalism Revisited"; Cohen, *Dimensions of American Jewish Liberalism*; Feingold, "From Equality to Liberty"; Glazer, "Anomalous Liberalism of American Jews"; Podhoretz, *Why Are Jews Liberals?*; Katznelson, "Between Separation and Disappearance"; Elazar, "American Political Theory and the Political Notions of American Jews"; Liebman, *Ambivalent American Jew*, chap. 7; Dollinger, *Quest for Inclusion*; Borowitz, *Liberal Judaism*, 403–7; Sklare and Greenblum, *Jewish Identity on the Suburban Frontier*, 322; Feingold, *American Jewish Political Culture and the Liberal Persuasion*; Jacobs, "Jewish Political Ethics in America"; Legge, "Understanding American Judaism"; Goren, *Politics and Public Culture of American Jews*, chap. 1; Svonkin, *Jews against Prejudice*; Medding, "General Theory of Jewish Political Interests and Behavior," 471–72; Dollinger, *Quest for Inclusion*; Shapiro, *A Time for Healing*; and Rynhold, *Arab-Israeli Conflict and American Political Culture*, chaps. 6 and 7.

37. Sarna, "American Jewish Political Conservatism in Historical Perspective."

38. For excellent discussions of the emergence of reform Jewry in Europe and the United States, see Meyer, *Response to Modernity*; Halpern, *American Jew: A Zionist Analysis*, chap. 4.

39. Luz, *Wrestling with an Angel*, 38–41.

40. Hirsch, "Religion Allied to Progress," 1854; cited from Mendes-Flohr and Reinharz, *Jew in the Modern World*, 197–202. Also see Meyer, *Jewish Identity in the Modern World*, 18.

41. For discussions of the concept of the chosen people, see Borowitz, "The Chosen People Concept as It Affects Life in the Diaspora"; Eisen, *Chosen People in America*; Eisen, "Rhetoric of Chosenness"; Novak, *Election of Israel*.

42. Cohen and Fein, "From Integration to Survival," 77. Also see Glazer, *American Judaism*, 47–48; Luz, *Wrestling with an Angel*, 32–34; Slezkine, *Jewish Century*, 93.

43. For overviews of the prophetic tradition, see Heschel, "Divine Pathos"; Heschel, "Prophetic Inspiration"; Jacob, "Prophetic Judaism"; Petuchowski, "Faith as a Leap of Action"; Legge, "Understanding American Judaism."

44. Heschel, *The Prophets*, 6.

45. Eisen, *Chosen People in America*, 47–48; Kristol, "Liberal Tradition of American Jews," 115; Herberg, "Prophetic Faith in an Age of Crisis"; Fein, *Where Are We?*; Jacob, "Prophetic Judaism"; Borowitz, *Liberal Judaism*, 403–7.

46. Leo Baeck, *The Essence of Judaism* (London: Macmillan, 1936). Quoted from Greene, "Chosen People in a Pluralist Nation," 163.

47. Walzer, *In God's Shadow*, 107.

48. There is no single definition of political theology. For Mark Lilla, conversations about political authority, the ends of politics, and the human condition often venture into the divine. Lilla, *Stillborn God*. William Cavanaugh and Peter Scott define it as: "The analysis and criticism of political arrangements (including

cultural-psychological, social, and economic aspects) from the perspective of dif-fering interpretations of God's ways with the world." Scott and Cavanaugh, intro-duction to *The Blackwell Companion to Political Theology*, 1. Their definition touches on Carl Schmitt's formulation that "all significant concepts of the modern theory of the state are secularized theological concepts not only because of their histori-cal development—in which they are transferred from theology to the theory of the state—but also because of their systemic structure." Schmitt, *Political Theology*, 36. Also see Meier, "What Is Political Theology?" 79–92. Following Émile Durkheim's concept of religion, others define political theology as the infusion of political con-cepts with the sacred. For collections on political theology, see Scott and Cava-naugh, *Blackwell Companion to Political Theology*, and Kessler, *Political Theology for a Plural Age*.

49. Mendelsohn, *On Modern Jewish Politics*.

50. Messinger, "Jewish Service and Global Citizenship," 6.

51. See, for instance, Walzer, *Law, Politics, and Morality in Judaism*; Walzer et al., *Jewish Political Tradition*, vol. 1, *Authority*; Walzer, *In God's Shadow*; Walzer et al., *Jewish Political Tradition*, vol. 2, *Membership*; Copulsky, "History and Essence."

52. Copulsky, "History and Essence," 63.

53. For other contributions that are torn between the descriptive and the pre-scriptive, see Walzer, "Anomalies of Jewish Political Identity"; Kahler, *Jews among the Nations*, 1–31; Borowitz, *Liberal Judaism*, 19–36.

54. For a similar discussion and conclusion of modern Jewish political theol-ogy, see Copulsky, "History and Essence," 62–98.

55. For various discussions of Reform Judaism in Europe, particularly as it re-lates to the nationalism question, see Aberbach, "Nationalism, Reform Judaism, and the Hebrew Prayer Book"; and Aberbach, "Nationalism and the Hebrew Bible."

56. Copulsky, "History and Essence," 65.

57. Eisen, "Rhetoric of Chosenness."

58. Lipset and Raab, *Jews and the New American Scene*, 7.

59. For the insidious view, see Mearsheimer and Walt, *Israel Lobby and US For-eign Policy*. For a more balanced assessment, see Feingold, *Jewish Power in America*; Lieberman, "'Israel Lobby' and American Politics."

60. For recent uses of the concept of Jewish foreign policy, see Waxman and Lazsenky, "Jewish Foreign Policy"; Sandler, "Towards a Conceptual Framework of World Jewish Politics"; Sandler, "Toward a Theory of World Jewish Politics and Jewish Foreign Policy"; Shain and Bristman, "Diaspora, Kinship, and Loyalty"; Klieman, "*Shtadlanut* as Statecraft by the Stateless"; Sandler, "Is There a Jewish For-eign Policy?"; Baron, "Diasporic Security and Jewish Identity."

61. Beker, "Diplomacy without Sovereignty"; Beker, "Sixty Years of World Jew-ish Congress Diplomacy." Despite setting out the case against, David Vital ulti-mately concedes that there are Jewish national interests and thus something akin to a Jewish diplomacy. Vital, "Diplomacy in the Jewish Interest."

62. Penkower, "Dr. Nahun Goldmann and the Policy of International Jewish Organizations."

63. See, for instance, Dowty, "Israeli Foreign Policy and the Jewish Question"; Waxman and Lasensky, "Jewish Foreign Policy," 234; Beilin, *His Brother's Keeper*; Avineri, "Ideology and Israel's Foreign Policy"; Inbar, "Jews, Jewishness, and Israel's

Foreign Policy"; Sheffer, "Elusive Question"; Sheffer, "A Nation and Its Diaspora"; Waxman, "Jewish Dimension in Israeli Foreign Policy"; Rynhold, "Israel's Foreign and Defense Policy and Diaspora Jewish Identity"; Mualem, "Israel's Foreign Policy"; Bayme, "American Jewry and the State of Israel," 3–4.

64. See, for instance, Liebman, *Pressure without Sanctions*, 42–43.

65. For overviews, see Elazar and Cohen, *Jewish Polity*; Wertheimer, "Jewish Organizational Life in the United States since 1945"; Wertheimer, *People Divided*; Elazar, *Community and Polity*. The figure is from Feingold, *American Jewish Political Culture and the Liberal Persuasion*, 57.

66. For a survey of pro-Israel organizations, see Waxman, "Israel Lobbies"; and Rynhold, *Arab-Israeli Conflict in American Political Culture*.

67. For a consideration of this characterization, see Telhami, "Israeli Foreign Policy."

68. Will Herberg calls this "survivalism." Herberg, "Assimilation in Militant Dress," 19.

69. Buber, "Jew in the World," 167.

70. Although Morgenthau is usually cited as a source for this form of realism, he also saw how Jewry embodied a prophetic spirit. See Mollov, *Power and Transcendence*.

71. For discussions of cosmopolitanism, see Appiah, *Cosmopolitanism*; Beck, "Cosmopolitan Society and Its Enemies"; Hannerz, "Cosmopolitans and Locals in World Culture"; Vertovec and Cohen, *Conceiving Cosmopolitanism*; Brennan, *At Home in the World*; Cheah and Robbins, *Cosmopolitics*; Beck, *Cosmopolitan Vision*; Pollack, "Cosmopolitanism and Vernacular in History"; Werbner, "Vernacular Cosmopolitanism"; Brock and Brighouse, *Political Philosophy of Cosmopolitanism*; Nussbaum, *For Love of Country?*; Benhabib et al., *Another Cosmopolitanism*; Waldron, "What Is Cosmopolitanism?"; Waldron, "Minority Cultures and the Cosmopolitan Alternative"; Kofman, "Figures of the Cosmopolitan"; Calhoun, "Cosmopolitanism and Nationalism"; Miller and Ury, "Cosmopolitanism: The End of Jewishness?"; Mehta, "Cosmopolitanism and the Circle of Reason."

72. David Hollinger, "Ethnic Diversity," in his *In the American Province*, 59; Mehta, "Cosmopolitanism and the Circle of Reason," 624; Hollinger, "Communalists and Dispersionist Approaches to Jewish History in an Increasingly Post-Jewish Era," 22, 23.

73. International Federation of Red Cross and Red Crescent Societies, "Humanity," http://www.ifrc.org/en/who-we-are/vision-and-mission/the-seven-fundamental-principles/humanity/. Accessed January 17, 2015.

74. Eisenstadt, *The Prophets*, 30.

75. Irving Horowitz emphatically pushes the point beyond the empirical to the categorical: "Thus, an attempt to answer my own question—what is the Jew?—I should note the following: He is a man who provides global society with an operational set of liberal values; and who in turn fares best in a global society that has a vested, legitimate interest in precisely fostering open-ended values for its own thoroughly non-Jewish reasons." Horowitz, *Israeli Ecstasies / Jewish Agonies*, 203.

76. Buber, "Jew in the World," 170.

77. Mack, "Zionism and the Palestinian Restoration Fund."

78. Kallen, *Zionism and World Politics*, 11–12.

79. Buber, "Jew in the World," 170.

80. Zipperstein, "Between Tribalism and Utopia"; Kohn, "Ahad Ha'am: Nationalist with a Difference."

81. For a compatible argument, see Sarna, introduction to *American Jewish Experience*, xvi; and Feingold, *American Jewish Political Culture and the Liberal Persuasion*, 51.

82. The first is from Scruton, *Dictionary of Political Thought*, 100. Both are cited from Mehta, "Cosmopolitanism and the Circle of Reason," 620.

83. Kofman, "Figures of the Cosmopolitan," 87–90.

84. Miller and Ury, "Cosmopolitanism: The End of Jewishness?"; Sznaider, "Hannah Arendt's Jewish Cosmopolitanism"; Kofman, "Figures of the Cosmopolitan."

85. For a sampling of this rather extensive literature on American Jews and Israel, see Halpern, "Political Significance of Israel for American Jews"; Urofsky, *American Zionism*; Cohen, *American Jews and the Zionist Idea*; Raider, *Emergence of American Zionism*; Berkowitz, *Western Jewry and the Zionist Project*; Wistrich, "Zionism and Its Jewish 'Assimilationist' Critics"; Feingold, *American Jewish Political Culture and the Liberal Persuasion*, esp. chap. 4; Gruen, "Aspects and Prospects of the Interaction between American Jews and Israel"; Eisen, "Israel at 50"; Eisen, "A New Role for Israel in American Jewish Identity"; Sasson, "Mass Mobilization to Direct Engagement"; Ben-Moshe and Segev, *Israel, the Diaspora, and Jewish Identity*; Livni, "Place of Israel in the Identity of Reform Jews."

86. Mendelsohn, *On Modern Jewish Politics*.

CHAPTER TWO: THE MAKING OF A PROPHETIC PEOPLE

1. Stuyvesant, "Petition to Expel Jews from New Amsterdam," 452.

2. "Reply to Stuyvesant's Petition," 453.

3. Diner, *Jews of the United States*, 23–24.

4. Ibid., 58. For the exchange of letters between the congregation at Newport and Washington, see "Message of Welcome to George Washington," August 17, 1790, and "A Reply to the Hebrew Congregation of Newport," c. August 17, 1790, 458–59.

5. Diner, *Jews of the United States*, 59.

6. Auerbach, "Liberalism and the Hebrew Prophets"; Mendelsohn, *On Modern Jewish Politics*, 14–17.

7. Ibid., 122.

8. Cited from Eisen, *Chosen People in America*, 137.

9. See ibid.; Eisen, "Rhetoric of Chosenness"; Greenstein, *Turning Point*, introduction.

10. Gurock, *History of Judaism in America*, 270.

11. *Yearbook of the Central Conference of American Rabbis*, 1899, vol. 9, p. 172, no place of publication; cited in Mendelsohn, *On Modern Jewish Politics*, 15.

12. Borowitz, "Chosen People Concept as It Affects Life in the Diaspora," 556–58.

13. Ibid., 556.

14. Eisen, *Chosen People in America*, 4; Eisen, "Rhetoric of Chosenness."

15. Greenstein, *Turning Point*, 4–6.

16. Ibid., 99.

17. Eisen, *Chosen People in America*, 25.

18. For discussions of exile, see Galchinsky, "Scattered Seeds."

19. The single best full-length study of the concept of chosen people in American Jewry is Eisen, *Chosen People in America*. For other discussions of the concept of chosenness in Jewish thought, see Hollander and Kaminsky, "Introduction: 'A Covenant to the People, a Light to the Nations.'"

20. Eisen, *Chosen People in America*, 40; Galchinsky, "Scattered Seeds," 198–207.

21. Halpern, *American Jew*, 97–104.

22. http://www.zionism-israel.com/hdoc/Philadelphia_Conference_1869.htm.

23. For a summary of the idea of the Wandering Jew, See Hasan-Rokem and Dundes, *Wandering Jew*.

24. Shiff, *Survival through Integration*, 36.

25. Woocher, *Sacred Survival*, 5.

26. Eisen, *Chosen People in America*, 68.

27. Goren, *American Jews*.

28. Eisen, *Chosen People in America*, 68.

29. Greenstein, *Turning Point*, 2.

30. Kristol, "Liberal Tradition of American Jews," 112.

31. Diner, *Jews in America*, 135.

32. Ibid., 97.

33. Ibid.

34. Glazer, *American Judaism*, 53.

35. Frankel, *Damascus Affair*.

36. For explicit discussions of the rise of Jewish internationalism at this moment, see Green, "Religious and Jewish Internationalism"; Green, "Old Networks, New Connections"; Dekel-Chen, "Activism as Engine"; Leff, *Sacred Bonds of Solidarity*, 2; Green, "Nationalism and the 'Jewish International'"; Moyn, "René Cassin, Human Rights, and Jewish Internationalism."

37. Klieman argues that now it is possible to speak of a "world Jewry." Klieman, "*Shtadlanut* as Statecraft by the Stateless," 109. Also see Troen and Pinkus, *Organizing Rescue*.

38. Leff, *Sacred Bonds of Solidarity*, 2.

39. Ibid. For overviews of the AIU, see Leff, *Sacred Bonds of Solidarity*; Winter, "René Cassin and the Alliance Israélite Universelle"; Schwarzfuchs, "Alliance Israélite Universelle and French Jewish Leadership vis-à-vis North African Jewry"; Szajkowski, "Alliance Israélite Universelle in the United States"; Bigart, "Alliance Israélite Universelle"; Bar-Chen, "Two Communities with a Sense of Mission."

40. Leff, *Sacred Bonds of Solidarity*, 181.

41. Ibid., 2–3.

42. For discussions on the relationship between Jewish internationalism and Great Power imperialism, see Moyn, "René Cassin, Human Rights, and Jewish Internationalism"; Green, "Intervening in the Jewish Question," 139–58.

43. Green, "Old Networks, New Connections," 64–68.

44. Klieman, "*Shtadlanut* as Statecraft by the Stateless," 107; Dekel-Chen, "Activism as Engine," 274; Poliakov, *Jewish Bankers and the Holy See*.

45. Green, "Religious and Jewish Internationalism," 13; Green, "Old Networks, New Connections."

46. Green, "Old Networks, New Connections," 72–73; Dekel-Chen, "Activism as Engine," 272–73.

47. Leff, *Sacred Bonds of Solidarity*, 183.

48. The important relationship between Jewish global action and imperialism is explored in the following articles by Abigail Green: "Nationalism and the 'Jewish International'"; "British Empire and the Jews"; "Rethinking Sir Moses Montefiore"; and "Limits of Intervention."

49. Wistrich, "Zionism and Its Jewish 'Assimilationist' Critics (1897–1948)," and esp. p. 64; Leff, *Sacred Bonds of Solidarity*.

50. Green, "Limits of Intervention."

51. Greene, "A Chosen People in a Pluralist Nation," 188.

52. Feinberg, "International Protection of Human Rights and the Jewish Question."

53. Fink, *Defending the Rights of Others*, 9.

54. Green, "Limits of Intervention, 2014.

55. Fink, *Defending the Rights of Others*, 30.

56. Handlin, *A Continuing Task*, chap. 3.

57. Sarna, *When General Grant Expelled the Jews*, 101.

58. Ibid.

59. Ibid., 102.

60. Silver, *Louis Marshall*, 88.

61. For a description of these early efforts, see Adler and Margalith, *With Firmness in the Right*.

62. For histories of the American Jewish Committee, see Cohen, *Not Free to Desist*; Goldbloom, "American Jewish Committee Abroad."

63. Marshall, "American Jewish Committee." See Silver, *Louis Marshall*, 107–24, for a detailed discussion of the AJC's creation.

64. Green, "Jewish Issues on the Human-Rights Agenda"; Woocher, *Sacred Survival*, 29.

65. "In the course of its own work the Committee had long since learned that prejudice was indivisible, and that in the United States it was less desirable to argue in favor of the rights of Jews than to defend the equality of all Americans, including Jews." Handlin, "American Jewish Committee," 7.

66. Handlin, "The American Jewish Committee: A Half Century View," 2.

67. Silver, *Louis Marshall*, 27.

68. For insightful discussions of Louis Marshall, see Silver, *Louis Marshall*; Silver, "Louis Marshall and the Democratization of Jewish Identity"; and Sarna, "Two Jewish Lawyers Named Louis."

69. Ibid., 3.

70. Fink, "Louis Marshall: An American Jewish Diplomat in Paris."

71. Woocher, *Sacred Survival*, 29.

72. For histories of the abrogation campaign, see Cohen, "Abrogation of the Russo-American Treaty of 1832"; Cohen, *Not Free to Desist*, chap. 4; Silver, *Louis Marshall*, 136–42, 194–21.

73. Silver, *Louis Marshall*, 137.

74. Cited from ibid., 195.

75. Kallen, *Zionism and World Politics*, 49.

76. Kohn, "Ahad Ha'am: Nationalist with a Difference"; Zipperstein, "Between Tribalism and Utopia." For various views on the relationship between Zionism and territory, see Alroey, "Zionism without Zion"; Davis, *Zionism in Transition*; Conforti, "East and West in Jewish Nationalism."

77. Arendt, "Jewish State: Fifty Years After," 7.

78. Kallen, *Zionism and World Politics*, 10.

79. For a selection of the rich literature on the anti-Zionism of American Jews, and especially those of the liberal and reform persuasions, see Laquer, "Zionism and Its Liberal Critics"; Kallen, *Zionism and World Politics*, 10; Cohen, "Reaction of Reform Judaism in America to Political Zionism"; Greenstein, *Turning Point*; Urofsky, *American Zionism*.

80. Balint, *Running Commentary*, 33.

81. Urofsky, *American Zionism*, 99–100.

82. Cited from Cohen, *American Jews and the Zionist Idea*, 6.

83. Greenstein, *Turning Point*, 10.

84. Wistrich, "Zionism and Its Jewish 'Assimilationist' Critics," 64.

85. Rischin, "Early Attitude of the American Jewish Committee to Zionism"; Cohen, *American Jews and the Zionist Idea*; Urofsky, *American Zionism*, 96.

86. Eisen, *Chosen People in America*.

87. Kallen, *Zionism and World Politics*, 132.

88. Alexander, *Irving Howe—Socialist, Critic, Jew*, 182. Also see Kallen, *Zionism and World Politics*, 132; Wistrich, "Zionism and Its Jewish 'Assimilationist' Critics."

89. Cited from Cohen, *American Jews and the Zionist Idea*, 6.

90. Peters, "Zionism and the Jewish Problem."

91. Ibid., 276.

92. Quoted from Cohen, *American Jews and the Zionist Idea*, 22.

CHAPTER THREE: PROPHETS MUGGED BY REALITY

1. Hyman, "Twenty-Five Years of American Aid"; Goldberg, *Jewish Power*, 106–7.

2. American Jewish Year Book, "Jewish War Relief Work"; Granick, "Waging Relief"; and Duker, "Jews in World War I." Silver, *Louis Marshall*, 254–65.

3. Ibid.

4. Woocher, *Sacred Survival*, 29.

5. For a brief overview of the first fifty years of the Joint, see Handlin, *Continuing Task*; and Handlin, "American Jewish Committee: A Half-Century View."

6. Woocher, *Sacred Survival*, 29.

7. Ibid., 31–32; Hyman, "Twenty-Five Years of American Aid to Jews Overseas"; Silver, *Louis Marshall*, 264.

8. Goldberg, *Jewish Power*, 106–7.

9. Handlin, *Continuing Task*, 20–25; American Jewish Year Book, "Jewish War Relief Work."

10. Halpern, *A Clash of Heroes*, 115.

11. Levin, "Zionism in America"; Cohen, *American Jews and the Zionist Idea*; Berkowitz, *Western Jewry and the Zionist Project*.

12. Cohen, *American Jews and the Zionist Idea.*

13. For discussions of Brandeis and his relationship to Zionism, see Urofsky, *Louis D. Brandeis: A Life*; Sarna, "Two Jewish Lawyers Named Louis"; Cohen, *American Jews and the Zionist Idea*, chap. 2. Over the 1920s and 1930s, Brandeis's ideas developed in a more unapologetically Zionist direction. He started believing that Zionism was not just a way for the Jews to contribute to the world, but that it was a way for the world to demonstrate its commitment to a more humane future. Gal, "Isaiah's Flame: Brandeis's Social-Liberal and Zionist Tradition."

14. Brandeis, "Jewish Problem: and How to Solve It."

15. Ibid.

16. Ibid.

17. Ibid.

18. For overviews of Horace Kallen, see Pianko, "The True Liberalism of Zionism"; Toll, "Horace M. Kallen: Pluralism and American Jewish Identity"; Greene, "Chosen People in a Pluralist Nation"; Greene, *Jewish Origins of Cultural Pluralism.*

19. Kallen, "Democracy versus the Melting Pot."

20. Greene, "Chosen People in a Pluralist Nation"; Bourne, "Jew and Trans-National America."

21. Quoted from Greene, "Chosen People in a Pluralist Nation," 173.

22. David Hollinger, "Ethnic Diversity, Cosmopolitanism, and the Emergence of the American Liberal Intelligentsia," in his *In the American Province*, 56–73. John Dewey opposed Kallen's pluralism on various grounds, including its neglect of the possibility that Jews, as Jews, might gain something from their interactions with other groups and from being constantly reminded of their relationship to the broader community.

23. Bourne, "Jew and Trans-National America," 279.

24. Ibid., 279.

25. Ibid., 279–80.

26. Ibid., 282.

27. This discussion of Kaplan draws from Pianko, *Zionism and the Roads Not Taken*; Novak, "Mordecai Kaplan's Rejection of Election"; Eisen, "Mordecai Kaplan's Judaism as a Civilization at 70"; Scult, "Americanism and Judaism in the Thought of Mordecai M. Kaplan"; and LaGrone, "Ethical Theories of Mordecai Kaplan and Abraham Joshua Heschel."

28. Pianko, *Zionism and the Roads Not Taken*, 97.

29. Cited in ibid., 118.

30. Urofsky, *American Zionism*, 213–20; Goldblatt, "Impact of the Balfour Declaration in America."

31. American Jewish Committee, "Jewish Post-War Problems: A Study Course," 11.

32. Urofsky, *American Zionism*, 213.

33. Janowsky, *Jews and Minority Rights.*

34. Capturing not only his views but also those of many on the committee, at this time Marshall wrote: "I am opposed to a Jewish state and always shall be. There is no likelihood that there will ever be a Jewish State in Palestine. There is, however, a strong possibility that, as a result of unified action, an outlet may be found in Palestine for the persecuted and suffering Jews of Eastern Europe. There

is no other outlet for them. The doors of Western Europe have been closed against them. . . . The opportunities afforded them of reestablishing themselves in our country are to be taken away from them [citing recent American legislation]. . . . What objections can there be, therefore, to an effort to establish for them a home in the land of their fathers and to enable them by the aid of wholesome sentiment to build up the waste places of the Holy Land and to bring about a renaissance?" Quoted from Goldman, "American Jewish Committee Abroad," 330. Also see Silver, *Louis Marshall*, 338–43.

35. For the statement, see http://israeled.org/american-jewish-committee-gives-qualified-endorsement-balfour-declaration/. Accessed February 3, 2015.

36. Kohler, "Jewish Rights at International Congresses"; Wolf, *Notes on the Diplomatic History of the Jewish Question*; Urofsky, *American Zionism*, 227–28; Feinberg, "International Protection of Human Rights and the Jewish Question."

37. Riga and Kennedy, "Tolerant Majorities, Loyal Minorities," 472, 476.

38. Silver, "Louis Marshall and the Democratization of Jewish Identity," 43. For overviews of this thinking, see Loeffler, "Between Zionism and Liberalism"; Alroey, "Zionism without Zion"; American Jewish Committee, "How the Jewish Communities Prepared for Peace during the First World War," Jewish Post-War Problems, A Study Course, Unit III.

39. American Jewish Committee, "Jewish Post-War Problems: A Study Course," 10, 14.

40. Marcus, *Social and Political History of the Jews of Poland*, 296.

41. American Jewish Committee, "Jewish Post-War Problems: A Study Course," 15–18.

42. According to Marshall, the AJC had a fairly good idea of what it wanted going into the meeting, the rest of the congress was confused and indecisive regarding the issue of Jewish rights, and Marshall pushed through a resolution that he believed gave him considerable autonomy to represent the American Jews on the question as he saw fit. Goldbloom, "American Jewish Committee Abroad."

43. Also see Levitas, "Reform Jews and Zionism."

44. Cohen, "Zionism: Tribalism or Liberalism?"

45. According to the "Abstract of Report of Meeting of Representative of Jewish Organizations Held in Paris, March 30–April 6, 1919," 227–28.

46. The following summary draws from Fink, *Defending the Rights of Others*; Fink, "Louis Marshall: An American Diplomat in Paris"; Riga and Kennedy, "Tolerant Majorities, Loyal Minorities"; Levene, *War, Jews, and the New Europe*; Levene, "Nationalism and Its Alternatives in the International Arena"; American Jewish Committee, "Jewish Post-War Problems: A Study Course," 24–29; Belth, "Minority Rights"; Marshall, "Report of the Delegates from the American Jewish Congress to the Peace Conference." Cited from American Jewish Committee, "Jewish Post-War Problems: A Study Course," 43–47; Duker, "Jews in World War I: A Brief Historical Sketch."

47. Letter from Louis Marshall to President Woodrow Wilson, May 23, 1919, Box 5, Louis Marshall, Correspondence, Peace Conference, 1919. American Jewish Committee.

48. Fink, *Defending the Rights of Others*, 148.

49. For discussions of the minorities treaties, see Mazower, "Minorities and the League of Nations in Interwar Europe"; Levene, "Nationalism and Its Alternatives in the International Arena"; Riga and Kennedy, "Tolerant Majorities, Loyal Minorities."

50. Goldbloom, "American Jewish Committee Abroad."

51. An irony, noticed at the time, was that religious liberty was not guaranteed by the League of Nations in sovereign states in Eastern Europe but it was for the mandatory countries in Central Africa; these peoples could appeal to the League, but not the Jews of Europe. Landman, "League of Nations and the Jews."

52. Read by Louis Marshall, "Report to the Delegates from the American Jewish Congress to the Peace Conference," May 30, 1920. Also see Halpern, "Jewish Nationalism: Self-Determination as a Human Right."

53. Parkes, *Emergence of the Jewish Problem.*

54. Cited from Fink, *Defending the Rights of Others,* 73n33.

55. Kallen, *National Solidarity and the Jewish Minority,* 89.

56. Feingold, *Time for Searching.*

57. Written to the Joint Foreign Committee of the Jewish Board of Deputies and the Anglo-Jewish Association, London.

58. There is no reason to think that American Jews were more focused on other peoples' problems than European Jewry's, but Jews made up a disproportionate percentage of the peace movement, the labor movement, and other such campaigns. Most strikingly, American Jews were overrepresented in the Lincoln Brigade, the American-organized military force that went to Spain to fight Franco and fascism and with the Republicans. The Spanish civil war was one of the great flashpoints of the 1930s, widely viewed as a last standing of progressive politics. And American Jews were not just picking sides, they were prepared to die for a "country that four centuries earlier expelled its Jews and for a cause which could only be viewed as part of a Jewish interest by a stretch of ideological imagination." For some American Jews, European Jews were among the many of worthy victims. Feingold, "Rescue and the Secular Perception," 156.

59. Feingold, *Time for Searching*; Silver, "Democratization of Jewish Identity," 56–59.

60. Cited from Urofsky, *American Zionism,* 302.

61. Kallen, *Zionism in World Politics,* 276.

62. Berkowitz, *Western Jewry and the Zionist Project.*

63. Cohen, *American Jews and the Zionist Idea,* 31.

64. Urofsky, *Louis D. Brandeis: A Life,* 534.

65. Halpern, *Clash of Heroes.*

66. Morgenthau, "Zionism a Fallacy."

67. Oder, "American Zionism and the Congressional Resolution."

68. *New York Times,* May 7, 1922, section II, p. 6. Cited from Oder, "American Zionism and the Congressional Resolution," 41.

69. Raider, Sarna, and Zweig, *Abba Hillel Silver and American Zionism.*

70. Shiff, *Survival through Integration,* 1–3.

71. Penkower, "American Jewry and the Holocaust."

CHAPTER FOUR: THE COSMOPOLITAN AND THE NATIONAL

1. Winter and Prost, *René Cassin and Human Rights*; Moyn, "René Cassin, Human Rights, and Jewish Internationalism."

2. Green, "Jewish Issues on the Human-Rights Agenda," 305–7; Lauterpacht, "International Bill of Rights."

3. Power, *Problem from Hell*.

4. Birmingham, *Hannah Arendt and Human Rights*.

5. Cohen, *In War's Wake*, 137; Cohen, "The Holocaust and the 'Human Rights Revolution'"; Mart, *Eye on Israel*, 17–19.

6. Dean, *Aversion and Erasure*; Levy and Sznaider, "Institutionalization of Cosmopolitan Morality; Levy and Sznaider, "Memory Unbound; Finkielkraut, *Imaginary Jew*, xii.

7. Alexander, *Remembering the Holocaust*, 26; Dean, *Aversion and Erasure*.

8. Niebuhr, "Jews after the War," 214.

9. Cited from Kallen, "National Solidarity and the Jewish Minority," 64.

10. Cited from Hitchens, *Hitch 22*, 384.

11. Finkielkraut, *Imaginary Jew*.

12. Deutscher, "The Non-Jewish Jew," 85–86.

13. Slezkine, *Jewish Century*, 328.

14. Halpern, *American Jew*, 33.

15. Sarna, *American Judaism: A History*; Goren, *Politics and Public Culture of American Jews*, chap. 9; Shapiro, *A Time for Healing*.

16. Sarna, *American Judaism: A History*, 262–93; Wertheimer, *People Divided*; Wrong, "Rise and Decline of Anti-Semitism in America"; Goren, "A 'Golden Decade' for American Jews."

17. Shapiro, *A Time for Healing*, 9–10; Mart, *Eye on Israel*, chap. 1.

18. See, for instance, Herberg, *Protestant-Catholic-Jew*.

19. Wall, *Inventing the American Way*; Alexander, *Remembering the Holocaust: A Debate*, 21; Dollinger, *Quest for Inclusion*, chaps. 2–4.

20. Wall, *Inventing the American Way*, 7.

21. Ibid., 9.

22. Quoted from Cohen, *Not Free to Desist*, 233–34.

23. Wall, *Inventing the American Way*, 78.

24. Eisen, *Chosen People in the United States*, 129.

25. Prell, "Triumph, Accommodation, and Resistance," 128–31.

26. Moore, "Reconsidering the Rosenbergs"; Shapiro, *A Time for Healing*, 35–36.

27. Svonkin, *Jews against Prejudice*, chap. 6.

28. Moore, "Reconsidering the Rosenbergs," 34; Dollinger, *Quest for Inclusion*, chap. 6; Prell, "Triumph, Accommodation, and Resistance."

29. In *Eye on Israel*, 57–77, Michelle Mart argues that American political culture during the Cold War shaped a growing image of a "tough Jew" and a more masculine Israeli, thus making inclusion of the Jew and the Israeli into American foreign policy increasingly possible.

30. Kaplan, *Contemporary American Judaism*, chap. 1; Gans, "American Jewry, Present and Future: Part I: Present," and Gans, "American Jewry, Present

and Future: Part II: Future"; Lipstadt, "From Noblesse Oblige to Personal Redemption."

31. Woocher, *Sacred Survival*, 58.

32. Baron, "Spiritual Reconstruction of European Jewry."

33. Glazer, *American Judaism*.

34. Shapiro, *A Time for Healing*, chap. 6; Prell, "Triumph, Accommodation, and Resistance," 122–26.

35. Lipstadt, "From Noblesse Oblige to Personal Redemption."

36. Mart, *Eye on Israel*, chap. 4.

37. Sklare and Greenblum, *Jewish Identity on the Suburban Frontier*; Lipstadt, "From Noblesse Oblige to Personal Redemption."

38. Sklare and Greenblum, *Jewish Identity on the Suburban Frontier*.

39. Vorspan and Lipman, *Justice and Judaism*.

40. Ibid., 63.

41. Imhof, "Between Home and Homeland," 89.

42. Sarna, introduction to *American Jewish Experience*; Diner, *In the Almost Promised Land*, xiv.

43. For overviews, see Cohen, *Not Free to Desist*, chap. 14; Dollinger, *Quest for Inclusion*, chaps. 6–8; Diner, *In the Almost Promised Land*.

44. Shapiro, *A Time of Healing*, 54.

45. Podhoretz, *Why Are Jews Liberals?*, 158; Goldstein, *Price of Whiteness*.

46. Sarna, *American Judaism*, 48.

47. Svonkin, *Jews against Prejudice*; Imhof, "Between Home and Homeland," 90–97.

48. For a brief review of the American Jewish organizations involved in international human rights, see Rosenfield, "Human Rights" (1948–49); Rosenfeld, "Human Rights" (1950); Hauser, "International Human-Rights Protection," 22–24.

49. Shiff, *Survival through Integration*; Dollinger, *Quest for Inclusion*, chap. 5.

50. Interview with Roberta Cohen, Washington DC.

51. Cohen, *Not Free to Desist*, 266.

52. The discussion draws heavily from the following documents by the American Jewish Committee: "Jewish Post-War Problems: A Study Course, Unit I: Why Study Post-War Problems"; "Readings on the Causes of Peace Failure, Unit II"; "Jewish Post-War Problems: A Study Course, Unit V: The Position of the Jews in the Post-War World"; "Jewish Post-War Problems: A Study Course, The Two World Wars—A Comparison and Contrast"; "How the Jewish Communities Prepared for Peace during the First World War, Jewish Post-War Problems, A Study Course, Unit III"; American Jewish Committee, "Jewish Post-War Problems: A Study Course"; "Proposed Provisions for the Peace Treaties"; "Protection of Human Rights"; Moscowitz, "Memorandum: A Brief Outline."

53. Also see Cohen, *Not Free to Desist*, 269–75.

54. Waldman, "Bill of Rights for All Nations," 14.

55. Loeffler, "The Conscience of America"; Waldman, "Bill of Rights for All Nations," 14, 48.

56. Halpern, "Jewish Nationalism."

57. Waldman, "Bill of Rights for All Nations."

58. Loeffler, "Between Zionism and Liberalism," 289–308.

59. Hirschberg, "Human Rights or Minority Rights?"

60. Correspondence from Jacob Landau to Albert Lusker, March 2, 1932; American Jewish Committee. Correspondence from Jacob Landau to Cyrus Adler, March 10, 1932, American Jewish Committee.

61. "Minutes of Meeting of German Advisory Group," April 12, 1944. American Jewish Committee.

62. American Jewish Committee, "Jewish Post-War Problems, Unit I," 14.

63. Emphasis in original. "Memorandum on Policy Related to Defense Program of American Jewish Committee," April 1946.

64. Waldman, "Bill of Rights for All Nations," 48.

65. American Jewish Committee, "Protection of Human Rights," 7, 17.

66. American Jewish Committee, "Jewish Postwar Problems: A Study Course, Unit V, The Position of the Jews in the Post-War World," 24.

67. Also see American Jewish Committee, "Protection of Human Rights," 4–5, 20.

68. For another sobering assessment, see American Jewish Committee, "The United Nations in 1946: Human Rights, Refugees, and Trusteeship."

69. American Jewish Committee, "Protection of Human Rights," 18.

70. The story has been told in many different versions over the years, including American Jewish Committee, "A World Charter for Human Rights"; Gaer, "To Reaffirm Faith in Fundamental Human Rights."

71. Gaer, "To Reaffirm Faith in Fundamental Human Rights," 7.

72. American Jewish Committee, "Proposed Provisions for the Peace Treaties," 6.

73. Gaer, "To Reaffirm Faith in Fundamental Human Rights," 8, 9; Shotwell, "American Jewish Committee Led Battle for Human Rights," 5.

74. Loeffler, "'Conscience of America.'"

75. Loeffler, "'Conscience of America,'" 402–3; and Loeffler, "In Pursuit of Universalism."

76. Loeffler, "'Conscience of America,'" 428.

77. Ibid., 408–409. Letter from Morris Waldman to Joseph Proskauer. Cited from ibid., 408–409.

78. Ibid., 425. This very liberal stance is also consistent with why the AJC was reluctant to advocate for inserting anti-Semitism into UN documents. Loeffler, "How Zionism Became Racism."

79. Eisen, "Israel at 50," 49; italics in original.

80. Arendt, "Jewish State: Fifty Years After," 8, and Gilboa, "Attitudes of American Jews toward Israel."

81. Halpern, "Impact of Israel on American Jewish Ideologies"; "Papers and Proceedings of the Joint Conference with the Theodor Herzl Institute on the Impact of Israel on the American Jewish Community"; Halpern, "Political Significance of Israel for American Jews"; Ganin, Uneasy Relationship, chap. 1.

82. See, for instance, Ganin, Truman, American Jewry, and Israel; Judis, Genesis.

83. Sklare, Observing America's Jews.

84. Cohen, Not Free to Desist, chap. 20.

85. Sarna, American Judaism: A History, 335; Gurin, "Impact of Israel on American Jewish Community Organization and Fund Raising"; Segev, "American Zionists' Place in Israel after Statehood"; Biale, Power and Powerlessness in Jewish History, 184; "The Impact of Israel on the American Jewish Community."

86. Sklare, "Lakeville and Israel," 438.

87. Eisen, "Israel at 50," 51.

88. Samuel, "Sundering of Israel and American Jewry," 199.

89. Gruen, "Aspects and Prospects of the Interaction between American Jews and Israel," 9.

90. From Hook, *Out of Step*; cited from Balint, *Running Commentary*, 37.

91. Galchinsky, "Scattered Seeds," 202; Grossman, "Transformation through Crisis"; Eisen, "Introduction: Four Questions concerning Peoplehood," 4.

92. Segev, "American Zionists' Place in Israel after Statehood"; Ganin, *Uneasy Relationship*, chap. 1.

93. Munz, "Nationalism Is the Enemy," 101, 106.

94. Herberg, "Assimilation in Militant Dress," 16.

95. For how particularism and nationalism related to universalism and humanitarianism in the American mindset, see Mart, *Eye on Israel*, chap. 2.

96. Proskauer, "Our Duty as Americans," 7.

97. Ben-Gurion and Dolgin, "Can We Stay Jews Outside the 'Land'? An Exchange."

98. Ben-Gurion and Dolgin, "Can We Stay Jews Outside the 'Land'?, 237.

99. Cited from Auerbach, "Liberalism and the Hebrew Prophets," 60.

100. Ben-Gurion and Dolgin, "Can We Stay Jews Outside the 'Land'?", 235.

101. Ibid.

102. Thompson, "America Demands a Single Loyalty"; Handlin, "America Recognizes Diverse Loyalties"; Samuel, "Why Israel Misunderstands American Jewry"; Weiser, "Ben-Gurion's Dispute with American Zionists"; Hertzberg, "American Jews through Israeli Eyes"; "Ben-Gurion against the Diaspora: Three Comments."

103. Rawidowicz, *Israel: The Ever-Dying People*, 113; Gorny, "Shilat ha Galut: Past and Present"; Cohen and Liebman, *Two Worlds of Judaism*, 89–91; Biale, *Power and Powerlessness in Jewish History*, 4–9. Kaufman, "Anti-Semitic Stereotypes in Zionism"; Ganin, *Uneasy Relationship*, chap. 3.

104. Zertal, *Israel's Holocaust and the Politics of Nationhood*, 25–31.

105. Rabin, *Rabin Memoirs*, 396–97.

106. Zertal, *Israel's Holocaust and the Politics of Nationhood*, 46.

107. Meyer, *Jewish Identity in the Modern World*, 74.

108. Although Zionist leaders might have shied away from a politics of victimhood, they were keenly sensitive to Jewish vulnerability. See Zerubavel, *Recovered Roots*.

109. Ben-Yehuda, *Masada Myth*, 74. Also see Zerubavel, *Recovered Roots*.

110. Katz, *Wrestling with an Angel*, 50–52. Also see Eisen, *Jewish Reflection on Homelessness and Homecoming*.

111. Halpern, "Political Significance of Israel for American Jews"; Weiser, "Ben-Gurion's Dispute with American Zionists."

112. Cited from Balint, *Running Commentary*, 40.

113. Ganin, *Uneasy Relationship*, chaps. 2, 4.

114. Ben-Gurion and Blaustein, "An Exchange of Views," 1950; cited in Mendes-Flohr and Reinharz, *Jew in the Modern World*, 524–28.

115. American Jewish Committee, *In Vigilant Brotherhood*; Sklare, "Lakeville and Israel," 413; Imhof, "Between Home and Homeland," 74–81.

116. For a first-person account of an international meeting between Diaspora Jews and the new Israeli state, recording the contempt the latter had for the former, see Handlin, "Zionist Ideology and World Jewry."

117. "State of Jewish Belief—A Symposium."

CHAPTER FIVE: THE NEW TRIBALISM

1. Cohen and Fein, "From Integration to Survival," 75; Sarna, *American Judaism: A History*, 307–18; Liebman, *Ambivalent American Jew*, 97; Shiff, *Survival through Integration*, 161.

2. Cohen and Fein, "From Integration to Survival," 80.

3. Woocher, *Sacred Survival*; Sarna, *American Judaism: A History*, 307; Goldberg, *Jewish Power*, 161–62; Sarna, *American Judaism: A History*, 336–37; Staub, "Holocaust Consciousness and American Jewish Politics," 324–31. See Walzer, "Multiculturalism and the Politics of Interest," 88–98, for a comparison of Kallen's cultural pluralism with contemporary multiculturalism.

4. Woocher, *Sacred Survival*, xxi; Goldberg, *Jewish Power*; Zeitz, "If I Am Not for Myself"; Lipstadt, "From Noblesse Oblige to Personal Redemption"; Biale, *Power and Powerlessness*, 146, 161, 199; Wertheimer, *People Divided*, 28–34.

5. See, for instance, the review in Whitfield, "Influence and Affluence."

6. Goldberg, *Jewish Power*, 138.

7. Glazer, *American Judaism*, 183, 192. Also see Zeitz, "If I Am Not for Myself"; Cohen and Fein, "From Integration to Survival."

8. Cited from Liebman and Cohen, *Two Worlds of Judaism*, 40.

9. Svonkin, *Jews against Prejudice*, 187.

10. Staub, *Torn at the Roots*; Knox, "Is America Exile or Home?"

11. Fackenheim, "Dilemma of Liberal Judaism"; also see his "Can We Believe in Judaism Religiously?"

12. Hertzberg, "Modern Jewish Dilemmas."

13. Staub, *Torn at the Roots*, 63.

14. Bell, "Reflections on Jewish Identity," 473.

15. Staub, *Torn at the Roots*, 66.

16. Also see Svonkin, *Jews against Prejudice*, 178–94.

17. Sarna, *American Judaism: A History*, 317; Staub, *Torn at the Roots*, 131–32.

18. Zeitz, "If I Am Not for Myself," 267–69; Saks, "Israel and the New Left."

19. See Rynhold, *Arab-Israeli Conflict and American Political Culture*, chap. 2, for the dramatic rise in support from Republicans.

20. Hertzberg, "Israel and American Jewry."

21. Sklare, "Lakeville and Israel," 438.

22. Quoted from Zeitz, "If I Am Not for Myself," 253.

23. Sklare, "Lakeville and Israel," 438.

24. Lipstadt, "From Noblesse Oblige to Personal Redemption," 299. Also see Sklare, "Lakeville and Israel," 438.

25. Staub, *Torn at the Roots*.

26. Hertzberg, "Israel and American Jewry," 72; Cohen and Fein, "From Integration to Survival," 81.

27. Finkielkraut, *Imaginary Jew*, 132; Lipstadt, "From Noblesse Oblige to Personal Redemption," 299–302. Yossi Shain characterizes this phase as the "Israelization" of the Jewish American diaspora. Shain, *Kinships and Diaspora*, 56.

28. Hertzberg, "Israel and American Jewry," 69.

29. Ibid., 72; Wertheimer, *People Divided*, 30, cited from Kaplan, *Contemporary American Judaism*, 45; Liebman, *Ambivalent American Jew*, 94; Shapiro, *A Time for Healing*, 201–13; Waxman, "Israel Lobbies," 14.

30. Liebman, *Ambivalent American Jew*, 92; Lipstadt, "From Noblesse Oblige to Personal Redemption," 302.

31. Lipstadt, "From Noblesse Oblige to Personal Redemption," 302–7.

32. See in particular the work by Hasia Diner, *We Remember with Reverence and Love*; "Post-World-War-II American Jewry and the Confrontation with Catastrophe"; and "Before the 'Holocaust.'" Also see Lipstadt, *Eichmann Trial*, 189–90.

33. Svonkin, *Jews against Prejudice*, 185–87.

34. Novick, *Holocaust in American Life*, 160, cited from Alexander, *Remembering the Holocaust*, 20.

35. Cole, *Selling the Holocaust*; Novick, *Holocaust in American Life*; and, the most polemical, Finkelstein, *Holocaust Industry*; and Flanzbaum, *Americanization of the Holocaust*.

36. See, for instance, Diner, "Before the 'Holocaust.'"

37. See, for instance, Berenbaum and Kramer, *World Must Know*; Linenthal, *Preserving Memory*; Gorny, *Between Auschwitz and Jerusalem*; Magid, "Holocaust and Jewish Identity in America."

38. Biale, "Melting Pot and Beyond"; Young, "America's Holocaust"; Berenbaum, *After Tragedy and Triumph*.

39. Berenbaum, *After Tragedy and Triumph*, 20. For a reaction to this strategy, see Rosenfeld, "Americanization of the Holocaust."

40. Woocher, *Sacred Survival*, 132.

41. Ibid.; Neusner, *Stranger at Home*; Shapiro, *A Time for Healing*, 217.

42. Kelner, "Ritualized Protest and Redemptive Politics."

43. Halpern, *American Jew*, 66–70.

44. Staub, *Torn at the Roots*, 131–32.

45. Benbassa, *Suffering as Identity*.

46. For various statements on the intimate relationship between Jews, suffering, and a sense of victimization, see Shiff, *Survival through Integration*, 142–47; Liebman and Cohen, *Two Worlds of Judaism*, 31–34; Ophir, "Identity of the Victims and the Victims of Identity."

47. Eban, Address by Abba Eban, 15.

48. Aharon Appelfeld, "Interview," *Jerusalem Post Magazine*, November 27, 1987, p. 4. Cited from Liebman and Cohen, *Two Worlds of Judaism*, 31.

49. Baron, "Newer Emphases in Jewish History."

50. Biale, *Power and Powerlessness*.

51. Berlin, *Against the Current*, 253.

52. Rawidowicz, *Israel: The Ever-Dying People*.

53. Also see Wieseltier, "Pariah and Politics"; Biale, *Power and Powerlessness*; Zertal, *Israel's Holocaust and the Politics of Nationhood*.

54. Klawans, "Josephus, the Rabbis, and Responses to Catastrophes Ancient and Modern"; Roskies, *Literature of Destruction*.

55. Liebman and Cohen, *Two Worlds of Judaism*, 31; also see Dean, *Aversion and Erasure*, 32.

56. Finkielkraut, *Imaginary Jew*, 11–16.

57. Zerubavel, *Recovered Roots*, 193; Wistrich, "Israel and the Holocaust Trauma."

58. Beinart, *Crisis of Zionism*, 38, 41.

59. Goldberg, *Jewish Power*, 162.

60. Woocher, *Sacred Survival*, 87.

61. Lipset and Raab, *Jews and the New American Scene*, 54.

62. Peretz, "American Left and Israel."

63. Liebman, "Leadership and Decision-Making in a Jewish Federation." Cited from Cohen and Fein, "From Integration to Survival," 81.

64. Staub, *Torn at the Roots*, 138.

65. Yaniv, *Deterrence without the Bomb*.

66. Gitlin and Leibovitz, *Chosen Peoples*, chap. 4.

67. Shapiro, *A Time for Healing*, 203.

68. Beckerman, *When They Come for Us*, 58.

69. Ibid., 62.

70. Ibid., 144–47; Chernin, "Making Soviet Jews an Issue"; Lazin, *Struggle for Soviet Jewry in American Politics*, chap. 2; Feingold, "Silent No More," chaps. 1–2.

71. Lazin, *Struggle for Soviet Jewry in American Politics*, 5–6.

72. Beckerman, *When They Come for Us*, 9.

73. Interview with author, June 11, 2014.

74. Ibid., 232.

75. Feingold, "Silent No More," 199–200.

76. Gitelman, "Soviet Jews: Creating a Cause and a Movement," 85.

77. Beckerman, *When They Come for Us*, 335, 395. Feingold, *Jewish Power in America*, 61; Feingold, "Silent No More," 219–20.

78. Beckerman, *When They Come for Us*, 95–97.

79. Feingold, *Jewish Power in America*, 50.

80. Interview with author, New York City, May 2014.

81. http://www.nytimes.com/2010/12/17/nyregion/17nyc.html?_r=0.

82. Beckerman, *When They Come for Us*, 284; Feingold, *Jewish Power in America*, 51.

83. Quoted from Beckerman, *When They Come for Us*, 284.

84. Interview with author, June 11, 2014, Washington, DC.

85. Feingold, "Silent No More," chap. 6.

86. Korey, "From Helsinki"; Golden, *O Powerful Western Star!*, 317–22.

87. Feingold, "Silent No More," 225–26.

88. Ibid., 188. However, commentary a few years later provides further evidence that Soviet Jews did not see themselves as natural allies with the dissident movement. Wolf, "Should Soviet Jews Join the Dissidents?"

89. Beckerman, *When They Come for Us*, 95–97.

90. Ibid., 325–30, 334–35.

91. Ibid., 328–30.

92. Friedman, "Introduction: The Jewish Community Comes of Age," 6.

93. Windmueller, "The 'Noshrim War': Dropping Out."

94. Blaustein, "Human Rights: A Challenge to Our Generation and the United Nations." American Jewish Yearbook, 469. Cotler, "Jewish NGOs, Human Rights, and Public Advocacy." For an account of the failed effort by American Jews to use the United Nations to raise their concerns about anti-Semitism, see Loeffler, "How Zionism Became Racism."

95. Interview with author.

96. Henkin, "Human Rights: Reappraisal and Readjustment," 85. Also see Henkin, "Judaism and Human Rights."

97. See the collection of essays in Sidorsky, *Essays on Human Rights*.

98. Interview with author, February 20, 2013.

99. Goldmann, Proceedings of the Fifth Plenary Assembly, 33.

100. Interview with Roberta Cohen, Washington, DC.

101. Galchinsky, *Jews and Human Rights*, 45.

102. Levy and Natan Sznaider, *Holocaust and Memory in the Global Age*.

103. Goldberg, *Jewish Power*, 175.

104. Henkin, "Human Rights: Reappraisal and Readjustment," i, 73. World Jewish Congress, Policy and Action, 60–76.

105. Sidorsky, introduction to *Essays on Human Rights*, xxxvii; Garment, "Majoritarianism at the United Nations and Human Rights."

106. American Jewish Committee, "World of the 1970s," 33–34.

107. Henkin, "Human Rights: Reappraisal and Readjustment," 68–87.

108. For a fascinating interpretation of this resolution's origins in the attempt by American Jews to insert the outlaw of anti-Semitism into UN documents, see Loeffler, "How Zionism Became Racism." Also see Liskofsky, "UN Resolution on Zionism."

109. Diner, *Jews of the United States*, 327.

110. The story is recounted in Galchinsky, "American Jewish Committee and the Birth of the Israeli Human Rights Movement."

111. Ibid., 305.

112. Ibid., 316–17.

113. Hagel and Peretz, "States and Transnational Actors," 476–78, 480; Dinstein, "Soviet Jewry and International Human Rights."

114. Lipset, "A Unique People in an Exceptional Country"; Glazer, *American Judaism*, 139; Shapiro, "Jews and the Conservative Rift."

115. Feingold, "From Equality to Liberty," 110; Glazer, "Anomalous Liberalism of American Jews," 139; Dollinger, *Quest for Inclusion*, 220; Cohen, *American Modernity and Jewish Identity*, 165–67; Glazer, *American Judaism*, xxiv; Zeitz, "If I Am Not for Myself," 258.

116. Shapiro, "Jews and the Conservative Rift"; Hacohen, "Strange Fact That the State of Israel Exists"; Balint, *Running Commentary*, 115.

117. Balint, *Running Commentary*, 115; Staub, *Torn at the Roots*; Buhle, "Crisis of Jewish Liberalism"; Dollinger, *Quest for Inclusion*, 225; Glazer, *American Judaism*, xiii; Goldberg, *Jewish Power*, 174–80.

118. For overviews, see Vaïsse, *Neoconservatism*.

119. Shapiro, "Jews and the Conservative Rift."

120. Friedman, *Neoconservative Revolution*; Shapiro, "Jews and the Conservative Rift."

121. *Commentary*, "Liberalism and the Jews."
122. Shapiro, *A Time for Healing*, 218.
123. Ibid., 221.

CHAPTER SIX: BACK TO THE FUTURE?

1. Cohen, "What American Jews Believe"; Goldstein, *Price of Whiteness*, 223–26.
2. See some of the reactions to Israel's 2014 invasion of Gaza. For instance, Goldberg, "Summer's Missing Question"; Lerman, "End of Liberal Zionism"; Avishai, "Is Liberal Zionism Impossible?"; Bruck, "Friends of Israel"; Strenger, "Unrequited Love Affair between Liberal Jews and an Illiberal Israel"; Beinart, "What Liberal Zionists Should Say When We're Called Naïve"; Gross, "Not the End of Liberal Zionism."
3. Shain, *Kinships and Diasporas in International Affairs*, 57; Feingold, *American Jewish Political Culture and the Liberal Persuasion*, esp. chap. 5.
4. Sasson, Phillips, Kadushin, and Saxe, "Still Connected? American Jewish Attitudes about Israel; Saxe and Boxer, "Loyalty and Love of Israel by Diasporan Jews"; Miller and Dashefsky, "Brandeis v Cohen et al.: The Distancing from Israel Debate"; Keysar, "Distancing from Israel: Evidence on Jews of No Religion"; Sasson, *New Realism*, 26–36; Rynhold, *Arab-Israeli Conflict and the American Political Culture*, chap. 6.
5. Fleisch and Sasson, "New Philanthropy."
6. Ibid.
7. For overviews of these trends, see Shain, *Kinships and Diasporas in International Affairs*, 60–61; Sasson, "Mass Mobilization to Direct Engagement"; and, especially, Fleisch, "Israeli NGOs and American Jewish Donors."
8. Fleisch, "Israeli NGOs and American Jewish Donors," 2, 90.
9. Massing, "Should Jews Be Parochial?"; Roberts, "American Jewish Donations to Israel."
10. Cohen and Liebman, "Israel and American Jewry in the Twenty-First Century," 5; Wald and Williams, "American Jews and Israel," esp. 210; Cohen and Kelman, "Beyond Distancing"; Sasson, "Mass Mobilization to Direct Engagement," 185.
11. Cohen and Abrams, "Israel off Their Minds," http://www.bjpa.org/Publications/details.cfm?PublicationID=207; Mellman, Strauss, and Wald, "Jewish American Voting Behavior 1972–2008"; Rynhold, *The Arab-Israeli Conflict in American Political Culture*, 155–57.
12. Wilkes, *And they Shall Be My People*, 224. Cited in Kaplan, *Contemporary American Judaism*.
13. Cohen, "Changing Conceptions of Jewish Collectivity among Young Adult Jews." The other study is by Luntz, *Israel in an Age of Eminem*, 14. Sheffer, *Diaspora Politics*, 233. All three pieces are cited from Wald and Williams, "American Jews and Israel," 210.
14. Jewish People Policy Institute, 2014, "Annual Assessment. 2013-14."
15. http://www.adl.org/press-center/press-releases/anti-semitism-usa/adl-audit-anti-semitic-incidents-2013.html#.VOtdXi5SK4k. However, it appears that the ADL has expanded the definition of anti-Semitic acts to include reports of harassment and other more subtle and subjective measures, which means that historical comparisons becomes much more complicated.

16. American Jewish Committee, "2006 Annual Survey of American Jewish Opinion."

17. Magid, *American Post-Judaism*; Cohen, Kelman, with Blitzer, "Beyond Distancing," 20; Cohen and Eisen, "Sovereign Self," http://www.jcpa.org/jl/vp453.htm.

18. Cohen and Eisen, *Jew Within*, 143. Also see Fischer and Stone, "Jewish Identity and Identification," 7; Goldberg, *Jewish Power*, 73; and Kaplan, *Contemporary American Judaism*.

19. Cohen, "Relationships of American Jews with Israel," 143.

20. Ginsburg, "Re-Anchoring Universalism to Particularism."

21. Beinart, *Crisis of Zionism*, 171.

22. Cohen, Kelman, with Blitzer, *Beyond Distancing*.

23. Luz, *Wrestling with an Angel*, 10–11.

24. Shafir and Peled, *Being Israel*, 1. Also see Kimmerling, *Invention and Decline of Israeliness*. Conforti, "Between Ethnic and Civic."

25. For one attempt to measure Israeli democracy, see the Israeli Democracy Index, http://en.idi.org.il/events/democracy-index/.

26. Reut Institute, "21st Century Tikkun Olam," 121–31.

27. Ibid., 2–3; Magid, "Holocaust and Jewish Identity in America," 104.

28. Cohen, "From Jewish People to Jewish Purpose"; Cohen, "Expressive, Progressive, and Protective."

29. Beinart, *Crisis of Zionism*, 170.

30. For an extended discussion of the impact of Israeli behavior on American Jewish attitudes, also see Jewish People Policy Institute, pp. 81–85; Jewish People Policy Institute, Jewish and Democratic: Perspectives from World Jewry," and especially 21-37.

31. Kimmerling, "Religion, Nationalism, and Democracy," 340.

32. The Jewish People Policy Institute, 2014, p. 100.

33. http://www.pewforum.org/2012/09/20/rising-tide-of-restrictions-on-religion-findings/.

34. Kimmerling, "Religion, Nationalism, and Democracy"; Ben-Yehuda, *Theocratic Democracy*; Porat, *Between State and Synagogue*.

35. "Who Owns Judaism?"

36. It has been this way since the founding of the State of Israel. See Liebman, *Pressure without Sanctions*, 61–117.

37. For a good overview of the diaspora struggle for religious pluralism in Israel, see Shain, *Kinships and Diasporas in International Affairs*, chap. 3.

38. Yeddia Stern and Jay Ruderman, March 3, 2014, Jewish Telegraphic Agency, "Is 'Israeli' a Nationality?" Cited from Jewish People Policy Institute, "Jewish and Democratic," p. 59.

39. For an extended discussion of these points, see Jewish People Policy Institute, Jewish and Democratic.

40. Wertheimer, "Generation of Change," 3–4.

41. Ibid., 39.

42. http://iengage.org.il/about_us_View.asp?Cat_Id=1. Accessed January 2, 2014.

43. Also see Cooper, "Assimilation of Tikkun Olam," 16–17.

44. Ibid., 172; Shain, *Kinships and Diasporas in International Affairs*, 58–62, and chap. 3.

45. Beinart, *Crisis of Zionism*, 177.

46. For a discussion of the New Israel Fund, see Steinberg, "Contesting Identities in Jewish Philanthropy," 256–75.

47. Shain, *Kinships and Diasporas in International Affairs*, 61.

48. Haklai, "Helping the Enemy?"

49. Also part of this trend is the growth in programming by American Jewish organizations that attempt to build bridges between Israeli Jews, on one side, and Israeli Arabs and Palestinians, on the other.

50. This discussion draws heavily from Kelner, *Tours That Bind*.

51. Ibid., 196.

52. Saxe, Shain, Wright, Hecht, Fishman, and Sasson, "Impact of Taglit-Birthright Israel: 2012 Update."

53. Kelner, *Tours That Bind*, 195.

54. Ibid., xix.

55. See for instance, Wertheimer, "Generation of Change," 3; and, Jager, "Are Young Rabbis Turning on Israel?"

56. Jacobs, *Where Justice Dwells*; Jacobs, *Their Shall Be No Needy*; Yanklowitz, *Jewish Ethics and Social Justice*; Mirsky, "*Tikkun Olam*: Basic Questions and Policy Directions"; Neumann, "Tikkun Olam: A Concept in Need of Repair."

57. See, for instance, Sacks, *To Heal a Fractured World*.

58. Kranson, "A Break with Spring Break."

59. The search was restricted to American Jewish newspapers with searchable archives.

60. Neumann, "Tikkun Olam: A Concept in Need of Repair," 32–33.

61. Although the following discussions talk generally about the rise of tikkun olam, the vast majority of programs and activities are national, not international.

62. Halkin, "How Not to Repair the World," *Commentary*, July 2008; Neumann, "Tikkun Olam: A Concept in Need of Repair"; Cooper, "Assimilation of Tikkun Olam."

63. Sacks, *To Heal a Fractured World*, 74.

64. Ibid., 75.

65. Maranz, "Crucial Question of Jewish Giving."

66. Wolf, "Repairing Tikkun Olam." Cited in Neumann, "Tikkun Olam: A Concept in Need of Repair," 32.

67. Alperson, "Judaism Is More Than 'Tikkun Olam.'"

68. Wertheimer, "Ten Commandments of America's Jews."

69. Steinberg, "Contesting Identities in Jewish Philanthropy."

70. Orthodox Jews volunteer at greater rates than non-Orthodox Jews, "but typically do most of their volunteering in the Jewish community and for Jewish causes." Chertok, Tobias, Rosin, and Boxer, *Volunteering + Values*, 38. As former British Chief Rabbi Jonathan Sacks observed: "The Orthodox community is very much concerned with particularism but gave up on universalism. . . . Phrases like 'light unto nations' or the 'Jewish mission' or 'ethical universalism,' all those things became code words for assimilation, reform, and the whole concept of *Tikkun Olam* became suspect." Sacks, "Tikkun Olam: Orthodoxy's Responsibility to Perfect G-d's World." Cited from Ginsburg, "Re-Anchoring Universalism to Particularism," 13.

71. Cohen and Fein, "American Jews and Their Social Justice Involvement."

72. Chertok, Tobias, Rosin, and Boxer, *Volunteering + Values*, 10.

73. Ibid., 39.

74. Ibid., 26, 28.

75. Ibid., 27.

76. Ibid., 38, 47. Also see Jones and Cox, "Chosen for What?"; Cohen and Wertheimer, "Whatever Happened to the Jewish People?," 36; Leibel, "Justice, Justice."

77. Gil and Wilf, *2030: Alternative Futures for the Jewish People*, 18.

78. Barnett and Stein, "Secularization and Sanctification of Humanitarianism."

79. Fischer and Stone, "Jewish Identity and Identification," 7.

80. Fischer and Stone, "Jewish Identity and Identification" 9.

81. Luxemburg, "No Room in My Heart for Jewish Suffering." Cited from Mendes-Flohr and Reinharz, *Jew in the Modern World*, 261–62.

82. Gitelman "Decline of the Diaspora Jewish Nation," 121. Quoted from Wald and Williams, "American Jews and Israel," 209.

83. Interview with author, December 20, 2012.

84. Eisner, J. (2009). "Not only for ourselves." *Jewish Daily Forward*. Retrieved from http://www.forward.com/articles/120018/. Cited from Morry Walfish, *Journal of Jewish Communal Service*, Volume 87, Nos. 1/2, Winter/Spring 2012, p. 26.

85. Messinger, *Currents*, September 2003.

86. For the argument that Israel is causing greater fissure within diasporic Jewish communities, see Kahn-Harris, *Uncivil War.*

87. Shachtman, *I Seek My Brethren*, 210.

88. Meeting notes from Jewish Agency for Israel / Makom consultation, February 8, 2012; quotes are from not for attribution names of participants. I also checked my summary of the meeting with two participants of the meeting.

89. "Background Papers on International Human Rights Questions," prepared for National Jewish Community Relations Advisory Council, April 7, 1992.

90. Interview with author, February 21, 2013; Pinto-Duschinsky, "Jews, Law, and Human Rights."

91. Besser, "Sad Silence."

92. October 9, 2009. http://www.nytimes.com/2009/10/20/opinion/20bernstein.html.

93. E-mail correspondence with author, June 3, 2015.

94. Neier, *International Human Rights: A Movement*, 219–24.

95. Sage, "JDC International Development Program."

96. "JDC Participating in National Appeal for Cambodian Refugees," 2.

97. Sage, "JDC International Development Program," 4.

98. Following the Israeli invasion, a major relief effort got underway. The Joint was part of the effort. Working through Lebanese ministries, Caritas, and other aid agencies, it channeled nearly $2 million for Lebanon, which surpassed the amount given by Christian and other nonsectarian agencies. Rubin, "Through Winter, Rain, and Mud." It also joined the caravan of relief agencies that entered from the Israeli-Lebanese border in the south, distributing mattresses, blankets, cookware, and kerosene stoves. "Aid Groups Appeal to Israel for Right to Enter Lebanon"; Rubin, "Through Winter, Rain, and Mud." Why would a Jewish agency provide relief to the Lebanese? One possibility is that it was intending to provide assistance to the population in southern Lebanon, primarily Shi'ite, and, at the time, allies because they had a mutual enemy in the PLO. However, I have spoken on the condition of anonymity with staff from the period, who insist that they went all the way into

Beirut and gave to all victims, including Palestinians. Perhaps reflecting the rather politically sensitive nature of their activities, the Joint's annual report does not discuss its role.

99.   Sage, "The JDC International Development Program."

100.   Ibid., 2. Interviews with current and former staff from the Joint.

101.   Also see Shachtman, *I Seek My Brethren*, 143–47. Rosen, *Mission, Meaning, and Money*, 93–96. Gideon Taylor, interview July 31, 2007; cited from Rosen, *Mission, Meaning, and Money*, 93.

102.   Sage, "The JDC International Development Program," 14.

103.   "Founding of the American Jewish World Service."

104.   Messinger, "Jewish Service and Global Citizenship," 6–7. Educational materials raise questions such as: "Who are the people I am obligated to, and how do I help them?" p. 6. American Jewish World Service, *Expanding the Universe of Obligations*. Also see Messinger and Dorfman, "Am I My Brother's Keeper If My Brother Lives Halfway around the World?"

105.   Messinger, *Currents*, September 2003.

106.   "Founding of the American Jewish World Service."

107.   Hamilton, *Fighting for Darfur*, 44.

108.   Walfish, "Jewish Service-Learning." Also see Messinger, "Twenty-First-Century Genocide."

109.   Eichler-Levine and Hicks, "As Americans against Genocide."

110.   "What's Jewish about It?"

111.   Hamilton, *Fighting for Darfur*, 124.

112.   Ibid., 110.

113.   Ibid., 63.

114.   Interview with official from the American Jewish World Service.

115.   Messinger, "Re: The Discussion about Poverty and Human Rights."

116.   Interview with official from American Jewish World Service.

CHAPTER SEVEN: THE FOREIGN POLICIES OF AN UNCERTAIN PEOPLE

1.   Vital, *Future of the Jews*; Eisen, "Introduction: Four Questions concerning Peoplehood," 2; Brown and Galperin, *Case for Jewish Peoplehood*; Ravid, *Peoplehood in an Age of Pluralism*; Ravid, *Peoplehood—Between "Charity Begins at Home" and "Repair the World."*

2.   Cited from Wertheimer, "Whatever Happened to the Jewish People?"

3.   Eisen, "Israel at 50"; Halpern, *American Jew*, 66.

4.   Eisen, *Chosen People in America*, 130.

5.   Ibid., 130.

6.   Dubnow, *Jewish History: An Essay in the Philosophy of History.*

7.   Hans Morgenthau, "The Jews and Soviet Foreign Policy," *Soviet Jewry* (1969): 85. Morgenthau Papers, Box 106. Cited from Mollov, "Jewry's Prophetic Challenge to Soviet and Other Totalitarian Regimes According to Hans J. Morgenthau."

8.   Miller and Ury, "Cosmopolitanism: The End of Jewishness?"

9.   Katz, "Post-Emancipation Development and Rights," 294.

10.   Slezkine, *The Jewish Century*; Mendelsohn, *On Modern Jewish Politics.*

11. Podhoretz, *Why Are Jews Liberals?*.

12. Bell, "Parable of Alienation."

13. Ibid., 14.

14. Ibid.

15. Veblen, "Intellectual Pre-Eminence of Jews in Modern Europe."

16. Ibid., 139.

17. Freud, "On Being of the B'nai B'rith."

18. Bell, "Parable of Alienation," 11, 15, 19.

19. Kaplan, *Religion of Ethical Nationhood*, 133.

20. Horowitz, *Israeli Ecstasies / Jewish Agonies*, 202.

21. Deutscher, *Non-Jewish Jew and Other Essays*, 25–27.

22. Fischer and Stone, "Jewish Identity and Identification," 141.

23. http://www.haaretz.com/jewish-world/u-s-jewish-groups-furious-over -campaign-to-bring-expat-israelis-back-home-1.399057.

24. American Jewish Committee, *Israel on My Mind*; Norich, *What Will Bind Us?*

25. Cited from Yaniv, *The Prime Ministers*, 399.

26. Liebman and Cohen, *Two Worlds of American Judaism*, 94–95. Also see Cohen and Liebman, "Israel and American Jewry in the Twenty-First Century"; Hammer, "Jewish Political Ethics in Israel"; Borowitz, *Liberal Judaism*, 97–99.

27. Fried, Bennett, and Keidan, "Toward a Tikkun Olam Policy for World Jewry and Israel."

28. Cited from Piterberg, "Zion's Rebel Daughter," 52.

29. Michael Oren, *Ally*. Cited from Jane Eisner, http://forward.com/opinion/ed itorial/310749/michael-oren-you-hardly-know-us/.

30. Weltsch, "Israel, Human Rights, and American Jewry," 355.

31. For discussions of diaspora-Israel relations, see Sheffer, *Diaspora Politics: At Home Abroad*; Sheffer, "Nation and Its Diaspora"; Shain and Bristman, "Diaspora, Kinship, and Loyalty"; Sheffer, "Loyalty and Criticism in Relations between World Jewry and Israel"; Liebman, "Moral and Symbolic Elements in the Politics of Israel-Diaspora Relations"; Liebman, *Pressure without Sanctions*; Shain, *Kinships and Diasporas in International Affairs*, 57–58, 99; Sufott, "Israel and the Diaspora"; Bayne, "American Jewry and the State of Israel"; Harman and Sarna, "American Jewish-Israeli Relations; Ben-Moshe and Segev, *Israel, the Diaspora, and Jewish Identity*.

32. Sklare, "Lakeville and Israel," 413.

33. Hertzberg, "Joint Responsibility Is No Picnic," 11.

34. Sarna, "Promised Land and Golden Land," 8. Also see Bayne, "American Jewry and the State of Israel"; Eisen, "New Jewish Role for Israel in American Jewish Identity"; Rynhold, *Arab-Israeli Conflict in American Political Culture*.

35. Jewish People Policy Planning Institute, *Arevut, Responsibility, and Partnership*, 20.

36. Ibid., 34.

37. For another perspective, see Eisen, "New Role for Israel in American Jewish Identity."

38. Rosner, *Shtetl, Bagel, and Baseball*.

39. Seliktar, "Changing Identity of American Jews, Israel, and the Peace Process"; Norich, *What Will Bind Us Now?*; Shain and Bristman, "Diaspora, Kinship, and Loyalty," 82–83.

40. Jewish Peoples Policy Institute, "Jewish and Democratic," 57-67.

41. See, for instance, Frank, *Jew in Our Day*.

42. Luz, *Wrestling with an Angel*, 240–41.

43. For other statements on victims, suffering, and violence see Thomas, "Suffering as a Moral Beacon." Benbassa, *Suffering as Identity*, 1; and Enns, *Violence of Victimhood*,

44. For the broader themes of particularism and universalism as they apply to Israel, see Ravid, *Peoplehood—Between "Charity Begins at Home" and "Repair the World."*

45. Interview with official from Jewish Agency; Grinstein, *Flexigidity: The Secret of Jewish Adaptability*, esp. pages 225–27. Beckerman, "Embattled Jewish Agency to Promote Identity over Aliyah."

46. Jewish People Policy Planning Institute, *Arevut, Responsibility, and Partnership*.

47. For a representative sample of opinion on the relationship between Jewish peoplehood and tikkun olam, see the collection of essays in Ravid, "The Peoplehood Papers," Also see Ginsburg, "Re-Anchoring Universalism to Particularism."

48. Jewish People Policy Planning Institute, *Arevut, Responsibility, and Partnership*, 40.

49. Friedman, "Jewish Soft Power"; Fried, Bennett, and Keidan, "Toward a Tikkun Olam Policy for World Jewry and Israel," 85.

50. Jewish People Policy Planning Institute, *Arevut, Responsibility, and Partnership*, 68.

51. Belman Inbal and Zahavi, "Rise and Fall of Israel's Bilateral Aid Budget." Cited in note 5, Reut Institute, "21st Century Tikkun Olam."

52. Jewish People Policy Planning Institute, *Arevut, Responsibility, and Partnership*, 38.

53. Ben-Moshe, "Darfurian Test."

54. Interview with author, Jerusalem, Israel.

55. Halpern, *American Jew*, 134.

56. Bell, "Reflections on Jewish Identity," 473.

57. Steinberg, "Politics of NGOs, Human Rights, and the Arab-Israeli Conflict"; Steinberg, "From Durban to the Goldstone Report"; also see Pollak, "The B'Tselem Witch Trials."

58. Weltsch, "Israel, Human Rights, and American Jewry," 358.

59. Pew Research Center, "A Portrait of Jewish Americans."

60. Beinart, *Crisis of Zionism*. Also see Nathan-Kazie, "Jews Express Wide Criticism of Israel in Pew Survey."

61. Magid, *American Post-Judaism*.

62. Gitelman, "Decline of the Diaspora Jewish Nation."

63. Quoted from Walzer, *In God's Shadow*, 125.

64. Cohen, *Israel: Is It Good for the Jews?*; Wolfe, *At Home in Exile*; Rabinovitch, *Jews and Diaspora Nationalism*; and Wettstein, *Diasporas and Exiles*.

65. Myers, "Rethinking Global Jewish Collectivity in a Post-Statist World."

66. Niebuhr, introduction to *The Jew in Our Day*, by Waldo Frank, 7.

67. Ibid.

68. Ibid., 13, 14.

BIBLIOGRAPHY

Aberbach, David. "Nationalism and the Hebrew Bible." *Nations and Nationalism* 11, no. 2 (2005): 223–42.

——. "Nationalism, Reform Judaism, and the Hebrew Prayer Book." *Nations and Nationalism* 12, no. 1 (2006): 139–59.

"Abstract of Report of Meeting of Representative of Jewish Organizations Held in Paris, March 30–April 6, 1919," 227–28.

Adler, Cyrus, and Aaron Morris Margalith. *With Firmness in the Right: American Diplomatic Action Affecting Jews, 1840–1945.* New York: American Jewish Committee, 1946.

"Aid Groups Appeal to Israel for Right to Enter Lebanon." *New York Times*, July 3, 1982, 5.

Alexander, Edward. *Irving Howe—Socialist, Critic, Jew.* Bloomington: Indiana University Press, 1998.

Alexander, Jeffrey C. *Remembering the Holocaust: A Debate.* New York: Oxford University Press, 2009.

Alperson, Joel. "Judaism Is More Than 'Tikkun Olam.'" Jewish Telegraphic Agency, July 27, 2011. http://www.jta.org/2011/07/27/news-opinion/opinion/op-ed-judaism -is-more-than-tikkun-olam.

Alroey, Gur. "'Zionism without Zion'? Territorialist Ideology and the Zionist Movement, 1882–1956." *Jewish Social Studies* 18, no. 1 (2011): 1–32.

American Jewish Committee. "2006 Annual Survey of American Jewish Opinion." Downloaded from http://www.ajc.org/site/apps/nlnet/content3.aspx?c=7oJILSP wFfJSG&b=8479755&ct=12483107 on February 15, 2015.

——. Correspondence from Jacob Landau to Cyrus Adler, March 10, 1932 New York: American Jewish Committee.

——. Correspondence from Jacob Landau to Albert Lusker, March 2, 1932. New York: American Jewish Committee.

——. "How the Jewish Communities Prepared for Peace during the First World War, Jewish Post-War Problems, A Study Course, Unit III." Research Institute on Peace and Post-War Problems, American Jewish Committee.

——. *In Vigilant Brotherhood: The American Jewish Committee's Relationship to Palestine and Israel.* New York: American Jewish Committee, 1964.

——. *Israel on My Mind: Israel's Role in World Jewish Identity.* Koppelman Institute on American-Jewish-Israeli Relations, American Jewish Committee, November 1995.

——. "Jewish Post-War Problems: A Study Course." Research Institute on Peace and Post-War Problems, American Jewish Committee, 1942.

——. "Jewish Post-War Problems, Unit I." Research Institute on Peace and Post-War Problems, American Jewish Committee, 1942.

——. "Jewish Post-War Problems: A Study Course, Unit I: Why Study Post-War Problems." Prepared by the Research Institute on Peace and Post-War Problems, American Jewish Committee, 1942.

——. "Jewish Post-War Problems: A Study Course, The Two World Wars—A Comparison and Contrast." American Jewish Committee, Research Institute on Peace and Post-War Problems, 1942.

——. "Jewish Post-War Problems: A Study Course, Unit V: The Position of the Jews in the Post-War World." Research Institute on Peace and Post-War Problems, American Jewish Committee, 1943.

——. "Proposed Provisions for the Peace Treaties." Second Session, January 31–February 1, 1946. Committee on Peace Problems.

——. "Protection of Human Rights." Preliminary Memorandum Prepared for the Conference, February 1–2, 1945. Committee on Peace Problems, New York: American Jewish Committee, December.

——. "Readings on the Causes of Peace Failure, Unit II." Prepared by the Research Institute on Peace and Post-War Problems, American Jewish Committee, 1942.

——. "The United Nations in 1946: Human Rights, Refugees, and Trusteeship." Committee on Peace Problems, Third Session, January 23–24, 1947.

——. "A World Charter for Human Rights," December 1948.

——. "The World of the 1970s: A Jewish Perspective." American Jewish Committee, September 1971.

American Jewish Committee and Anglo-Jewish Association. London Conference of Jewish Organizations: Report of the Programme Committee, 1946.

American Jewish World Service. *Expanding the Universe of Obligation: Judaism, Justice and Global Responsibility.* 3rd ed. New York: American Jewish World Service, 2009.

American Jewish Year Book. "Jewish War Relief Work." *American Jewish Year Book* 19 (1918): 194–226. Philadelphia: Jewish Publication Society of America.

Amyot, Robert P., and Lee Sigelman. "Jews without Judaism? Assimilation and Jewish Identity in the United States." *Social Science Quarterly* 77 (1996): 177–89.

Appiah, Kwame Anthony. 2010. *Cosmopolitanism: Ethics in a World of Strangers.* New York: W. W. Norton, 2010.

Arendt, Hannah. "The Jewish State: Fifty Years After: Where Have Herzl's Politics Led?" *Commentary* 1 (1946): 1–8.

Auerbach, Jerold S. *Are We One? Jewish Identity in the United States and Israel.* New Brunswick, NJ: Transaction Publishers, 2001.

——. "Liberalism and the Hebrew Prophets." *Commentary* (August 1987): 58–60.

——. "Liberalism, Judaism, and American Jews: A Response." In *The Americanization of the Jews,* edited by Robert Seltzer and Norman Cohen, 144–48. New York: New York University Press, 1995.

Avineri, Shlomo. "Ideology and Israel's Foreign Policy." *Jerusalem Quarterly* 37 (1986): 3–13.

Avishai, Bernard. "Is Liberal Zionism Impossible?" *New Yorker*, September 5, 2014. http://www.newyorker.com/news/news-desk/liberal-zionist. Accessed December 22, 2014.

Avner, Yehuda. *The Prime Ministers: An Intimate Narrative of Israeli Leadership* (New Milford, CT: Toby Press, 2010).

"Background Papers on International Human Rights Questions." Prepared for National Jewish Community Relations Advisory Council, April 7, 1992.

Balint, Benjamin. *Running Commentary: The Contentious Magazine That Transformed the Jewish Left into the Neoconservative Right.* New York: PublicAffairs, 2010.

Bar-Chen, Eli. "Two Communities with a Sense of Mission: The Alliance Israélite Universelle and the Hilfsverein der Deutschen Juden." In *Jewish Emancipation Reconsidered: The French and German Models*, edited by Michael Brenner, Vicki Caron, and Uri Kaufmann, 111–21. Tübingen: Mohr Siebeck, 2003.

Barnett, Michael, and Janice Gross Stein. "The Secularization and Sanctification of Humanitarianism." In *Sacred Aid: Faith and Humanitarianism*, edited by Michael Barnett and Janice Gross Stein, 3–36. New York: Oxford University Press, 2012.

Baron, Ilan Zvi. "Diasporic Security and Jewish Identity." *Journal of Modern Jewish Studies* 13, no. 2 (2014): 292–309.

Baron, Salo W. "Newer Emphases in Jewish History." *Jewish Social Studies* 25, no. 4 (1963): 235–48.

———. "The Spiritual Reconstruction of European Jewry." *Commentary* (November 1945): 4–12.

Batnitzky, Leora. *How Judaism Became a Religion: An Introduction to Modern Jewish Thought.* Princeton, NJ: Princeton University Press, 2011.

Bayme, Steven. "American Jewry and the State of Israel: How Intense the Bonds of Peoplehood?" *Jewish Political Studies Review* 20, no. 1–2 (2008): 7–21.

Beck, Ulrich. "The Cosmopolitan Society and Its Enemies." *Theory, Culture, and Society* 19, no. 1–2 (2002): 17–44.

———. *Cosmopolitan Vision.* Boston: Polity, 2006.

Beckerman, Gal. "Embattled Jewish Agency to Promote Identity over Aliyah: New Emphasis on 'Peoplehood' Reflects Economic Reality and Russian Roots." *Forward*, March 12, 2010. http://forward.com/articles/126458/embattled-jewish-agency-to-promote-identity-over-a/.

———. *When They Come for Us, We'll Be Gone: The Epic Struggle to Save Soviet Jewry.* Boston: Houghton Mifflin Harcourt, 2010.

Beilin, Yossi. *His Brother's Keeper: Israel and Diaspora Jewry in the Twenty-First Century.* New York: Schocken Books, 2000.

Beinart, Peter. *The Crisis of Zionism.* New York: Macmillan, 2012.

———. "What Liberal Zionists Should Say When We're Called Naïve." February 19, 2014. *Ha'aretz.* http://www.haaretz.com/opinion/.premium-1.575091.

Beker, Avi. "Diplomacy without Sovereignty: The World Jewish Congress Rescue Activities." In *Organizing Rescue: Jewish National Solidarity in the Modern Period*, edited by Selwyn Ilan Troen and Benjamin Pinkus, 343–60. Portland OR: Frank Cass, 1992.

———. "Sixty Years of World Jewish Congress Diplomacy: From Foreign Policy to the Soul of the Nation." In *Jewish Centers and Peripheries: Europe between American and Israel Fifty Years after World War II*, edited by S. Ilan Troen, 373–96. New Brunswick, NJ: Transaction Publishers, 1998.

Bell, Daniel. "A Parable of Alienation." *Jewish Frontier* 13 (1946): 12–19.

——. "Reflections on Jewish Identity." In *The Ghetto and Beyond: Essays on Jewish Life in America*, edited by Peter I. Rose, 465–76. New York: Random House, 1969.

Belman Inbal, Aliza, and Shachar Zahavi. *The Rise and Fall of Israel's Bilateral Aid Budget, 1958–2008*. Tel-Aviv University, the Harold Hartog School of Government and Policy, 2009.

Belth, Nathan. "Minority Rights." In *Universal Jewish Encyclopedia*, by Isaac Landman, vol. 3, 574–75. New York: Ktav, 1969.

"Ben Gurion against the Diaspora: Three Comments." *Commentary* (1961): 193–202.

Ben-Gurion, David, and Simon A. Dolgin. "Can We Stay Jews Outside 'The Land'? An Exchange." *Commentary* 16 (September 1953): 233–39.

Ben-Moshe, Danny. "The Darfurian Test." *Jerusalem Report*, August 20, 2007, 47.

Ben-Moshe, Danny, and Zohar Segev, eds. *Israel, the Diaspora, and Jewish Identity*. Portland, OR: Sussex Academic Press, 2007.

Ben-Yehuda, Nachman. *The Masada Myth: Collective Memory and Mythmaking in Israel*. Madison: University of Wisconsin Press, 1996.

——. *Theocratic Democracy: The Social Construction of Religious and Secular Extremism*. New York: Oxford University Press, 2010.

Benbassa, Esther. *Suffering as Identity: The Jewish Paradigm*. London: Verso, 2010.

Benhabib, Seyla, Jeremy Waldron, Bonnie Honig, and Will Kymlicka. *Another Cosmopolitanism*. Edited by Robert Post. Vol. 3. Oxford: Oxford University Press, 2006.

Berenbaum, Michael. *After Tragedy and Triumph: Essays in Modern Jewish Thought and the American Experience*. New York: Cambridge University Press, 2009.

Berenbaum, Michael, and Arnold Kramer. *The World Must Know: The History of the Holocaust as Told in the United States Holocaust Memorial Museum*. Boston: Little, Brown, 1993.

Berkowitz, Michael. *Western Jewry and the Zionist Project, 1914–1933*. New York: Cambridge University Press, 1997.

Berlin, Isaiah. *Against the Current: Essays in the History of Ideas*. New York: Random House, 2012.

Bernstein, Richard J. *Hannah Arendt and the Jewish Question*. Cambridge, MA: MIT Press, 1996.

Bernstein, Robert. "Rights Watchdog, Lost in the Mideast." October 19, 2009. http://www.nytimes.com/2009/10/20/opinion/20bernstein.html.

Besser, James D. "Sad Silence: The Lack of Jewish Voices on Detainee Abuse Is Not a Good Mark on the Community." *Baltimore Jewish Times*, August 5, 2005, 24.

Biale, David. "The Melting Pot and Beyond: Conflicting Narratives of American Jewish History." In *Insider/Outsider: American Jews and Multiculturalism*, edited by David Biale, Michael Galchinsky, and Susannah Heschel. Berkeley: University of California Press, 1998.

——. *Power and Powerlessness in Jewish History*. New York: Schocken Books, 2010.

Bigart, Jacques. "The Alliance Israélite Universelle." *American Jewish Year Book* (1900): 45–65.

Birmingham, Peg. *Hannah Arendt and Human Rights: The Predicament of Common Responsibility*. Bloomington: Indiana University Press, 2006.

Birnbaum, Ben. "Minority Report." *New Republic*, April 27, 2010. http://www.newrepublic.com/article/minority-report-2.

Birnbaum, Pierre. *Geography of Hope: Exile, the Enlightenment, Disassimilation.* Stanford, CA: Stanford University Press, 2008.

Blaustein, Jacob. "Human Rights: A Challenge to Our Generation and the United Nations." In *The Quest for Peace: The Dag Hammarskjold Memorial Lectures,* edited by Andrew Cordier and Wilder Foote. New York: Columbia University Press, 1965.

Borowitz, Eugene B. "The Chosen People Concept as It Affects Life in the Diaspora." *Journal of Ecumenical Studies* 12, no. 4 (1975): 553–68.

———. "The Dialects of Jewish Particularity." *Journal of Ecumenical Studies* 8 (1971): 560–74.

———. *Liberal Judaism.* New York: Union of American Hebrew Congregations, 1984.

Bourne, Randolph. "The Jew and Trans-National America." *Menorah Journal* (December 1916): 277–84.

Brandeis, Louis. "The Jewish Problem: How to Solve It." Speech to the Conference of Eastern Council of Reform Rabbis, April 25, 1915. Downloaded from http://www .law.louisville.edu/library/collections/brandeis/node/234 on February 3, 2015.

Breitman, Richard, and Allan Lichtman. *FDR and the Jews.* Cambridge, MA: Belknap Press of Harvard University Press, 2013.

Brennan, Timothy. *At Home in the World: Cosmopolitanism Now.* Cambridge, MA: Harvard University Press, 1997.

Brenner, Michael, Vicki Caron, and Uri R. Kaufmann, eds. *Jewish Emancipation Reconsidered: The French and German Models.* Tübingen: Mohr Siebeck, 2003.

British Observer. "The Consultative Conference in London: Landmark in International Jewish Relations." *Commentary* (September 1955): 212–18.

Brock, Gillian, and Harry Brighouse, eds. *The Political Philosophy of Cosmopolitanism.* New York: Cambridge University Press, 2005.

Brown, Erica, and Misha Galperin. *The Case for Jewish Peoplehood: Can We Be One?* Woodstock, VT: Jewish Lights Publishing, 2009.

Broyde, Michael J., and John Witte, eds. *Human Rights in Judaism: Cultural, Religious, and Political Perspectives.* Northvale, NJ: Jason Aronson, 1998.

Bruck, Connie. "Friends of Israel." September 1, 2014. http://www.newyorker.com/ magazine/2014/09/01/friends-israel. Accessed December 22, 2014.

Buber, Martin. *For the Sake of Heaven.* New York: Harper and Row, 1966.

———. *Israel and the World: Essays in a Time of Crisis.* Syracuse, NY: Syracuse University Press, 1997.

Buhle, Paul, and Michael E. Staub. "The Crisis of Jewish Liberalism." *Tikkun* 18, no. 2 (2003): 71–74.

Burg, Avraham. *The Holocaust Is Over; We Must Rise from Its Ashes.* New York: Palgrave Macmillan, 2008.

Calhoun, Craig. "Cosmopolitanism and Nationalism." *Nations and Nationalism* 14, no. 3 (2008): 427–48.

Central Conference of American Rabbis. *Yearbook of the Central Conference of American Rabbis.* Vol. 9. University of Michigan Library, 1899.

Cheah, Pheng, and Bruce Robbins, eds. *Cosmopolitics: Thinking and Feeling beyond the Nation.* Minneapolis: University of Minnesota Press, 1998.

Chernin, Albert. "Making Soviet Jews an Issue: A History." In *A Second Exodus: The American Movement to Free Soviet Jews,* edited by Murray Friedman and Albert D. Chernin, 15–69. Hanover, NH: University Press of New England for Brandeis University Press, 1999.

Chertok, Fern, Joshua Tobias, Shirah Rosin, and Matthew Boxer. *Volunteering + Values: A Repair the World Report on Jewish Young Adults*. New York: Repair the World, 2011.

Cohen, Gerard Daniel. *In War's Wake: Europe's Displaced Persons in the Postwar Order*. New York: Oxford University Press, 2011.

———. "The Holocaust and The Human Rights Revolution: A Reassessment." In *The Human Rights Revolution: An International History*, edited by A. Irye, P. Goedde, and W. Hitchcock, 53–72. New York: Oxford University Press, 2012.

Cohen, Mitchell. "A Preface to the Study of Modern Jewish Political Thought." *Jewish Social Studies* 9, no. 2 (2003): 1–27.

Cohen, Morris R. "Zionism: Tribalism or Liberalism?" *New Republic*, March 8, 1919, 182–83.

Cohen, Naomi Wiener. "The Abrogation of the Russo-American Treaty of 1832." *Jewish Social Studies* 25 (1963): 3–41.

———. *American Jews and the Zionist Idea*. Tel-Aviv: Ktav, 1975.

———. *Not Free to Desist: The American Jewish Committee, 1906–1966*. Philadelphia: Jewish Publication Society of America, 1972.

———. "The Reaction of Reform Judaism in America to Political Zionism (1897–1922)." *Publications of the American Jewish Historical Society* (1951): 361–94.

Cohen, Richard. *Israel: Is It Good for the Jews?* New York: Simon and Schuster, 2014.

Cohen, Steven Martin. *American Modernity and Jewish Identity*. New York: Routledge, 1983.

———. "Changing Conceptions of Jewish Collectivity among Young Adult Jews and Their Implications for Jewish Education: A Dual Research Project." Jerusalem: The Research Unit, Department of Jewish-Zionist Education, Jewish Agency for Israel, 2002, 14.

———. *The Dimensions of American Jewish Liberalism*. American Jewish Committee, 1989.

———. "Expressive, Progressive, and Protective: Three Impulses for Innovative Organizing among Young Jews Today." In *The New Jewish Leaders: Reshaping the American Jewish Landscape*, edited by Jack Wertheimer, 84–112. Waltham, MA: Brandeis University Press, 2011.

———. "From Jewish People to Jewish Purpose: Establishment Leaders and Their Non-Establishment Successors." In *The New Jewish Leaders: Reshaping the American Jewish Landscape*, edited by Jack Wertheimer, 45–83. Waltham, MA: Brandeis University Press, 2011.

———. "Relationships of American Jews with Israel: What We Know and What We Need to Know." *Contemporary Jewry* 23, no. 1 (2002): 132–55.

———. "What American Jews Believe." *Moment* 7, no. 7 (1982): 23–27.

Cohen, Steven M., and Sam Abrams. "Israel off Their Minds: The Diminished Place of Israel in the Political Thinking of Young Jews." Berman Jewish Policy Archive at NYU Wagner. New York: New York University, 2008.

Cohen, Steven Martin, and Arnold M. Eisen. *The Jew Within: Self, Family, and Community in America*. Bloomington: Indiana University Press, 2000.

———. "The Sovereign Self: Jewish Identity in Post-Modern America." *Jerusalem Letter / Viewpoints* 453 (2001): 1–18.

Cohen, Steven M., and Leonard Fein. "American Jews and Their Social Justice Involvement: Evidence from a National Survey." Amos—The National Jewish Part-

nership for Social Justice, November 21, 2001. Downloaded from http://www.bjpa
.org/Publications/details.cfm?PublicationID=4692 on August 24, 2013.
——. "From Integration to Survival: American Jewish Anxieties in Transition." *Annals of the American Academy of Political and Social Science* (July 1985): 75–88.
Cohen, Steven Martin, Ari Y. Kelman, with Lauren Blitzer. *Beyond Distancing: Young Adult American Jews and Their Alienation from Israel.* Jewish Identity Project of Reboot, 2007. http://www.jidaily.com/tNqOnZm.
Cohen, Steven M., and Charles S. Liebman. "Israel and American Jewry in the Twenty-First Century, A Search for New Relationships." In *Beyond Survival and Philanthropy: American Jewry and Israel,* edited by Allon Gal and Alfred Gottschalkpp, 3–24, New York: Hebrew Union College Press, 2000.
Cohen, Steven M., and Jack Wertheimer. "Whatever Happened to the Jewish People?" *Commentary* 121, no. 6 (2006): 33–37.
Cole, Tim. *Selling the Holocaust: From Auschwitz to Schindler: How History Is Bought, Packaged, and Sold.* New York: Routledge, 1999.
Commentary. "Liberalism and the Jews: A Symposium." (January 1980): 15–82.
Conforti, Yitzhak. "Between Ethnic and Civic: The Realistic Utopia of Zionism." *Israel Affairs* 17, no. 4 (2011): 563–82.
——. "East and West in Jewish Nationalism: Conflicting Types in the Zionist Vision?" *Nations and Nationalism* 16, no. 2 (2010): 201–19.
Cooper, Levi. "The Assimilation of Tikkun Olam." *Jewish Political Studies Review* 25 (2014): 3–4.
Copulsky, Jerome. "History and Essence: The Construction of a Modern Jewish Political Theology." In *Political Theology for a Plural Age,* edited by Michael Jon Kessler, 62–98. New York: Oxford University Press, 2013.
Cotler, Irwin. "Jewish NGOs, Human Rights, and Public Advocacy: A Comparative Inquiry." *Jewish Political Studies Review* (Fall 1999): 61–95.
Crane, Jonathan. "Why Rights? Why Me?" *Journal of Religious Ethics* 35, no. 4 (2007): 559–89.
Davis, Moshe, ed. *Zionism in Transition.* Publications of the Continuing Seminar on World Jewry, vol. 3. New York: Herzl Press, 1980.
Dean, Carolyn. *Aversion and Erasure: The Fate of the Victim after the Holocaust* (Ithaca: Cornell University Press, 2010).
Dekel-Chen, Jonathan. "Activism as Engine: Jewish Internationalism, 1880s–1980s." In *Religious Internationals in the Modern World: Globalization and Faith Communities since 1750,* edited by Abigail Green and Vincent Viaene. New York: Palgrave Macmillan, 2012.
Deutscher, Isaac. "The Non-Jewish Jew." In *Zionism Reconsidered: The Rejection of Jewish Normalcy,* edited by Michael Selzer, 85–86. New York: Macmillan, 1970.
——. *The Non-Jewish Jew and Other Essays.* New York: Oxford University Press, 1968.
Diner, Hasia R. "Before the 'Holocaust': American Jews Confront the Catastrophe, 1945–62." In *American Jewish Identity Politics,* edited by Deborah Dash Moore, 45–82. Ann Arbor: University of Michigan Press, 2004.
——. *In the Almost Promised Land: American Jews and Blacks, 1915–1935.* Baltimore: Johns Hopkins University Press, 1995.
——. *The Jews of the United States, 1654 to 2000.* Berkeley: University of California Press, 2004.

——. "Post-World-War-II American Jewry and the Confrontation with Catastrophe." *American Jewish History* 91, no. 3–4 (2003): 439–67.

——. *We Remember with Reverence and Love: American Jews and the Myth of Silence after the Holocaust, 1945–1962.* New York: New York University Press, 2009.

Dinstein, Yoram. "Soviet Jewry and International Human Rights." In *Essays on Human Rights: Contemporary Issues and Jewish Perspectives,* edited by David Sidorsky, 126–43. Philadelphia: Jewish Publication Society of America, 1979.

Dollinger, Marc. "American Jewish Liberalism Revisited: Two Perspectives Exceptionalism and Jewish Liberalism." *American Jewish History* 90, no. 2 (2002): 161–64.

——. *Quest for Inclusion: Jews and Liberalism in Modern American.* Princeton, NJ: Princeton University Press, 2000.

Dowty, Alan. "Israeli Foreign Policy and the Jewish Question." *Middle East Review of International Affairs* 3, no. 1 (1999): 1–11.

Dubnov, Arie. "Anti-Cosmopolitan Liberalism: Isaiah Berlin, Jacob Talmon, and the Dilemma of National Identity." *Nations and Nationalism* 16, no. 4 (2010): 559–78.

——. *Isaiah Berlin: The Journey of a Jewish Liberal.* New York: Palgrave, 2012.

——. "A Tale of Trees and Crooked Timbers: Jacob Talmon and Isaiah Berlin on the Question of Jewish Nationalism." *History of European Ideas* 34, no. 2 (2008): 220–38.

Dubnow, Simon. *Jewish History: An Essay in the Philosophy of History.* Philadelphia: Jewish Publication Society of America, 1927.

Duker, Abraham. "Jews in World War I: A Brief Historical Sketch." Unit II, Jewish Post-War Problems, Research Institute on Peace and Post-War Studies, 17–21. New York: American Jewish Committee, 1942.

Eban, Abba. Address by Abba Eban, Proceedings of the Fifth Plenary Assembly of the World Jewish Congress, p. 15. Brussels; Geneva: World Jewish Congress, 1966.

Eichler-Levine, Jodi, and Rosemary Hicks. "'As Americans against Genocide': The Crisis in Darfur and Interreligious Activism." *American Quarterly* 59, no. 3 (2007): 711–35.

Eisen, Arnold. *The Chosen People in America: A Study in Jewish Religious Ideology.* Bloomington: Indiana University Press, 1983.

—— "Introduction: Four Questions concerning Peoplehood—and Just as Many Answers." In *Jewish Peoplehood: Change and Challenge,* edited by Menachem Revivi and Ezra Kopelowitz, 1–11. Brighton, MA: Boston Academic Studies Press, 2009.

——. "Israel at 50: An American Jewish Perspective." *American Jewish Year Book* (1998): 47–71.

——. *Jewish Reflection on Homelessness and Homecoming.* Bloomington: Indiana University Press, 1986.

——. "Mordecai Kaplan's Judaism as a Civilization at 70: Setting the Stage for Reappraisal." *Jewish Social Studies* 12, no. 2 (2006): 1–16.

——. "A New Role for Israel in American Jewish Identity." Institute on American Jewish-Israeli Relations, American Jewish Committee, 1992.

——. "The Rhetoric of Chosenness and the Fabrication of American Jewish Identity." *American Pluralism and the Jewish Community,* edited by S. M. Lipset 53–69. New York: Transaction Publishers, 1990.

Eisenstadt, Shmuel. 1990. "The American Jewish Experience and American Pluralism: A Comparative Perspective." In *American Pluralism and the Jewish Community,* edited by S. M. Lipset, 43–52. New York: Transaction Publishers, 1990.

——. *The Prophets: Their Times and Social Ideas*. Chicago: Charles H. Kerr Publishing, 1971.

Elazar, Daniel. "American Political Theory and the Political Notions of American Jews: Convergences and Contradictions." In *The Ghetto and Beyond: Essays on Jewish Life in America*, edited by Peter Rose, 203–27. New York: Random House, 1969.

——. *Community and Polity: The Organizational Dynamics of American Jewry*. Philadelphia: Jewish Publication Society, 1995. The figure is from Feingold, *American Jewish Political Culture and the Liberal Persuasion*, 57.

Elazar, Daniel, and Stuart Cohen. *The Jewish Polity*. Bloomington: Indiana University Press, 1985.

Enns, Diane. *The Violence of Victimhood*. University Park: Pennsylvania State University Press, 2012.

Fackenheim, Emil. "Can We Believe in Judaism Religiously? An Ethical Faith Is Not Enough." *Commentary* (1948): 521–27.

——. "The Dilemma of Liberal Judaism." *Commentary* (October 1960): 301–10.

Fein, Leonard. *Where Are We?* New York: Harper and Row, 1988.

Feinberg, Nathan. "The International Protection of Human Rights and the Jewish Question." *Israel Law Review* 3, no. 4 (1968): 487–500.

Feingold, Henry. *American Jewish Political Culture and the Liberal Persuasion*. Syracuse, NY: Syracuse University Press, 2014.

——. "From Equality to Liberty: The Changing Political Culture of American Jews." In *The Americanization of the Jews*, edited by Robert Seltzer and Norman Cohen, 110–13. New York: New York University Press, 1995.

——. *Jewish Power in America: Myth and Reality*. New Brunswick, NJ: Transaction Publishers, 2011.

——. "Rescue and the Secular Perception: American Jewry and the Holocaust." In *Organizing Rescue: Jewish National Solidarity in the Modern Period*, edited by Selwyn Ilan Troen and Benjamin Pinkus, 154–66. Portland OR: Frank Cass, 1992.

——. *"Silent No More": Saving the Jews of Russia, the American Jewish Effort, 1967–1989*. Syracuse, NY: Syracuse University Press, 2007.

——. *A Time for Searching: Entering the Mainstream, 1920–1945*. Baltimore: Johns Hopkins University Press, 1992.

Fine, Robert. "Two Faces of Universalism: Jewish Emancipation and the Jewish Question." *Jewish Journal of Sociology* 56, nos. 1 and 2 (2014): 29–47.

Fink, Carole. *Defending the Rights of Others: The Great Powers, the Jews, and International Minority Protection, 1878–1938*. New York: Cambridge University Press, 2006.

——. "Louis Marshall: An American Jewish Diplomat in Paris, 1919." *American Jewish History* 94, no. 1–2 (2008): 21–40.

Finkelstein, Norman. *The Holocaust Industry: Reflections on the Exploitation of Jewish Suffering*. London: Verso, 2000.

Finkielkraut, Alain. *The Imaginary Jew*. Lincoln: University of Nebraska Press, Bison Books, 1997.

Fischer, Shlomo, and Suzanne Last Stone. "Jewish Identity and Identification: New Patterns, Meanings, and Networks." Jerusalem: Jewish People Policy Institute, 2012.

Flanzbaum, Hilene, ed. *The Americanization of the Holocaust*. Baltimore: Johns Hopkins University Press, 1999.

Fleisch, Eric. "Israeli NGOs and American Jewish Donors: The Structures and Dynamics of Power Sharing in a New Philanthropic Era." PhD diss., Brandeis University, 2014.

Fleisch, Eric, and Theodore Sasson. "The New Philanthropy: American Jewish Giving to Israeli NGOs." Cohen Center for Modern Jewish Studies, Brandies University, April 2012, p. 10.

"The Founding of the American Jewish World Service: A Fund for International Relief and Development." Prospectus, March 1985. N.p.

Frank, Waldo. *The Jew in Our Day*. New York: Duell, Sloan, and Pearce, 1944.

Frankel, Jonathan. *The Damascus Affair: "Ritual Murder," Politics, and the Jews in 1840.* New York: Cambridge University Press, 1997.

French National Assembly. "Debate on the Eligibility of Jews for Citizenship." December 23, 1789; cited from Paul Mendes-Flohr and Jehuda Reinharz, eds. *The Jew in the Modern World: A Documentary History*, 2nd ed. New York: Oxford University Press, 1995, 114–16.

Freud, Sigmund. "On Being of the B'nai B'rith: An Address to the Society in Vienna," May 6, 1926. Reprinted in *Commentary* (March 1946): 23–24.

Fried, Eli, Roger Bennett, and Charles Keidan. "Toward a Tikkun Olam Policy for World Jewry and Israel." *Journal of Jewish Communal Service* 84, no. 1–2 (2009): 82.

Friedman, Ina. "Jewish Soft Power." *Jerusalem Report*, July 24, 2006, 11–12.

Friedman, Murray. "Introduction: The Jewish Community Comes of Age." In *A Second Exodus: The American Movement to Free Soviet Jews*, edited by Murray Friedman and Albert D. Chernin, 6. Hanover, NH: University Press of New England for Brandeis University Press, 1999.

———. *The Neoconservative Revolution: Jewish Intellectuals and the Shaping of Public Policy*. New York: Cambridge University Press, 2005.

"The Future Agenda of the Jewish People." Peoplehood Papers. EJewishphilanthropy. Downloaded on August 24, 2013 at http://ejewishphilanthropy.com/the-future-agenda-of-the-jewish-people/.

Gaer, Felice. "To Reaffirm Faith in Fundamental Human Rights: The UN and Human Rights, 1945–95." Jacob Blaustein Institute for the Advancement of Human Rights, the American Jewish Committee, Presented by Barbara Blaustein Hirschhorn to the "We the Peoples," Conference San Francisco, California, June 22, 1995.

Gal, Allon. "Isaiah's Flame: Brandeis's Social-Liberal and Zionist Tradition." *Journal of Modern Jewish Studies* 11, no. 2 (2012): 207–20.

Gal, Allon, and Alfred Gottschalk, eds. *Beyond Survival and Philanthropy: American Jewry and Israel*. New York: Hebrew Union College Press, 2000.

Galchinsky, Michael, "The American Jewish Committee and the Birth of the Israeli Human Rights Movement." *Journal of Human Rights* 5 (2006): 303–21.

———. *Jews and Human Rights: Dancing at Three Weddings*. Lanham, MD: Rowman and Littlefield, 2007.

———. "Scattered Seeds: A Dialogue of Diasporas." In *Insider/Outsider: American Jews and Multiculturalism*, edited by David Biale, Michael Galchinsky, and Susannah Heschel, 185–211. Berkeley: University of California Press, 1998.

Ganin, Zvi. *Truman, American Jewry, and Israel, 1945–1948*. New York: Holmes and Meier, 1979.

——. *An Uneasy Relationship: American Jewish Leadership and Israel, 1948–1957.* Syracuse, NY: Syracuse University Press, 2005.

Gans, Chaim. *The Limits of Nationalism.* New York: Cambridge University Press, 2003.

Gans, Herbert. "American Jewry, Present and Future: Part I: Present." *Commentary* 21 (May 1956): 422–30.

——. "American Jewry, Present and Future: Part II: Future." *Commentary* 21 (May 1956): 555–63.

Garment, Leonard. "Majoritarianism at the United Nations and Human Rights." In *Essays on Human Rights: Contemporary Issues and Jewish Perspectives,* edited by David Sidorsky, 30–36. Philadelphia: Jewish Publication Society of America, 1979.

Gil, Avi, and Einat Wilf. *2030: Alternative Futures for the Jewish People.* Jerusalem: Jewish People Policy Planning Institute, January 2010.

Gilboa, Eitan. "Attitudes of American Jews toward Israel: Trends over Time." *American Jewish Year Book* (1986): 110–25.

Ginsburg, Dyonna. "Re-Anchoring Universalism to Particularism: The Potential Contribution of Orthodoxy to the Pursuit of Tikkun Olam." Downloaded from http://www.yutorah.org/lectures/lecture.cfm/777837/Ms-_Dyonna_Ginsburg/Re-anchoring_Universalism_to_Particularism-_The_Potential_Contribution_of_Orthodoxy_to_the_Pursuit_of_Tikkun_Olam on August 24, 2013.

Gitelman, Zvi. "The Decline of the Diaspora Jewish Nation: Boundaries, Content, and Jewish Identity." *Jewish Social Studies* 4, no. 2 (1998): 112–32.

——. "Soviet Jews: Creating a Cause and a Movement." In *A Second Exodus: The American Movement to Free Soviet Jews,* edited by Murray Friedman and Albert D. Chernin, 84–96. Hanover, NH: University Press of New England for Brandeis University Press.

Gitlin, Todd, and Liel Leibovitz. *The Chosen Peoples: America, Israel, and the Ordeals of Divine Election.* New York: Simon and Schuster, 2010.

Glazer, Nathan. *American Judaism,* 2nd ed. Chicago: University of Chicago Press, 1988.

——. "The Anomalous Liberalism of American Jews." In *The Americanization of the Jews,* edited by Robert Seltzer and Norman Cohen, 133–48. New York: New York University Press, 1995.

Goldberg, J. J. *Jewish Power: Inside the American Jewish Establishment.* New York: Basic Books, 1997.

——. "Summer's Missing Question: What Is Zionism? A Fundamental Disconnect Accentuated by War." *Forward,* September 7, 2014. http://forward.com/articles/205200/summers-missing-question-what-is-zionism/, accessed December 22, 2014.

Goldblatt, Charles Israel. "The Impact of the Balfour Declaration in America." *American Jewish Historical Quarterly* 57, no. 4 (1968): 455–515.

Goldbloom, Maurice. "The American Jewish Committee Abroad: In the Midst of War and Revolution." *Commentary* (October 1957): 3–19.

Golden, Peter. *O Powerful Western Star! American Jews, Russian Jews, and the Final Battle of the Cold War.* Jerusalem: Geffen Publishing House, 2012.

Goldmann, Nahun. Proceedings of the Fifth Plenary Assembly of the World Jewish Congress, Brussels. Geneva: World Jewish Congress, 1966.

Goldstein, Eric. *The Price of Whiteness: Jews Race, and American Identity.* Princeton, NJ: Princeton University Press, 2006.

Goren, Arthur. *The American Jews: Dimensions of Ethnicity*. Cambridge, MA: Harvard University Press, 1980.

———. "A 'Golden Decade' for American Jews, 1945–1955." In *The American Jewish Experience*, 2nd ed., edited by Jonathan Sarna, 294–311. New York: Holmes and Meier, 1997.

———. *The Politics and Public Culture of American Jews*. Bloomington: Indiana University Press, 1999.

Gorny, Yosef. *Between Auschwitz and Jerusalem: Jewish Collective Identity in Crisis*. Portland, OR: Vallentine Mitchell, 2003.

———. "Shilat ha Galut: Past and Present." In *Beyond Survival and Philanthropy: American Jewry and Israel*, edited by Allon Gal and Alfred Gottschalk, 41–47. Cincinnati: Hebrew Union College Press, 2000.

Gottlieb, Micah. "Interview with Michael Walzer." *AJS Perspectives* (Fall 2006): 10.

Granick, Jaclyn. "Waging Relief: The Politics and Logistics of American Jewish War Relief in Europe and the Near East (1914–1918)." *First World War Studies* 5, no. 1 (2014): 55–68.

Green, Abigail. "The British Empire and the Jews: An Imperialism of Human Rights?" *Past and Present* 199 (May 2008): 175–205.

———. "Intervening in the Jewish Question, 1840–1878." In *Humanitarian Intervention: A History*, edited by Brendan Simms and D.J.D. Trimm, 139–58. New York: Cambridge University Press, 2010.

———. "The Limits of Intervention: Coercive Diplomacy and the Jewish Question in the Nineteenth Century." *International History Review* 36, no. 3 (2014): 473–92.

———. "Nationalism and the 'Jewish International': Religious Internationalism in Europe and the Middle East, c. 1840–c. 1880." *Comparative Studies in Society and History* 50, no. 2 (2008): 535–58.

———. "Old Networks, New Connections: The Emergence of the Jewish International." In *Religious Internationals in the Modern World: Globalization and Faith Communities since 1750*, edited by A. Green and V. Viaene, 53–81. New York: Palgrave Macmillan, 2012.

———. "Religious and Jewish Internationalism." Unpublished manuscript, 2014.

———. "Rethinking Sir Moses Montefiore: Religion, Nationhood, and International Philanthropy in the Nineteenth Century." *American Historical Review* (June 2005): 631–58.

Green, Leslie C. "Jewish Issues on the Human-Rights Agenda in the First Half of the Twentieth Century." In *Essays on Human Rights: Contemporary Issues and Jewish Perspectives*, edited by David Sidorsky, 297–308. Philadelphia: Jewish Publication Society of America, 1979.

———. "The Judaic Contribution to Human Rights." *Canadian Yearbook of International Law* 28 (1990): 3.

Greene, Daniel. "A Chosen People in a Pluralist Nation: Horace Kallen and the Jewish-American Experience." *Religion and American Culture: A Journal of Interpretation* 16, no. 2 (2006): 161–94.

———. *The Jewish Origins of Cultural Pluralism: The Menorah Society and American Diversity*. Bloomington: Indiana University Press, 2011.

Greenstein, Howard. *Turning Point: Zionism and Reform Judaism*. Ann Arbor, MI: Scholars Press, 1981.

Grinstein, Gidi. *Flexigidity: The Secret of Jewish Adaptability.* Gidi Grinstein, 2013.

Gross, Michael. "Not the End of Liberal Zionism." *Ha'aretz,* August 25, 2014.

Grossman, Lawrence. "Transformation through Crisis: The American Jewish Committee and the Six-Day War." *American Jewish History* 86, no. 1 (1998): 27–54.

Gruen, George. "Aspects and Prospects of the Interaction between American Jews and Israel." Conference on American Jewish Dilemmas. New York: American Jewish Committee, American Federation of Jews from Europe, 1971.

Gurin, Arnold. "Impact of Israel on American Jewish Community Organization and Fund Raising." *Jewish Social Studies* 21, no. 1 (1959): 46–59.

Gurock, Jeffrey, ed. *The History of Judaism in America: Transplantations, Transformations, and Reconciliations.* Vol. 5. New York: Routledge, 1998.

Hacohen, Malachi Haim. "Dilemmas of Cosmopolitanism: Karl Popper, Jewish Identity, and 'Central European Culture.'" *Journal of Modern History* 71 (March 1999): 105–49.

——. "'The Strange Fact That the State of Israel Exists': The Cold War Liberals between Cosmopolitanism and Nationalism." *Jewish Social Studies* 15, no. 2 (2009): 37–81.

Hagel, Peter, and Pauline Peretz. "States and Transnational Actors: Who's Influencing Whom? A Case Study of Jewish Diaspora Politics during the Cold War." *European Journal of International Relations* 11, no. 4 (2005): 467–93.

Haklai, Oded. "Helping the Enemy? Why Transnational Jewish Philanthropic Foundations Donate to Palestinian NGOs in Israel." *Nations and Nationalism* 14, no. 3 (2008): 581–99.

Halkin, Hillel. "How Not to Repair the World." *Commentary* 126 (July–August 2008): 22–23.

Halpern, Ben. "America Is Different." In *American Jews: A Reader,* edited by Marshall Sklare, 25–46. New York: Berhman House, 1983.

——. *The American Jew: A Zionist Analysis.* New York: Schocken Books, 1956.

——. *A Clash of Heroes: Brandeis, Weizmann, and American Zionism.* New York: Oxford University Press, 1987.

——. "The Impact of Israel on American Jewish Ideologies." *Jewish Social Studies* 21, no. 1 (1956): 62–81.

——. "Jewish Nationalism: Self-Determination as a Human Right." In *Essays on Human Rights: Contemporary Issues and Jewish Perspectives,* edited by David Sidorsky, 309–35. Philadelphia: Jewish Publication Society of America, 1979.

——. "The Political Significance of Israel for American Jews." Conference on American Jewish Dilemmas. New York: American Jewish Committee, American Federation of Jews from Europe, 1971.

Hamilton, Rebecca. *Fighting for Darfur: Public Action and the Struggle to Stop Genocide.* New York: Palgrave Macmillan, 2011.

Hammer, Reuven. "Jewish Political Ethics in Israel." In *The Oxford Handbook of Jewish Ethics and Morality,* edited by Elliot Dorff and Jonathan Crane, 459–71. New York: Oxford University Press, 2013.

Hammerschlag, Sarah. *The Figural Jew: Politics and Identity in Postwar French Thought.* Chicago: University of Chicago Press, 2010.

Handlin, Oscar. "America Recognizes Diverse Loyalties: 'External' Ties Are Not Necessarily Dangerous." *Commentary* (March 1950): 220–26.

——. "The American Jewish Committee: A Half-Century View." *Commentary* (January 1957): 1–10.

——. *A Continuing Task: The American Jewish Joint Distribution Committee, 1914–64.* New York: Random House, 1964.

——. "Zionist Ideology and World Jewry: Reflections on a Conference." *Commentary* (February 1958): 105–9.

Hannerz, Ulf. "Cosmopolitans and Locals in World Culture." In *Global Culture: Nationalism, Globalization, and Modernity,* edited by Mike Featherstone, 237–52. Beverly Hills, CA: Sage.

Harman, David, and Jonathan Sarna. "American Jewish-Israeli Relations: Two Perspectives." New York: Institute on American Jewish Israeli Relations, the American Jewish Committee, 1995.

Hasan-Rokem, Galit, and Alan Dundes, eds. *The Wandering Jew: Essays in the Interpretation of a Christian Legend.* Bloomington: Indiana University Press, 1986.

Hauser, Rita. "International Human-Rights Protection: The Dream and the Deceptions." In *Essays on Human Rights: Contemporary Issues and Jewish Perspectives,* edited by David Sidorsky, 21–29. Philadelphia: Jewish Publication Society of America, 1979.

Henkin, Louis. "Human Rights: Reappraisal and Readjustment," In *Essays on Human Rights: Contemporary Issues and Jewish Perspectives,* edited by David Sidorsky, 68–87. Philadelphia: Jewish Publication Society of America, 1979.

——. Introduction to *World Politics and the Jewish Condition,* 3–36. New York: Quadrangle Books, 1972.

——. "Judaism and Human Rights." *Judaism* 25 (1976): 436–46.

——, ed. *World Politics and the Jewish Condition.* New York: Quadrangle Books, 1972.

Herberg, Will. "Assimilation in Militant Dress: Should the Jews Be 'Like unto the Nations?'" *Commentary* (July 1947): 16, 19.

——. "Prophetic Faith in an Age of Crisis" *Judaism* (1952): 195–202.

——. *Protestant-Catholic-Jew.* New York: Doubleday, 1955.

Hertzberg, Arthur. "American Jews through Israeli Eyes: A Traveler's Report on Some Current Attitudes." *Commentary* (January 1950): 1–7.

——. *Being Jewish in America: The Modern Experience.* New York: Schocken Books, 1987.

——. "Israel and American Jewry." *Commentary* (August 1967): 170–71.

——. "Joint Responsibility Is No Picnic." In *Israel on My Mind: Israel's Role in World Jewish Identity,* 10–13. New York: Dorothy and Julius Koppelman Institute on American Jewish-Israel Relations, American Jewish Committee, 2005.

——. "Modern Jewish Dilemmas." *Commentary* (February 1963): 172–73.

Heschel, Abraham Joshua. "The Divine Pathos: The Basic Category of Prophetic Theology." *Judaism* 2 (1955): 61–67.

——. "Prophetic Inspiration: An Analysis of Prophetic Consciousness." *Judaism* 11, no. 1 (1962): 3–13.

——. *The Prophets.* New York: Harper Perennial Modern Classics, 2001.

Hirsch, Samson Raphael. "Religion Allied to Progress," 1854; cited from Paul Mendes-Flohr and Jehuda Reinharz, eds. *The Jew in the Modern World: A Documentary History,* 2nd ed. New York: Oxford University Press, 1995, 197–202.

Hirschberg, Albert. "Human Rights or Minority Rights?" *Contemporary Jewish Record* 8 (1945): 43–47.

Hitchens, Christopher. *Hitch 22: A Memoir.* New York: Twelve Press, 2010.

Hollander, Dana, and Joel Kaminsky. "Introduction: 'A Covenant to the People, a Light to the Nations': Universalism, Exceptionalism, and the Problem of Chosenness in Jewish Thought." *Jewish Studies Quarterly* 16 (March 2009): 1–5.

Hollinger, David. "Communalists and Dispersionist Approaches to Jewish History in an Increasingly Post-Jewish Era." *American Jewish History* (March 2009): 1–32.

———. *In the American Province: Studies in the History and Historiography of Ideas.* Baltimore: Johns Hopkins University Press, 1985.

Hook, Sidney. *Out of Step: An Unquiet Life in the 20th Century.* New York: Harper-Collins, 1987.

Horowitz, Irving. *Israeli Ecstasies / Jewish Agonies.* New York: Oxford University Press, 1977.

———. 1999. "Who Owns Judaism?" *Society* (May–June 1999): 29.

Howe, Irving. "The New York Intellectuals: A Chronicle and Critique." *Commentary* (October 1968): 29–51.

http://www.adl.org/press-center/press-releases/anti-semitism-usa/adl-audit-anti-se mitic-incidents-2013.html#.VOtdXi5SK4k.

http://www.haaretz.com/jewish-world/u-s-jewish-groups-furious-over-campaign -to-bring-expat-israelis-back-home-1.399057.

http://www.zionism-israel.com/hdoc/Philadelphia_Conference_1869.htm.

Hyman, Joseph. "Twenty-Five Years of American Aid to Jews Overseas: A Record of the Joint Distribution Committee." *American Jewish Year Book* 41 (1940): 141–79. Philadelphia: Jewish Publication Society of America.

Ignatieff, Michael. *Blood and Belonging.* New York: Farrar Straus and Giroux, 1995.

Imhof, Elizabeth Mizrahi. "Between Home and Homeland: The Transformation of American Jewish Political Identity, 1945–1973." PhD diss., University of Chicago, 2012.

"The Impact of Israel on the American Jewish Community." Proceedings of a Conference Convened by the Theodor Herzl Institute and the Conference on Jewish Social Studies at the Herzl Institute in New York City, December 22–23, 1956. New York: Herzl Press, 1959.

Inbar, Ephraim. "Jews, Jewishness, and Israel's Foreign Policy." *Jewish Political Studies Review* 2, no. 3–4 (1990): 70–82.

International Federation of Red Cross and Red Crescent Societies. "Humanity." http:// www.ifrc.org/en/who-we-are/vision-and-mission/the-seven-fundamental-princi ples/humanity/. Accessed January 17, 2015.

Interview with Yitzhak Rabin on the *MacNeil-Lehrer Newshour*, September 13, 1993.

Jacob, Walter. "Prophetic Judaism: The History of a Term." *Journal of Reform Judaism* 26, no. 2 (1979): 33–46.

Jacobs, Jill. "Jewish Political Ethics in America." In *The Oxford Handbook of Jewish Ethics and Morality*, edited by Elliot Dorff and Jonathan Crane, 445–49. New York: Oxford University Press, 2013.

———. "Justice and Human Rights." *Sh'ma*, November 2011, 15.

———. *There Shall Be No Needy: Pursuing Social Justice through Jewish Law and Tradition.* Woodstock, VT: Jewish Lights Publishing, 2010.

———. *Where Justice Dwells: A Hands-On Guide to Doing Social Justice in Your Jewish Community.* Woodstock, VT: Jewish Lights Publishing, 2011.

Jager, Elliott. "Are Young Rabbis Turning on Israel?" *Jewish Ideas Daily*, October 24, 2011. http://www.jewishideasdaily.com/989/features/are-young-rabbis-turning-on -israel/.

Janowsky, Oscar J. *The Jews and Minority Rights, 1898–1919.* New York: Columbia University Press, 1933.

"JDC Participating in National Appeal for Cambodian Refugees." *Jewish Telegraphic Agency*, February 1, 1980.

Jewish People Policy Institute. Jewish Solidarity in an Age of Polarization. Background Policy Documents. Brainstorming Conference, May 18-19, 2015, Glen Cove, NY. Jerusalem: Jewish People Policy Institute, 2015.

Jewish People Policy Institute. *Jewish and Democratic: Perspectives from World Jewry.* Jerusalem: Jewish People Policy Institute, 2014.

Jewish People Policy Institute. Annual Assessment, 2012-2013. Jerusalem: Jewish People Policy Institute, 2013.

Jewish People Policy Planning Institute. *Arevut, Responsibility, and Partnership.* Jerusalem: Jewish People Policy Planning Institute, November 2009.

Jones, Robert P., and Daniel Cox. "Chosen for What? Jewish Values in 2012." Public Religion Research Institute, Washington, DC, 2012.

Judis, John. *Genesis: Truman, American Jews, and the Origins of the Arab/Israeli Conflict.* New York: Farrar, Straus, and Giroux, 2014.

Kahler, Erich. *The Jews among the Nations.* New Brunswick, NJ: Transaction Publishers, 1989.

Kahn-Harris, K. *Uncivil War: The Israel Conflict in the Jewish Community.* London: David Paul, 2014.

Kallen, Horace. "Democracy versus the Melting Pot: A Study of American Nationality." *The Nation*, February 25, 1915.

———. "Judaism as Disaster." In his *Of Them Which Say They Are Jews.* New York: Bloch Publishing, 1954.

———. "National Solidarity and the Jewish Minority." In his *Of Them Which Say They Are Jews.* New York: Bloch Publishing, 1954.

———. *Zionism and World Politics: A Study in History and Social Psychology.* Garden City, NY: Doubleday Page, 1921.

Kaplan, Dana Evan. *Contemporary American Judaism: Transformation and Renewal.* New York: Columbia University Press, 2009.

Kaplan, Mordecai. *The Religion of Ethical Nationhood: Judaism's Contribution to World Peace.* New York: Macmillan, 1970.

Katz, Jacob. *Out of the Ghetto: The Social Background of Jewish Emancipation (1770–1870).* Syracuse, NY: Syracuse University Press, 1973.

———. "Post-Emancipation Development and Rights: Liberalism and Universalism." In *Essays on Human Rights: Contemporary Issues and Jewish Perspectives*, edited by David Siforsky, 282–96. Philadelphia: Jewish Publication Society of America, 1979.

Katznelson, Ira. "Between Separation and Disappearance: Jews on the Margins of American Liberalism." In *Paths of Emancipation: Jews, States, and Citizenship*, edited by Ira Katznelson and Pierre Birnbaum, 157–205. Princeton, NJ: Princeton University Press, 1995.

Katznelson, Ira, and Pierre Birnbaum, eds. *Paths of Emancipation: Jews, States, and Citizenship*. Princeton, NJ: Princeton University Press, 1995.

Kaufman, Yehezkel. "Anti-Semitic Stereotypes in Zionism: The Nationalist Rejection of Diaspora Jewry." *Commentary* (March 1949): 239–45.

Kelner, Shaul. "Ritualized Protest and Redemptive Politics: Cultural Consequences of the American Mobilization to Free Soviet Jewry." *Jewish Social Studies: History, Culture, Society* 14, no. 3 (2008): 1–37.

———. *Tours That Bind: Diaspora, Pilgrimage, and Israeli Birthright Tourism*. New York: New York University Press, 2010.

Kessler, Michael Jon, ed. *Political Theology for a Plural Age*. New York: Oxford University Press, 2013.

Keysar, Ariela. "Distancing from Israel: Evidence on Jews of No Religion." *Contemporary Jewry* 30, no. 2–3 (2010): 199–204.

Kimmerling, Baruch. *The Invention and Decline of Israeliness: State, Society, and the Military*. Berkeley: University of California Press, 2001.

———. "Religion, Nationalism, and Democracy in Israel." *Constellations* 6, no. 3 (1999): 339–63.

Klawans, Jonathan. "Josephus, the Rabbis, and Responses to Catastrophes Ancient and Modern." *Jewish Quarterly Review* 100, no. 2 (2010): 278–309.

Klieman, Aharon. "*Shtadlanut* as Statecraft by the Stateless." *Israel Journal of Foreign Affairs* 2, no. 3 (2008): 99–113.

Knepper, Paul. "Polanyi, 'Jewish Problems,' and Zionism." *Tradition and Discovery: The Polanyi Society Periodical* 32, no. 1 (2005): 6–19.

Knox, Israel. "Is America Exile or Home? We Must Begin to Build for Permanence." *Commentary* (November 1946): 401–8.

Kofman, Eleonore. "Figures of the Cosmopolitan: Privileged Nations and National Outsiders." *Innovation* 18, no. 1 (2005): 83–97.

Kohler, Max. "Jewish Rights at International Congresses." *American Jewish Year Book* (1917): 1–55. Philadelphia: Jewish Publication Society of America.

Kohn, Hans. "Ahad Ha'am: Nationalist with a Difference: A Zionism to Fulfill Judaism." *Commentary* (1951): 558–66.

———. *The Idea of Nationalism: A Study in Its Origins and Background*. New Brunswick, NJ: Transaction Publishers, 2005. Originally published: New York: Macmillan, 1944.

Konvitz, Milton, ed. *Judaism and Human Rights*. 2nd ed. New Brunswick, NJ: Transaction Publishers, 2001.

Korey, William. "From Helsinki: A Salute to Human Rights." In *A Second Exodus: The American Movement to Free Soviet Jews*, edited by Murray Friedman and Albert D. Chernin, 124–35. Hanover, NH: University Press of New England for Brandeis University Press, 1999.

Kranson, Rachel. "A Break with Spring Break." *Lilith* 27, no. 2 (2002): 5.

Kristol, Irving. "The Liberal Tradition of American Jews." In *American Pluralism and the Jewish Community*, edited by Seymour Martin Lipset, 109–16. New Brunswick, NJ: Transaction Publishers, 1990.

LaGrone, Matthew. "Ethical Theories of Mordecai Kaplan and Abraham Joshua Heschel." In *The Oxford Handbook of Jewish Ethics and Morality*, edited by Elliot Dorff and Jonathan Crane, 151–65. New York: Oxford University Press, 2013.

Landman, Isaac. "The League of Nations and the Jews." *American Hebrew*, May 23, 1919, 740–71.

Langdum, Robert. "Liberal Judaism as a Living Faith." *Commentary* (July 1952): 8–14.

Laquer, Walter. "Zionism and Its Liberal Critics, 1896–1948." *Contemporary History* 6, no. 4 (1971): 161–82.

Lauterpacht, Hersch. "International Bill of Rights: Second Phase." *Commentary* (September 1946): 255–64.

Lazin, Fred. *The Struggle for Soviet Jewry in American Politics: Israel versus the American Jewish Establishment*. New York: Lexington Books, 2005.

Leff, Lisa. *Sacred Bonds of Solidarity: The Rise of Jewish Foreign Policy in Nineteenth-Century France*. Palo Alto, CA: Stanford University Press, 2006.

Legge, Jerome. "Understanding American Judaism: Revisiting the Concept of 'Social Justice.'" *Contemporary Jewry* 16, no. 1 (1995): 97–109.

Leibel, Aaron. "Justice, Justice: Can It Bring Disaffected Jews Back Home?" *Washington Jewish Week*, November 2, 2006, 28.

Lerman, Antony. "The End of Liberal Zionism: Israel's Move to the Right Challenges Diaspora Jews." *New York Times*, August 22, 2014. http://www.nytimes.com/2014/08/23/opinion/sunday/israels-move-to-the-right-challenges-diaspora-jews.html?_r=0. Accessed December 22, 2014.

Letter from Louis Marshall to President Woodrow Wilson, May 23, 1919. Box 5, Louis Marshall, Correspondence, Peace Conference, 1919. American Jewish Committee.

Levanon, Nehemiah. "Israel's Role in the Campaign." In *A Second Exodus: The American Movement to Free Soviet Jews*, edited by Murray Friedman and Albert D. Chernin, 70–83. Hanover, NH: University Press of New England for Brandies University Press, 1999.

Levene, Mark. "Nationalism and Its Alternatives in the International Arena: The Jewish Question at Paris, 1919." *Journal of Contemporary History* 28, no. 3 (1993): 511–31.

———. *War, Jews, and the New Europe: The Diplomacy of Lucien Wolf, 1914–1919*. Portland, OR: Littman Library of Jewish Civilization, 1992.

Levin, N. Gordon, Jr. "Zionism in America." *Reviews in American History* (December 1975): 511–15.

Levitas, Irving. "Reform Jews and Zionism—1919–1921." *American Jewish Archives*, April 1962, 3–19.

Levitt, Laura. "Impossible Assimilations, American Liberalism, and Jewish Difference: Revisiting Jewish Secularism." *American Quarterly* 59, no. 3 (2007): 807–32.

Levy, Daniel, and Natan Sznaider. "The Institutionalization of Cosmopolitan Morality: The Holocaust and Human Rights." *Journal of Human Rights* 3, no. 2 (2004): 143–57.

———. *Holocaust and Memory in the Global Age*. Philadelphia: Temple University Press, 2005.

———. "Memory Unbound: The Holocaust and the Formation of Cosmopolitan Memory." *European Journal of Social Theory* 5, no. 1 (2002): 87–106.

"Liberalism and American Jews." Special issue of *Journal of Modern Jewish Studies*, August 2012.

Lieberman, Robert. "The 'Israel Lobby' and American Politics." *Perspectives on Politics* 7, no. 2 (2009): 235–57.

Liebman, Charles. *The Ambivalent American Jew: Politics, Religion, and Family in American Jewish Life*. Philadelphia: Jewish Publication Society of America, 1973.

——. "Leadership and Decision-Making in a Jewish Federation: The New York Federation of Jewish Philanthropies." *American Jewish Year Book* 79 (1982): 149–69.

——. "Moral and Symbolic Elements in the Politics of Israel-Diaspora Relations." In *Kinship and Consent: The Jewish Political Tradition and Its Contemporary Uses*, edited by Daniel Elazar, 345–56. New Brunswick, NJ: Transaction Publishers, 1997.

——. *Pressure without Sanctions: The Influence of World Jewry on Israeli Policy*. Rutherford, NJ: Fairleigh Dickinson University Press.

Liebman, Charles, and Steven Cohen. *Two Worlds of Judaism: The Israeli and American Experiences*. New Haven, CT: Yale University Press, 1990.

Lilla, Mark. *The Stillborn God: Religion, Politics, and the Modern West*. New York: Alfred A. Knopf, 2007.

Linenthal, Edward. *Preserving Memory: The Struggle to Create America's Holocaust Museum*. New York: Viking Penguin, 1995.

Lipset, Seymour Martin. "A Unique People in an Exceptional Country." In *American Pluralism and the Jewish Community*, edited by S. M. Lipset, 3–31. New York: Transaction Publishers, 1990.

Lipset, Seymour Martin, and Earl Raab. *Jews and the New American Scene*. Cambridge, MA: Harvard University Press, 1995.

Lipstadt, Deborah. *The Eichmann Trial*. New York: Schocken Books, 2011.

——. "From Noblesse Oblige to Personal Redemption: The Changing Profile and Agenda of American Jewish Leaders." *Modern Judaism* 4, no. 3 (1984): 295–309.

——. "The Holocaust: Symbol and 'Myth' in American Jewish Life." *Forum on the Jewish People, Zionism, and Israel* 40 (Winter 1980/81).

Liskofsky, Sidney. "International Protection of Human Rights." In *World Politics and the Jewish Condition*, edited by Louis Henkin, 277–328. New York: Quadrangle Books, 1972.

——. "UN Resolution on Zionism." *American Jewish Year Book* 77 (1977): 97–126.

Livni, Michael. "The Place of Israel in the Identity of Reform Jews: Examining the Spectrum of Passive Identification with Israel to Active Jewish-Zionist Commitment." In *Israel, the Diaspora, and Jewish Identity*, edited by Danny Ben-Moshe and Zohar Segev, 86–101. Portland, OR: Sussex Academic Press, 2007.

Loeffler, James. "Between Zionism and Liberalism: Oscar Janowsky and Diaspora Nationalism in America." *Association for Jewish Studies Review* 34, no. 2 (2010): 289–308.

——. " 'The Conscience of America': Human Rights, Jewish Politics, and American Foreign Policy at the 1945 United Nations San Francisco Conference." *Journal of American History* (September 2013): 401–28.

——. "How Zionism Became Racism: International Law, Anti-Semitism, and Jewish Lawyering at the United Nations, 1945–1975." Unpublished manuscript, 2014.

——. "In Pursuit of Universalism: The American Jewish Committee's 1944 'Declaration on Human Rights,' " unpublished manuscript, 2012.

——. "The Particularist Pursuit of American Universalism: The American Jewish Committee's 1944 Declaration on Human Rights." *Journal of Contemporary History* (April 2015): 274–95.

Luntz, Frank. *Israel in an Age of Eminem.* Philadelphia: Andrea and Charles Bronfman Philanthropies, 2003.

Luxemburg, Rosa. "No Room in My Heart for Jewish Suffering" (1916). In *The Jew in the Modern World: A Documentary History,* 2nd ed., edited by Paul Mendes-Flohr and Jehuda Reinharz, 261. New York: Oxford University Press, 1995.

Luz, Ehud. *Wrestling with an Angel: Power, Morality, and Jewish Identity.* New Haven, CT: Yale University Press, 2003.

Mack, Julian. "Zionism and the Palestinian Restoration Fund." *The Maccabæan: A Magazine of Jewish Life and Letters* 33–34 (June 1920): 189–91.

Magid, Shaul. *American Post-Judaism: Identity and Renewal in a Postethnic Society.* Bloomington: Indiana University Press, 2013.

———. "The Holocaust and Jewish Identity in America: Memory, the Unique, and the Universal." *Jewish Social Studies* 18, no. 2 (2012): 100–135.

Mahler, Joseph. *Jewish Emancipation: A Selection of Documents.* Jews and the Post-War World, No. 1. New York: American Jewish Committee, 1942.

Maoz, Asher. "Can Judaism Serve as a Source of Human Rights?" Tel Aviv University Law School Faculty Papers, 2005, Paper 7.

Maranz, Felice. "A Crucial Question of Jewish Giving; to Jews or not to Jews?" *Moment* 28, no. 6 (2003).

Marcus, Joseph. *Social and Political History of the Jews of Poland.* Berlin: Walter de Gruyter, 1983.

Markowitz, Fran. "Plaiting the Strands of Jewish Identity: A Review Article." *Comparative Studies in Society and History* 32 (1990): 181–89.

Marshall, Louis. "The American Jewish Committee." Address to the 21st Biennial Convention of the Union of American Hebrew Congregations, January 20, 1909.

———. "Report of the Delegates from the American Jewish Congress to the Peace Conference." Philadelphia, May 20, 1920.

———. "Report of the Delegates from the American Jewish Congress to the Peace Conference." May 30, 1920.

Mart, Michelle. *Eye on Israel: How America Came to View Israel as an Ally.* Albany: State University of New York Press, 2006.

Marx, Karl. "On the Jewish Question" (1843). In *The Marx-Engels Reader,* edited by Robert Tucker, 26–46. New York: Norton, 1978.

Marx, Robert. *The People In Between: The Paradox of Jewish Interstitiality.* NY: C2C Publishing, 2014.

Massing, Michael. "Should Jews Be Parochial?" *American Prospect* (November 2000): 30–35.

Mazower, Mark. "Minorities and the League of Nations in Interwar Europe." *Daedulus* 2 (Spring 1997): 47–63.

———. "The Strange Triumph of Human Rights, 1933–1950." *Historical Journal* 47, no. 2 (2004): 379–98.

Mearsheimer, John, and Stephen M. Walt. *The Israel Lobby and US Foreign Policy.* New York: Macmillan, 2007.

Medding, Peter. "A General Theory of Jewish Political Interests and Behavior." *Jewish Journal of Sociology* 19, no. 2 (1977): 115–44.

Mehta, Pratap Bhau. "Cosmopolitanism and the Circle of Reason." *Political Theory* 28, no. 5 (2000): 619–39.

Meier, Heinrich. "What Is Political Theology?" *Interpretation* 30, no. 1 (2001): 79–92.

Mellman, Mark S., Aaron Strauss, and Kenneth D. Wald. "Jewish American Voting Behavior 1972–2008: Just the Facts." The Solomon Project, July 2012. http://bjpa .org/Publications/details.cfm?PublicationID=14234.

Memorandum of interview had at Paris with President Wilson, Monday, May 26, 1919, by Louis Marshall and Cyrus Adler. Box 5, Louis Marshall, Correspondence, Peace Conference, 1919. American Jewish Committee.

"Memorandum on Policy Related to Defense Program of American Jewish Committee." April 1946.

Mendelsohn, Ezra. *On Modern Jewish Politics*. New York: Oxford University Press, 1993.

Mendes-Flohr, Paul R., and Jehuda Reinharz, eds. *The Jew in the Modern World: A Documentary History*, 2nd ed. New York: Oxford University Press, 1995.

"Message of Welcome to George Washington," August 17, 1790, and "A Reply to the Hebrew Congregation of Newport," ca. August 17, 1790; cited from Paul Mendes-Flohr and Jehuda Reinharz, eds. *The Jew in the Modern World: A Documentary History*, 2nd ed. New York: Oxford University Press, 1995, 458–59.

Messinger, Ruth. *Currents*, September 2003; unedited version is in Messinger, "Jewish Service: A Vision for 21st Century American Judaism." http://ajws.org/who_we _are/news/archives/viewpoints/jewish_service_-_a_vision.html. Accessed August 26, 2012.

——. "Jewish Service: A Vision for 21st Century American Judaism." http://ajws .org/who_we_are/news/archives/viewpoints/jewish_service_-_a_vision.html. Accessed August 26, 2012.

——. "Jewish Service and Global Citizenship: Transforming Experience into Action." *Contact* (Winter 2008): 6–7.

——. "Re: The Discussion about Poverty and Human Rights." N.p., n.d.

——. "The Twenty-First-Century Genocide: The Imperative of a Jewish Response." *Sh'ma* (October 2007): 1–2.

Messinger, Ruth, and Aron Dorfman. "Am I My Brother's Keeper If My Brother Lives Halfway around the World?" In *Righteous Indignation: A Jewish Call for Justice*, edited by Rabbi Or N. Rose, Jo Ellen Green Kaiser, and Margie Klein. Woodstock, VT: Jewish Lights Publishing, 2008.

Meyer, Michael. *Jewish Identity in the Modern World*. Seattle: University of Washington Press, 1990.

——. *Response to Modernity: A History of the Reform Movement in Judaism*. Detroit: Wayne State University Press, 1988.

Michels, Tony. "Is America Different? A Critique of American Jewish Exceptionalism." *American Jewish History* 96, no. 3 (2011): 201–24.

Miller, Michael, and Scott Ury. 2010. "Cosmopolitanism: The End of Jewishness?" *European History Review*, 17, 3, June, 337–59.

Miller, Ron, and Arnold Dashefsky. "Brandeis v Cohen et al.: The Distancing from Israel Debate." *Contemporary Jewry* 2/3, no. 30 (2010): 155–64.

"Minutes of Meeting of German Advisory Group." April 12, 1944. American Jewish Committee.

Mirsky, Yehudah. "*Tikkun Olam*: Basic Questions and Policy Directions." *Jewish People Public Policy Institute* (2008): 213–29.

Mollov, M. Benjamin. "Jewry's Prophetic Challenge to Soviet and Other Totalitarian Regimes According to Hans J. Morgenthau." *Journal of Church and State* 39, no. 3 (1997): 561–78.

———. *Power and Transcendence: Hans. J. Morgenthau and the Jewish Experience*. Lanham, MD: Lexington Books, 2002.

Moore, Deborah Dash. "Reconsidering the Rosenbergs: Symbol and Substance in Second Generation American Jewish Consciousness." *Journal of American Ethnic History* 8, no. 1 (1988): 21–37.

Morgenthau, Henry. "Zionism a Fallacy, Says Morgenthau." *New York Times*, June 27, 1921.

Moscowitz, Moses. "Memorandum: A Brief Outline of the steps leading up to the adoption of the minorities clauses, the meaning of these clauses, and the causes of their failure in practical life." October 12, 1939; Box 5, Louis Marshall, Correspondence, Peace Conference, 1919. American Jewish Committee.

Moyn, Samuel. "René Cassin, Human Rights, and Jewish Internationalism." In *Thinking Jewish Modernity*, edited by Jacques Picard et al., forthcoming. http://www .brandeis.edu/tauber/events/CassinMoyn.pdf.

Mualem, Yitzhak. "Israel's Foreign Policy: Military-Economic Aid and Assisting Jewish Communities in Distress—Can the Two Coexist?" *Israel Affairs* 18, no. 2 (2012): 201–18.

Munz, Ernest. "Nationalism Is the Enemy: Has Zionism Taken the Wrong Road?" *Commentary* (August 1946): 101–6.

Myers, David. "Rethinking Global Jewish Collectivity in a Post-Statist World." April 18, 2010. Downloaded from jpeoplehood.org. http://jpeoplehood.org/library-item/ rethinking-global-jewish-collectivity-post-statist-world/.

Naraniecki, Alexander. "Karl Popper on Jewish Nationalism and Cosmopolitanism." *European Legacy: Toward New Paradigms* 17, no. 5 (2012): 623–37.

Nathan-Kazie, Josh. "Jews Express Wide Criticism of Israel in Pew Survey but Leaders Dismiss Findings: Establishment Sticks to Its Guns." *Forward*, October 2, 2013.

Neier, Aryeh. *The International Human Rights: A Movement*. Princeton, NJ: Princeton University Press, 2012.

Neumann, Jonathan. "Tikkun Olam: A Concept in Need of Repair." *Degel: Torah and Jewish Studies from Alei Tzion* 3, no. 2 (2010): 32–43.

Neusner, Jacob. *Stranger at Home: "The Holocaust," Zionism, and American Judaism*. Atlanta, GA: Scholars Press, 1997.

New York Times, May 7, 1922, Section II, p. 6. Cited from Irwin Oder, "American Zionism and the Congressional Resolution of 1922 on Palestine." *Publications of the American Jewish Historical Society* 45, no. 1 (1955): 35–47, at 41.

Niebuhr, Reinhold. Introduction to *The Jew in Our Day*, by Waldo Frank, 3–14. New York: Duell, Sloan, and Pearce, 1944.

———. "Jews after the War, I." *The Nation*, February 21, 1942, 214–16.

Nordau, Max. "The Jewish Return to Palestine." An address delivered on January 11, 1920, p. 6. Reprinted by Keesings Publishing Rare Prints.

Norich, Sam. *What Will Bind Us Now? A Report on the Institutional Ties between Israel and American Jewry*. Center for Middle East Peace and Economic Cooperation, 1994.

Novak, David. *The Election of Israel: The Idea of the Chosen People*. New York: Cambridge University Press, 1995.

———. "Mordecai Kaplan's Rejection of Election." *Modern Judaism* 15, no. 1 (1995): 1–19.

Novick, Peter. *The Holocaust in American Life*. Boston: Houghton Mifflin, 1999.

Nussbaum, Martha. *For Love of Country?* Edited by Joshua Cohen. Boston: Beacon Press, 2002.

Oder, Irwin. 1955–56. "American Zionism and the Congressional Resolution of 1922 on Palestine." *Publications of the American Jewish Historical Society* 45, no. 1 (1955): 35–47.

Ophir, Adi. "The Identity of the Victims and the Victims of Identity: A Critique of Zionist Ideology for a Postzionist Age." In *Postzionism: A Reader*, edited by Laurence Silberstein, 81–101. New Brunswick, NJ: Rutgers University Press, 2008.

Oz, Amos. "The Discreet Charm of Zionism." In *Under This Blazing Light*. New York: Cambridge University Press, 1995.

"Papers and Proceedings of the Joint Conference with the Theodor Herzl Institute on the Impact of Israel on the American Jewish Community." *Jewish Social Studies* 21 (1959): 1–88.

Papers of Louis Marshall. Correspondence Box 5. Peace Conference, 1919 (1).

Parkes, James. *The Emergence of the Jewish Problem, 1878–1939*. New York: Oxford University Press, 1946.

Penkower, Monty Noam. "American Jewry and the Holocaust: From Biltmore to the American Jewish Conference." *Jewish Social Studies* 47 no. 2 (1985): 95–114.

———. "Dr. Nahun Goldmann and the Policy of International Jewish Organizations." In *Organizing Rescue: Jewish National Solidarity in the Modern Period*, edited by Selwyn Ilan Troen and Benjamin Pinkus, 141–53. Portland OR: Frank Cass, 1992.

Penslar, Derek Jonathan. "An Unlikely Internationalism." *Journal of Modern Jewish Studies* 7, no. 3 (2008): 309–23.

Peretz, Martin. "The American Left and Israel." *Commentary* (November 1967): 27–34.

Peters, John Punnett. "Zionism and the Jewish Problem." *Sewanee Review* 29, no. 3 (1921): 268–94.

Petuchowski, Jakob. "Faith as a Leap of Action: The Theology of Abraham Joshua Heschel." *Commentary* (May 1958): 390–97.

Pew Research Center. "A Portrait of Jewish Americans." October 1, 2013. http://www.pewforum.org/2013/10/01/jewish-american-beliefs-attitudes-culture-survey/.

———. "Rising Tide of Restrictions on Religion." September 20, 2012. http://www.pewforum.org/2012/09/20/rising-tide-of-restrictions-on-religion-findings/.

Pianko, Noam. "'Make Room for Us': Jewish Collective Solidarity in Contemporary Political Thought." *Journal of Modern Jewish Studies* 11, no. 2 (2012): 191–205.

———. "'The True Liberalism of Zionism': Horace Kallen, Jewish Nationalism, and the Limits of American Pluralism." *American Jewish History* 94, no. 4 (2008): 299–329.

———. *Zionism and the Roads Not Taken: Rawidowicz, Kaplan, Kohn*. Bloomington: Indiana University Press, 2010.

Pinkus, Benjamin. "Israeli Activity on Behalf of Soviet Jewry." In *Organizing Rescue: Jewish National Solidarity in the Modern Period*, edited by Selwyn Ilan Troen and Benjamin Pinkus, 373–402. Portland OR: Frank Cass, 1992.

Pinto-Duschinsky, Michael. "Jews, Law, and Human Rights." *Jewish Ideas Daily*, December 27, 2012. http://www.jewishideasdaily.com/5643/features/jews-law-and -human-rights/.

Piterberg, Gabriel. "Zion's Rebel Daughter: Hannah Arendt on Palestine and Jewish Politics." *New Left Review* 48 (November–December 2007): 39–57.

Podhoretz, Norman. *Why Are Jews Liberals?* New York: Vintage Books, 2010.

Poliakov, Leon. *Jewish Bankers and the Holy See from the Thirteenth to the Seventeenth Century.* London: Routledge, 1977.

Pollack, Sheldon. "Cosmopolitanism and Vernacular in History." *Public Culture* 12, no. 3 (2000): 591–625.

Pollak, Noah. "The B'Tselem Witch Trials." *Commentary* (May 2011). https://www .commentarymagazine.com/article/the-btselem-witch-trials/.

Porat, Guy. *Between State and Synagogue: The Secularization of Contemporary Israel.* New York: Cambridge University Press, 2013.

Power, Samantha. *A Problem from Hell: America in an Age of Genocide.* New York: Basic Books, 2002.

Prell, Riv-Ellen. "Against the Cultural Grain: Jewish Peoplehood for the 21st Century." ,In *Jewish Peoplehood: Change and Challenge*, edited by Menachem Revivi and Ezra Kopelowitz, 117–28. Brighton, MA: Boston Academic Studies Press, 2009.

——. "Triumph, Accommodation, and Resistance: American Jewish Life from the End of World War Two to the Six-Day War." In *The Columbia History of Jews and Judaism*, edited by Marc Rafael, 114–41. New York: Columbia University Press, 2008.

Proskauer, Joseph. "Our Duty as Americans—Our Responsibility as Jews." Forty-first Annual Meeting of the American Jewish Committee, January 18, 1948, p. 7.

Rabin, Yitzhak. *The Rabin Memoirs.* Berkeley: University of California Press, 1966.

Rabinovitch, Simon. *Jews and Diaspora Nationalism: Writings on Jewish People in Europe and the United States* (Waltham, MA: Brandeis University Press, 2012).

Raider, Mark. *The Emergence of American Zionism.* New York: New York University Press, 1998.

Raider, Mark, Jonathan Sarna, and Ronald Zweig, eds. *Abba Hillel Silver and American Zionism.* New York: Routledge, 1997.

Ravid, Shlomi, ed. *Peoplehood—Between "Charity Begins at Home" and "Repair the World."* Vol. 6 of the Peoplehood Papers, Center for Jewish Peoplehood Education, 2010. http://jpeoplehood.org/library-item/peoplehood-between-charity-begins-at -home-and-repair-the-world/, 2007. Accessed May 8, 2015.

——. *Peoplehood in an Age of Pluralism: How Do We Embrace Pluralism While Keeping Us Whole?* Vol. 10 of the Peoplehood Papers, Center for Jewish Peoplehood Education, 2013. http://ejewishphilanthropy.com/peoplehood-in-the-age-of-pluralism -how-do-we-embrace-pluralism-while-keeping-us-whole/. Accessed January 15, 2015.

Rawidowicz, Simon. *Israel: The Ever-Dying People, and Other Essays.* Rutherford, NJ: Farleigh Dickinson University Press, 1986.

"Reply to Stuyvesant's Petition," April 26, 1655; cited from Paul Mendes-Flohr and Jehuda Reinharz, eds., *The Jew in the Modern World: A Documentary History*, 2nd ed. New York: Oxford University Press, 1995, 453.

Reut Institute. "21st Century Tikkun Olam: Improving the Lives of a Quarter Billion People in a Decade." Executive Summary of a Conceptual Framework. A Global Engagement Strategy for the State of Israel and the Jewish People, Tel-Aviv, Israel, April 2012.

Riga, Liliana, and James Kennedy. "Tolerant Majorities, Loyal Minorities, and 'Ethnic Reversals': Constructing Minority Rights at Versailles 1919." *Nations and Nationalism* 15, no. 3 (2009): 461–82.

Rischin, Moses. "The Early Attitude of the American Jewish Committee to Zionism (1906–22)." *Publication of the American Jewish Historical Society* 49 (1959–60): 188–201.

Roberts, Helen. "American Jewish Donations to Israel." *Contemporary Jewry* 20 (1999): 201–13.

Rose, Or N. "Jewish Seminarians for Justice." *Tikkun* 21, no. 4 (2006): 57.

Rosen, Mark. *Mission, Meaning, and Money: How the Joint Distribution Committee Became a Fundraising Innovator.* Brandeis University, 2010.

Rosenfeld, Alvin. "The Americanization of the Holocaust." *Commentary* (June 1995): 35–40.

———. "The Americanization of the Holocaust." In *American Jewish Identity Politics*, edited by Deborah Dash Moore, 45–82. Ann Arbor: University of Michigan Press, 2008.

Rosenfeld, Geraldine. "Human Rights." *American Jewish Year Book* 50 (1948–49): 483–93.

———. "Human Rights." *American Jewish Year Book* 51 (1950): 433–43.

Roshwald, Aviel. *The Endurance of Nationalism.* New York: Cambridge University Press, 2006.

Roskies, David. *The Literature of Destruction: Jewish Responses to Catastrophe.* Philadelphia: Jewish Publication Society.

Rosner, Shmuel. *Shtetl, Bagel, and Baseball: On the Dreadful, Wonderful State of America's Jews .* Hebrew. Jerusalem: Keter Publishing, 2011.

Rubin, Trudy. "Through Winter, Rain, and Mud, Lebanon's Palestinian Refugees Rebuild." *Christian Science Monitor*, January 10, 1983.

Rynhold, Jonathan. *The Arab-Israeli Conflict and American Political Culture.* New York: Cambridge University Press, 2015.

———. "Israel's Foreign and Defense Policy and Diaspora Jewish Identity." In *Israel, the Diaspora, and Jewish Identity*, edited by Danny Ben-Moshe and Zohar Segev, 144–63. Portland, OR: Sussex Academic Press.

Sacks, Rabbi Jonathan. *To Heal a Fractured World: The Ethics of Responsibility.* New York: Schocken Books, 2005.

Sage, Naomi. "The JDC International Development Program: The Decision by the American Jewish Joint Distribution Committee to Formulate Its Non-Sectarian Efforts." *Jewish Philanthropy and Collective Responsibility in the 19th and 20th Centuries.* (Spring 2006).

Saks, Robert. "Israel and the New Left." Presented at the Annual Meeting of the National Conference of Jewish Communal Service, Detroit, Michigan, June 10, 1968.

Samuel, Maurice. "The Sundering of Israel and American Jewry: Has the New State Rejected Its Jewish Past?" *Commentary* (September 1953): 199–206.

———. "Why Israel Misunderstands American Jewry: Some Ways of Closing the Rift." *Commentary* (1953): 300–310.

Sandler, Shmuel. "Is There a Jewish Foreign Policy?" *Jewish Journal of Sociology* 29, no. 2 (1987): 115–21.

——. "Toward a Theory of World Jewish Politics and Jewish Foreign Policy." *Hebraic Political Studies* 2, no. 3 (2007): 326–60.

——. "Towards a Conceptual Framework of World Jewish Politics: State, Nation, and Diaspora in a Jewish Foreign Policy." *Israel Affairs* 10, no. 1–2 (2004): 301–12.

Sarna, Jonathan. "American Jewish Political Conservatism in Historical Perspective." *American Jewish History* 87, no. 2 and 3 (1999): 113–22.

——. Introduction to *American Jewish Experience*, edited by Jonathan Sarna. New York: Holmes and Meier, 1997.

——. "Promised Land and Golden Land." In *Two Perspectives: American Jewish-Israeli Relations*, by David Harman and Jonathan Sarna, 7. The Institute on American Jewish Israeli Relations, American Jewish Committee. New York: American Jewish Committee, September 1995.

——. "Two Jewish Lawyers Named Louis." *American Jewish History* 94, no. 1–2 (2008): 1–19.

——. *When General Grant Expelled the Jews.* New York: Schocken Books, 2012.

——, ed. *American Judaism: A History.* New Haven, CT: Yale University Press, 2004.

Sasson, Theodore. "Mass Mobilization to Direct Engagement: American Jews' Changing Relationship to Israel." *Israel Studies* 15, no. 2 (2010): 173–95.

——. *The New Realism: American Jews' Views about Israel* (New York: American Jewish Committee, 2009).

Sasson, Theodore, Benjamin Phillips, Charles Kadushin, and Leonard Saxe. "Still Connected? American Jewish Attitudes about Israel." Cohen Center for Modern Jewish Studies, Brandeis University, 2010.

Sasson, Theodore, Benjamin Phillips, Graham Wright, Charles Kadushin, and Leonard Saxe. "Understanding Young Adult Attachment to Israel: Period, Life Cycle, and Generational Dynamics." *Contemporary Jewry* (January 2012) 297–319.

Sasson, Theodore, Leonard Saxe, and Michelle Shain. 2015. "How Do Young American Jews Feel About Israel?" *Tablet Magazine*, February 14, 2015. http://www.tabletmag.com/scroll/189210/how-do-young-american-jews-feel-about-israel

Saxe, Leonard, and Matthew Boxer. "Loyalty and Love of Israel by Diasporan Jews." *Israel Studies* 17, no. 2 (2012): 92–101.

Saxe, Leonard, Michelle Shain, Graham Wright, Shahar Hecht, Shira Fishman, and Theodore Sasson. "The Impact of Taglit-Birthright Israel: 2012 Update." Cohen Center for Modern Jewish Studies, Brandeis University, October 2012. http://www.brandeis.edu/cmjs/noteworthy/jewish_futures_taglit_2012.html.

Schmitt, Carl. *Political Theology.* Chicago: University of Chicago Press, 2005.

Schwarzfuchs, Simon. "The Alliance Israélite Universelle and French Jewish Leadership vis-à-vis North African Jewry, 1860–1914." In *Organizing Rescue: Jewish National Solidarity in the Modern Period*, edited by Selwyn Ilan Troen and Benjamin Pinkus, 77–90. Portland, OR: Frank Cass, 1992.

Scott, Peter, and William T. Cavanaugh, eds. *The Blackwell Companion to Political Theology.* Malden, MA: Blackwell, 2004.

Scruton, Roger. *A Dictionary of Political Thought.* London: Macmillan, 1980.

Scult, Mel. "Americanism and Judaism in the Thought of Mordecai M. Kaplan." In *The Americanization of the Jews*, edited by Robert Seltzer and Norman Cohen, 339–54. New York: New York University Press, 1995.

Segev, Zohar. 2007. "American Zionists' Place in Israel after Statehood: From Involved Partners to Outside Supporters." *American Jewish History* 93, no. 3 (2007): 277–302.

Seliktar, Ofira. "The Changing Identity of American Jews, Israel, and the Peace Process." In *Israel, the Diaspora, and Jewish Identity*, edited by Danny Ben-Moshe and Zohar Segev, 124–37. Portland, OR: Sussex Academic Press, 2007.

Seltzer, Robert, and Norman Cohen, eds. *The Americanization of the Jews*. New York: New York University Press, 1995.

Shachtman, Tom. *I Seek My Brethren: Ralph Goldman and "The Joint": Rescue, Relief, and Reconstruction—The Work of the American Jewish Joint Distribution Committee*. New York: Newmarket Press, 2001, p. 210.

Shafir, Gershon, and Yoav Peled. *Being Israeli: The Dynamics of Israeli Citizenship*. New York: Cambridge University Press, 2001.

Shain, Yossi. *Kinships and Diasporas in International Affairs*. Ann Arbor: University of Michigan Press, 2008.

Shain, Yossi, and Barry Bristman. "Diaspora, Kinship, and Loyalty: The Renewal of Jewish National Security." *International Affairs* 78, no. 1 (2002): 69–95.

Shapiro, Edward. "Jews and the Conservative Rift." *American Jewish History* 87, no. 2–3 (1999): 195–215.

———. *A Time for Healing: American Jewry since World War II*. Baltimore: Johns Hopkins University Press, 1995.

Sheffer, Gabriel. *Diaspora Politics: At Home Abroad*. New York: Cambridge University Press, 2003.

———. "The Elusive Question: Jews and Jewry in Israeli Foreign Policy." *Jerusalem Quarterly* 46 (Spring 1988): 104–14.

———. "Loyalty and Criticism in Relations between World Jewry and Israel." *Israel Studies* 17, no. 2 (2012): 77–85.

———. "A Nation and Its Diaspora: A Re-Examination of Israeli Jewish Diaspora Relations." *Diaspora* 11, no. 3 (2002): 331–57.

Shiff, Ofer. *Survival through Integration: American Reform Jewish Universalism and the Holocaust*. Boston: Brill, 2005.

Shotwell, James. "American Jewish Committee Led Battle for Human Rights." *Committee Reporter*, July 1945, 5.

Sidorsky, David. Introduction to *Essays on Human Rights: Contemporary Issues and Jewish Perspectives*, edited by David Sidorsky, xvii–xlv. Philadelphia: Jewish Publication Society of America, 1979.

———, ed. *Essays on Human Rights: Contemporary Issues and Jewish Perspective*. Philadelphia: Jewish Publication Society of America, 1979.

Silver, Matthew. "Louis Marshall and the Democratization of Jewish Identity." *American Jewish History* 94, no. 1–2 (2008): 41–69.

———. *Louis Marshall and the Rise of Jewish Ethnicity*. Syracuse, NY: Syracuse University Press, 2013.

Sklare, Marshall. "Lakeville and Israel: The Six-Day War and Its Aftermath." In *American Jews: A Reader*, edited by Marshall Sklare, 413–39. New York: Behrman House, 1983.

———. *Observing America's Jews*. Waltham, MA: Brandeis University Press, 1993.

Sklare, Marshall, and Joseph Greenblum. *Jewish Identity on the Suburban Frontier.* New York: Basic Books, 1967.

Slezkine, Yuri. *The Jewish Century.* Princeton, NJ: Princeton University Press, 2004.

Sorkin, David. "Between Messianism and Survival." *Journal of Modern Jewish Studies* 3, no. 1 (2004): 73–86.

"The State of Jewish Belief—A Symposium." *Commentary* (August 1966).

Staub, Michael. "Holocaust Consciousness and American Jewish Politics." In *The Columbia History of Jews and Judaism,* edited by Marc Rafael, 324–31. New York: Columbia University Press, 2008.

———. *Torn at the Roots: The Crisis of Jewish Liberalism in Postwar America.* New York: Columbia University Press, 2002.

Stein, Ken, and Rich Walter. "Today in Israel History." http://israeled.org/american-jewish-committee-gives-qualified-endorsement-balfour-declaration/. Accessed February 3, 2015.

Steinberg, Gerald. "From Durban to the Goldstone Report: The Centrality of Human Rights NGOs in the Political Dimension of the Arab-Israeli Conflict." *Israel Affairs* 18, no. 3 (2012): 372–88.

———. "The Politics of NGOs, Human Rights, and the Arab-Israeli Conflict." *Israel Studies* 16, no. 2 (2011): 24–54.

Steinberg, Kerri. "Contesting Identities in Jewish Philanthropy." In *Diasporas and Exiles,* edited by Howard Wettstein, 253–78. Berkeley: University of California Press, 2002.

Stone, Suzanne Last. "A Jewish Perspective on Human Rights." *Society* (January–February 2004): 17–22.

———. "Tolerance versus Pluralism in Judaism." *Journal of Human Rights* 2, no. 1 (2003): 105–17.

Strenger, Carlo. "The Unrequited Love Affair between Liberal Jews and an Illiberal Israel." *Ha'aretz,* August 27, 2014.

Stuyvesant, Peter. "Petition to Expel Jews from New Amsterdam, September 22, 1654." In *The Jew in the Modern World: A Documentary History,* 2nd ed., edited by Paul Mendes-Flohr and Jehuda Reinharz, 452. New York: Oxford University Press, 1995.

Sufott, E. Zev. "Israel and the Diaspora: Roles and Responsibilities." In *Jewish Centers and Peripheries: Europe between America and Israel Fifty Years after World War II,* edited by S. Ilan Troen, 397–417. New Brunswick, NJ: Transaction Publishers, 1998.

Svonkin, Stuart. *Jews against Prejudice: American Jews and the Fight for Civil Liberties.* New York: Columbia University Press, 1997.

Szajkowski, Z. "The Alliance Israélite Universelle in the United States, 1860–1949." *Publications of the American Jewish Historical Society* 39, no. 4 (1950): 389–443.

Sznaider, Natan. "Hannah Arendt's Jewish Cosmopolitanism: Between the Universal and the Particular." *European Journal of Social Theory* 10, no. 1 (2007): 112–22.

Talmon, J. L. "Uniqueness and Universality of Jewish History." *Commentary* (July 1957): 1–14.

Tamir, Yael. "A Strange Alliance: Isaiah Berlin and the Liberalism of the Fringes." *Ethical Theory and Moral Practice* 1 (1998): 279–89.

Telhami, Shibley. "Israeli Foreign Policy: A Realist Ideal-Type or a Breed of Its Own?" In *Israel in Comparative Perspective*, edited by Michael Barnett, 29–51. Albany: State University of New York Press, 1996.

Thomas, Laurence Mordekhai. "Suffering as a Moral Beacon." In *The Americanization of the Holocaust*, edited by Hilene Flanzbaum, 198–210. Baltimore: Johns Hopkins University Press, 1999.

Thompson, Dorothy. "America Demands a Single Loyalty: The Perils of a 'Favorite' Foreign Nation." *Commentary* (March 1950); 210–19.

Toll, William. "Horace M. Kallen: Pluralism and American Jewish Identity." *American Jewish History* 85, no. 1 (1997): 57–74.

Trevor-Roper, Hugh R. "Jewish and Other Nationalisms." *Commentary* (January 1963): 15–21.

Troen, Selwyn Ilan, and Benjamin Pinkus, eds., *Organizing Rescue: Jewish National Solidarity in the Modern Period*. Portland OR: Frank Cass, 1992.

Urofsky, Melvin. *American Zionism: From Herzl to the Holocaust*. Lincoln: University of Nebraska Press, 1975.

———. *Louis D. Brandeis: A Life*. New York: Pantheon, 2009.

Vaïsse, Justin. *Neoconservatism: The Biography of a Movement*. Cambridge, MA: Belknap Press of Harvard University Press, 2010.

Veblen, Thorstein. "The Intellectual Pre-Eminence of Jews in Modern Europe." *Political Science Quarterly* 34, no. 1 (1919): 33–42.

Vertovec, Steven, and Robin Cohen, eds. *Conceiving Cosmopolitanism: Theory, Context, and Practice*. New York: Oxford University Press, 2002.

Vital, David. "Diplomacy in the Jewish Interest." In *Jewish History: Essays in Honour of Chimen Abramsky*, edited by Ada Rapaport-Albert and Steven Zipperstein, 683–95. London: Peter Halban, 1989.

———. *The Future of the Jews: A People at the Crossroads?* Cambridge, MA: Harvard University Press, 1990.

Vorspan, Albert, and Eugene Lipman. *Justice and Judaism: The Work of Social Action*. New York: Union of Hebrew Congregations, 1956.

Vromen, Suzanna. "Hannah Arendt's Jewish Identity: Neither Parvenu nor Pariah." *European Journal of Political Theory* 3, no. 2 (2004): 177–90.

Wald, Kenneth, and Bryan Williams. "American Jews and Israel: The Sources of Politicized Ethnic Identity." *Nationalism and Ethnic Politics* 12 (2006): 205–37.

Waldman, Morris. "A Bill of Rights for All Nations." *New York Times Magazine*, November 19, 1944, 14, 48.

Waldron, Jeremy. "Minority Cultures and the Cosmopolitan Alternative." *University of Michigan Journal of Law Reform* 25 (1992): 751–93.

———. "What Is Cosmopolitanism?" *Journal of Political Philosophy* 8, no. 2 (2000): 227–43.

Walfish, Mordecai. "Jewish Service-Learning: History and Landscape." http://jpro .org/dev/pdf-files/old-journals/18.pdf.

Wall, Wendy L. *Inventing the American Way: The Politics of Consensus from the New Deal to the Civil Rights Movement*. New York: Oxford University Press, 2009.

Walzer, Michael. "The Anomalies of Jewish Political Identity." In *Jewish Peoplehood: Change and Challenge*, edited by Menachem Revivi and Ezra Kopelowitz, 33–37. Brighton, MA: Boston Academic Studies Press, 2009.

——. *In God's Shadow: Politics in the Hebrew Bible*. New Haven, CT: Yale University Press, 2012.

——. "Multiculturalism and the Politics of Interest." In *Insider/Outsider: American Jews and Multiculturalism*, edited by David Biale, Michael Galchinsky, and Susannah Heschel, 88–98. Berkeley: University of California Press, 1998.

——. "Universalism and Jewish Values." Delivered at the twentieth annual Hans Morgenthau Lecture on Ethics and Foreign Policy, Carnegie Council on Ethics and International Affairs, New York City, May 15, 2001.

——, ed. *Law, Politics, and Morality in Judaism*. Princeton, NJ: Princeton University Press, 2006.

——, et al., eds. *The Jewish Political Tradition*. Vol. 1, *Authority*. New Haven, CT: Yale University Press, 2000.

——, et. al., eds. *The Jewish Political Tradition*. Vol. 2, *Membership*. New Haven, CT: Yale University Press, 2012.

Waxman, Dov. "The Israel Lobbies: A Survey of the Pro-Israel Community in the United States." *Israel Studies Forum* 25, no. 1 (2010): 5–28.

——. "The Jewish Dimension in Israeli Foreign Policy." *Israel Studies Forum* 19, no. 1 (2003): 34–56.

Waxman, Dov, and Scott Lasensky. "Jewish Foreign Policy: Israel, World Jewry, and the Defense of 'Jewish Interests.' " *Journal of Modern Jewish Studies* 12, no. 2 (2013): 232–52.

Weiser, Benno. "Ben-Gurion's Dispute with American Zionists: Why They Reject the 'Duty to Emigrate.' " *Commentary* (August 1954): 93–101.

Weltsch, Robert. "Israel, Human Rights, and American Jewry: New Roles in the Centuries-Old Struggle." *Commentary* (April 1950): 354–58.

Werbner, Pnina. "Vernacular Cosmopolitanism." *Theory, Culture, and Society* 23, no. 2–3 (2006): 496–98.

Wermuth, David. "Human Rights in Jewish Law: Contemporary Juristic and Rabbinic Conceptions." *University of Pennsylvania Journal of International Law* 32, no. 4 (2010): 1101–32.

Wertheimer, Jack. "Generation of Change: How Leaders in Their Twenties and Thirties Are Reshaping American Jewish Life." Avi Chai Foundation, September 2010.

——. "Jewish Organizational Life in the United States since 1945." *American Jewish Year Book* 95 (1995): 3–98.

——. *A People Divided: Judaism in Contemporary America*. Hanover, NH: University Press of New England; Waltham, MA: Brandeis University Press, 1997.

——. "The Ten Commandments of America's Jews." *Commentary* (June 1, 2012): 35–40.

——. "Whatever Happened to the Jewish People?" *Commentary* (June 2006). https://www.commentarymagazine.com/article/whatever-happened-to-the-jewish-people/.

——, ed. *The New Jewish Leaders: Reshaping the American Jewish Landscape*. Waltham, MA: Brandeis University Press, 2011.

"What's Jewish about It? *Baltimore Jewish Times*, April 28, 2006, 70–75.

Wettstein, Howard, ed. *Diasporas and Exiles: Varieties of Jewish Identity* (Berkeley: University of California Press, 2002).

Whitfield, Stephen. "Influence and Affluence, 1967–2000." In *The Columbia History of Jews and Judaism*, edited by Marc Rafael, 142–63. New York: Columbia University Press, 2008.

Wieseltier, Leon. "Pariah and Politics: Hannah Arendt and the Jews, Part II." *New Republic*, October 14, 1981. http://www.newrepublic.com/article/books-and-arts/75453/pariahs-and-politics.

Wilkes, Paul. *And They Shall Be My People*. New York: Atlantic Monthly Press, 1994.

Windmueller, Steven. "The 'Noshrim War': Dropping Out." In *A Second Exodus: The American Movement to Free Soviet Jews*, edited by Murray Friedman and Albert D. Chernin, 161–72. Hanover, NH: University Press of New England for Brandeis University Press, 1999.

Winter, Jay. "René Cassin and the Alliance Israelite Universelle." *Modern Judaism* 32, no. 1 (2012): 1–21.

Winter, Jay, and Antoine Prost. *René Cassin and Human Rights: From the Great War to the Universal Declaration*. Cambridge: Cambridge University Press, 2013.

Wistrich, Robert. "Israel and the Holocaust Trauma." *Jewish History* 11, no. 2 (1997): 13–20.

——. "Zionism and Its Jewish 'Assimilationist' Critics (1897–1948)," *Jewish Social Studies* 4, no. 2 (1998): 59–111.

Wolf, Arnold Jacob. "Repairing Tikkun Olam—Current Theological Writing." *Judaism* (Fall 2001): 479–82.

——. "Should Soviet Jews Join the Dissidents?" *Sh'ma* 8, no. 153 (1978): 116–20.

Wolf, Lucien. *Notes on the Diplomatic History of the Jewish Question*. Jewish Historical Society of England, University College. London: Filiquarian Publishing, 1919.

Wolfe, Alan. *At Home in Exile: Why Diaspora Is Good for the Jews*. Boston: Beacon Press, 2014.

Woocher, Jonathan S. *Sacred Survival: The Civil Religion of American Jews*. Bloomington: Indiana University Press, 1986.

World Jewish Congress. Policy and Action of the World Jewish Congress, 1966–1974, Report to the Sixth Plenary Assembly. Geneva: Office of the Secretary-General, 1974.

Wrong, Dennis. "The Rise and Decline of Anti-Semitism in America." In *The Ghetto and Beyond: Essays on Jewish Life in America*, edited by Peter Rose, 313–34. New York: Random House, 1969.

Yakobson, Alexander, and Amnon Rubinstein. *Israel and the Family of Nations: The Jewish Nation-State and Human Rights*. New York: Routledge, 2009.

Yaniv, Avner. *Deterrence without the Bomb: The Politics of Israeli Strategy*. Lexington, MA: Lexington Books, 1987.

Yanklowitz, Shmuly. *Jewish Ethics and Social Justice: A Guide for the 21st Century*. Pompano Beach, FL: Derusha Publishing, 2012.

Young, Bette Roth. "Emma Lazarus and Her Jewish Problem." *American Jewish History* 84, no. 4 (1996): 291–313.

Young, James. "America's Holocaust: Memory and the Politics of Identity." In *The Americanization of the Holocaust*, edited by Hilene Flanzbaum, 68–82. Baltimore: Johns Hopkins University Press, 1999.

Zeitz, Joshua Michael. "'If I Am Not for Myself . . .': The American Jewish Establishment in the Aftermath of the Six Day War." *American Jewish History* 88, no. 2 (2000): 253–86.

Zertal, Idith. *Israel's Holocaust and the Politics of Nationhood.* New York: Cambridge University Press, 2005.

Zerubavel, Yael. *Recovered Roots: Collective Memory and the Making of Israeli National Tradition.* Chicago: University of Chicago Press, 1995.

Zipperstein, Steven. 1993. "Between Tribalism and Utopia: Ahad Ha'am and the Making of Jewish Cultural Politics." *Modern Judaism* 13, no. 3 (1993): 231–47.

INDEX

Lightning Source UK Ltd.
Milton Keynes UK
UKHW011826010422
400964UK00003B/303